A history of the New Zealand fiction feature film

Manchester University Press

A history of the New Zealand fiction feature film

Bruce Babington

Manchester University Press

Copyright © Bruce Babington 2007
The right of Bruce Babington to be identified as the author of this work has been asserted by him in accordance with the Copyright, Designs and Patents Act 1988.

Published by Manchester University Press
Altrincham Street, Manchester M1 7JA, UK
www.manchesteruniversitypress.co.uk

British Library Cataloguing-in-Publication Data
A catalogue record for this book is available from the British Library

Library of Congress Cataloging-in-Publication Data applied for

ISBN   978 0 7190 7541 4 *hardback*
ISBN   978 0 7190 7542 1 *paperback*

First published 2007

This edition first published 2018

Typeset by
Action Publishing Technology Limited, Gloucester
Printed in Great Britain
by Lightning Source

'Come along to the pitchers tonight, Sandra?'
'Pictures, Daddy.'
'Pitchers, that's what I said. Come on down to the Gigantic, I believe it's a pretty good pitcher.'
'Not pitchers, pictures.'
'Pitcher. Pitchers. Then how do you pronounce it? You're all too bloody superior for me.'
(Robin Hyde, The Godwits Fly, 1938)

Our town, you know that place Raggleton, way down there by the sea, was a big place, no village in the country. It had a hotel two stories high, and with two barber shops, and there were pictures twice a week.
(Ian Cross, The God Boy, 1957)

If ever a post-mortem is performed on us, I think they will find there are three words written on New Zealand's heart – ANZAC, HOLLYWOOD and HOME. But only a very rash prophet would venture to suggest which will be carved the deepest.
(Gordon Mirams, Speaking Candidly: Films and People in New Zealand, 1945)

Theatre is dignifying Klynham's cinema somewhat. It was a big draughty barn of a place, but many happy hours we spent therein. The building has had a great face-lift recently, but I recall it fondly the way it was in the days when Les and I sat enthralled by a serial picture called 'The King of Diamonds', and the kids stamped on the floor and whistled at each certificate of approval, unless it was a travel film and then they hooted and groaned. There was always a chance of my bare arm brushing against the electrically charged flesh of Josephine McClinton again as we crowded down the stairs at interval, or even maybe, some day, fluking a seat alongside her. There were big pictures of Tom Mix and Robert Montgomery and June Withers on the walls of the stairway ...
(Ronald Hugh Morrieson, The Scarecrow, 1963)

It was the strangest thing to sit down there and look up and see ourselves as others did. We stared at these shadows of ourselves. These likenesses. Fred looked like Fred. Billy Wallace looked like Billy Wallace. Jimmy Hunter himself but only more so. We watched our shadows perform knowledgeable tricks; and when you thought about it you realised that the shadows had to know their owners in order to be so convincing. Our shadows remembered their origins spectacularly well. Things, personal things, previously intimate to ourselves. Fred Newton scratching himself. Billy Stead holding the front of his shorts out from himself to look down. Massa closing one nostril to blow snot out the other. Now it was up there for all to see. There was some initial discomfort, but this soon passed and pleasure set in.
(The 1905 All Blacks watch themselves on the screen of a London theatre in
Lloyd Jones, The Book of Fame, 2000)

Contents

List of illustrations	*Page* ix
Acknowledgements	xi
1 Introduction: the New Zealand fiction feature film: history, theory, practice	1
2 Forgotten nitrate: feature film-making in New Zealand 1912–1940	28
3 Fifty years a pioneer: the cinema of Rudall Hayward 1921–1972	55
4 Sustaining the dream: the age of O'Shea	85
5 Living white males: New Zealand cinema 1975–1985	113
6 'World famous in New Zealand': contemporary cinema 1986–2005	179
7 Wandering stars: New Zealand cinema on the world screen – Vincent Ward, Peter Jackson, Jane Campion	257
Filmography of fiction feature films	272
Select bibliography	279
Index	283

Illustrations

1 Hera Tawhai-Rogers as Hinemoa in the first feature film made by a New Zealander, Tarr's lost *Hinemoa* (1914), the image taken from the accompanying programme, which outlived the film.   *page* 48
2 Rudall Hayward (centre), towards the end of his life in 1970, with Barry Barclay (left) and James McNeish (right) during the making of a Pacific Films documentary.   56
3 Frame enlargement of early New Zealand cinema's nearest approach to a star, Dale Austen, in the mother aspect of her dual mother–daughter role in Hayward's melodrama *The Bush Cinderella* (1928).   61
4 Hayward's silent masterpiece *The Te Kooti Trail* (1927) 1. 'Soldiers three': left to right, Jules Vidoux (James Warner), Eric Mantell (Arthur Lord), Barney O'Halloran (Joe Tennant).   68
5 *The Te Kooti Trail* 2. Minatory choker close-up of Te Kooti (Te Pairi Oterangi), whose rebellion gives the film its title.   69
6 *The Te Kooti Trail* 3. Romantic 'Maoriland' with indigenous lovers Taranahi (Patiti Warbrick) and Monika (Tina Hunt).   70
7 The second father of New Zealand film, John O'Shea, working at his Pacific Films in 1992. Photographer: Paul Estcourt.   86
8 Original poster for O'Shea's groundbreaking race-relations romance *Broken Barrier* (1952), featuring Terence Bayler and Kay Ngārimu.   89
9 Conflict between David (Colin Broadley) and Laura (imported Bond girl Nadja Regin) in O'Shea's odyssey of alienation, *Runaway* (1964).   97
10 Deliriously mixed whakapapas as rising opera diva, Kiri Te Kanawa, treats a bicultural children's audience to 'Una voce poco fa' in O'Shea's musical *Don't Let It Get You* (1966).   106

11 Ethan (Frank Whitten) and Toss (Fiona Kay), enigmatic against a forbidding landscape in Vincent Ward's *Vigil* (1984), the first New Zealand production to gain art-film applause overseas. 131
12 Antic roadies at historical turning point. John (Tony Barry, right) and Gerry (Kelly Johnson) hitting the tarmac in Geoff Murphy's *Goodbye Pork Pie* (1981). 135
13 Requiem for a heroic fuckwit: Al (Bruno Lawrence) in a grotesque variant of the bonds of homosocial mateship with Ray (Keith Aberdein) in Roger Donaldson's male melodrama, *Smash Palace* (1982). 149
14 Director Geoff Murphy, the key figure of the early post-1977 industry, on set with kūpapa soldiers in his reworking of Hayward's New Zealand Wars epics, *Utu* (1983). 156
15 The allegorical white male/white woman/Māori triangle at the centre of the later part of Murphy's *The Quiet Earth* (1985): left to right, Api (Pete Smith), Joanne (Alison Routledge) and Zac (Bruno Lawrence). 163
16 The unconventionally sited bathing arrangements of Lucinda (Danielle Cormack) catch the oneiric, mildly surrealistic ambiance of Harry Sinclair's *The Price of Milk* (2000). 205
17 Sayo (Yuri Kinugawa) sitting at the global signpost suggests a near allegory of a 'glocal' New Zealand cinema in a transnational age in *Memory and Desire* (Niki Caro, 1997). 221
18 A pastoral moment amidst the angst of cultural displacement in Merita Mita's *Mauri* (1988): right to left, Awatea (Rangimarie Delamere) and her grandparents Kara and Hemi (Eva Rickard and Sonny Waru). 232
19 No indigenous pastoral here, but urban disintegration and violence in Lee Tamahori's version of Alan Duff's controversial novel: Jake (Temuera Morrison) and Beth (Rena Owen) in *Once Were Warriors* (1994). 238
20 Pauline (Melanie Lynskey, left) and Juliet (Kate Winslet) recreate for the 1990s, 1950s *folie à deux* and suburban matricide in Jackson's masterpiece *Heavenly Creatures* (1996). 263

All illustrations from The New Zealand Film Archive: Ngā Kaitiaki O Ngā Taonga Whitiāhua.

Acknowledgements

Much of the research for this book was done on a semester's leave from the English Department at the University of Newcastle upon Tyne, and on a supplementary semester made possible by an AHRB replacement teaching award. Thanks to Roger Horrocks and Nick Perry for organizing a three-month visiting research professorship at Auckland University, for a room, a video player and access to the Department's video collection and the university library; also to Adam White, who was as helpful as anyone could have been in helping me settle in, to Roger also for his selfless sharing of his great knowledge of New Zealand film. Next, thanks to the National Film Archive in Wellington for also giving me a room and video player for three months and access to their film and other collections; in particular to Virginia Callanan for her constant help in obtaining material, even after I had returned to England. Thanks to all the other staff for their pleasantness and helpfulness, to Frank Stark who alerted me to Robert Steele, also to Russell Campbell at Victoria University for various help. Thanks to three film-makers – Gaylene Preston, John Reid and Don Selwyn – for their time and help; also to Matt Horrocks at the NZFC for helping me to see some very recent films and answering various queries. Not least a salute to Aro Video, 'world famous in New Zealand' and beyond for finding me copies of so many films and helping me spend what was left of my grant money so happily. Finally, I couldn't have stayed anything like six months in New Zealand without the hospitality of my sister Sue in Dunedin, and two pairs of dear friends, Michael and Mary Munro in Ngaio, and Michael and Ann Morrissey in Avondale. Thanks also to another dear friend, Josie Karavasil, for visiting the archive for me when I found too late things that still needed checking; also to John Saunders at Newcastle University, with whom it has been a pleasure to teach film for twenty-five years.

1

Introduction: the New Zealand fiction feature film: history, theory, practice

History

An ordinary evening in Auckland, 1959

In 1959, at the height of this author's adolescent cinema-going, a year before the arrival of television, which, as elsewhere, changed the situation of cinema profoundly, Auckland, like other smaller New Zealand cities and towns, was a place of mass film-going. In the city's evening paper, the *Auckland Star* of Friday 22 May, the entertainment advertisements were as usual dominated by 13 metropolitan and 36 suburban cinemas, one, sometimes two, for every suburb: all those States, Royals, Britannias, New Orpheuses, Gaieties, Mayfairs and Victorias; a litany of once-familiar names. These were impressive numbers for a city of 400,000, and, repeated on a smaller scale nationwide, support Gordon Mirams' claim in his *Speaking Candidly: Films and People in New Zealand* (1945), the first book about film published in New Zealand, that 'we adopted the motion picture earlier and more enthusiastically than most other nations, and today we spend as much time and money at the pictures, per head of population as any other people in the world, except the Americans – and even they are not far ahead of us'.[1] *The Official New Zealand Year Book, 1959* gives New Zealand a population of just under 3 million, supporting 578 cinemas with 37.5 million admissions per year, an average of 17 cinema visits per annum by each person. The *Year Book* also asserted that New Zealand cinema-going had overtaken American per capita by 1953 and was the world's second highest per capita, trailing only Britain.

Such widespread cinema-going owed its existence to a number of factors that remove the need for theorizing an indigenous scopophilia in excess of other nations. Because of television's late arrival, the great age of cinema-going lasted longer than in most developed nations. New Zealand was also a country with relatively few highly developed non-sporting leisure activities to compete. As Mirams noted of New

Zealand's many film venues: 'An Englishman may ask, "What cinema are you going to tonight?" to differentiate between picture-theatres and "stage" theatres. But New Zealanders say, "What theatre are you going to tonight?" because to us all theatres are cinemas'.[2] In the pre-television and pre-internet worlds, films were one of a geographically isolated country's primary windows on the world – the large windows of a small room, to adapt the poet Allen Curnow's phrase. From about 1959 the European art cinema was becoming a fixture of arts festivals. But as the groundbreaking successes of the new New Zealand cinema, when they came, revealed, American films had the most far-reaching popularity and influence. This is reflected, even exaggerated, in those 22 May 1959 advertisements, where only two British films are showing besides eleven American in the metropolitan cinemas, and in the suburbs there is hardly a British film in sight.

Two early writers on the cinema: Gordon Mirams and J.C. Reid
Like Mirams, J.C. Reid, a professor of English at Auckland University, and the *Star*'s influential film critic around 1959, was concerned with educating audiences in critical and, in Reid's case (as his book *Catholics and the Films*, 1949,[3] the second work on film published in New Zealand, suggests), moral directions. Both, following a long tradition of New Zealand cultural criticism, tried to inculcate resistance to American popular art. What these critics of an age before film studies shared with general audiences was their identification of feature films with overseas. Only towards the end of his book does Mirams mention New Zealand film production as distinct from New Zealand audiences, and then it is to address as the hope of the future the documentary tradition, laying emphasis on the 1940 government-sponsored New Zealand visit of the leading British documentarist John Grierson, and his much quoted remarks about the importance of New Zealand making documentaries that went beyond dairy and tourist propaganda and exhibitions of Rotorua Māori, to show 'the faces' and 'the native genius of New Zealand'.[4] Grierson's referent here was solely documentary; neither he nor the government was interested in a feature film industry. Understandably, especially in wartime, it was the long tradition of propaganda and human interest documentaries which prevailed in the setting up of the government National Film Unit in 1941. For Mirams, as for most others, film was still 'in the toddling stage' and 'the documentary is the only branch of film production in which this country has any chance of making a contribution of real value and the successful production in New Zealand of features which compare with even the most modest Hollywood efforts cannot

be expected within any measurable space of time'.⁵ Reid, despite his proselytizing for New Zealand literature, made no mention at all of New Zealand film in his booklet.

Hindsight makes brilliant critics of us all, and neither writer could have been expected on the evidence available to see many feature film possibilities. Would we have done better in their situation? On the other hand, Mirams displays a selectively distorting memory in the dismissive account of New Zealand non-documentary film-making which justifies his assertions. Dividing the 'so-called' features into two classes, he specified on the one hand 'the work of adventurers who saw the chance to turn to some profit the vanity and gullibility of simple souls who fancied they would be hailed as embryo stars and given immediate Hollywood contracts if they could only get in front of a movie camera ...' (though this ignores three New Zealanders of his time, two of them graduates of beauty or talent contests – Dale Austen, Colin Tapley, and the child star, Ra Hould – who actually did land Hollywood contracts), and on the other 'the work of well-meaning amateurs with much more enthusiasm than knowledge of how to make films'.⁶ The alternatives are hardly elevating: exploiters of naïveté or incompetent amateurs. The major figure of early New Zealand film, Rudall Hayward, fell, it would appear, into both categories, into the first presumably for his cheerfully hyped auditions for 'community comedies', and into the second with 'several features centred around the Maori and local history'.⁷ Hayward's *Rewi's Last Stand* (1940) was released only five years before Mirams' book, so his view was imperceptive. But rather than too easily berating him, we should see the amnesia of this committed cinephile as representative, caused by his own zealous commitment to documentary and, more generally, by the culturally dependent mentality, understandable in a colonial society, unable to conceive of worthwhile production in New Zealand, at least in the field where Hollywood was dominant. A recurrent feature of early critical writing on the emerging New Zealand cinema of the 1980s was to purvey anecdotes about only marginally earlier audiences' self-conscious embarrassment at hearing New Zealand accents in the cinema.

Of course, in one way Mirams was right: there had been few feature films made when he wrote, and fewer of more than archival interest. The emptiness was dramatic in comparison with the trans-Tasman rival, Australia, which sustained a significant silent industry almost from the century's beginning; Pike and Cooper's filmography lists 106 features (or proto-features) made between 1900 and 1913 and another 151 between 1914 and 1929, though output declined throughout the sound era until the 1970s renaissance.[8] In the early 1920s Australia produced films of an impressive standard (for example, *The Sentimental Bloke*, 1920, *A Girl of the Bush*, 1921). By comparison there was only *one* New Zealand-produced feature made in New Zealand before Hayward's earliest (1922), George Tarr's lost *Hinemoa* (1914), which, whatever the interest of its unique position, clearly failed to match early Australian productions in sophistication. In the whole of the period up to the beginning of the Second World War there were only twelve fiction feature films which by most standards qualify as New Zealand-made films.

It was therefore, despite the documentary tradition which took early root under government direction at the Department of Tourism, a rather empty scene, and the basic explanation is simple enough. New Zealand's population in 1912, the year Méliès shot the first fiction films made in the country, was just over 1 million, with under a quarter of a million living in the four main urban centres. The 1911 census gave Australia's non-aboriginal population as about 4.5 million, with Sydney and Melbourne contributing 650,000 and 600,000 respectively. By the 1921 census Sydney had over a million people and Melbourne nearly a million, while New Zealand's population was only slightly more than Sydney's, and similar ratios continue into the present, where New Zealand's population of nearly 4 million is slightly less than Sydney's. What these statistics show is that from early days Australia had urban populations and infrastructures large enough to sustain a non- subsidized film industry, whereas New Zealand did not. An associated factor was the potency of late nineteenth-century Australian nationalism, which developed in more strident mythmaking ways than in New Zealand, where 'Better Britons' flourished. Australian culture promoted its self-images more vibrantly and successfully than New Zealand. Through novels, ballads and then films various 'myths' were robustly projected – of the outback, the 'girl of the bush', 'the sentimental bloke', the anti-authoritarian digger, the swagman defying police and squatters, and the legend of the bushranger – in a way that New Zealanders registered complicatedly, half-enviously and, in the image of their own idealized laconic even-headedness, half-condescendingly.

The long wait for 1977

Despite the the achievements of the two great originating figures Rudall Hayward and John O'Shea, the primary reality in the history of New Zealand feature film production is that it only became viable as a sustainable enterprise from 1977 onwards with the investment of public monies, albeit on a small scale, into enabling mechanisms. The programme for the premiere of Tarr's *Hinemoa* (1914) had its promoters addressing with extreme optimism 'those who welcome yet another industry in "God's Own Country"'.[9] Hayward certainly didn't experience cinema as an emerging industry when he attempted to get minor government aid for the first *Rewi's Last Stand*; the realities he encountered were quite different. On 26 August 1924 – writing to Sir Maui Pomare, Minister of Health in the Massey administration, asking him to take up shares in the film and allow use of his name to influence people, and requesting help in obtaining uniforms and weapons from the Māori Wars and from the staging of the Siege of Orakau at the British Empire Exhibition of 1924 – Hayward pleaded: 'I might mention that in America and in England film producers are given every possible assistance by the authorities, in an undertaking of this nature'.[10] The bureaucratic response unsympathetically advised making duplicates instead.

Historically there were two moments where New Zealand governments briefly addressed the possibilities of an entertainment film industry: the first in 1934 when the Committee of Enquiry into the Motion Picture Industry replied to representations that footage levies should be reimposed to support the setting up of a film industry, by making no recommendation at all; the second in 1949 when The Motion Picture Industry Committee replied to the question 'Whether it is desirable in the national interest to foster the production of films in NZ, and if so, by what means', with the statement that 'The evidence discloses no hindrances upon the production of entertainment film in NZ beyond the necessity of providing considerable capital for what must be a speculative return ... but there is nothing to prevent anyone from making the venture. There is, however, no case to be made out for the expenditure of public money on such a project'.[11] The 1949 response restricted itself to economic considerations, but did not ask whether there were strategies that might make returns less speculative, and certainly never broached (despite the longstanding sense of documentary as a useful ideological tool) anything like the later favoured ideas of 'cultural capital' and 'spectatorial rights' as a worthy target for economic capital. To be fair, it was a very different world in which only a very few visionaries thought otherwise. In 1928, aware that the extra costs of sound technology would shortly make film-making in New Zealand even more hazardous, Rudall Hayward had put forward strenuous arguments, both cultural and economic, for measures to support a native film industry. In the brief optimism of the release of *The Bush Cinderella* (1928) – with its New Zealand star,

Dale Austen, back from minor parts at MGM – Hayward, in a one-issue broadsheet, *The New Zealand Film Pioneer: dedicated to the Interest of Our Own Motion Pictures*, argued anonymously for the establishment of a national feature film industry. 'New Zealand films. Valuable infant industry. Battle for existence'. He optimistically put forward a four-point proposal arguing use of 'the Dominion's material advantages for film purposes': (i) employment for local talent and tradesmen; (ii) savings on the £250,000 per annum spent on importing foreign films; (iii) revenue from the sale of New Zealand films overseas; (iv) the role New Zealand films overseas would have in attracting tourists. These arguments (not uniformly convincing, for Hayward's own films conspicuously failed to bring in foreign revenue and the later showing of local films has never significantly cut into the number of imported films) were buttressed by cultural ones in an article attributed to 'WBM', 'Is New Zealand becoming Americanized? Baleful influence on [sic] American films. Why we want good New Zealand pictures'. The argument for films from the 'Britain of the South' employed familiar imperial tones, but with a nationalist inflection, 'We have plenty of incidents in our island story worthy to rank with any on the pages of British heroism'.[12] But these arguments fell on deaf ears if they were even remembered in 1934, and the 1949 committee seemed to have no memory of *Rewi's Last Stand* (1940), or recalled it only as an unsuccessful economic venture.

The New Zealand Film Commission

It was not until the late 1970s that the question 'whether it is desirable in the national interest to foster the production of films in NZ, and if so, by what means?' was answered in the affirmative, in the setting up of the New Zealand Film Commission, 1977–1978, to oversee film funding. The route to these historic moments involved the confluence of several factors: (i) the increasing sense in New Zealand of film as a prestigious medium; (ii) the enviable success of the big sibling Australia's revival of its film industry, to immediate international applause in the mid-1970s, and the success of the Australian Film Commission, Australian state funding mechanisms and tax advantages for film investment, prompting the question: if there, why not in New Zealand? (iii) the emergence of screen talent even in unpropitious circumstances with the early features of Geoff Steven, Paul Maunder, Tony Williams, the Academy Award nomination of Michael Firth's feature-length winter-sports documentary *Off The Edge* (1977) and especially the commercial success of *Sleeping Dogs* (1977), all suggesting around 1975–1977 that film had potential; (iv) a belated realization by politicians of national cinema as 'cultural capital' – a concept now in the air as it had not been in 1934 and 1949 – that fiction film, as much as if not more than documentary, might have propaganda uses advertising New Zealand in the widest sense.

Since 1977, feature-film funding mechanisms have centred on the New Zealand Film Commission (NZFC), augmented by NZ On Air funding where TV showings have been negotiated as part of the package. Though a small percentage of films made have been funded from private-sector sources alone (*The Piano* and *The Lord of the Rings*, completely funded 'off-shore' are the best-known examples) and some others by a mixture of NZFC and private-sector funding, the overwhelming majority of films have been solely NZFC funded. The Commission's policies, involving dispersal of monies at differing stages of development from script to post-production, have remained basically constant, though passing through various phases of greater or lesser populist emphasis,[13] with greater or lesser (more often lesser) amounts of government money available, international co-production deals (both one-off and more sustained), and various schemes aimed at encouraging production from both ends of the spectrum of directorial experience. (Though it lacks critical acumen, Lindsay Shelton's recent 'insider' account *The Selling of New Zealand Movies*, offers gossipy insights into the world of producers, funders and vendors).[14]

Basically this is the situation that has prevailed. Famously, there was a brief period in the early 1980s where tax loopholes made film investment riskless and profitable, and relatively large numbers of films were made (29 in the period 1983–1985), some without any government contribution, but the 1982 budget closed the loopholes, though projects already under way were allowed to continue. By 1985 the last of the boom was over, and, despite predictions that the industry would fold, seven films were released in 1986, six in 1987, and seven in 1988. And though 1989 was a disastrous year, with only one release, by and large production thereafter has been sustained at a reasonable level.

Theory and practice
A small English-language cinema

In *Australian National Cinema* Tom O'Regan writes of Australia as a 'medium sized English language cinema'.[15] Among huge cinemas (for example Hollywood, Bollywood), big ones (Japan, France, Italy, Britain), and medium-sized ones (Australia), New Zealand ranks among the smallest, sustained by a population of only 4 million, producing on average about five films a year, increasing with the advent of cheap digital production from seven in 2002 to an unprecedented sixteen in 2003 (though making is not necessarily to be equated with theatrical, or even commercial video or DVD, release). Despite this smallness, New Zealand has made a significant impact upon the relatively newly constituted audience for 'world cinema', most obviously through several high-profile film-makers (Vincent Ward, Jane Campion and Peter Jackson), but also through films disseminated around the world in 'art house' cinemas, on television, then on video and now DVD, feeding a market for new national cinemas; films felt to exhibit some kind of freshness and difference while still basically operating within the parameters of mainstream legibility, whether from Afghanistan, Vietnam, Ireland, Australia, China, Iran or New Zealand.

Small cinemas, big problems

The situation of the New Zealand cinema is defined, however, not just by desirable newness, but by problems besetting all small cinemas and, most specifically, small English-language cinemas. The most persistent of these problems are as follows.

(i) The small size of the home audience, with its age-old preference for Hollywood productions, which makes it almost impossible for local films to take a substantial share of the home box office, and for even successful ones to recover costs through local exhibition.

(ii) The consequent impossibility, despite various governmental gestures towards ending the industry's 'cycle of dependency', of it existing apart from government funding, especially since New Zealand governments have been traditionally averse to quotas and levies, as well as to legislating tax incentives to private-sector film investment. This only ever existed in New Zealand briefly in the early 1980s by accident, not by design, and later in the one-off case of the NZ$219 million (at least) tax write-off allowed *The Lord of the Rings*, after a change in the law to close another loophole. However, around 2005 the question of tax incentives seems now to be opening up again, after arguments for them led by Peter Jackson, a powerful voice in a small public arena.

(iii) The very low rates of pay for most personnel in the industry not employed on 'off-shore' financed projects – actors, directors, creative and technical personnel – as well as low film-making budgets.

(iv) The consequent likelihood of any director or actor achieving international recognition taking up overseas offers. Among successful local directors, Geoff Murphy, Roger Donaldson, Lee Tamahori, Alison Maclean, Vincent Ward and Jane Campion have all moved overseas. Peter Jackson's unprecedented position as a Hollywood director in Wellington is too freakish to be more than an unrepeatable exception. Among actors, Bruno Lawrence, though regarded at home as the quintessential New Zealand actor, spent significant parts of his career in Australia; Sam Neill, internationally the busiest of New Zealand actors, has in nearly thirty years made only three New Zealand films; the London-based Kerry Fox has, after *An Angel at My Table*, only made a single local film. The situation in the contemporary film world of one-off projects rather than long-term contracts now allows more flexibility for the émigré actor and director, who can, while operating overseas, more easily return to make films, as Murphy with his recent *Spooked* (2004), Donaldson with *The World's Fastest Indian* (2005), and Ward with *River Queen* (2006) have lately done. At the same time, actors like Cliff Curtis, Temuera Morrison and Karl Urban can commute profitably to minor Hollywood parts, while pursuing careers in New Zealand. Minor, though, is the defining term, because if their Hollywood careers accelerated, their New Zealand careers could hardly be sustained in parallel. As a result of such movements New Zealand cinema has often been called a cinema of first-time directors. Though this is sometimes treated as an unambiguous positive, ensuring constant injections of unconventionality, the situation has drawbacks in terms of lack of experience and consolidated wisdom, some of the consequences of which are discussed later in this book.

(v) The 'which audience' dilemma. Like the Australian, English/British and Canadian cinemas and the two small anglophone cinemas with which in terms of population it has even more in common – Ireland (5 million) and Scotland (4 million) – the New Zealand cinema has the advantage over non-anglophone cinemas of relatively uncomplicated linguistic access to American markets. Caught between two desires – to gain success through what is felt as authentically local for home audiences, or by breaking into the major foreign markets, primarily the American, intimidatingly difficult though that may be on any but a minor art-house scale – the consequence is the particular inflection of an identical argument endlessly staged by other small cinemas: should films be made with the home audience primarily in mind? Or should they be tailored to the possibility of breaking into greater markets? The economic problem with the first is that the home market is so small, and that films made for it may be too idiosyncratic to appeal overseas to any but committed, minority art-house audiences looking for different 'world cinema' experiences. The problem with the second is the likelihood of films that are cut-rate Hollywood clones, rejected both at home and abroad for the real deal. The sustaining dream is, of course, a cinema, or more modestly, the occasional film, the authentic localness of which appeals to the greater audience. This is not impossible, but relatively rare, and where it has happened – without doubting the enormous importance of their success for the whole New Zealand industry of the films in question – one might argue that *Once Were Warriors* and *Whale Rider* (though not, I believe, *Heavenly Creatures*) compromise their local realities to some degree in the search for wider audiences. (This is too purist a view to be much shared: there is little evidence that it worried more than a small minority of the films' big home audiences.) Inescapably, small cinemas have the home/away dilemma as part of their inevitable landscape. The majority of films will continue to be made with an eye on the two audiences, internal and external, with the best that can be usually hoped for – leaving aside the dreamed of exception that penetrates the wider market – being overseas art-house success buttressed by television and DVD sales to that audience looking for different national 'authenticities' (at least as they understand them), which makes the local but international film possible on a moderate commercial scale. (Another route – the largely video, now DVD, penetration of an international market by local horror-film makers – is too genre-specific to be generally applicable.)

(vi) 'The whole world in one country' – the problematic of New Zealand as a site for foreign 'off-shore' film-making. In *The Whole World in One Country* promotional booklet, published by Film New Zealand in 1999, two elements are heavily promoted: (a) the extraordinary variety of the New Zealand landscape (its 'English Summer lanes, Welsh hillsides and forest ... Cretan and Grecian coastlines', as well as 'Fantasy landscapes'[16] – *The Lord of The Rings* is of course the obvious instance of the last – with recent instances of location mimicry being Taranaki as Japan in *The Last Samurai* and Dunedin as New England in Christine Jeffs' *Sylvia*), and (b) the experience, 'competitive crew costs' and adaptability (no problems with strict demarcation) of New Zealand technicians.[17] Although there are now cheaper places in which to film (as noted by Mark De Wayne's *Making Your Films for Less Outside the US*, which mentions Canada, Singapore, France, South Africa, the Philippines, Hong Kong and Australia, but not New Zealand),[18] the combination of relatively low costs in 'a highly deregulated economy', geographical variety, and experienced crew – along with the formidable local CGI expertise recently developed through Jackson's later special-effects-dominated films – makes it a desirable location. This is not a new phenomenon but the accelerated continuation (with Bollywood's now established and South Korea's even more recent use of New Zealand settings the latest additions)[19] of one visible much earlier: for instance, the Australian *The Mutiny of the Bounty*'s made-over Rotorua as Tahiti and Pitcairn Island (1916), and the Nelson production site standing in for a Pacific island in the American production *Venus of the South Seas* (1924), centring on the Australian aquatic star Annette Kellerman, and sardonically referred to by Hayward in his *New Zealand Film Pioneer* as never even being credited in the film. 'Off-shore' film-making (lately further boosted by local digital expertise developed out of Jackson's recent films) provokes two antithetical responses. The first, affirmative, stresses economic benefits: the provision of constant employment for the industry, or at least its technical sector. The opposite view, voiced by the filmmaker Sam Pillsbury, forsees negative consequences, in which New Zealand's primary cinematic role could become 'the runaway [off-shore film-making] haven of the South Pacific'. 'While they [runaway productions] have a place, says Pillsbury, as a training ground for industry new entrants and as guaranteed employment for industry professionals, they must be viewed critically: "By imposing formulaic story-lines and systems that leave little room for the growth and development of indigenous stories, the lure of the 'runaway bonus' could stifle New Zealand's unique film perspective, slowly turning it into just another service industry."'[20]

From low to no – small-budget film-making the New Zealand way: constraints, creativity and costs on poverty row

Though lately a number of films have been budgeted at around NZ$5 million and even, in co-production deals, up to NZ$10 (with the expenditure on *River Queen* and *Perfect Creature* near double this), the standard New Zealand film-making experience is working on very low budgets with all the associated constraints. Some of the not too distant major successes of the industry were made astonishingly cheaply: for instance, *Once Were Warriors* for NZ$1.4 million, *Mauri* for NZ$2 million, and *Meet The Feebles* for NZ$ 750,000.[21] In some respects the more democratic end of the digital revolution has already altered things, allowing radically cheap shooting in ways impossible before, with, in the commercial sector, films like Jason Stutter's *Tongan Ninja* and John Laing's *The Shirt* showing the way. However, the production values expected by mainstream audiences cannot be replicated by cheap digital shooting, and while these technologies have already increased the variety of local production, they cannot solve the budgetary problematic of most New Zealand films, which is operating as a very small-budget player in a higher-budget market.

The situation is ambiguous. Should we celebrate it as helping to prevent New Zealand cinema from becoming a largely anonymous player in transnational cinema, and as spurring creativity in an affirmatively 'poor' cinema? Or should we see its 'poverty row' aspects as promoting a regime of short cuts and temporary repairs, conventional solutions (mainstream without the money) rather than creativity? As with several of the endemic problems of New Zealand cinema, there is no simple answer. There is, anyway, no quick-fix solution to low budget problems, even though they could be mitigated by tax incentives and superior co-productions. The New Zealand cinema, even under better circumstances of more private investment, cannot – as a basically government-subsidized industry, protected from the rigours of the marketplace – expect markedly increased subsidies, and therefore has to live as best it can with low-budget film-making the norm. The two instances below illustrate different practitioners' responses to the problem in two films where creativity rather than mediocrity is observable.

A young film-maker, Vanessa Alexander, the writer-director of *Magik and Rose* (2000), wrote an Auckland University thesis detailing the making of the film under conditions which were an extreme version of the usual New Zealand experience of working with a small budget of under or around NZ$2 million.[22] She got her opportunity under Larry Parr's short-lived, financially unstable Kahukura Productions scheme to increase local film production by so-called 'no-budget' films, funded initially at no more than NZ$250,000. The rough cuts of these films were then shown to organizations (in reality the New Zealand Film Commission) in the hope of receiving post-production funding, which happened here to the extent of an extra NZ$500,000, bringing the total budget to NZ$750,000: still very low even by New Zealand standards of the time, but close enough to the average lowest budget to make her experiences a perspective from which generalization is possible. Some of her economic breakdowns are extremely revealing. Alexander received NZ$5,000 as writer and another NZ$5,000 as director, and the director of photography NZ$3,000. The actors and technicians were paid a flat NZ$500 a week, though the actors were also guaranteed some share of profits, if any.[23] Clearly, no one gets rich working on New Zealand films, unless gold is struck overseas. The film was made to a very tight schedule: 3 weeks of rehearsals, 4 weeks pre-production, and a short shoot of 28 days (22 of them active), but followed by nearly a year's post-production.[24] Under these constraints Alexander made a quirkily charming,

Introduction 13

off-beat film that looks as if it cost considerably more. She is, however, a film-maker happy to work within the New Zealand Film Commission's 'dominant ideology' of 'bums on seats' through 'a strong emphasis on humour and entertainment': 'I felt I could still steer the film I wanted to make through the industry's maze of commercial expectations'. The low shooting budget ordained that money spent in one place had to be saved in others, meaning that many scenes consisted of only one shot and that 'many of the more visual, cinematic methods of story telling are often unattainable ... The very nature of a low budget project tends to emphasize character and dialogue driven narrative'.[25] Given that she found herself able to work happily within such constraints – which also included a compulsory test screening and much work on 'branding', 'target audience' and 'niche market' – it is interesting that the one conflict she reports was her insistence against marketing advice on not replacing the lead male, Oliver Driver, with a more glamorous-looking actor. In justifying her choice, Alexander made her only 'ideological' statement, differentiating her film from Hollywood films: 'I feel simply that casting by physical attributes is the domain of the Hollywood star system and should be openly kept out of New Zealand films'.[26] Implicit in this is a whole 'local-real' versus Hollywood aesthetic, though within formal parameters more adapted from Hollywood than any more radical aesthetic, that many New Zealand film-makers would share, though Alexander's statement of difference is also given a pragmatic twist in her suggestion that glamour castings are useless given the short art-house overseas runs that New Zealand films get.

If *Magik and Rose* presents a largely affirmative instance of what can be done under severe constraints, Leon Narbey's *The Footstep Man*, one of the most ambitious New Zealand films of the 1990s, made on a three-times larger but still restricted budget, tells a different story. Cairns and Martin quote Narbey as having for budgetary reasons to shorten the script by 20 minutes, cutting out completely the film-within-the-film's producer, Walter, thus deleting in a New Zealand film about film-making the always vital producer's role in mediating between aspiration and economic reality, which, ironically played a particularly major part in the making of *The Footstep Man*.[27] As distinct from Alexander's expressions of relative ease in working with her even greater constraints, Narbey's view was 'The simple answer to "what are the difficulties and challenges of making a film in New Zealand?" is "Not enough money."' Narbey's film is more complex than Alexander's; as he himself said, 'it was a very ambitious film. It probably shouldn't have been made for less than five million dollars'.[28] Despite its tribulations, *The Footstep Man* is still one of the best local films of the 1990s, but its vicissitudes show another side to the constraints that Alexander, with a less ambitious project, was able to deal with more easily.

Mythologies of difference

To listen to some voices, one might think that problems were non-existent. And in one sense optimism is justified: over the last few years considerable new talents have made feature films, arguing a reservoir of talent and desire for cinematic expression running unexpectedly deep in a culture often reluctant to support local films (as evidenced in some of the abysmally poor box-office figures revealed in Lindsay Shelton's *The Selling of New Zealand Movies*). The most extreme declarations of almost unconditional optimism for the New Zealand cinema tend to come, not surprisingly, as its practitioners respond to the spotlight of premieres and festivals. For instance, at the 2004 London Film Festival, where three New Zealand female film-makers' films were highlighted, multiple tributes to the industry were made. The festival's director announced that 'New Zealand film makers had succeeded by telling their own stories rather than following typical Hollywood storylines' and the distinguished director Gaylene Preston said 'film-making in New Zealand relied more on the individuality of the director than elsewhere. Movies in America and elsewhere were driven by the "committee process" and boardroom meetings, while in New Zealand they were often cooked up around the kitchen table ... Our film making is genuine, we stand staunch'.[29] These statements are paralleled by those from Nicki Caro (the director of *Whale Rider*): 'She was repeatedly asked how New Zealand continued to produce such extraordinary cinema? "That thrills me. I'm so proud of and inspired by features from my own country because they are unique and audacious and they don't compromise and they aren't mediocre. There's a kind of persistent originality here that I really connect with". She believed part of the reason was that New Zealand was a nation of first film-makers'.[30]

Such statements, however affecting, demand qualification. An equal case could be made that much New Zealand cinema is more derivative than original; suffers, as frequently asserted, from poor screenwriting; and is less a director's than a producer's cinema, tailored to the more commercial inflections of funding policy, with films typically hammered out less round kitchen than round committee room tables, often with mediocre results. This would be as much a negative exaggeration as the others are positive, but any balanced view must include it. For instance, it is salutary to observe that such well-known films as *Sleeping Dogs, Once were Warriors, What Becomes of the Broken Hearted?, The Scarecrow* and *Came a Hot Friday* share the characteristic of reducing elements of darkness, conflict and difficulty in their sources (providing a counter-tendency to claims of a 'cinema of unease'): for example, *The Scarecrow*'s omission of its source's darkest protracted joke (the absolute apex of the novelist Ronald Hugh Morrieson's 'Kiwi Gothic'), the muddling of the funeral times and indeed bodies of old Mr Fitzherbert and the teenage victim of Salter's rape and murder. *The Scarecrow* survives such softenings to be a not inconsiderable film, and *Came a Hot Friday* has a deserved classic status, which, however, also involves processes of comparable softening. The crux of the argument here is not the films' metamorphoses of their origins away from literal illustration, but their tendency to play down rather than to inventively expand areas of conflict and difficulty. At times *Came a Hot Friday* even transcends its source, particularly in its reinvention of its conmen protagonists. This said, there is still something to be pondered, and not all positively, in the report that 'before the shoot, Mune [the director] was still wrestling with the hard, vicious, bitter side of Morrieson which he was uncomfortable with. So Mune, Parker, and composer and friend Stephen McCurdy got together and beat and beat and beat the story', a story Mune earlier described as 'sad and on the side of death' and 'not what I was about'.[31]

Seen as a not uncommon tendency across many films, such instances do raise questions about filmic mythologies of constant independence. To say this is not to deny that independence and inventiveness are often present in New Zealand films, but rather that practitioners understandably exaggerate their ubiquity. As we shall see, with Nick Perry's essay 'Antipodean Camp' below, there are certain myths of New Zealand 'difference', creativity, end-of-the-world lastness becoming firstness, of a handmade, improvised, do-it-yourself cinema, positively individualistic and unregulated, that may, irrespective of their only partial truth, actually need to be sustained, disregarding evidence to the contrary, in order for a precarious film industry to prosper. By contrast, think how much of a downer an emphasis on New Zealand sameness, conventionality, imitation, lastness without claim to primacy, would be.

Questions of nation and national cinema

In writing about New Zealand cinema, one can hardly proceed unaware that nation and nationalism are now much debated subjects and that their relation to cinema, encapsulated in the term 'national cinema', is no longer seen as transparent. From recent theorizing a number of points are immediately relevant. These centre around: (i) questions of the legitimacy of the idea of boundaried national cinema in an age of globalization in which the transnational is pervasive; (ii) critiques of the narrowness with which national cinemas have been described; (iii) various defences of national cinema, growingly in contemporary writing associated with a contemporary cinema underpinned by subsidies from governments committed to cinema as national expression. As regards (i), this book accepts the view that 'If the concept of national cinema is considered troublesome at the level of theoretical debate, it is still a considerable force at the level of state policy';[32] not just a force in state policy, it should be added, but for many viewers and supporters of the cinema, as well as many film-makers. It also agrees that in the age of globalism, the immediate cinematic consequences of which are international co-production, and, paradoxically, a particular manifestation of 'glocalism', whereby tendencies towards globalism create the conditions for a transnational high valuing of local cinemas, boundaries have to be seen as fluid, though this does not at all mean they have no reality. As regards (ii), it may well be true that various constructions of national cinema have repressed contesting and marginal voices. Though this is often assumed to be a conservative vice, it is a fault that equally belongs to the left, where what are seen as valuably 'progressive' films may be foregrounded to the exclusion of ones judged 'regressive'. Here it is interesting to read Andrew Higson's worries that, in defending a subsidized British cinema, John Hill argues 'less for a national cinema than what may be called a critical (and implicitly left wing) cinema'.[33] Yet one can still agree with Hill that 'it is important that a national cinema is maintained in Britain' (or New Zealand), one 'capable of registering the lived complexities of British [or New Zealand] "national life"',[34] though such a cinema should be seen as more pluralistic than he suggests. Though I elsewhere find O'Regan's *Australian National Cinema* lacking, one of its positive features is its stress on the hybridity and heterogeneity of Australian (and by implication other) national cinemas.[35] Thus this book attempts to record the instabilities as well as stabilities in New Zealand cinema, its mundanities as well as exceptionalities. Higson writes how traditional views of national cinema have seen its importance in offering 'coherent images of the nation, sustaining the nation at an ideological level, exploring what is understood to be the "indigenous culture"' (a complicated term in the New Zealand context with a double, even triple meaning: Māori, indigenous Pākehā [Māori term, now mainstream, for white New Zealanders] and indigenous New Zealander, encompassing both and more). 'Of equal importance today', he continues, 'is the role cinema is felt to play in terms of promoting the nation as a tourist destination, to the benefit of the tourism and service industries',[36] something particularly true of New Zealand in the age of *The Lord of the Rings*. This book is naturally aware of the intertwining of the cinema with these phenomena, but is more interested in the textuality of its films than their more extrinsic uses.

How do you define a New Zealand (fiction feature) film?

A book of this kind faces problems in defining exactly what is and is not a New Zealand film. The New Zealand Film Commission can only support films with 'a significant New Zealand content', so how it publicly defines this 'content', in its most extended sense, is at least a beginning: 'a. the subject matter of the film b. the locations at which the film is or is to be made c. the nationalities and places of residence of – (i) The authors, scriptwriters, composers, producers, directors, actors, technicians, editors and other persons who took part or are to take part in the making of the film (ii) The persons who own or are to have the copyright of the film'. Further criteria relate to (d) the film's money sources, (e) the ownership of equipment and technical facilities, and a wide statement of 'any other matters' that are 'relevant'.[37] What are generally, commonsensically, considered New Zealand films fulfil various combinations of the above, particularly a, b, c and d, many all of them. The possible complications more marginal cases present can only be hinted at here. The abstract geography of New Zealand cinema can best be envisaged as a series of concentric circles, spreading from wider inner circles occupied by a majority of films fulfilling most of the criteria above uncontentiously, to narrower ones occupied at the furthest extremes by films that perhaps fulfil only one or two, perhaps made in New Zealand with local money in the tax-break period, with a very minor New Zealand element in production, technical and marginal acting areas, like the unreleased film *Prisoners* (1982), oriented to the American market. *A Soldier's Tale*, directed by the New Zealand producer/director/screenwriter Larry Parr, has a wholly overseas cast, and subject matter with no New Zealand element, though it adapted a novel by the New Zealand author M.K. Joseph, and had New Zealand financing and some New Zealand technicians working on it. Though it lacks New Zealand subject matter, actors and shooting sites, there can be little argument here (as with the parallel cases of recent novels by New Zealand writers with wholly non-New Zealand settings and characters, such as Elizabeth Knox's *The Vintner's Luck* and Catherine Chidgey's *The Transformation*), that *A Soldier's Tale* is a New Zealand film, rather more clearly than Anna Campion's *Loaded* (1995). This latter film was made in England by an expatriate New Zealander without other connections to the home industry, except through her sister Jane Campion, centred on English characters and subject matter played out by English actors, but was, however, jointly financed by the NZFC with British Screen, with post-production in New Zealand, expatriate New Zealanders on the crew, and the involvement of the leading local art-film producers John Maynard and Bridget Ikin. *Loaded* must be situated at some distance from the central circles envisaged above, but there are situations in which it might be integral to the discussion of New Zealand cinema – a study of Jane Campion, involving her sibling, the history of international co-production in the New Zealand cinema, a study of the producer's role in New Zealand cinema, a study of expatriate film-makers – though these are outnumbered by the contexts in which it would not be treated as a New Zealand film. Since we are talking not of a single criterion, but multiple overlapping ones, common sense should be applied. An Australian producer and French funding, do not make *The Piano* either a French or Australian film, at least in the most culturally central ways, and while Ward's *The Navigator* is a trans-Tasman co-production, the director's nationality, the subject matter and the place of shooting combine to make it more a New Zealand than Australian film (whereas the director's nationality and past and broadly shared antipodean elements are the only aspects that give, with Campion's *Sweetie* or *Holy Smoke*, New Zealand connections to dominantly Australian films). These examples raise the difficult question: how are the foreign cinema films of expatriate directors to be classified? Are, for instance, Donaldson's, Murphy's and Ward's overseas films 'New Zealand films' in some unofficial cultural rather than financial-industrial sense, because of the directors' New Zealand connections? Again, answers may be more or less complicated depending on the context (authorship studies of New Zealand directors working in Hollywood or other cinemas, more general studies of New Zealand's relationship with other cinemas), and recently in the cases of Murphy, Ward and Donaldson, the matter has been redefined by the directors' return to at least isolated instances of film-making in New Zealand, which has suddenly reinvigorated questions of the relationship between their home and overseas films. It is likely that closer links exist between art or art-house directors like Ward's and Campion's New Zealand films and their non-New Zealand ones, a function of the auteuristic film encouraging the expression of more personal motifs (which may be connected to nationality), than is the case with expatriate directors working in post-studio Hollywood film-making where – and it has to be remembered that Murphy and Donaldson surrendered their screenwriting roles when they moved – there is little or no space for such material. That is, however, unless we believe Dr George Miller that some essential Australianness, or, by extension, New Zealandness, cannot but express itself even in these circumstances, like the revelatory diphthongs and high-rising terminal contours the expatriate's speech patterns may retain.[38]

Because this book deals with the early periods of New Zealand film-making, it includes, for those early periods, under the rubric New Zealand film, those made in New Zealand by foreigners, such as Méliès' productions (the first fiction films made in New Zealand) and other early overseas productions between 1916 and 1935. The justification of this expanded definition is that such films constituted a major part of the landscape of the earliest New Zealand cinema, which cannot be understood without reference to them. (Instances of a few much later films by overseas directors with local participation and thematics substantial enough for them to be treated as part of the local cinema are traced in chapters 5 and 6.)

On critical analysis and on not joining the search for a grand theory of everything

Film-making in New Zealand, as elsewhere, is the generative centre of many activities (think of those three multi postage stamp issues of characters from *The Lord of the Rings* – our favourite, of course, Gollum NZ$2, December 2003), both commercial and ideological, from touristic advertising of the country, to the promotion of knowledge about its films in journalism, archives, and academic film studies. Though the bulk of valuable work in the latter has been small scale, patient archival research, studies of single films or limited topics, some of the most interesting, though not necessarily the most successful, instances of local criticism have produced not so much theories as generative metaphors for New Zealand film. The most influential of these has been the concept, encapsulated in its title, of a *Cinema of Unease*, a television documentary in the British Film Institute's *Centenary of Cinema* national cinemas series made by the most internationally prestigious of New Zealand actors, Sam Neill, and the documentarist Judy Rymer, with an audience much greater than that of academic writers. Generally speaking, this film essay was well received overseas, because of its appealingly graspable argument. At home it was critically less liked, and reproved for being out of touch with more varied recent movements and for its narrow view of, as Roger Horrocks put it in a lucid summary of the case for and against, 'New Zealand as a Southern Hemisphere equivalent of the dark Sweden of Ingmar Bergman's films'.[39] Though its view of later New Zealand cinema as reacting against the blandness of 1950s and 1960s New Zealand life is out of touch with many changes, it is, nevertheless, a strong view, foregrounding a real, though subdominant, strand of New Zealand cinema, and one that has passed into popular currency, for example, in the video cover blurb for *Snakeskin* (Gillian Ashurst, 2000), which speaks of that film as one that 'boots the cinema of unease into the new century'. Two other views may be seen as variants on this, in finding related kinds of unease at the core of the cinema. In a short overview of New Zealand film written for an American academic publication, David Gerstner and Sarah Greenlees identify 'anxiety' over national and filmic identity as the generating principle of New Zealand cinema.[40] Again, like a 'cinema of unease', the idea of a cinema generated by identity anxieties is not lacking in force, for in a small new nation recently passing from settler colonial to post-colonial identity, and in its small and vulnerable cinema, overshadowed by more dominant cinemas, most of all Hollywood, it would be strange not to find such concerns manifested. Yet, beyond the vagueness of its articulation, the idea is unsatisfactory as a generative account, partly because, as with the cinema of unease, so many films evade its grasp. Another problem in seeing it as more than a useful partial insight is that similar anxieties must logically afflict all post-colonial societies and cinemas (and even all small cinemas, whether post-colonial or not), so that the generating identity anxiety said to characterize New Zealand cinema must be shared with many others, and even with larger societies and cinemas, thus losing much of its specificity of application. A third, again impressionistic, variant on the 'cinema of unease' is found in the labelling by Merata Mita, the Māori director of *Mauri* and *Patu!*, of the New Zealand film industry as 'a white neurotic one' in its presentation of 'the white man or woman at odds with his/her country and himself/herself', interpreted as the unanalysed and unarticulated filmic embodiment of 'the colonial syndrome of dislocation', enacted in symptoms of malaise that film narratives displace from their origins in 'the fear and repression caused by political guilt' onto the purely personal.[41] This, then, is a variation of the cinema of unease and identity anxiety translated into political terms, distinctly different, in Mita's interpretation from Māori cinema, which is seen as driven by the antithetical qualities of 'identity, resolution and survival' (though these are terms equally applicable to Hayward's films, and ones that – looking at two recent films, *Rain* and *In My Father's Den* – still have resonance for some later Pākehā cinema).[42] While – like the other two statements, of which it is a racial variant – the claim has it points in referring to the still living issue of the colonial state's expropriation of Māori land, its application to mainstream New Zealand cinema is far from unproblematic in its ascription of all psychological conflict to a single deflected cause. It may be felt that Mita's claim (which might also be seen as more moral exhortation than analysis – in other words, you ought to feel more guilt and dislocation than you do!), works better with the mainly literary products of the nationalist period, with their constant tropes of unease with an unlived-in landscape and of envy of the indigene's longer tenure, than with later films. Lastly, it might be said that symptoms of malaise are too common and various in complex societies to be ascribed simply to colonial guilt. All three tropes (unease, identity anxiety and deflected guilt) have considerable limitations as fundamental, generative accounts, yet at the same time suggest perspectives that are part of the critical endeavour the contemporary film analyst inherits.

The same may be said of Nick Perry's 'Antipodean Camp' (where 'Camp' loses its usual connotations, becoming the politically subdominant's response to politico- cultural rather than heterosexual dominance). While the tropes discussed above are primarily attempts to diagnose subject matter, Perry's suggests a formal peculiarity of Australasian art as residing affirmatively in conditions often perceived negatively – lastness, isolation, distance from the centres, powerlessness, reimagined as a creative act of post-modern 'bricolage', a gathering of other cultures' driftwood to form new image combinations on the beaches of the edge of the world, in films of a highly hybridic, cross-generic nature. Perry's argument is expressed, through a remarkable density of allusion (depending on your view, either illuminatingly illustrative of the complexity of Australasian post-modern intertextuality, or defensively camouflaging slightness of argument) but also, with a boldness which will either seem invigorating or lacking, through an extremely small range of illustrations, though it must be said that he has a great gift for the telling instance: for instance, his brief meta-cinematic allegorizing of Al's use of bits and pieces from all over the world to repair Ray's car in *Smash Palace*.[43] 'Antipodean Camp', like the other instances referred to, has flaws as an argument, it being, for instance, unclear whether it can really be claimed that New Zealand (and/or Australian, the argument tends to slip between Australasian and singularly New Zealand) cinema is more post-generically hybridic than others. It may be that Perry's influential trope, which manoeuvres round the poet Bill Manhire's assertion of New Zealand as the site for the artist of 'diversities, disjunctions, juxtapositions and incongruities',[44] is less powerful as an analytical precept, than as another necessary enabling myth of significance and creativity for New Zealand film.

Two other critics should also be mentioned. Martin Blythe's book *Naming the Other* (1994) is much the most interesting of the few books written about New Zealand film, an account up to the mid-1980s not of the whole terrain but of representations of Māori across the whole cinema, documentaries as much as feature films, which has many groundbreaking things to say about its important subject. In particular its delineation of categories of the early cinema – particularly the 'Maoriland Romance' (the timeless ahistorical portraits of pre-European life), and the 'Historical or Nationalist Romance' (the fall into history, the encounter of Pākehā and Māori), as well as its definitions of various generic subspecies, 'ethnological romance', 'pakeha pilgrimage genre', and so forth – are so strong that they will doubtless be adopted into general critical usage.[45] In an area where analysis is sometimes equated with hostility, Blythe's book was not particularly well received in New Zealand on publication. However, his scepticism about a whole range of essentialisms – Pākehā, Māori, masculinist, feminist – and his treating of various dogmas as myths – such as the integration myth, the bicultural myth, the Māori separatist myth, and so on – are enormously valuable in a minefield bestrewn with essentialist arguments. Roger Horrocks, the New Zealand critic with the longest spread of publication, commands respect for work, particularly a series of overviews of the New Zealand film scene, that resist the chimera of a single generative principle. His 'Cultures, Policies, Films' essay is an exemplary survey of the local film scene circa 1998, with its emphasis on New Zealand, and, by extension, New Zealand cinema, not as (if it ever was quite that) 'stolid [and] never-changing',[46] but as a place of cultures and identities in contention as well as relation, and its ability to bring into relation, multiple social, economic, cultural and cinematic factors.

Organization and categorization: genre via Schopenhauer

As a history this book's organization is broadly, but not minutely, chronological. Unsurprisingly, problems of organization and categorization become more pressing in its contemporary sections, especially for the period 1986–2005 with its greater output of films. Organization by individuals, with its largely misleading suggestions of a cinema of auteurs, is used sparingly, with only Hayward and O'Shea given sections to themselves, and Murphy, Donaldson, Ward, Campion, Jackson and Sinclair being dealt with in subsections. There are few others for whom auteurial approaches are particularly productive; other candidates include Gaylene Preston, Peter Wells, Florian Habicht, Alison Maclean, Garth Maxwell, Niki Caro and Christine Jeffs. Organization, then, along generic and modal lines has been chosen as generally the best approach, but has difficulties which must be briefly sounded. The most basic delineation of the problem of generic classification – insoluble because it involves two competing paradigms neither of which can claim superiority – is Schopenhauer's in *On the Fourfold Root of the Principle of Sufficient Reason* where he sets out the two competing laws of Homogeneity and Specification: 'Entities should not be multiplied unnecessarily' and 'the number and variety of entities is not to be limited without good reason'.[47] Given the antithetical desires, on the one hand, to work with the most fundamental and inclusive categories and, on the other to avoid subsuming the individual in the genus, it is not surprising that most generic categorization in works on national cinemas is inconsistent. For instance, though Dermody and Jacka's study of Australian cinema[48] is marred by arrogant opinionatedness, the inconsistency of its generic organization is not, it seems to me, a ground for criticism, since it proves serviceable enough. The same may be said of the thematic pseudo-genres that organize Kevin Rockett's book on the Irish Film Board ('Childhood', 'Rites of Passage', 'Migration', and so on).[49] As these remarks suggest, this book's largely generic organization does not pursue the spectre of absolute consistency, but moves between the twin poles of homogeneity and specification, employing traditional generic categories, along with newer elastic ones such as the 'road movie', various hybrids, and, especially in the 1986–2005 section where the number of films prohibits over-specification, larger categories such as 'melodrama', 'comedy' and 'two-culture and Maori-made films', divided into various subspecies.

Me, Clark, Wilder and this book

A few final notes on the aims and ambitions of this book. (i) As a history, it attempts to combine two approaches often felt to be antithetical, the textual (with its close reading of individual films) and the historical (with its marginalizing of the individual text to comprehensiveness and generalization). O'Regan's *Australian National Cinema*, for all its exhaustiveness in various contemporary directions (contemporary only because one of its oddities is that it addresses only the later third of Australian film production, as if identifying 'national cinema' with state-subsidized cinema, though it nowhere argues this), admits to cutting out any emphasis on textuality[50] – surely an enormous limitation. The writer on New Zealand cinema has the advantage of a much smaller field of production, allowing this book to give more films more extensive attention than is usual in a text of this kind. Detailed discussion is given to films of demonstrable textual complexity and/or that are historically central to the New Zealand cinema, though word limits mean that casualties are inevitable in the later period. (ii) It should be emphasized that this book is not a history of production practices, of producers and production companies, or of the subsidizing mechanisms so important in contemporary New Zealand cinema. Such matters are raised where necessary, but my primary emphases are textual, of meaning, of cultural contribution, of aesthetic particularity. (iii) This book, written by an expatriate, addresses New Zealand readers and a wider overseas audience interested in New Zealand and the New Zealand cinema simultaneously. This has its difficulties, particularly where material familiar to the local reader needs to be explained, though as concisely as possible. At the same time, however, it has to be remembered that what one credits an ideal New Zealand reader as knowing (a quick test: the films of Hayward and O'Shea; the works of the historians Cowan, Sinclair, King; the Māori prophets; the Hunn Report; Baxter's poems; the novels of Mander, Devanny, Morrieson and Duff; the iconicity of John Rowles; the political theorizing of André Siegfried; those references to the 1986 rugby World Cup and to Mark Greatbatch's batting in the 1992 cricket World Cup in the boys' history highlights in *Stickmen*), he or she may in some cases be as innocent of as all but the exceptional overseas reader. Expatriatism has been in some ways a disadvantage in writing this book – distance from new films (in particular recent cheap, commercially unreleased digital productions) and other source materials being the most obvious – but it has the advantages of freeing the writer from parochial pressures and internecine quarrels. Given that this book addresses both a New Zealand and an overseas audience, it may have another difficulty. When writing about John Reid's films for a different book, I referred to the character 'Old Mac', the escaped convict folk hero in *Carry Me Back*, interpreting him as parodying the 'Man Alone' myth. My account was, I believe, perfectly good, except that it lacked one touch of local knowledge because I had forgotten the real-life prototype Reid referred to. What reminded me was reading the New Zealand writer Lloyd Jones's short story 'Me, Clark and Wilder', a wittily poignant cautionary tale of the local in the age of the transnational, about experience too intimate to be easily translated.⁵¹ George Wilder, a minor criminal, escaped from prison in New Plymouth, then from Mount Eden Prison twice in the early 1960s, and attained an ambiguous folk-hero status by evading the police for sixty-two days in the first case and one hundred and seventy-two in the second. Memories flooded back of the escapee's fame and even of Howard Morrison's pastiche recording 'George the Wilder Colonial Boy'. My once vivid, lapsed but latent, then revived, memories of Wilder, have functioned for me through what has been a difficult project, as an emblem of turning disadvantage to advantage, seeing my erratic hold on them, inasmuch as they were experiences I shared with Lloyd Jones and many of his audience, as binding me to the local scene in a way blocked to the overseas critic, but in their fragility, at times apparent non-existence, linking me to the outsiders for whom this book is also written.

Notes

1 Gordon Mirams, *Speaking Candidly: Films and People in New Zealand*, Paul's Book Arcade, Hamilton, 1945, 5.
2 Mirams, 10.
3 J.C. Reid, *Catholics and the Films*, Auckland Diocesan Council of the Holy Name Society/Whitcombe and Tombs, Auckland, 1949.
4 Mirams, 203.
5 *Ibid.*, 207.
6 *Ibid.*, 203.
7 *Ibid.*
8 A. Pike and R.Cooper, *Australian Film 1900–1977: A Guide to Feature Film Production*, Oxford University Press, Melbourne, 1980.
9 Tarr material, New Zealand Film Archive (NZFA).
10 Department of Internal Affairs document, Hayward material, NZFA.
11 Clive Sowry, 'The Arts: Film', *The New Zealand Book of Events*, G. McLauchlan, M. King, et al., eds, Methuen, Auckland, 1986, 415–16.
12 *The New Zealand Film Pioneer: Dedicated to the Interest of our Motion Pictures*, vol. 1, no. 1, Hayward material, NZFA.
13 Ruth Harley, the NZFA's Chief Executive was quoted as encouraging 'movies you'll want to see, as opposed to the gloomy art-house films that have dogged the industry for years', Lindsey Dawson, 'Hot Off The Satellite', *Grace*, October/November, 1998.
14 Lindsay Shelton, *The Selling of New Zealand Movies*, Awa Press, Wellington, 2005.
15 Tom O'Regan, *Australian National Cinema*, Routledge, London, 1996, 77ff.
16 Jane Gilbert, Desiree Keown, et al., *The Production Guide to the World in*

One Country, Film New Zealand, Wellington, 1999, 21.
17 Ibid., 11.
18 Mark De Wayne, Making Your Films For Less Outside the USA, Allworth Press, New York, 2002.
19 On Film, May 2003, 6.
20 Interview by Barbara Sumner, Metro, September 2000, 80.
21 Figures from Helen Martin and Sam Edwards, New Zealand Film 1912–1996, Oxford University Press (NZ), Auckland, 1997.
22 Vanessa Alexander, 'Magik and Rose': A Case Study in 'No-Budget' Filmmaking', unpublished MA Thesis, Auckland University, 2000.
23 Ibid., Appendix B.
24 Ibid., 23–42.
25 Ibid., 69.
26 Ibid., 15.
27 Barbara Cairns and Helen Martin, Shadows on the Wall: A Study of Seven New Zealand Feature Films, Longman Paul, Auckland, 1994, 309.
28 Ibid., 309.
29 New Zealand Herald, 6 November 2003.
30 Otago Daily Times, 5 August 1998.
31 On Film, April 1985.
32 Andrew Higson, 'The Limiting Imagination of National Cinema', Cinema and Nation, Mette Hjort and Scott Mackenzie, eds, Routledge, London, 2000, 69.
33 Ibid., 71.
34 Quoted by Higson, ibid., 71.
35 O'Regan, especially 2–3.
36 Higson, 69.
37 New Zealand Film Commission Act 1978.
38 Dr George Miller, quoted in O'Regan, 102.
39 Roger Horrocks, 'New Zealand Cinema: Cultures, Policies, Films', Twin Peeks: Australian and New Zealand Feature Films, ed. Deb Verhoeven, Damned publishing, Melbourne, 2000, 129–37.
40 David Gerstner and Sarah Greenlees, 'Cinema By Fits and Starts: New Zealand Film Practices in the Twentieth Century', CineAction 51, February 2000, 37–47.
41 Merata Mita, 'The Soul and the Image', Film in Aotearoa, New Zealand, Jonathan Dennis and Jan Bieringa, eds, 2nd ed., 1996, 36–54.
42 Ibid., 48.
43 Nick Perry, 'Antipodean Camp', Hyperreality and Global Culture, Routledge, London, 1988, 4–28.
44 Bill Manhire, quoted by Perry in 'Antipodean Camp', 13.
45 Martin Blythe, Naming the Other: Images of the Maori in New Zealand Film and Television, The Scarecrow Press, Metuchen NJ, 1994.
46 Horrocks, 131.
47 'Abstract of Schopenhauer's On the Fourfold Root of the Principle of Sufficient Reason', Arthur Schopenhauer, The World As Will and Idea,

Everyman/J.M. Dent, London, 267–8.
48 Susan Dermody and Elizabeth Jacka, *The Screening of Australia: Anatomy of a Film Industry*, vol. 1, Currency Press, Sydney, 1981.
49 Kevin Rockett, *Ten Years After: The Irish Film Board 1993–2003*, Irish Film Board, Galway, 2003.
50 O'Regan, 3.
51 Lloyd Jones, 'Me, Clark and Wilder', in *The Flamingo Book of New Zealand Short Stories*, ed. Michael Morrissey, Flamingo, Auckland, ext. ed., 2004, 455–66.

2

Forgotten nitrate: feature film-making in New Zealand 1912–1940

Absolute beginners: actuality films at the turn of the century

In New Zealand's earliest surviving film footage, you can see moving images more than a hundred years old. These tiny films, marked by the same formal simplicity and viewing their subjects from single static camera positions, exhibit overarching similarities to those collected in the archives of other film cultures around the world, yet those of each culture capture scenes which, for all their sameness, register the differences of uniquely inflected ways of life. In New Zealand, where films were exhibited as early as 1896, and first made in 1898, the oldest that survives is the *Departure of the Second Contingent for the Boer War* (1900). It was shot by an Aucklander, A.H. Whitehouse, who became the country's first film-maker in December 1898 with a series of films on various subjects including a horse called Uhlan winning the Auckland Cup, the Governor General opening the Auckland Exhibition, and the Māori Canoe Hurdle Race at Ngaruawahia. In *The Visit of the Duke and Duchess of Cornwall to Rotorua* (1901, filmed by Joseph Perry of the Limelight Department of the Australian Salvation Army), the royal party inspect Rotorua's scenic wonders and a 3,000-strong ceremonial assembly of Māori iwi (tribes). A third film, *New Zealand Footballers: The All Blacks Arrival and Reception at Auckland 1906* (1906), shot by a local cameraman Brandon Haughton, peacefully inflects the first's military masculinity as Prime Minister Seddon greets the returning warriors of the first All Black rugby side to tour Britain, in 1905. Departures from and returns to a small isolated country, self-definition through imperial ties, military prowess, sporting excellence, celebrations of colonial manhood, the extraordinary geography of New Zealand, the two population strands and the denial of tensions with Māori in the ceremonial place of the latter: these fragmentary moments concentrate important aspects of early New Zealand culture. That two of them were made by locals shows the early presence of small-scale film-making, though when entertainment films eventuated they would, with their larger scale, be largely the work of visiting film-makers. It is hard to estimate exactly how much small-scale home activity there was prior to the 1920s, though the Tourist Department was making government films by 1907, and the growing number of cinemas must have wanted local images among the overseas ones shown; these local images might have included *Poi Dances at Whakarewarewa* (1910), *World Championship Axemen's Carnival, Taumata Park, Eltham, New Zealand* (Brandon Haughton, 1912), or the films produced by Garnett Saunders for the Empire Theatre in New Plymouth, such as *Taranaki Jockey Club's Annual Meeting* (1912), for which Haughton also was cameraman.[1] The last was too local for export, but space existed for short 'topicals' and 'scenics' like the other two in the British market, as evidenced by advertisements in 1912 in *Bioscope* for *A Trip on the Mokau River New Zealand* (Heron Films, 270 feet), *Naval and Military Tournament New Zealand* (Urbanora Films, 440 feet), and *A Visit to Plymouth (New Zealand)* (Urbanora Films, 260 feet).[2] Such films must have been made by New Zealanders, and sold to British companies. Another *Bioscope* piece, advertising T.J. West's Australian operations, says that the New Zealand government has lent 'a series of New Zealand views ... of the thermal area of Mount Ngaurahoe, now in active eruption, and this is proving a special attraction'.[3] Similarly the NZFA catalogue notes that *New Zealand's Thermal Wonderland* (1910, James McDonald?) was probably sent to the High Commission in London 'to advertise New Zealand as a tourist destination'.[4]

That film-watching was becoming a national habit is evident from *Bioscope*'s occasional New Zealand reports. One at the end of 1908 says 'That the moving picture is becoming much more popular at our antipodes is beyond question. The crowds are increasing in volume every week'.[5] A promotional article slightly later reports T.J. West's shows in Wellington, Auckland and Dunedin, with Christchurch about to open.[6] Another *Bioscope* issue notes in 1911 that Fuller and Sons' new Auckland theatre holds 1,800 people.[7] Fascinatingly, the British *Kinematograph and Lantern Weekly* in 1907 printed a letter from a 'Fred Foley of Otaki', obviously an early exhibitor, expressing pleasure in receiving the 'latest doings of the trade in England or London, every 'Frisco mail'.[8] A rarely documented American view is found in a 1913 issue of *Moving Picture World* in which a correspondent (E. Miles Samuels) reports on the Wellington scene, noting five cinemas for a population of 70,000, three of them running continuous shows, all with small orchestras in the evening, and generally 'comfortable', though without central heating in winter. Samuels also reported smaller screens than in America, 'fair' projection, lack of consciousness of fire dangers, backwardness in theatre management, unoriginality in advertising, and the lack of film criticism in the press.[9]

The emergence of the fiction film

Such notations underline the rapid expansion of film-viewing in New Zealand; the early dependency on overseas film material; the place of early New Zealand films in an early transnational cinematic economy, though much more by import than export; and the difficulties for local film-makers to work outside of the smallest formats. This latter situation hardly changed by the 1920s, so that the early work of H.C. Gore, Edwin Coubray, Lee Hill and Jack Welsh was pioneering in the most arduous sense: land-clearing, with little production beyond the ephemeral, but with a belief in future growth. Of these pragmatic experimenters, generally more technologically than aesthetically driven, only Coubray directed a feature: the lost *Carbine's Heritage* (1927), on which he was also screenwriter, photographer and in charge of sound (an early instance of that non-demarcated New Zealand crewman advertised in *The Whole World in One Country*!) The exception was Rudall Hayward, whose six feature films, 1922–1940, underline his pre-eminence over his fellow pioneers.

From 1912 to 1940, the overwhelming majority of films produced in New Zealand, were short government-sponsored documentaries. In *The Tin Shed*, a history of government film-making 1922–1941, 355 films are claimed, some 80 surviving.[10] Their titles indicate the characteristic subgenres, shared with independent productions, that were the backdrop to the fiction features that emerged: agricultural and industrial celebration (*Irrigation in Otago*, 1923, *Condensed Milk Industry*, 1924); scenic celebration (*Over the Huka Falls*, 1928); imperial celebration (*Their Royal Highnesses the Duke and Duchess of York Visit New Zealand*, 1927); Māori celebration (*Whakarewarewa*, 1927); and social welfare celebrations (*Health Camps for Happiness*, 1937), a tradition carried on by the National Film Unit from 1941. Most of these subgenres combined in several large-scale documentaries glorifying the young nation – the independent *The Birth of New Zealand* (Harrington Reynolds, 1922), and the government films *Glorious New Zealand* (1925) and *Romantic New Zealand* (1934). *The Birth of New Zealand*, some of which survives recycled in E.T. Brown's *The Romance of Maoriland* (1930), is interesting in its push towards docudrama re-enactment of historical moments 'The Landing of Captain

Cook', 'The Signing of the Historic Treaty of Waitangi', and 'Gabriel's Gully Gold Rush', with its fragmentary equivalent of the Australian bush-ranging film. These are early instances of film-makers unable to make fiction films finding ways of customizing documentary, true also of the government Centennial film *One Hundred Crowded Years* (1940), with its dramatized pivotal moments, including a statuesque pioneer family surviving breaking in the land and the Māori Wars.

From 1912 to 1940 there were only twenty-seven fiction feature films (some of the earlier are what are called here 'proto-features') made in New Zealand, only fourteen of which were by New Zealanders (six of them Hayward's). Jonathan Dennis stressed the 'local, personal and irregular' nature of early New Zealand film in a period 'uncluttered by masterpieces',[11] but while only Hayward's features could contest this claim, others do not lack in interest.

The account below observes three principles. First, it reserves Rudall Hayward for extended attention later. Second, it bends (for Méliès, as for Hayward's 'community comedies' later) archival definitions of 'feature', for reasons of historical primacy, inclusivity and influence.[12] Third, it includes made-in-New Zealand films alongside films made by New Zealanders. The rationale here is that foreign features that were made in New Zealand at a time when there was no (then almost no) local feature production were imbued with a significance in New Zealand film history that later foreign-made films with New Zealand settings could not generate (for instance, the Hollywood melodramas *Green Dolphin Street* (Victor Saville, 1947), *Spinster* (a.k.a. *Two Loves*, Charles Walters, 1961) and *Until They Sail* (Robert Wise, 1957), and the British imperial adventure *The Seekers* (Ken Annakin, 1954), only the last of which, apart from fragments of *Until They Sail*, was actually filmed locally). These late arrivers lacked the force of firstness, and played to later local audiences which, if half flattered by filmic attention, were critical of their almost surreal inauthenticities, for New Zealanders if not their intended audiences (Sandra Dee as a Christchurch teenager?!).

Méliès's magical mystery tour: Gaston Méliès in New Zealand, 1912

Loved By A Maori Chieftess (1913); *Hinemoa* (1913); *How Chief Te Ponga Won His Bride* (1913)

The first film-maker to make fiction films in New Zealand was the Frenchman Gaston Méliès. The older brother of the more famous Georges, Gaston moved to New York in 1903 to represent his brother's interests. As Georges's career declined, Gaston went into American film production from 1909, making eventually an estimated 150 short productions, specializing in westerns.

In July 1912, Méliès, with between eighteen and twenty actors and crew, began an unprecedented expedition to make films in Tahiti, New Zealand, Australia, Java, Siam and Japan, before returning to America the next summer.[13] The New Zealand visit, restricted to the North Island, took place from mid-September to mid-October 1912. Méliès was in his late fifties, and his obituary noted that 'the hardships of this tour proved too much for his health' and that 'he returned to [the US] in the summer of 1913, a wreck of his former self', dying in Corsica after retiring.[14]

After making dramas and documentaries in Tahiti, Méliès's company sailed to Wellington, The *New Zealand Herald* (16 September 1912) reported their arrival on the *Aorangi*: 'The Craze For Pictures Film Company On Tour: In Search of Novel Settings for Photo Plays ... An American Touring Company of Film Producers Reached New Zealand Yesterday.' As the Wellington *Evening Post*'s well-briefed writer (12 September) noted, 'So vast is the output of moving pictures in America – and yet it does not meet the demand – and so well exploited is even the material of the vast Continent, that enterprising firms of film manufacturers are looking further afield ... and there is nothing for it to get something fresh but to set sail in the Pacific for the land of the sunny south'. Méliès's tour was, then, part of the time's vogue for exotic documentary, as well as for exotic fictions.[15] The *Evening Post* article concluded by describing Méliès's methods of developing film on site in a portable darkroom and forwarding it to New York for printing, adding, 'As possible items on local picture programmes they will be looked forward to with interest', though in fact, ironically, the films were never locally released. The *New Zealand Herald* article also reported Méliès's intention to use the white actors as leads, and 'natives' as 'supers' for 'local colour', concluding 'in all probability particular attention will be paid to Rotorua, which is regarded as an excellent field for exploitation'.

The journalist Doré Hoffman who publicized the trip in the American film weekly *Moving Picture World*, used letters from Méliès for his articles, one of which was written specifically to introduce the New Zealand films. The trip, costing $US250,000,[16] was thus highly planned as regards publicity.

'Authenticity', though a negotiable concept, was clearly a value, and one of the company, Edward Mitchell, given visiting personality coverage in the *Dominion* (13 September 1912), was an Australian novelist and journalist resident in Los Angeles, with some likely knowledge of New Zealand as well as his homeland.

The company quickly moved on to Rotorua. Méliès obviously made swift local contacts, for the *Evening Post* (17 September) noted that 'Mr James Cowan of Wellington, the authority on Māori legend and custom, has been engaged as general Advisor and interpreter to the Méliès Picture Expedition and will leave with the party for Rotorua today'. Probably Cowan and Mitchell worked together. While the 'scenic' specialists in the party made *The River Whanganui, A Trip to the Waitomo Caves of New Zealand, The Maoris of New Zealand* and *A Trip through the 'North Island' of New Zealand* (the last focusing on such modern material as the Takapuna ferry, striking wharfies, Albert Park, Grafton Bridge, kauri logging, ostrich farming, a 'present day Maori village' and the Wellington waterfront),[17] Méliès worked on three fiction films: the one-reel *Hinemoa* and *How Chief Te Ponga Won His Bride* and the two-reel *Loved by A Maori Chieftess*, the first two with all-Māori casts

None of Méliès's New Zealand films survive, but enough records remain in newspaper reports, advertisements, reviews, synopses and Hoffman's publicity – alongside Méliès's letters to his son Paul, working for him in New York – to illuminate the films and point some enduring significances.

The material displayed in *Moving Picture World* in early 1913 shows, unsurprisingly, that New Zealand was valued as an exotic site, with the Māori the chief attraction, analogous in their exoticism to volcanic Rotorua, where filming took place. Reviewing *Loved By A Maori Chieftess*, W. Stephen Bush wrote that 'Of all the savage races none has accepted more readily the fruits of modern civilization than the Maori', to the point where they 'are even represented in the white man's parliament', but adaptation to modernity was clearly less interesting than that 'there is enough of the primitive about them to make them uncommonly interesting ... a people so wholly and strangely different from ourselves'.[18] Hoffman could be inconsistent, sometimes seriously educational, sometimes sensational. His article 'Méliès in New Zealand: The first Visit of a Motion Picture Company to that Part of the Antipodes', overwhelmingly emphasized the cannibalism which threatened the hero of *Loved By A Maori Chieftess*.[19] That two of the films had all-Māori casts (with apparently just one white lead in the other) was seen as a major enticement for viewers: the advertisement for the 'scenic' *The Maoris of New Zealand* described the Māori as 'one of the most wonderful but least known, races in existence ... the original natives of New Zealand, ... though conquered by the English, still retain their savage manners and instincts'.[20] Bush's review of *Loved by a Maori Chieftess* dwelled fascinatedly on difference, with its noting of 'Glimpses of the strange rude architecture of the Maoris, quaint figures carved out of wood with infinite patience and not without skill; the "totems" injected by savage fancy with supernatural power, the picturesque dwellings, the fantastic dances, the strong, well-knit statues of the Maori man and woman'.[21]

Film-making in early New Zealand, outside the major centres, was a rough business, and was here exacerbated by atrocious weather and poor communications (Méliès wrote 'We're in a foul country, cold, rainy and windy'),[22] which made shooting doubly difficult. Not surprisingly, there were technical problems, and damage to some nitrate stock was discovered in New York.[23] In New Zealand the company was also beset by serious disputes, resulting in Méliès shedding seven actors for a combination of laziness, uncooperativeness and abusive behaviour, while one of the party ('Johnny') had to be 'left in Wellington with syphilis caught in Tahiti'. 'You can imagine' he wrote to Paul 'how pleased I am to be rid of these brutes of Americans'.[24] This crisis seems to have led to a change of direction from plots dominated by white actors to two out of three with all-Māori casts, consolidated by Méliès's discovery in Rotorua of the 'half-blood maori Minister', the Reverend F. Bennett, and his troupe of 'Mahoris' 'who do all sorts of performance', of and Bennett's ability to co-direct the Māori actors with him. In the same letter, writing of *Loved by a Maori Chieftess*, Méliès noted that 'Ray has the only white role' and that he proposed to use the three white actors who remain 'as little as possible'. It is clear that the films Méliès made later in Australia, where an Australian actress augmented the troupe, differed from the New Zealand ones in being dominated by white actors. Probably the aboriginals were considered less photogenic, and were perhaps less amenable than Māori, whose histrionic traditions in hui provided a bridge between them and acting, further mediated by their performing in the Reverend Bennett's troupe. One of the Americans who stayed with the company told the Australian journal *Theatre* that 'The Maoris are born actors. In this respect they knock all the other natives we ever came across endways'.[25] Bush agreed with this, while arguing that the story had to be simple, so as not to take Māori actors 'out of their element', adding that 'the personality and acting of the simple Maori girl who took the leading part [certainly Māta Horomona, who played Hinemoa] hold a strange charm of their own'.[26]

While *Hinemoa* and *How Chief Te Ponga* belonged to Blythe's genre of pre-European 'Maoriland Romance', like Acheson's once famous novel *Plume of the Arawas* (1930), set in a land of noble savagery untouched by Europeans, *Loved by a Maori Chieftess* entered the world of interracial history found in 'Historical Romance'. *Moving Picture World*'s summary reads: 'Just after the Maori uprising of 1870, when the bitter feeling against the British was growing, a young English trapper [sic] was taken captive by a Maori tribe. The influence of the Chief's daughter who loved him to the point where she believed him the man she was predestined to marry, saved him from death by burning. Their escape through the treacherous land of hot geysers, recapture and final union are told in a series of exciting scenes that make the film a real thriller'. This can be given further detail from another synopsis, naming the white man as Chadwick, the chief's daughter as Wena, Chadwick's Maori rival as Chief Te Heuheu, and clarifying such plot details as Wena being told by a sorceress that she will marry a white man, and Chadwick threatened by cannibalism and being made a chief of the tribe at the narrative's end.[27] *Hinemoa*, at the other extreme, was advertised as 'the Romeo and Juliet of [oral] Maori Literature', and a 'Maori Idyl'.[28] *Chief Te Ponga*'s narrative of the young Chief abducting the beautiful Puhuhu [Puhihuia], daughter of the Chief of an enemy tribe, like the others was a love story, allowing western fantasies of the exotic-erotic Polynesian lovers (like Murnau's Reri and Matahi in *Tabu*) untouched by western corruption, or white man with 'dusky maiden'. Bush's review of *Loved by a Maori Chieftess* has already been quoted, and the others also gained good reviews, *Hinemoa* being praised for its non-theatricality, and 'a quality something like stories in Homer', and *Chief Te Ponga* for being 'instructive and valuable'.[29]

Méliès seems to have worked well with the Māori, comparing Māta Horomona more than favourably to a white actress: 'While it was necessary to drum things into Mildred [Bracken] in order for her to understand what she should do, I had only to explain very slowly to Martha [Māta] what I wanted from her and she would immediately do it with a natural grace that you will notice in her acting'.[30] Rudall Hayward much later claimed that Méliès 'rather than trust the principle [sic] role to a Maori girl, decided to use his wife and she was browned up with cocoa and was the first Hinemoa, this French actress'.[31] But this was either a joke or a doing-down of Méliès to advance Hayward's own claims, though Lottie Lyell did play a half-Māori character in Raymond Longford's lost *A Maori Maid's Love* (1916), and in an interview Hayward said that, assisting on Beaumont Smith's *The Betrayer*, his duties included 'painting the legs of an Australian actress [Stella Southern] with red ochre to keep her looking like a Maori girl'.[32] Incidents seem to have been confused in the cause of a good story!

Méliès's cameo of him and his wife farewelling his leading actress has embarrassing aspects for the post-colonial reader, but demonstrates artistic respect:

> I gave Martha her photo together with a £2 note [sic]; she was very worked up and you could feel that she was close to tears; she slid to the floor of the hotel lounge, sat at Hortense's feet like a little dog and sweetly kissed her hands, while the chief came to me with great sympathy and displaying very good English ... I thank you in the name of my Maori brothers, never in our life have we met with such good people as you. One of those who stuck out his tongue in one of the groups was also there, and he made horrible grimaces to show his friendship. All in all, very fine people; very intelligent, who seem to understand nothing when one explains to them what must be done and who carry out to the letter and with intelligence what one asks.[33]

Méliès's adventures established patterns and significances for the immediate future: (i) Until much later most fiction films made in New Zealand were made by foreign film-makers. (ii) Although a minority of his 'scenics' portrayed contemporary New Zealand, Méliès's and his audience's interest in New Zealand and the Māori was overwhelmingly for their exoticism. Another earlier (1899) French visitor, the sociologist André Siegfried, was attracted by the idiosyncrasies of white colonial New Zealand, especially its political-industrial reforms.[34] Méliès took the opposite route, shared by most visiting film-makers (excepting the Australians, too close to see New Zealand wholly exotically). (iii) The authentic indigeneity of the films' Māori casts, stressed in advertisements and reviews (which hid their theatrical experience), would be equally emphasized by Pauli's *Romance of Hine-moa* (1927), Collins' *The Devil's Pit* (1929/1930)[35] and Markey's *Hei Tiki* (1935), which, forgetting Méliès, all claimed to be the first film with an all-Māori cast. (iv) Méliès's fictions between them embody the two basic genres of narratives based on Māori material, to borrow Blythe's powerful terminology: the 'Maoriland Romance', set in a dehistoricized pre-European past, and the 'Historical Romance' of the 'fall into history', involving the relationship and clash of the races. The first eventually disappeared under the weight of historical problematics, though late-mutated quasi-variants on the type have recently appeared in such films as *Whale Rider*, and the second became dominant, especially as New Zealand directors took over. (v) Méliès's dramas were set in Rotorua, whose thermal wonders provided a geographical synecdoche for the country, and metaphors for the human action, as well as spectacle. Bush's *Chieftess* review specially praised 'the scenic parts of this feature' such as 'The steaming and spouting geysers of Maoriland peculiar to that part of the world alone', and celebrated the cameraman's fortuitous shooting of an erupting geyser during one of the dramatic scenes, which he claimed the actors only narrowly escaped.[36] From then through to *The Lord of the Rings*, landscape has been a dominant feature of New Zealand film-making. (vi) Méliès's experiences dramatized the difficulties of early film-making in New Zealand, not just in terms of communications, which would rapidly improve, but with respect to the lack of other infrastructures necessary to film-making, which would take seventy years to develop to small industrial proportions. (vii) Though Méliès's films stressed the exotic, some of the 'scenics' presented a modern New Zealand, and the advertisement for *The River Whanganui*, in seeking similarity rather than difference[37] by calling its subject 'The Rhine of New Zealand', suggests the exotic/familiar duality characteristic of later New Zealand cinema, and its reception at home and overseas.

'Maoriland' revisited

The Romance of Hine-moa (Gustav Pauli, 1927); *The Devil's Pit*, a.k.a. *Under the Southern Cross*, a.k.a. *Tamango* (Lew Collins, 1929/1930); *Hei Tiki* (Alexander Markey, 1935)

Just as Méliès's films were part of an early international cinema of the exotic, those of his successors – minor Carl Denhams, visiting fifteen and more years later to make films with all-Māori casts, first the British director Gustav Pauli, then the two Americans, Lew Collins and Alexander Markey – pursued a continuing cinematic interest. Though lacking the same force and sensuous beauty, these New-Zealand-set films are closer to the greatest of Pacific ethnographic fictions, Murnau and Flaherty's *Tabu* (1931), in their use of indigenous casts and settings, than to a film like King Vidor's *Bird of Paradise* (1932), with its white hero, Joel McCrae, and its south seas heroine played by Dolores Del Rio. In *Tabu*, what Blythe calls the 'Timeless' and 'Historical' Romances combine, this intersection of 'Paradise' and 'Paradise Lost' being a major reason for the film's extraordinary power. Avoiding the intersection of their ambivalent Paradises with History, however, all the New Zealand films present, like Acheson's once well-known novel *Plume of the Arawas* (1930), a Māori world set long before the coming of the European. Notably – though filmed on the spot and with the opportunity of local knowledge (the great ethnographer Elsdon Best reportedly had an advisory role on Pauli's *Romance of Hine-moa*[38]) – they tend to elide the Māori with fantasies of a more generalized Polynesian romance, deploying stock motifs that take precedence over indigenous particulars, with the danger, as expressed in the *New York Times*' judgement on *Hei Tiki*, that 'For all the conviction it carries, the picture might as well have been filmed on Staten Island or in Hollywood'.[39] Also, given the largely unerotic nature of Māori dance and ritual, especially when compared to the Tahitian, combined with all three directors' inability to find players with the physical beauty of *Tabu*'s Matahi and Reri, the films are too stolidly unsensual to convince as the lost realms of the innocent body that the genre dreams, and with which the realities of Māori culture hardly coincide, making ancient New Zealand an uneasy fit for erotic fantasy.

While Markey's *Hei Tiki* survives intact, only the first reel remains of Pauli's *Hine-moa* and mere out-takes of Collins' *The Devil's Pit*, first released silent (1929), then with soundtrack (1930). All three directors remain obscure figures, itself a register of Maoriland's minor status as a site for popular ethnography: Alexander Markey, of whom there is no record after his single venture into film; Lew Collins (a.k.a. Lewis Collins and Lewis D. Collins), who pursued a long, undistinguished career until 1951 at Universal and minor studios; and Gustav Pauli, a cameraman on a number of English films 1923–1929, whose location experience in Africa for *Livingstone Fifty Years After* (1925) led to his New Zealand visit and his only directing projects, and who was the most talented. The surviving single reel of *The Romance of Hine-moa* reveals a film-maker of sensitivity, with scenes of gentle forest pastoral matching the idyllic prescriptions of such intertitles as 'Cool sunrise dimmed the stars and gilded the murmuring ripples of Lake Rotorua'. Tūtānekai, travelling on a mission to the Arawa, sleeps in the ferns by the lake shore and is woken by singing. Unobserved, he first sees Hinemoa (Māta Hurihanganui) and her girl companions gathering small crustaceans at the seashore. All three films use almost identical plots – lovers from different (even warring) tribes, prevented from marriage, overcoming varying obstacles to union: in *The Romance of Hine-moa*, a jealous rival has Tūtānekai (Akuhato) accused of stealing the chief's tapu (taboo) food (if no part of the Hinemoa story, a convincing instance of tapu which Elsdon Best perhaps suggested), and, before the heroine comes to him on her famous swim, he has to undergo an ordeal in the volcanic 'Valley of Fire'. This is a similar site to the volcano in *The Devil's Pit* where Patiti (Patiti Warbrick) himself made tapu by another jealous rival, throws him, after himself crossing a lake (rowing not swimming) to be with Miro (Witarina Mitchell). In *Hei Tiki*, Manui (Ben Biddle) rescues Mara (Nowara Kereti) from her fate as the war god's bride, by impersonating the god and abducting her, the ensuing battle giving way to the inter-tribal unity which characterized these narratives' closures.

Hei Tiki (Alexander Markey, US, 1935)

The outlandish narrative surrounding Alexander Markey and the making of *Hei Tiki* almost overshadows the film itself, especially since Geoff Steven's excellent documentary *Adventures in Maoriland: Alexander Markey and the Making of Hei Tiki* (1985) made the facts more widely known. Markey, an American, first visited New Zealand in 1925 inauspiciously peddling a cancer cure. A former 'lecturer' and editor,[40] Markey persuaded Universal Studios to let him undertake a feature film built around Māori, albeit with a co-director (Lew Collins) because of his inexperience. Disagreements caused Markey to be recalled, with Collins completing the film, *The Devil's Pit* (1929/1930 a.k.a. *Under the Southern Cross*, a.k.a. *Tamango*). Markey then started his own production company with £10,000 from New Zealand investors. Two full-scale forts were built on the southern edges of Lake Taupo.[41] The *Waikato Independent* (20 October 1931) described the production camp near Takamai:

> Venerable tohungas who might have orated at tribal councils, smoking a gasper after their day's work was done, and impressive tattoed chieftains who might have let [sic] ancient tribes in war and peace, discussing the latest racing by medium of a newspaper a week old. It was perhaps the strangest mixture of old and new which has ever been compounded in New Zealand.

The film-making was marked by problems and controversies: money ran out; Māori extras were unpaid; and Coubray's sound tests failed, meaning that the film was eventually released, without synchronized dialogue, as late as 1935, by which time it must have seemed very old-fashioned. Markey seems to have acted unscrupulously towards both Coubray and Alfred Hill, the composer, and when he left New Zealand failed to return Māori artefacts lent to him by the Ngāti Tūwharatoa. The film, when released in America, gained poor reviews, perceived as failing on grounds of both authenticity and entertainment.[42]

Hei Tiki's narrative moves initially between two different tribal sites, allegiance to one of which separates the young hero and heroine. Mara is to be dedicated as virgin bride to the war god, who will make her tribe the rulers of the area. Her father, the chief, decrees death for any man who approaches her. Manui is sent by his father, the other tribe's chief, on a reconnaissance mission. Tera, the older woman who watches over Mara, is an inefficient guard and also lets slip the existence of a secret passageway from the pā (fortified village) into the bush used by warriors in past battles. On one of Mara's secret journeys into the bush she is encountered by Manui, leading to love trysts, one of which nearly proves fatal as they are seen – they only just escape through the tunnel. Manui, with four companions, rescues Mara by impersonating the war god. With the help of smoke and a sacred weapon, he successfully executes his plan, but the couple are pursued and his tribe's pā attacked. In a moment of intense conflict for Mara, Manui and her avenging father seem doomed to fatal conflict. However, when the father learns that she is no longer a virgin, he spares the couple, announcing that the war god has ensured his tribe's invincibility by joining it to Manui's. The film's final trope announces that 'the icy pendant of the war god makes way for the living warmth of the hei tiki' and the lovers are happily 'allowed to return to the tranquil seclusion of their beloved forest'.

The film's opening ceremony of the war god's bride-to-be stepping over the bodies of young warriors is spectacularly inauthentic (and seems to have offended the participants), underlining Markey's and the other directors' willingness to invent ritual unconstrained by the anthropological actual with its less photogenic codes and practices. Markey's 'native melodies', for instance, owe much to Hawaian models, and Mara's charming dances have a hula-like quality. At the same time, the bustling life of the pā is packed full of semi-authentic weaving, spinning of tops, and stick games, as well as native cuisine: Manui's bush pigeon filled with hot stones and cooked wrapped in fragrant leaves, with Manui cooking his speared fish in a hot spring (as Tūtānekai is seen cooking his crayfish when Hinemoa's companions report seeing him in *The Romance of Hine-moa*). The idyllic side of the myth of Maoriland calls up a prettified nature, with Mara conversing with a kea (native parrot) and a pair of lovebirds presiding over Mara and Manui's implied lovemaking, much like the fantails that watch over the lovers in *Plume of the Arawas*. The dark side is, of course, the rule of savage gods and war, always threatening the idyll.

Hei Tiki's lack of synchronized dialogue gives extra licence for Markey to leave his imprint as narrator, especially in the fascinating prologue. Inviting the spectator on a tour similar to the earlier half of Méliès's route, Markey conducts images of a journey from New York to San Francisco, to Hawaii, to the South Seas, and finally 'further in the direction of the South Pole until we come to Aotearoa, the land of the long white cloud, the bottom of the world'. Then follows Markey's description of Aotearoa as 'the isle of ghosts ... covered with thousands of sacred burial caves of their bold ancestors'. This past, though, is not to be discovered in the present, but only regained through a fiction, acted by the descendants of those who supposedly lived it. 'It was there we found the remnants of a vanishing race of native noble men and women, the stalwart people of Maoriland', who 'consented to relive a legendary love romance of their buried past'. These re-enactments' 'authenticity' is guaranteed by the film's boldest inventions, the offscreen testaments supposedly made by two actors, Tonga and Terani. Thus, 'Terani the proud chieftain who on first seeing his image on the screen, hot tears in his eyes for the vanished glory of his race, exclaimed "There is a real man. I am only the shadow"'. And thus Tonga, 'whose sincerity was so intense', that 'he ended his life with his own hand when the last reel was finished, so that his make-believe death in the picture might become an actuality'. The imaginative excess of Markey's romantic imaginings of the artist dying to give his artwork life suggests that Steven was fair enough when he answered his own question, 'Was he [Markey] a crook?' with 'Probably not. A romantic with a dream of creation that got out of control'.

Settler romances
'While Aussie barmen milk the till': early Australian film-making in New Zealand

The Test (Rawdon Blandford, 1916); *A Maori Maid's Love* (Raymond Longford, 1916); *The Mutiny of the Bounty* (Raymond Longford, 1916); *The Betrayer* (Beaumont Smith, 1921); *The Adventures of Algy* (Beaumont Smith, 1925)

Between the New-Zealand-made *Hinemoa* (Tarr, 1914) and Hayward's *My Lady of the Cave* (1922), feature production was dominated by Australians, utilizing the nearby part-exotic for the larger audience. In *The Mutiny of the Bounty*, New Zealand's geographical variety for the first time mimicked somewhere else, with Rotorua Tahiti and Pitcairn Island, and Māori Tahitians. In the others New Zealand represents itself in a series of melodramas of pioneer life – the comedy *The Adventures of Algy* the only modal exception – similar enough to Australian experience to provoke recognition, but different enough to incite curiosity. Unfortunately no footage of the first four films survives. The happy exception is again *The Adventures of Algy*, intact in a restored version.

The Test differed from *The Betrayer* and *A Maori Maid's Love* in confining its melodrama to the white settler world. The test was the test of love between the heroine's two suitors when all three are lost in the bush (a situation with trans-Tasman resonances), which the favoured one fails by secretly hoarding food not offered to the other two. The tragic outcome had the heroine and the faithful rejected rival dying of starvation while the untrustworthy fiancé survives, consumed with guilt. Conversely, *A Maori Maid's Love* and *The Betrayer* pushed towards optimistic endings with a young couple united: surprisingly, in both cases, a mixed-race heroine (white father, Māori mother) and a white man. This treatment of miscegenation differed from the norm and is particularly interesting in the light of its pulling back from full realization, even in the Māori-conscious films of Hayward, as late as 1940. The situation is tangled in complexities. There was, of course, no legal barrier to intermarriage in New Zealand, and mixed marriages were not infrequent, though more common down the social scale. But New Zealand film-makers clearly were gripped by an internal constraint, prompted by the audience's preference for interracial union to be acted out in national images and celebrations, rather than more intimately. Satchell's novel *The Greenstone Door* (1914) is typical in flirting with such romance at the centre by having the hero fall in love in his youth with a Māori girl, Reremoa, but eventually unite with the white, aristocratic Heleonora. It seems to have been psychically easier for Australian directors, as outsiders, to present successful miscegenation in New Zealand fictions, than for New Zealanders. For those Australians, New Zealand may have been a setting in which they could experiment with interracial fictions in a way unlikely in Australia, where not only were indigenous Australians considered the most backward of races, but legal mechanisms existed preventing intermarriage, except where children already existed. Notably, though, as distinct from the Maoriland romances with their all-Māori casts, in these films Australians Lottie Lyell and Stella Southern, chosen for their Australasian 'star' appeal, assumed Polynesian colouring, and only minor parts were played by Māori.

The Adventures of Algy (1925)

The Adventures of Algy is an Australian film, but its New Zealand 'star', Bathie Stuart ('our own New Zealand girl' in one New Zealand advertisement[43]) means it is geared towards New Zealand as well as Australian audiences, and that it is pushing towards, if not quite literally, being an Australasian co-production. It is true that with its heroine, the charmingly named Kiwi McGill (Bathie Stuart, 'the girl who does the Maori songs') finding fame on the Sydney stage doing intensely inauthentic Māori dances, the film's distortion of indigenous material might be criticized, but the 'crazy mirror' of comedy both suggests an indulgent licence and a degree of self-awareness at work.

In the first comedy made in New Zealand (apart from Hayward's lost short *The Bloke from Freeman's Bay*, 1921, and perhaps another short film noted by Edwards, Barry Marschel's *The Kid from Timaru*, 1917[44]), the journey of the comically upper-class, seemingly effete Algy (the English comedian Claude Dampier) from London to New Zealand, via Sydney, is precipitated by his uncle leaving him property, though a crooked lawyer, favouring his own son, omits to tell Algy that there are two properties and whoever arrives first will inherit the desirable Moana Station, as opposed to the loser's rundown Taranaki section. At the Moana Station, near Rotorua, run by John McGill, Algy discovers he has been cheated by the conniving lawyer's son, Murray Watson, who is aggressively courting the station manager's daughter, Kiwi. Algy falls for her, but is too naïve to realize it or her willingness, pleasantly expressed by his narrative-long attempts to fill in the crossword clue, L—E, 'a popular illness'.

Kiwi's father runs into financial problems, tempting her to give in to Murray's marriage proposals. After Algy has departed for his barren property, she visits her Māori friend, Mary. Instead of Kiwi and the external audience watching Māori dancing in the pā, Mary entreats her 'Dance for us, Kiwi, and forget your troubles!', an incongruity registered by Minette Hillyer, who persuasively sees Kiwi's appropriation of the indigenous in terms of the settler culture's need for self-definition through assimilation of native elements.[45] The admiring Māori audience for Kiwi's dance is joined by another, an Australian theatrical entrepreneur who offers her a contract for a Sydney revue.

While this happens Algy views his disastrous inheritance, though a hopeful intertitle says it is believed there may be oil in the region. Trying to forget Kiwi, Algy tours the four main centres, experiencing, for instance, Wellington's wind and cable car, and Scottish Dunedin, where children laugh at Algy's kilt, forcing him into trousers, a reminder that even Scottishness undergoes hemispheric inflections. In the film's last phase all four main characters converge on Sydney: Kiwi to rehearse her show, Algy to seek money from England to subsidize oil drilling, Murray on a chance visit, and Murray's ex-mistress, Mollie (Billie Carlisle), arriving from England to seek her treacherous lover. Through various coincidences, Mollie gets a job in Kiwi's company's theatre, and becomes not only her roommate but her understudy; Algy is reacquainted with Kiwi; Murray, finding Kiwi, resumes his marriage demands, rejecting Mollie, and using his Moana Station wealth to gain financial control of the show to undermine the new 'independence' Kiwi has asserted. Attempting 'to break her spirit', he has her sacked. Molly, offered her part, refuses it out of loyalty then, when Kiwi supports her, takes it. At the gala opening the loyal Mollie feigns intoxication so that Kiwi, replacing her, triumphs. Still unaware of his love for Kiwi, Algy returns to Taranaki. Murray pushes Kiwi, now unemployed because he has withdrawn his money from the show, to the point of surrender, but a telegram arrives from Algy saying oil has been struck. Kiwi rescues Molly, who has fallen on bad times, and, realizing that Kiwi loves Algy, Murray attempts to discredit him in a ludicrous trick, which misfires, publishing a lonely hearts advertisement in his name (a microplot Hayward opportunistically re-employs in the 'community comedies'). Finally, Kiwi, taking the initiative, calls on Algy. As he sits still puzzling over the crossword, she enters in a Māori skirt to dance a sort of hula in front of him. He asks 'Kiwi, Kiwi, what does this mean?' She replies 'It means LOVE, Algy'. He fills in the missing word.

Among the comedy's concerns that have largely vanished are the placing of the plot beginnings back in the mother country, asserting still strongly felt relationships and antagonisms, and equally the vicissitudes of the 'new chum' settling into the new world with its opportunities for local superiorities to balance inferiorities. Arriving in Sydney, Algy has his top hat bumped by a workman, telling the effete 'homey' that he cannot get away with anything here, but also suggesting deep-seated inferiorities in the need to do it. Algy's overdressed upper-class English innocence provides much fun, as when scared stiff in Auckland's Queen Street of meeting the warlike Māori he has read about. His initial appearance in the film, while highlighting the fact that it is a vehicle for Claude Dampier the English comedian, memorably hyperbolizes his sillyassness. Like the ship that sails into the screen in a famous shot in *Nosferatu*, Dampier's prominent nose enters the screen ahead of his profile, which when it reaches centre screen turns in large close-up to the audience, eyes wide open, huge soppy but benevolent grin, buck teeth creating an irresistibly comic face, completed when he screws a monocle into his eye-socket. Clottish, but good at heart, and willing to give it a go, Algy finally makes good, generating audience goodwill alongside condecension.

In the lively Kiwi McGill, *The Adventures of Algy* finds a way of dealing with the paradox presented by the desire to use the Māori presence in New Zealand as definitive of the place – *The Adventures of Algy in Maoriland* is after all the film's apparent alternative title – and even of Pākehā New Zealandness. Thus, without the complications of being mixed race, Kiwi manages oxymoronically to be both Māori and not Māori. Hyperbolically associated with the indigenous through her name, Kiwi is further inscribed as such when in Māori costume she performs a poi dance which the ever willing Algy tries to imitate, only succeeding in hitting himself in the eye and her father in the face. In the last scene, as a prelude to marrying Algy to herself and the country, she puts on a Māori skirt and dances for him. Both in this film, and in Hayward's *The Bush Cinderella*, Minette Hillyer argues, it is the heroine who embodies essential New Zealandness: 'Kiwi McGill [like Mary Makepeace Cameron] is made desirable by what seems to be her inalienable sense of belonging ... Kiwi represents an almost hyperbolically determined model "New Zealander"'.[46]

Under the Southern Cross (Gustav Pauli, 1926)
There is a beguiling description which picks up much of the optimistic charm of *Under the Southern Cross* in *Le giornate de cinema muto*, which talks of 'the film's major appeal now as then' lying

> in the wealth of local colour, it's packed full of crowds riding the witch's hat at the A & P show, filling the members' stand at the races, two-stepping round the tennis court at an afternoon dance party, and feasting on tables laden with local produce. Here is a rural New Zealand swarming with activity, where farmers are gentlemen, their daughters are good sports, the farm manager wears a three-piece suit and Maori are depicted as fun-loving rascals politely kept at arms' length.[47]

Confusable because *Under the Southern Cross*, a generic antipodean title if ever there was one, is one of the several titles of Lew Collins's film, Pauli's *Under the Southern Cross* is *The Romance of Hine-moa*'s companion piece, a settler romance in a settled white world, balancing the other's equally unruptured pre-European life.

In its simple narrative David Byrne (Charles Aubrey Ashford) 'just arrived from the Old Country', where he has suffered an unexplained setback, takes up a job as farm manager on the failing McDermott farm, gaining expertise as he works. Journeying out to New Zealand he has met a brother and sister, Garrick and Hazel Carlisle (Moata Doughty, Tui Fryer), the owners of the nearby Carlisle Station, a wonderfully civilized place, approached by a poplar-planted road, and heir to all the verandahed graces of genteel landowner life. At the Hawke's Bay Spring Show, amidst the activities described above, David runs into Garrick and Hazel again, and Garrick introduces him to Robert Fenton (Ginger Barton), although it transpires that David and Fenton knew each other in London. David and Fenton become rivals for Hazel. Fenton threatens to reveal David's mysterious past if he continues courting Hazel, so David leaves and sends a letter to say he cannot attend a party to which he's been invited. A cable arrives announcing that David has been cleared of the forgery for which he went to gaol, and that Fenton's guilt has been proved. As he is united with Hazel, the film concludes with his happy rhetorical question 'Am I to stay under the Southern Cross?'

This closing question is uttered in a fern-fringed garden like that of the Campbells' house in Hayward's *The Bush Cinderella*, an image of New Zealand's desirability, a *locus amoenus* that skirts the wilderness but tames it without wholly excluding it. While the film, like *The Adventures of Algy*, constantly evokes 'the old country' in its plot, its melodrama of wrongfully attributed past crimes (as in *The Te Kooti Trail*) suggests it is a world well left. Like *The Adventures of Algy*, this is a rites-of-passage film, with the hero adapting to a physically demanding new life which, however, includes surprising refinements (afternoon tea on the verandah, with a servant rather ambiguously in attendance). Harsher elements prevent the picture from becoming too utopian: after all, Fenton the villain has snaked entry to paradise, suggesting that what has been left behind may follow into the new world, and life on Springfield Farm where David works has few of the amenities of the Carlisle Estate and many more difficulties. But in moments like the dreamlike softenings of *The Price of Milk* many years later, both the harsher aspects of farming and the just-glimpsable Māori world are sweetened in Hazel's bringing in a lamb with a fractured leg to recover amidst the little cluster of similarly wounded creatures she nurses in a pastoral hospital, while at Springfield David feeds a little Māori boy's lambs. Significantly, the main Māori presence in the film is a cared-for child. Twice, there are curious moments that might be taken to reflect on the latter of the softenings: the first when Hazel's sister asks if David and the Māori boy he has brought to the show are related, on the surface a laughable mistake which fails to register the obvious signs that they are not, but which, taken at another level (not intended by the speaker), has more troubling connotations. The second is the maladroit phrasing by which Garrick explains to Hazel that David is innocent, 'Hazel, David's a white man who's had a bad time', a common enough cliché of an earlier time, said innocently enough, but at least retrospectively slightly troubling the idyll.

New Zealand-made feature films

Hinemoa (George Tarr, 1914)

Given the predominance of documentary over fiction in New Zealand cinema's first seventy years, it is fitting that when George Tarr, an Australian settled in Auckland, moved from theatre and cinema management into film production with the photographer Charles

Newnham, the resulting fiction proto-feature (2,500 feet) was a second thought, replacing a planned documentary on Māori customs, aimed at a British market no longer beckoning as the Great War began.[48] These original British market ambitions, and the nationwide tour that the film undertook, contrast with the one other local feature film in the following ten years (apart from Hayward's *My Lady of the Cave*, 1922), of which only a poster survives: *The Romance of Sleepy Hollow* (1923, 'Written and Directed by Henry J. Makepeace'), advertised as 'A Bright, Sparkling Comedy-Drama in Four Reels'. Almost everything about the poster suggests a production so intensely local that Auckland's suburbs were the furthest reach of its ambitions, with the actors all geographically identified, the Hollywood (and jokey?) sounding Francis X. Bouzaid '(of Onehunga)' and June Philips '(Of Dominion Road)', with supporting players from Remuera, Onehunga, Ellerslie, Newmarket, Mount Eden, Devonport, Ponsonby and Parnell. Such unremitting localism makes Hayward's ambitious logo 'Made in New Zealand for the World' and his unsuccessful attempt to break into the mainstream British market with *My Lady of the Cave* all the more remarkable.

Like Méliès, Tarr filmed the most romantic of Māori stories, the Arawa legend of Hinemoa, already, as suggested by Alfred Hill's cantata *Hinemoa*, composed to words by the poet Arthur Adams, a text that had 'captured the colonial imagination'.[49] No footage of Tarr's *Hinemoa* survives, but background information elucidates something of its nature. The programme that accompanied it (Figure 1) has a 'Managerial Note' expressing pride in being 'the first photo-play produced in New Zealand by entirely local enterprise', and emphasizing not just the correctness of 'native costume', but that it was 'filmed in Rotorua' 'on the original spots, which have been handed down by generations of Māoris as authentic landmarks in the lives of their ancestors'. This assertion of 'authenticity' of place and actors was common in early New Zealand features, and was present as late as Hayward's second *Rewi's Last Stand* (1940), in the epigraph of which the amateur actors of Te Kuiti are described as 'reenacting on the actual locations the parts played by their pioneering forefathers'.

The film's narrative was based on the version of the story collected by Governor Grey (scholar as well as governor) in his *Polynesian Mythology* (1854/1855),[50] as shown by details in the programme's synopsis which follow that particular telling, suggesting an attempt at fidelity to indigenous tradition very different from films like Markey's *Hei Tiki*. One of these details is the prominence of the hero Tūtānekai's friend Tiki, who sorrowfully exclaims when Tūtānekai wins Hinemoa,

1. Hera Tawhai-Rogers as Hinemoa in the first feature film made by a New Zealander, Tarr's lost *Hinemoa* (1914), the image taken from the accompanying programme, which outlived the film.

'but as for me, alas! I have no wife', and is awarded Tūtānekai's younger sister, Tipa, while the film apparently began with an enactment of some of the original story's starting complications, with the illegitimate hero's mother returning with her son to her husband after a long adulterous liaison, the bridge to the present made when 'Eighteen years later Tiki brings news of Hinemoa' and her beauty. Tutanekei's desire for her, though reciprocated, seems impossible because of his low status. In sections labelled 'The Meeting of the Maoris', 'Meeting of the Lovers' and 'Maori Customs', the pair's falling in love must have taken place in contexts originally visualized for the lapsed documentary project, probably scenes on the marae (meeting area), the warriors' games and the women's poi dances and stick games familiar from many later films. The rest, according to the synopsis, followed the basics of most versions of the story: Tūtānekai's courting of Hinemoa with his flute, and Hinemoa swimming across the lake to Mokoia island to join her lover – a surviving image from the film has Hera Tawhai-Rogers sitting by and gazing across Lake Rotorua – the swim itself providing dramatic opportunities. (As Grey's version puts it, 'and there she threw off her clothes and cast herself into the water, and she reached the stump of a sunken tree which used to stand in the lake, and was called Hinewhata, and she clung to it with her hands, and rested to take breath'.[51]) Then, after her landing, followed the sequence where Tūtānekai's servant repeatedly comes to the water to fill his master's calabash, only to have it broken by Hinemoa as a device for bringing the unsuspecting Tūtānekai to her; Tūtānekai's angry arrival to kill the culprit; his meeting with Hinemoa; some version of the union (would the comic erotic suggestions of the visitor entering Tūtānekai's dwelling and being surprised by four feet instead of two have been filmed?); followed by 'Happiness of All'.[52]

Tarr's film was shot in eight days on a budget of £50, a forerunner of the ubiquitous low-budget film in later New Zealand cinema. Though the film was apparently tinted, 'semi-coloured and containing all the natural tints appertaining to the climate of New Zealand',[53] the project was otherwise obviously quick and modest, Tarr's statement that there was almost no cutting[54] suggesting mundane cinematic ambitions. Through his partnership with the Reverend F. Bennett, the superintendant of Māori Music in Rotorua, whose troupe of Māori entertainers had acted tableaux of the Hinemoa story in his stage pageant 'The Maori at Home, at Play, at War and Under the Pakeha Regime',[55] Tarr preserved a link with Méliès's *Hinemoa* of two years earlier. The film listed as its cast four Māori players: Hera Tawhai-Rogers as Hinemoa, her husband Rua Tawhai as Tūtānekai, Miro

Omahau as Tiki, and Taimai Omahau as Ngaranui. It was taken by Tarr on a five-month nationwide tour and played a week in each of the four main centres. A certain vulgarity, more likely the copywriter's than the film's, is suggested by the *Stratford* (Central Taranaki) *Times* advertisement, 'A Romantic love story in dusky toning, rivalling the famous narrative of Hero and Leander, a beautiful belle in bronze braves all'.[56] The advertisement has a familiar ring, the comparison with romantic European analogues of the tale (Méliès's advertising cited *Romeo and Juliet*), the authentic 'picked cast of fifty Maoris', and Rotorua's 'wonder sights'. The well-known surviving image of Hera Tawhai-Rogers as Hinemoa is impressive rather than erotic, showing her seated by the lake, with chin moko (tattoo) and fully clad in native costume – quite unlike the 1899 painting by Gotttfried Lindauer, which shows her with naked torso and impressive breasts – an exception to the tradition of largely untitillating pictorial representation of the Māori woman in early New Zealand art.

Tarr made one other feature-length film, a documentary travelogue about Melanesia titled *10,000 Miles in the Southern Cross* (1923), then returned to the theatre as a scenic artist.[57] The surviving image of Hera Tawhai-Rogers' Hinemoa, though the film is irretrievably lost, was commemorated as one of the four key New Zealand film moments (with *Broken Barrier*, *Goodbye Pork Pie* and *Once Were Warriors*) on stamps commemorating New Zealand cinema's centenary in 1996. Compared with those other films all the indications are that Tarr's was a modest and artless production, but as the first feature film made in New Zealand it has a historical position that cannot be challenged.

Song of the south

Carbine's Heritage (Edwin Coubray, 1927); *Down on the Farm* (Stewart Pitt, 1935); *Phar Lap's Son?* (Dr A.L. Lewis, 1936); *The Wagon and The Star* (J.J.W. Pollard, 1936)

Edwin Coubray's *Carbine's Heritage* (1927) was the only feature made by a local film-maker other than Hayward between 1923 and 1935. As its title indicates – Carbine was a racehorse only slightly less famous than the Phar Lap of the later film's title – it belonged to the genre of 'sporting' (in other words horseracing) pictures (which flourished in the early British cinema). The narrative, as related by Coubray[58] sounds conventional enough: promising horse, problems over its ownership, resolved in a love story, comic interludes, crooks kidnapping it, and the winning of the climactic race where Coubray's gifts as an actuality cinematographer came into play as he used the actual Auckland Cup of 1926 as the film's climax.

A spurt of feature film-making took place in 1935–1936, encouraged by the piecemeal local development of sound systems (such as Coubray had unsuccessfully attempted for *Hei Tiki*) necessary because of the unavailability under Hollywood patents of the new technology. In 1934 Rudall Hayward made a comedy short, *Hamilton Talks*, and in 1936 he released his first sound feature, *On the Friendly Road*. Just ahead of him in chronology, though not in attainment, were New Zealand's first sound feature films, *Down on the Farm* (Stewart Pitt, 1935), *Phar Lap's Son?* (A.L. Lewis, 1936), and *The Wagon and the Star* (J.J.W. Pollard, 1936), all made in the country's far south, the first two in Otago, the third in Southland, and all with contemporary subjects.[59] Of these, *Phar Lap's Son?* is completely lost, *The Wagon and the Star* survives only in one reel, and *Down on the Farm* only in fragmentary out-takes. All had major contributions from two other of New Zealand film-making's pioneers – minor Colin McKenzies: less talented than Hayward, but important in the local scene – Jack Welsh (sound) and Lee Hill (photography). The films' emergence demonstrated an optimistic will to make local films which commands sympathetic respect, but they were unskilled amateur efforts, not much above the level of the local operatic societies that provided cast members able to participate in their musical numbers. The most substantial surviving footage – from the last of the films, *The Wagon and The Star* – displays extreme limitations of film-making technique, exposed all the more by the exigencies of the new sound medium, resulting in static scenes of dialogue in medium shot with little camera movement, variation of angle, or cutting, hardly helped by amateurish acting (the last of which underlines Hayward's achievements with equally untrained players). Not unexpectedly, the most impressive segments are in silent documentary mode, the local colour of the agricultural games with Highland dancing shot from a low angle and a sprint race with competitors running towards the camera. Thematically, these films were very much in an optimistic settler-romance mode. Two interacting trains of meaning can be traced. On the one hand, there is a clinging to an increasingly old-fashioned class hierarchy (perhaps more typical of the more traditional South Island) – the presence of which André Siegfried back in 1899 had noted curiously accompanying democratic egalitarianism[60] – expressed in plots involving a two-tiered society[61] featuring wealthy landowners or other semi-aristocracy, such as Sir Henry Hicks in *Down on the Farm*, the debt-ridden Colonel in *Phar Lap's Son*, and the wealthy Peter Tyson in *The Wagon and The Star*. On the other hand, there are plot mechanisms which tend to dissolve hierarchies, as in *Down on the Farm* and *The Wagon and the Star*, where the daughters of the landowners marry less established characters, while in *Phar Lap's Son?* the Colonel marries an American actress, which perhaps carries some over-hopeful meta-cinematic allegory. The plot of *The Wagon and The Star* – like those of *The Adventures of Algy*, Pauli's *Under the Southern Cross* and Hayward's *The Te Kooti Trail* – manipulates late variations on the motif of the 'homey' doing his rites of passage to become a New Zealander. In parallel to the main love plots, there appears to have been second tier comedy in all the films, played out by yokels, the odd maid and stable hands, an indubitable expression of hierarchy, yet which also, as Edwards suggests, 'showed the beginnings of the irreverent and egalitarian humour which has since become a hallmark of New Zealand films'.[62] Two of the films ambitiously and unsuccessfully attempted the British market, but *Kinematograph Weekly*'s embarrassing judgement on *Down On The Farm* ('a feeble story, indifferent treatment, inferior acting, and indistinct photography'[63]) was obviously registered by Gordon Mirams, powerfully contributing to his view that fiction film-making was impossible in New Zealand.

Notes

1 All held in the New Zealand Film Archive.
2 *Bioscope*, 15 February 1912; 4 April, 1912.
3 *Bioscope*, 22 April 1909, 17. See also the 'Fuller's Pictures' report, 29 April 1908, 22.
4 www.filmarchive.org.nz (accessed 23 April 2007).
5 *Bioscope*, 4 December 1908, 17.
6 *Bioscope*, 14 January 1909.
7 *Bioscope*, 26 January 1911, 47.
8 *Kinematograph and Lantern Weekly*, 22 August 1907, 230.
9 'Conditions in New Zealand', *Moving Picture World*, 7 June 1913, 1021.
10 Jonathan Dennis, ed., *The Tin Shed: The Origins of the National Film Unit*, research Clive Sowry, New Zealand Film Unit/New Zealand Film Archive, Wellington, 1981, 5.
11 Jonathan Dennis, ed., *Aotearoa and the Sentimental Strine: Making Films in Australia and New Zealand in the Silent Period*, Moa Books, Wellington, 1993, 6.
12 'Feature film' definitions for pre-1977 films are fluid, with 40 minutes being the Library of Congress's definition. Martin and Edwards' departure from this for some earlier films is paralleled by Pike and Cooper (see chapter 1) with whom they implicitly – and this book, explicitly – share the concept of shorter 'proto-features'.

13 *Evening Post*, 12 September 1912, 8; *Moving Picture World*, 3 August 1912, 438, and 17 August 1912, 647.
14 Méliès Obituary, *Moving Picture World*, 24 April 1915, 532.
15 Richard Barsam, *Non Fiction Film: A Critical History*, rev. ed., Indiana University Press, Bloomington, 1992, 42–55.
16 *Moving Picture World*, 24 April 1915, 532.
17 Advertisement, *Moving Picture World*, 10 May 1913; *Moving Picture World* synopsis, circa May 1913, in NZFA.
18 *Moving Picture World*, 8 March 1913, 1001.
19 *Moving Picture World*, 8 February 1913, 553–4.
20 *Moving Picture World*, advertisement 'The Maoris of New Zealand', 12 April 1913, 231.
21 *Moving Picture World*, 8 March 1913, 1001.
22 Letter, 2 October 1912; also 26 September 1912: Méliès material, NZFA.
23 Patrick McInray, 'The American Méliès', *Sight and Sound*, autumn 1979, 254.
24 Letter 26 September 1912: Méliès material, NZFA.
25 *Theatre* (Sydney), 2 December 1912, 37/a.
26 *Moving Picture World*, 8 March 1913, 1001.
27 *Moving Picture World*, synopsis, circa early March 1913, copy in NZFA. Martin and Edwards, 20.
28 *Moving Picture World*, 29 March 1913, 1395.
29 Review of *Hinemoa*, *Moving Picture World*, 12 April 1913, 165; review of *How Chief Te Ponga Won His Bride*, in *Moving Picture World*, quoted (undated) in Martin and Edwards, 22.
30 Letter 12 October 1912: Méliès material, NZFA.
31 Interview with Walter Harris, Hayward material, NZFA.
32 *Auckland Star*, 3 October 1970.
33 Letter 12 October 1912: Méliès material, NZFA.
34 André Siegfried, *Democracy in New Zealand*, translated E.V. Burns, Bell, London, 1914.
35 Collins' film had three different titles, *Under The Southern Cross*, *The Devil's Pit*, and *Tamanga*. The first is avoided here because of potential confusion with Pauli's film.
36 *Moving Picture World*, 8 March 1913, 1001.
37 *Moving Picture World*, 5 April 1913, 115.
38 *Romance of Hine-moa* material, NZFA.
39 Also 'Mr Markey described his story as a dramatization of a native legend. The same legend appears to be native to Hollywood, so many versions of it having been filmed there', *New York Times Film Reviews*, 2 vols, New York Times and Arno Press, New York, 1970, vol. 2, 1142.
40 *AFI Catalogue of Feature Films 1931–40*, 883.
41 Sam Edwards, *Waikato Times*, 9 February 1996.
42 While the *New York Times*' review attacked the film's inauthenticity, *Variety*, 5 February 1935, found a lack of 'sufficient entertainment value

in a primitive romance to propel unusual enthusiasm commercially'. *The Devil's Pit* had a better *New York Times* review than both *Hei Tiki* (*New York Times Film Reviews* 2, 563) and *The Romance of Hine-moa* (1, 558), though the latter is interesting in describing 'Irma Caron, an exponent of Maori music' dressed in Māori costume performing on stage before the film.
43 *New Zealand Theatre and Motion Picture*, 1 September 1925.
44 Sam Edwards, *A Chronology of New Zealand Film* (inhouse, Waikato University Department of Screen Studies, 2000, 27). However, there are arguments that the film may have been based on Timaru's famous Cornish immigrant, Bob Fitzsimmons, the world heavyweight champion, 1897–99.
45 Minette Hillyer, 'We Calmly and Adventurously Go Travelling: New Zealand Film 1925–1935', unpublished MA thesis, Auckland University, 55.
46 *Ibid.*, 54.
47 *Le giornate del cinema muto*, Pordenone Silent Film Festival, XVIII Edizione 10–17 October 1998, Cinema Verdi, 18.
48 Clive Sowry and Jonathan Dennis 'Hinemoa', *On Film*, December 1983, 40.
49 Martin and Edwards, 23.
50 Sir George Grey, 'The Story of Hine-moa (The Maiden of Rotorua)', *Polynesian Mythology and Ancient Traditional History of the New Zealanders as Furnished by Their Priest and Chiefs*, 1854. Interpret Sacred Text Archive, www.sacred-texts.com/pac (accessed 28 March 2007).
51 *Ibid.*
52 *Hinemoa* Programme, Tarr material, NZFA.
53 Dennis, *Aotearoa and the Sentimental Strine*, 8.
54 Interview with Tarr, Tarr material, NZFA.
55 Clive Sowry and Jonathan Dennis, *On Film*, December 1983, 40.
56 Advertisement, *Stratford Times* (undated), Tarr material, NZFA.
57 Clive Sowry, 'George Tarr', *Dictionary of New Zealand Biography*, available online at www.dnzb.govt.nz/dnzb (accessed 28 March 2007).
58 Martin and Edwards, 37.
59 Simon Price, *New Zealand's First Talkies: Early Film – Making in Otago and Southland, 1896–1939*, Otago Heritage Books, Dunedin, 1996.
60 Siegfried, 270–9.
61 Martin and Edwards, 45.
62 Martin and Edwards, 45.
63 *Kinematograph Weekly* review quoted in *Dunedin Evening Star*, 4 March 1978, 11: 'After this, our colonial cousins will be well advised to restrict their exports to mutton'. See also the *Monthly Film Bulletin* review of *Phar Lap's Son* (20 February 1938, 69): 'The photography is very inferior and it is often impossible to hear what is said. The actors stand in the picture and recite their parts strictly in turn'.

3

Fifty years a pioneer: the cinema of Rudall Hayward 1921–1972

Introduction: laureate, official and unofficial

When Rudall Hayward (1900–1974; Figure 2) died, two years after his last feature *To Love a Maori* (1972), the extraordinariness of his fifty-year career was hardly registered except in terms of clichéd longevity. This was unsurprising, given that four of his seven features made in New Zealand were largely forgotten silents. Rediscovery was inevitable, but it took an 'overseas expert' – the American Robert Sklar, writing in *Landfall* in 1971,[1] making comparisons with early Hollywood – to remind locals of this half-forgotten taonga (treasure). Sklar's remarks were largely confined to the sound version of *Rewi's Last Stand* (1940) and *On The Friendly Road* (1936), a fraction of Hayward's output. While his view that the British distributor's cutting of *Rewi* – the only, truncated, surviving copy – resulted in an improved film (better than Hayward's silents)[2] was aberrant, his high estimation of the films he knew was not. Sklar asserted that 'his career is not simply of local interest', making comparisons with Ford, King and Dwan. Emphasizing that 'none of them had to overcome, as Rudall Hayward did, the lack of funds, of equipment and of a professional company',[3] Sklar asserted Hayward's stature without excessive special pleading. 'Most historical films demean our sense of history, *Rewi's Last Stand* is one of the few I know which can enhance our feeling for the past'.[4]

Born in England, Hayward came to New Zealand as a child in 1905, and was brought up in his father's and uncle's film-exhibition company. He worked with Raymond Longford in Australia on *Rudd's New Selection* (1920), for Beaumont Smith on *The Betrayer* (1921), and on the documentary feature *The Birth of New Zealand* (1922). His own films included the New Zealand, or Māori, Wars features (*Rewi's Last Stand*, 1925; *The Te Kooti Trail*, 1927; *Rewi's Last Stand*, 1940), melodramas (*My Lady of the Cave*, 1922; *The Bush Cinderella*, 1928), numerous short comedies mostly made in 1928–1929, 'social problem' films (*On The Friendly Road*, 1936; *To Love a Maori*, 1972), and doc-

2. Rudall Hayward (centre), towards the end of his life in 1970, with Barry Barclay (left) and James McNeish (right) during the making of a Pacific Films documentary.

umentary shorts, made with his second wife Ramai Te Miha Hayward, on Māori subjects, New Zealand flora, fauna, geography and history, and Chinese topics shot on his visit there in 1957.[5]

In a radio talk,[6] Hayward traced his inspiration back to his schooldays, where he 'read, by chance, James Cowan's *Adventures of Kimble Bent* [1911].[7] 'Kimball Bent [an American turned British soldier turned deserter] fought throughout the Taranaki wars on the Maori side, and I still think his is one of the most thrilling biographies ever written. In New Zealand, it suddenly occurred to me, was material for film plays just as exciting and colourful as any Hollywood western'. Hayward's debt to Cowan, the author also of *The New Zealand Wars*,[8] the major source for his New Zealand epics, visualized with turning pages in the second *Rewi*, unpacks interestingly. All three historical films (epics if not in mass resources, certainly in dramatizing foundational moments of national history) have elements of primitive 'docudrama'– actual historical locations, historical characters impersonated by look-alikes, in the first *Rewi* 'historical facsimile' announcements like Griffith's in *Birth of a Nation*, in the second *Rewi* an occasional commentating voiceover. But 'docudrama' suggests an antiquarian dryness foreign to Hayward's emotional response to Cowan's own emotiveness both in his 'official' accounts of the Orakau and Te Poronu sieges, and in those later popular works which reformulate them even more heroically and nostalgically: relating, for instance, how the Orakau siege took place on his father's property where, as a child, he searched for bullets.[9] Hayward's recalling of *The Adventures of Kimble Bent* as the decisive text in his artistic evolution is highly interesting. It was episodes from Cowan's mainline history that he filmed, citing Cowan as 'official historian' in the titles of *Rewi's Last Stand* (1940). *Kimble Bent*'s unofficial picaresque was too sardonically tangential to the pieties of Pākehā progress and Māori nobility to displace his idealized colonists and mostly chivalrous Māori warriors. However, Hayward's recalling of *Kimble Bent*, with its anti-hero deserting to a Māori tribe, and its racially muddled lines of battle, suggests his films' complicated cross-empathies. Hayward shares much of the official Cowan's mythology, the building of a chivalrous past for the new nation, the celebration of burgeoning national identity through the distinctiveness of Māori material, the invocation of pioneer destiny crossed with ambivalent admiration for the supposedly disappearing Māori, the last of these with the sentimental limitations noted by Michael King.[10] But regarding these limitations, two things should be remembered. The first is that Cowan (and Hayward) are not alone: that modern historians like Sinclair, Belich and King are no less national mythmakers too, whose histories 'serve a contemporary function', as a look at the stirring final paragraph of King's *Penguin History of New Zealand*, makes clear, where it substitutes for Cowan's pioneering values of 'enterprise, ruggedness and settler bravery' settled-world qualities like 'good hearted, practical, commonsensical and tolerant'.[11] The second is that with both Hayward's historical inspiration and his films there are multifarious currents which resist too simple reduction.

Ladies of the cave and bush: the melodramas *My Lady of the* Cave (1922), *The Bush Cinderella* (1928)

In Hayward's settler romances, the New Zealand Wars ended, nation building is the agenda, though a nostalgia for a more colourful past, something like F.E. Maning's famous *Old New Zealand*,[12] pervades *My Lady of the Cave* and, at least subterraneanly, the New Zealand Wars films. The titles of both melodramas gesture to heroines more indigenous than the Northumbrian Alice Wingate journeying to the Ureweras in *The Te Kooti Trail*; both are associated with native terrain (the Bay of Plenty Coast in *My Lady of the Cave*, the native bush in *The Bush Cinderella*), the first with religious Madonna echoes, the second with resonances of transplanted fairytale. Minette Hillyer links *The Bush Cinderella*'s Mary Makepeace Cameron, found in one sweetly improbable shot petting a tame kiwi, with *The Adventures of Algy*'s Kiwi McGill, as a female embodiment of a utopian already-settled New Zealandness.[13] Both as a rich Cameron and a poor but cheerful Codlin (the farmers who have adopted her), she encompasses both the ordinary and the special. The other heroine, shrouded in mystery, is altogether more odd, revealed in the narrative's finale as the daughter of settlers whose Australian guest broke a tapu, leading to his and the parents' death in a Māori attack; she is smuggled away by a faithful Māori boy, Rau, who still guards her on the isolated island where she lives wearing a dress suggestive of eurhythmic classes. A mixture of innocence, natural impulse and, in a stranger mode than Kiwi's in *The Adventures of Algy*, of contact with Māori, she is claimed by the hero as his settler bride. Both films operate double-time schemes linking their 1920s audiences to earlier history. *The Bush Cinderella*'s prologue pushes back a quarter of a century to 1901 as the heroine's mother becomes pregnant, on the eve of his embarkation for the Boer War, by an officer later killed on the *veldt*. More complicatedly, *My Lady of the Cave* structures a double temporal regression from the film's addressed present (1922) to a narrative set in 1890, but whose hermeneutic resides in events thirty years before, bringing back the New Zealand Wars as a kind of local 'return of the repressed'.

My Lady of the Cave's weird narrative immediately summons up an oneiric mode. Although a prologue title apparently promises old-fashioned simplicities –'Forget this artificial age of the super-civilized with its "Cubist" Jazz and "problem plays". Say goodbye to the smoking city and sleepy town – and let us tread back over the leaves of other years to a time not so long ago' [1890] – this invocation of the complex through over-denial should alert us to the film's curious wish-fulfilment strategies. For all its bright, fair-weather shooting – much of the action taking place on or by water – the dreamlike is immediately suggested as the Mill Clerk (Gordon Campbell) 'a dreaming soul', is 'lured' out of his 'drab existence' by 'Romance and Wanderlust'. A sailing accident propels him into the sea, from where he is washed up on an island beach where he meets 'the wildest dream eclipsed on a lonely isle! A sea-nymph, beauteous, timid, her childish simplicity (seemingly) of another world'. As, largely worldlessly (because she speaks no English), they establish contact, they are interrupted by a baleful presence all but hidden from the camera's view, leading her to hurry her visitor to a canoe in which he escapes. A title preserves the event's mystery as he regrets his 'cowardice in leaving her with this strange creature whose hideous cries still rang into the night'. A very long shot from the hero's point of view sees the lady (Hazel West) on the beach with a distant undecipherable male figure ('the lady alone with her hideous beast-companion!-gaoler?-husband?') Later, journeying through the bush, the hero experiences two dreamlike visions: first, 'out of the past', a spectral band of Māori warriors (prefiguring the ultimate plot revelations), second, as he sits meditating, the girl from 'the fairy island' gently touches him.

In rough, smalltown Ohuna, the hero's reveries are mocked by his mate Dick as adolescent dreams. The mill clerk makes further voyages to the island, its hazards now including criminals protecting their territory. On the second he rescues the lady, bringing her back to Ohuna, from where, however, she disappears, the only clue being her guardian's giant footprint. Returning to the island again, with Dick, he finds that the criminals are sly-groggers, buying illicit liquor from the lady's Māori keeper (Rau), who uses the money to buy supplies and clothes for his ward. Dangers culminate in a gunfight in which the hero shoots Rau as he guards his prisoner, then has his own life saved when the fatally wounded Māori kills the memorable villain, 'Edward Perret Clarence of the Public Schools Club'. Before dying, the Māori hands over a packet 'to be opened by Rau's ward' (that is, the lady). As the mill clerk leaves the island with her he uses dynamite to blast the entrance to the cave to seal it in.

Plot denouements are retarded as the hero agrees to his mate Dick's fiancée, the widow Meredith, taking the girl to Sydney for a crash course in colonial culture – 'to learn the difference between A and Z and a few other things a girl ought to know', leaving the two mates to live a 'bachelorized existence'. The girl's achievement of literacy results in a letter outlining her education, in which, in a phrase that has New Zealand's first melodrama serendipitously prefiguring its most famous, she writes 'But the pianos, oh sweet sound'. Though she relates meeting other men, she has rejected their touches for 'you, the man who found me'. After two years she returns to Ohuna and the information in the Māori's package is revealed. Letters from a Queenslander visiting the infant heroine's parents in New Zealand recount the visitor's accidental breaking of a tapu which leads to Māori massacring the family – except for the little girl, who is saved by a Māori boy (Rau). He is tortured by the attackers – the graphic details of the description explaining his inhuman cries and the description of him as 'the deaf and dumb bloke – the big Maori eunuch': 'They cut off the tip of his tongue – poured boiling fat into his ears and, wreaking a worse revenge, made certain mutilations until I fear for his sanity'. The girl is thus revealed as a pioneer's daughter with the curiously unappealing name of Beryl Trite, and the Māori's protective aggression is explained. A year later the now-married Gordon and Beryl imagine revisiting the island on a pleasure yacht.

Under examination, the narrative's strangeness increases. In its remarkable fantasy the hero discovers in the wilds not a dusky maiden but an untouched white Hinemoa, who undergoes education to prepare her as pioneer wife and mother. This might seem to have little to do with Māori matters, but the narrative plunges back into the New Zealand Wars for its traumatic source, attaching to its central mystery a native figure who, in an extraordinary concentration of feelings about the 'other', is both threatening and friendly, dangerous and life preserving. As Rau lies dying, the heroine's ambivalence towards him resolves into gratitude as she nurses him, a role also tenderly adopted by the hero. Yet his castration seems a necessary element in some dark psychic scenario in which the Māori's representation goes through wild subjective changes – at first imaged as a wild beast, then horribly imagined as the lady's husband, then shown as loyally protective, and in the end treated lovingly (at least when dying) by the Pākehā. Remarkably, the film's closing images refuse to let him disappear from the narrative as a close up of the lovers' clasped hands has superimposed on it the deathbed handclasp between the hero and Rau. It is a wholly unpredictable moment, and its contradictions forcefully illustrate the reductiveness of reading Hayward through a simple ideological framework. Even the ending's optimistic forward gaze is ambivalent as it presents the future world as one in which dull pleasure-cruisers rather than adventurers will visit the island.

The Bush Cinderella (1928), unlike *My Lady of the Cave*, evolves its narrative without reference to Māori, its regression being to 1901, the moment of New Zealand's imperial Boer War glory. Aligned to the woman's film, it centres on a double female protagonist – first the mother, Margaret Cameron, then the daughter, Mary Makepeace Cameron, both played by early New Zealand cinema's nearest approach to a star, Dale Austen (Figure 3). The mother, already orphaned and under her puritanical uncle's care, reads of her fiancé's war death in a newspaper just after she has happily bought a pair of booties for their unborn child. Her secret revealed, her uncle Andrew Cameron (Walter Gray) banishes the 'Jezebel'. She is taken in by poor

3. Frame enlargement of early New Zealand cinema's nearest approach to a star, Dale Austen, in the mother aspect of her dual mother–daughter role in Hayward's melodrama *The Bush Cinderella* (1928).

farmers, the Codlins, who raise her daughter after she dies in childbirth. Before dying, she names her daughter Mary Makepeace Cameron, and asks the family, if the child needs help, to write to Cameron, enclosing the booties. Time then elides to Mary's young womanhood, at which point the Codlins write to Margaret's uncle asking for help with her education.

In the ensuing narrative Mary is comically courted by the drongoish Sammy (Al Mack), while genteelly flirting with the stalwart Neal Harrison RN (Cecil Scott), a handsome pipe-smoking naval man, given to solitary fishing. Both courtships, like much of the film and *My Lady of the Cave*, take place outdoors, with a shoeless Mary presenting herself with sweet forwardness to the naval officer. Unknown to her, the Codlins' letter reaches Cameron's secretary, who gives his employer the booties, but conceals the accompanying letter. Much affected, Cameron instructs his lawyer that a will benefiting his secretary, Michael Murgatroyd (Ernest Yadall), should only stand if Mary cannot be found. Murgatroyd, overhearing this, hires his own investigator to find her, poisons Cameron, then has Mary kidnapped. Climactically, Harrison rescues Mary from the ship on which she is imprisoned, and the pair race to their lawyer's office, arriving just in time for 'the Bush Cinderella' to claim her inheritance and for Murgatroyd to be arrested.

Just as the title *My Lady of the Cave* encapsulates that narrative's desire to combine older traditions (the invocation of the Madonna) with New Zealand subject matter (the cave as synecdoche), so does the title of *The Bush Cinderella* with its indigenizing of the fairy story. Notably the localizing synecdoche is in both cases natural and fresh-aired, reflecting pride rather than inferiority in all those early descriptions of New Zealanders as outdoor types (for example Sir Robert Stout's statement that 'our climate will evolve a different variety [of person], and that he will be fonder of outdoor life and amusements').[14] Hayward's outdoor filming was in part enforced, but it also underlines his intuitive attunement as national artist. Both films swing between the poles of affirming and dismissing the past and of celebrating or criticizing the new culture's positives and negatives. That Cameron's Puritanism was a bad import was a constant refrain of New Zealand cultural criticism till recently; otherwise, British types may be either good or bad. *The Bush Cinderella*'s stalwart hero is highly English and associated with imperial naval power. Conversely, *My Lady*'s colourful chief villain is thoroughly ambivalent. An upper-class Englishman, Edward Perret Clarence of 'the Public Schools Club' is the product of privilege gone bad. He is terminally banished as unfit for the new democratic colony by his death at the Māori's hands, yet there is something perversely admirable, an old-world style beyond the new, in his unregenerate death, true to himself and to his origins as, hallucinating London crowds, he expires saluting 'Piccadilly, dear old Piccadilly'. Clarence is clearly too privileged, but the no-contest between the urbane (though still outdoorsy) Harrison and poor rural Sammy, 'the hired hand', reflects a preference for refinement and a disdain for a cowcocky who takes the colonial make-do spirit too far in improvising a belt with barbed wire, that is not at odds with the Cinderella story's upward trajectory.

Here there is much to admire cinematically, from the idealized pastoral of the Cameron mansion, where the ornate domestic garden gently intermingles with not-too-hostile bush, an early cinematic version of a New Zealand dream, to scenes cultivating high melodrama. As befits a film where the heroine borrows her name from *Birth of a Nation*, there are strong Griffithian effects, as when Cameron's conscience is struck as he reads his niece's middle name, Makepeace. If occasionally the imitations seem old-fashionedly over-direct, as in God's hand's forming Mary's child out of clay to a gothically lettered devotional text, the moment where Mary walks along the street, reading about her fiancé's death, with the word 'Dead!' appearing over the image, is the emotive equal of anything by Hayward's mentor. In another moment, Murgatroyd, after poisoning Cameron, notices a piece of wire hanging outside the window in the warning shape of a hangman's noose, an effect comparable to one in Hitchcock's *Blackmail* (1929). Both directors may have adapted a stage melodrama effect that preceded them, but each pursues his personal noir in his own way – Hitchcock via lighting with a noose-like shadow forming around Annie Ondra's neck as she stands up after writing her confession, Hayward by crossing the melodramatic with the New Zealand quotidian domestic, a piece of wire from some do-it-yourself job dangling on an outside wall providing the omen.

'Hard seeds' and 'Eye-school graduates': Hayward's two-reel 'community comedies'

Hayward's first (lost) film was a short comedy, *The Bloke from Freeman's Bay* (1921). A poster, advertising George Forde as 'NZ's First Screen Comedian ... the Original "Hard Seed"', claimed 'More Real Humour in its two reels than all the "Million Dollar Comedies" ever perpetrated'. Slightly differing synopses suggest in its topical 'monkey gland' rejuvenation narrative, in which 'the bloke' Heck Ramley and a preacher have nightmares of receiving each other's thyroid glands from a careless transplant mad doctor,[15] a comic critique of the new society's Puritanism. While Hayward then dropped the purely comic for his melodramas and silent New Zealand Wars films, both cultivate comedy peripherally. The 'Birth of a Nation' epics feature 'crew culture' humour – like Ben Horton getting drunk on the rum supposedly used for softening new boots in *Rewi's Last Stand* (1940), or Barney's bush dentistry in *The Te Kooti Trail*. Less 'crew' oriented is the gently erotic comedy, playing on native elements in the lovers' flirtatious kissing and tapu dialogue in the former. The melodramas have their comic moments too – *The Bush Cinderella*'s sequence of Mary's ridiculous suitor, Sammy, observed by mocking kids gauchely practising courting, a very antipodean humour of embarrassment with love's softnesses, shamelessly borrowed from Dave's antics in the Australian classic *On Our Selection* (1920), or *My Lady of the Cave*'s vignette of the two 'bachelorized' males frenziedly spring-cleaning for the ladies' arrival.

Hayward's most extended comic phase came between the end of the silent and the beginning of the sound eras. Forseeing the disastrous rise in costs talkies would cause New Zealand feature production, he embarked on a series of more than twenty short two-reel comedies in 1928–1929 to maximize expiring opportunities. Hayward's enterprise is broadly burlesqued in Jackson and Botes' *Forgotten Silver* (1995), as their mythical film pioneer Colin McKenzie (a Rudall Hayward with knobs on) joins a local comedian to make comedies whose titles *Stan The Man in Levin*, *Stan The Man in Buller*, and so on, allude to Hayward's.

These formulaic 'community comedies' (only *A Takapuna Scandal* and the lost and apparently rather risqué *Hamilton's Hectic Husbands* (1928) exhibit significant difference) took a predetermined script (the copyrighted version in the NZFA, 'A Girl of Our Town', lists 75 shots) from town to town, filling in the template with mostly identical events and characters acted by townspeople after much publicized auditions. There were only two basic differentiating elements, exchangeable localities and casts. Contemporary newspapers suggest considerable excitement. The *Napier Daily Times* reports Hilda, Hayward's first wife, making arrangements ahead of her husband: 'Picking Screen types for Napier's First Film Production: Mrs Rudall Hayward Interviewed'.[16] An advertisement asks for: 'A Young Lady with good even features, dark eyes, good teeth, slender and graceful ... a typical NZ Outdoor Man, able to ride well ... A smart young Man About Town, well dressed, able to drive a car'.[17] A typical review reported that at *Betty of Blenheim*'s premiere 'the audience's chief interest centred, not in the story, but in the incidental camera studies of different quarters of Blenheim and its residents ... [the audience] greeted with applause the appearance in street and mob scenes of many well-known local citizens'.[18]

In *Forgotten Silver*'s burlesque, the comedies of 'Stan the Man' are primitive practical jokes, surprise assaults on innocent victims. Cruder than Hayward's, their burlesque nevertheless suggests something of his melange of fights, chases, abductions and pranks like the villain infecting society ladies with itching powder, or discrediting the hero with a lonely hearts advertisement in his name. The scapegoat villain's punishment is physically enforced by a posse, satirizing the vigilante impulses of a young society. Just as *My Lady of the Cave* gestured to modernist art, marking as self-conscious the film's oneiric modes, so *A Takapuna Scandal* – the most intricate of these two reelers, with a visiting comedian playing the lead, its scene on the Luna Park roller coaster, and the trick-photography spectacle of the hero, his umbrella caught in the wind, floating above Auckland – initially addresses the viewer with 'You have seen "The Birth of a Nation". You were amazed by "Intolerance". You were thrilled by "Ben Hur". This film has nothing to do with any of them ... By the way, we forgot to mention that the title has nothing to do with the picture, neither is there a plot, which shows how modern we are.' The effect, comparing the greatest with the smallest show on earth, may be bathetic, but also enacts what New Zealanders also know, that stationed at the edge one may survey, and in a sense possess, the whole world, that conceptually – if not materially – Takapuna can subsume Hollywood. Another element of the comedies, their groan-eliciting punning intertitles (for example, after Hyacinth has rejected Hector's proposal, 'But Hector's hopes have risen Hya-cint-th (he lispths)') embodies a variation on the films' conjunction of obviousness and self-consciousness.

The term 'community comedies' underlines the importance of the local in these films, in each of whose titles a girl's name or the generic 'A Daughter of ...' is followed by a place name, sometimes a city, but often a smallish town like Gisborne or Te Kuiti, where, no less than with the conurbations, local sites and citizens were featured. The local emphasis invited a split response from audiences. On the one hand, there was pride in locality, as when Hector floats over Auckland in *A Takapuna Scandal*, though his reference to the (Westfield) freezing works' stench is one only an Aucklander might ambivalently celebrate. On the other hand, there are constant jokes about insignificance: for example, both *A Daughter of Dunedin* and *Hamilton Talks* introduce their city ironically with 'this Saturday afternoon in the Great throbbing Metropolis ... Getting more like New York every day', and Dunedin is labelled 'A very progressive little town – Always Forward in Going Backward', with a street full of inhabitants walking in trick-shot reverse. Clearly the response called-up is mixed, celebrating particularity (Dunedin or Te Kuiti are themselves and nowhere else) but also masochistically recognizing them as the back of beyond.

These comedies are invariably structured around a love plot, in the most formulaic instances (for example *A Daughter of Dunedin*, *A Daughter of Christchurch*) where two rivals compete for the local schoolteacher. Both William Cowcocky (cow cocky was slang for dairy farmer) and Freddy Fishface are grotesque types: Fishface a newspaper reporter, effete, cowardly, mendacious; Cowcocky, though physically impressive, parodically hypermasculine, simply knocking Freddy down whenever they meet. Freddy is effeminately associated with words, apparently varsity educated, his LLB stands (with homosexual implications?) for 'Lupin Lovers Brotherhood', and his seemingly ardent heterosexuality seems unreal: 'he knew all about women. He'd read [Marie Stopes's] *Married Love*'. In *Hamilton Talks*, the villain

Crispin is even more effete, gate-crashing a women's party in drag as 'Mrs Fifi DeLacey', but the aviator hero, Darrell Hargreaves, is presented, exceptionally, relatively unironized. Viewed through Peter Wollen's structuralist–auteurist model, which saw Howard Hawks' comedies as the inverse of his action films,[19] Hayward's comedies parody his serious concerns, particularly heroic settler masculinity, with the homosocial colonial male's unease with the feminine antically displayed, through both effeminate villain and grotesquely over-masculine hero. The somewhat ambivalent heroine ('she was an eye-school graduate who knew her business') hesitates between her unenviable choice of rural muscle and urban effeteness, but hypermasculinity wins, and after Cowcocky rescues her from Fishface's abduction, the pair are united. But while love triumphs, the internal male audience has little time for it, in both *Dunedin* and *Christchurch* the posses which have pursued the villain head for the bar, with an 'Aw cripes, let's get a spot'. The plot of polarized masculinities is hardly present in *A Takapuna Scandal*, where the hero (the English comedian Hector St Clair) is physically more like the usual villain, epicene, small, and here slightly elderly, a typical child-adult comic. Lacking the usual antitheses, *A Takapuna Scandal* is structured around Hector's brushes with authority and his eventual entry into the heroine's socially superior world where her parents dress formally for the beach, pursuing her until 'Miss Manners' becomes enamoured of 'her funny little boy friend'.

There has been little analytical writing about these films. One view has seen them as disempowered local cinema challenging Hollywood hegemony through its emphasis on home-madeness, and unusual distribution and exhibition mechanisms.[20] The idea has its attractions. At all events, Hayward's 'Hollywood on Tour' road-trip was the opposite of the boast of the title frame of *The Te Kooti Trail* ('Made in New Zealand for the World'), being made rather in, say, Gisborne, for audiences in Gisborne alone. Minette Hillyer argues a further significance in the comedies' 'capacity to capture moving, transitory life', seeing them as having a near uniqueness in the absence of films dealing with contemporary life (though Pauli's *Under the Southern Cross*, *The Adventures of Algy* and parts of *The Bush Cinderella* must be exceptions to this).[21]

'Our brooding bush'

The New Zealand wars pics: *Rewi's Last Stand* (1925); *The Te Kooti Trail* (1927); *Rewi's Last Stand* (1940)

Hayward's greatest achievement is in the local filmic genre of the New Zealand Wars, derived from the western, but with its own differing history, landscape, iconography and ethos. Of his three films, two restage the siege of Orakau (1864), where 300 Waikato and Ngāti Maniapoto Māori defenders, including women and children, refused to surrender to a force of British militia six times larger. The third film foregrounds the siege at Te Poronu (1869), where a tiny group of settlers and friendly Ngāti Pukeko defended a mill until overwhelmed by Te Kooti's forces. Hayward inherited Cowan's almost sacramental view of these incidents. 'The story of the last day in Orakau imperishably remains an inspiration to deeds of courage and fortitude. Nowhere in history does the spirit of pure patriotism blaze up more brightly than in that little earthwork redoubt',[22] and 'No stone, no memorial of any kind marks the spot defended by "John the Frenchman" with such heroic valour. In a few years, but for this record, the memory of Jean Guerren's gallant stand would have perished. New Zealand should mark as one of its national monuments the ground made sacred by a brave son of France who defended his post to the death'.[23] When Hayward was embroiled in censorship controversies over *The Te Kooti Trail* (Figures 4–6), with the government delaying its premiere until Whakatane elders (of the church Te Kooti founded) had seen it, he argued that his 1925 film had been 'nothing but one long eulogy of their [Māori] courage and bravery',[24] and he undoubtedly sincerely believed in the films' balance, the earlier celebrating oppositional Māori, the later Pākehā and kūpapa (friendly Māori) heroism. Deconstructing the view of the Wars as dominated by chivalrous heroism, James Belich writes of them being massaged 'into the least disagreeable shapes possible ... a good clean fight, dotted with incidents of courage and chivalry, after which the two peoples shook hands and made up'.[25] One might add that it is easy to celebrate the vanquished's nobility when they are dying out, as the misapprehension was even in the 1920s. Thus in *The Te Kooti Trail*'s coda, the aged Captain Gilbert Mair (whose actual life prototype died as close to the film as 1923) writes to his Arawa allies invoking a joint future 'under the law and loving one another ... the greatest nation, the English, here side by side with the smallest race, the Maori.' The prototype of such stories of interracial strife and nostalgia, Fenimore Cooper's *The Last of the Mohicans* (1826), is built on the same foundation, there the

4. Hayward's silent masterpiece *The Te Kooti Trail* (1927) 1. 'Soldiers three': left to right, Jules Vidoux (James Warner), Eric Mantell (Arthur Lord), Barney O'Halloran (Joe Tennant).

vanishing red man. Like Cooper's, Hayward's epics cannot do otherwise than celebrate the ground of their being, the victory of European civilization over indigenous savagery, involving the expropriation of the indigenes' land. Yet like Cooper's foundational art they cannot be reduced to such simple statements, redolent as they are not only of heroic, sacrificial progress but of melancholy and nostalgia, contradictions and ambivalences. The films may be made with amateur actors and sometimes pitiable resources, but they have a compelling technical flair, seen in Hayward's penchant for sweeping travelling shots; his use of outdoor and bush settings, often carrying poetic atmospheres in moments both of action and meditative lull; and his masterful employment of Griffithian techniques, particularly the intercutting of parallel actions, as in Taranahi's and Mair's journeys to help the mill's defenders in *The Te Kooti Trail*, and sometimes brilliant editing, as in the awful moment of Nika's execution.

The Te Kooti Trail is a complexly structured narrative with multiple overlapping centres of interest enfolded within its story of Te Kooti's attack on the Te Poronu mill, and Gilbert Mair's subsequent attempt to capture him, which, though unsuccessful, ends the revolt. Though

5. *The Te Kooti Trail* 2. Minatory choker close-up of Te Kooti (Te Pairi Oterangi), whose rebellion gives the film its title.

Eric Mantell is the obvious protagonist, at times other characters take on at least momentary centrality (Jean Guerren, the manager of the Māori-owned mill; his wife Erihapeta (Peti) and her sister Monika (Nika); Monika's lover Taranahi; Eric's soldier companions Jules Vidoux and Barney O'Halloran; Alice Winslow, Eric's true love; and Gilbert Mair, the real-life leader of the Arawa Flying Column), while Te Kooti is a brooding presence behind the action, and there is some concentration on another real-life figure, Peka Makarini (Baker McLean, Te Kooti's lieutenant). John Grierson in 1940 expressed surprise at 'how near to producing a Cecil B. DeMille spectacle Mr Hayward had come [in the second *Rewi*] with the resources at his disposal',[26] a tribute to the battle scenes' impressive logistics, but *The Te Kooti Trail*'s multiple centres also create an epic feel, covering colonial society from its English origins in the Northumberland opening to various manifestations of civilian and military, Pākehā and Māori, and Pākehā-Māori life in New Zealand, though the grounds of Te Kooti's rebellion and its religious dimension are left unexplored, with the Māori leader remaining a shadowy character. Both the first and second

6. *The Te Kooti Trail* 3. Romantic 'Maoriland' with indigenous lovers Taranahi (Patiti Warbrick) and Monika (Tina Hunt).

*Rewi*s have similar epic ambitions. The first's surviving scenes show more of Auckland civilian and military life, and through Kenneth Gordon's (Edmund Finney) contact with Takiri (Miss Tina), the aristocratic Māori girl he meets on his travels, some sense of Māori life outside battle. Since Kenneth becomes a prisoner in the Orakau pā when it is attacked, the lost footage would justify Edwards' statement that he gains 'a view of Maori quite different from that of his fellow colonials'.[27] The surviving battle footage grants the Māori moments of Griffithian pathos with shots of a mother and child in the trenches ('And through it all the eternal mystery') and a child asleep ('the dreamless sleep of exhaustion'). Like the first, the second *Rewi* shows more from a non-friendly Māori viewpoint than *The Te Kooti Trail*, including Ariana's grandfather persuasively telling her why she must stay with the tribe, and stages the siege (possibly even more so than the first) so that the audience is encouraged to switch identifications repeatedly through changes of camera viewpoint and the mixed blood heroine's choosing to stay with the Māori.

The Te Kooti Trail's primary love plot, between Eric (Arthur Lord) and Alice (Billie Andreasson), largely taking place offscreen, and by letter, is in visual terms less pre-eminent than the Māori idyll of Nika (Tina Hunt) and Taranahi (Patiti Warbrick), and the cosy interracial marriage of Guerren (Captain H. Redmond) and Erihapeta (Mary Kingi). Rather than reaching across the races, Eric and Alice reach across imperial geography, eventually bringing Alice from England to New Zealand. *The Te Kooti Trail* is more centred on visions of white settler origins transmuted into a hoped-for future than on racial relations, though the latter are inescapable and dealt with by the film through an almost Manichean split between the kūpapa (with whom no problems exist) and the largely uninvestigated rebel Māori (brave but savage, regressive to the former's progressive). James Belich argues that such early local nationalism as existed was the assertion of New Zealandness as 'Better Britishness', not so much national difference as the same but better. This explains how *The Te Kooti Trail* can pursue processes of national becoming within a British framework. *The Te Kooti Trail* begins in England with Eric's enforced leaving for the colony, and returns spasmodically until Alice's redoubtable journey, undertaken 'with that great faith and fortitude that ever upheld our pioneer mothers'. Britain is the new colony's source, and its sons and daughters become the patriarchs and matriarchs of the later generations watching the film. Additionally, the (Anglo-Scottish) legend of the 'Lost Legion' is sounded at the film's beginning – a Roman Legion disappears after marching into Scotland to put down a rebellion, paralleling the 'Lost Legion' of forgotten soldiers who have formed Pākehā New Zealand; there are echoes here of Kipling, his poem 'The Lost Legion' (1895) with its celebration of 'gentlemen rovers abroad' in the outposts of Empire, and in the way the three legionnaires, Eric, Jules Vidoux (James Warner) and Barney O'Halloran (Joe Tennant) recall the trio in Kipling's army stories, *Soldiers Three* (1888).

Nevertheless, through this anglocentric prism, the focus is the new land. When from 'back Home in Northumberland' Alice writes telling Eric that he has been cleared, she assumes 'then you will come home to your own, my soldier boy'. But Eric stays and Alice journeys. When Jules is dying he urges Eric to return since 'there is no honour, no glory in this – only ze grave in ze bush – where I go – lost – forgotten'. Eric replies, 'There is honour, old chap, there is honour – We're helping to make this beautiful country a place where generations to come will live in peace'. Jules seems convinced enough by this to ask, 'Will they think of us, Eric, these people to come?' When Jules dies, his companions bury him in a bush grave. In a funerary intertitle, the poet Arthur Adams' lines appended to his obscure interment suggest that posthumously Jules has become a New Zealander ('And till all time shall cease / Our brooding bush shall fold them / In her broad-bosomed peace'). This nationalist inflection of the imperial recurs again in the footrace between the New Zealander Mair (Thomas McDermott) and the Irish Barney, who runs for the honour of 'the ould sod', which is won by Mair. And though the bush campaign is dominated by stirring action, there are quiet moments that more allusively signify at-homeness, one where the legionnaires relax on the beach while Jules cooks for them, a brief *mise-en-scène* of open-air proto-barbecuing lifestyle, a dream of fair weather and beachside contentment echoed in Mair's alfresco beachside situation as he writes his final letter.

In one unchangeable aspect of the account Hayward inherited, the Te Poronu mill, a gift from Governor Grey to local Māori, is managed by Jean Guerren, a Frenchman. Rather than minimizing this slightly disruptive detail, Hayward doubles it by inventing a fictive Frenchman, Jules Vidoux, as one of Eric's comrades. The doubling underlines local audience knowledge of early French connections, and the possibility that New Zealand might have become a French colony. At the film's close both Frenchmen are dead, leaving the British and Irish (Barney) to inherit. But the point is not simply imperial victory; the Frenchmen's presence constitutes part of the new country's already rich history, and is celebrated for that, as well as gesturing inclusively towards the small European minorities in the country. What, however, of the larger minority, the Māori?

As the government's concern suggested, Hayward's Te Kooti was contentious, at least for Ringatū Māori, for whom he was a prophet reliving the Israelites' struggle against Pharoah. Hayward, who was forced to amend two intertitles, insisted that he had portrayed Te Kooti 'in his true character as a misguided patriot'.[28] He kept in his papers a statement by the Māori leader Sir Āpirana Ngata, which he undoubtedly saw as proof that the progressive Māori shared his opinion. Ngata's aristocratic view was that Te Kooti was 'the last and greatest representative of the worst side of the Māori character, its subtlety, cunning and treachery, and love of bloodshed – its immorality and its fanaticism'.[29] Hayward was carefully accurate with Te Kooti's external details, such as his famous white horse, but he was less interested in internal motivation, simplifying his religious beliefs down to the drama of him (Te Pairi Oterangi) clutching his mission bible and orating in large gestures, or swearing the vengeance on the Arawa kūpapa that his 'atua' (God) has commanded. Perhaps to deflect some blame from Te Kooti, Hayward foregrounds another historical figure, Peka Makarini (Baker McLean, played by Tipene Hotene), with details from Cowan underwritten by reminiscences of Griffith's mulatto villain in *Birth of a Nation*. In Cowan's account of Monika's execution and Peti's forced remarriage, the decisions are Te Kooti's; in the film they are the sadistic and histrionic Peka's. But, though Peka may be used for local colour (Hayward cannot resist including his little dog, the only creature he loves) and to deflect blame from Te Kooti, nothing is made of his mixed race as Hayward steers clear of the fears played upon in *Birth of a Nation*'s mulatto mistresses and attempted rapes, and indeed presents Guerren's and Peti's marriage pleasantly. It is as if Hayward, propelled by his admiration for Griffith into a region of unfamiliarly extreme racial attitudes, backs off, finding his mentor's beliefs less admirable than his aesthetics. There is a moment of miscegenetic burlesque near the end where the burly Barney, approached by two rather comically plump Māori women, becomes so excited that he tumbles over backward, feet in the air. The women are hardly presented as desirable with their bulk and heavy facial mokos (which neither Monika nor Peti, nor Ariana in the later *Rewi* have) but then neither is Barney, and the scene evokes relatively even-handed comedy rather than prejudice beyond a dislike of the facial moko. Such details should remind us that although the film creates benevolent mythologies of what are often contradictory and less benign realities, the Griffithian template of obsessive racial fear hardly fitted the New Zealand situation.

Guerren and Peti live one way, while Nika chooses another, her relationship with Taranahi echoing the Hinemoa legend particularly in Taranahi's flute playing and the lovers' association with the water. While *The Te Kooti Trail* is less searching in one respect, in presenting no oppositional Māori in the briefly impressive way the *Rewi* films do, it gives the couple the narrative's most idyllic moments as they float along the river. Later, when the dying Taranahi, having revenged Nika by killing Peka, looks up from Mair's supporting embrace, the audience shares his point of view as he sees Nika waiting for him on Cape Reinga (the Māori soul's stepping-off place), and then watches himself joining her. Earlier Nika wears both a tiki (greenstone ornament) and a cross, fusing Christianity with Māori culture. But here Hayward allows Taranahi's ancient belief system – dying, he seems to have reverted to it – a moving visualization, partly because like Jules' burial it provides a metaphor for living and dying in the new land. Taranahi's vision is also distinct enough not to clash with more orthodox religious beliefs, whereas Te Kooti's indigenous adaptation of Christianity is too disturbing to be foregrounded. Notably, the plot ends with Barney and the wounded Eric, followed by Alice, arriving at a friendly marae, again enacting that appropriation of Māori elements which, as well as enacting the reconciliation of the races, is typical of the settler culture striving to distinguish itself from its origins. Reconciliatory meanings are also in some degree contradictorily transferred onto the historical character Gilbert Mair. When he rides through Matata to raise Arawa men for his flying column, he shouts his message in the Māori language (which, like the best settler characters from Hayward's Ken Gordon and Bob Beaumont to Scott in *Utu* to Baines in *The Piano*, he speaks) 'E ara! E ara! Maranga! Maranga! Tatua! Tatua!: Rise up! Rise up! Up, up with you! Gird yourselves!' There being no interracial romance at the centre of the film, Mair's role (paradoxical, of course, for a military officer fighting Māori) as a kind of Pākehā Māori – as the lover not of a single Māori woman, but, in a more diffused sense, of the Māori people – is, from the film's viewpoint, not wholly facile, though it tends to equate the Arawa with other Māori where convenient.

Mair in fact did speak Māori, maintained his mana and his Arawa connections, and at his death his body rested on several marae.[30] In the film he is portrayed as particularly devoted to Taranahi, who dies in his arms. After he writes to his Arawa friends, recalling the sacrifice of both Māori and Pākehā in the Wars, the last shot of the film moves from 1923 to the present (1927): 'Down by the dreaming Lake of Romance [i.e the place of Hinemoa's swim] stands a lone monument'. A close-up of the obelisque shows the words 'in Memory of an English gentleman / And soldier / Who loved the Maori race / Captain Gilbert Mair'. Touching, utopian, naïve, mendacious, hopeful, the contradictions and ambiguities attendant on this attempt to create a wholly positive ending are a microcosm of this wonderful, neglected film.

For two reasons the later *Rewi's Last Stand* (1940) is the most popular of Hayward's New Zealand Wars films. First, as a sound film, it has been more widely seen than *The Te Kooti Trail*, while the fragments of the first *Rewi* are known only to scholars and archivists; second, its central love relationship between Bob Beaumont and the half-Māori rangatira (aristocrat), Ariana, appeals to audiences' romantic sensibilities, though some watchers have viewed the love plot unsympathetically as a cover for assimilation-domination. In the 1925 prototype Kenneth rescues Takiri, a 'proud, sensitive Maori maid' from the river, and journeys with her. Their relationship of mutual aid cannot be completely reconstructed, but while it is clear that he, in love with Cecily Wake (Nola Casselli), is not erotically bound up with her, she may have unrequited amorous feelings for the man she calls 'my Pakeha' and 'a good soft Pakeha'. It is possible then to see the first *Rewi* as suggesting, if only by the characters' proximity, then disavowing, an interracial love plot, half allowed in *The Te Kooti Trail* with Guerren and Peti, but only in a homely version. No doubt in the later film there was some autobiographical impetus to turn hints of a love plot into a central romance, since Hayward met (and later married) Ramai Te Miha, who played Ariana, during the film. While this might be read as a foregrounding of what was previously filmically repressed, we should guard against a simple progressive versus reactionary interpretation of the three texts that celebrates the third at the expense of the other two, or, on the contrary, elevates the earlier films over the third for forgoing the temptation to stage a central assimilationist romance.

In fact, each of the three has surprising moments unparalleled in the others. Only in the earlier *Rewi* does Te Waro, the tohunga, make to extract the heart of a dead soldier as a sacrifice to the god of war. When Rewi Maniopoto (Chief Abe) stops him, he declares, 'Unless I make a sacrifice in blood, the Maori Gods will desert us'. Up to this point the scene contrasts ancient Māori barbarity with the more advanced Rewi who, though opposing the white man, represents the Māori moving towards civilization. Less expected, though, is Rewi's reply, 'I care not for your Maori Gods, we are fighting under the religion of Christ!', a riposte that relativizes the conflict disturbingly, setting Christian against Christian. This nuance of the 1925 film argues strongly against seeing it, and by extension *The Te Kooti Trail*, simply as rehearsals for the later film.

The later *Rewi*'s narrative is more concentrated than *The Te Kooti Trail*'s. In 1864 the Reverend Morgan (Mr C.S. Wood) abandons his Waikato mission amidst threats of war, stemming from the Māori King movement's attempt at autonomy. In the face of the Ngāti Maniapotos' declaration that all mixed-race children must be returned to the tribe, Bob Beaumont (Leo Pilcher), a local merchant, helps the missionaries to smuggle out Ariana (Ramai Te Miha), with whom his romance is blooming. Ngāti Maniapoto warriors, however, force Ariana back to her tribe. Bob meets Governor Grey (A.J.C. Fisher) in Auckland and undertakes a mission for him, during which he meets Ariana again. Despite loving Bob, she feels bound by tribal loyalty and returns to the pā. During the siege, Bob (or Ropata, the Māori version of his name) and 'Old Ben' Horton (Stanley Knight), later to be revealed as Ariana's unknown father, are in the force attacking the pā. When the defenders break out, Ariana is fatally wounded (or so it seems; the treatment is ambiguous enough to provoke differing interpretations). Found by Bob and 'Old Ben', she learns her father's identity, and the film ends.

The only surviving version of the film presents problems. Shortened from 112 minutes to just over an hour, for British release as a B-supporting feature, it certainly lost waiata (songs) sung by Ariana, and probably parts of the siege. What else was lost is unclear, and unfortunately, as far as its value as evidence goes, A.W. Reed's novel of the film is more of a fantasia on its themes than a copy of it, with Bishop Selwyn (not in the film) a major figure at the end, and Ariana indubitably surviving.[31] The film's unfortunate shortening also results in an extremely bare narrative, easy for the unwary to read as undiluted regressive ideology. This is not to deny that the film operates within expected ideological parameters (civilization versus savagery, rationality versus emotion, and so forth), but it is to resist a monolithic notion of ideology that fails to see the text as made up of contested, sometimes contradictory movements, ambivalences and ironies as well as certainties.

Bob and Ariana's romance causes problems as the Ngāti Maniapoto reclaim all mixed-race children, including Ariana. Bob's split loyalties clearly do not present him with insoluble dilemmas, even though he has been brought up as the Ngā Puhis' blood brother, since he is, implicitly, able to rationalize fighting against Māori on the grounds, presumably, that defeat will be benefit them in the long run. His attitude perhaps parallels that attributed to Gilbert Mair in the *Dictionary of New Zealand Biography*, where it is said that though Mair 'was a willing participant in the New Zealand Wars, and a ruthless enemy in battle, he was aware of the complexities and moral implications of the campaigns and sensitive to the views of his Māori antagonists'.[32] Early on Bob's only immediate problem is to get Ariana to Auckland. However, circumstances quickly change as Ariana is forced to confront her mixed blood. As the whites leave the mission, it is assumed that she will accompany them. Her passive agreement is then more actively stated as, clutching Bob, she echoes his 'Her choice is to go with me and seek her [white] father', with an affirmative 'Ay'. When she changes her mind, it is initially only to try to prevent Bob fighting with Tama, and then, when Tama wins, to prevent Tama killing him. Her choice of Bob is clear when she asks her grandfather 'Why have you taken me from the people I love?' But he answers 'Our people need you', and the sequence closes on her meditating his words in thoughtful close-up. When the lovers meet later by the Waikato river, Bob assumes that she will accompany him, but she explains that she cannot, that 'Maori women fight beside their men', and asks him 'What would they think of me, a Rangatira ... [if I failed to join them]? I can't change what is in me'. Though shots of her in the siege suggest that she cannot bring herself to shoot at the attackers, as some other of the Māori women are shown to, she acts as nurse and comforter to wounded warriors and children. However, there is no question of the narrative following the older American pattern from Cooper's *Last of the Mohicans*, of cutting off the possibility of sexual relations by death. In the earlier scene, before they part, it is clear that they are about to make love as she tells him 'There's so little time. Tonight we are lovers ...', before they kiss passionately. Ariana may or may not die, marriage may be prevented, but she is by then already Bob's lover.

Bob Beaumont, the ideal colonist, is presented affirmatively: a trader, connecting both small town and city New Zealand, civilized yet also a man of action eager to join up to fight, and undertake dangerous missions on his own. Fluent in Māori (the first words he speaks in the film are in Te Reo and he translates the Orakau exchanges for 'Old Ben'), his Māori credentials include having an impressive ability to fight with the taiaha (wooden weapon).

It is difficult to tell, with all the positives Bob embodies, whether Hayward intended a degree of irony in certain of his actions, or whether ambiguity results from contradictions in Hayward's views, sympathetic but paternalist, which the text reproduces. Bob reminds (the historical) Reverend Morgan enthusiastically, that he is known as Governor Grey's 'Watchman of the Waikato', seemingly approving his double role, as spiritual advisor to the Māori and government informer.[33] Perhaps we are asked to see Morgan's doubleness as caringly paternal towards his 'children', a proper joining of the spheres of government and church, but the alacrity with which he threatens Māori who have taken mixed-race children with land confiscation seems more political than purely Christian, and the mission sign chalked over with writing announcing it as the headquarters of the 60th regiment, suggests some critical irony. Bob is presented as a happily two-sided figure: Pākehā, but as near to a Māori as a Pākehā can be with his Māori language and uses of such terms as 'mana', 'tapu' and 'rangatira'. But when Governor Grey sends him off on his mission, attention is forced on his deception when Old Ben asks him chidingly, of his civilian clothes, if he is ashamed of his army uniform. Bob explains that he is known to the Ngāti Maniapoto as a trader (the implication being that they will therefore treat him as a friendly trader rather than as a government official). It is difficult not to see this as a breach of trust, reflecting, consciously or unconsciously, on Bob's position.

The film's ending has generated disagreement as to what on the most literal level happens, whether Ariana dies or survives. It has been argued that Ariana survives, possessed by Bob.[34] When the defenders break out of the pā, Ariana and Tama escape together, Tama firing at the pursuers, and Ariana being wounded. After the battle, when Bob and Ben look for her, they find Tama's body, and his heroic death is recounted. They eventually discover Ariana and a double reunion takes place, of the two lovers, and of father and daughter, though Ben's shaking of his head signals that she is doomed. Bob and Ariana greet each other, she ecstatically ('Ropata, oh darling'), he sadly. Then the attention switches from the lovers to father and daughter, and Ben's uttering the words 'God Forgive me' over his leaving of Takiri, Ariana's mother, many years before. The cutting (presumably recutting) of these last moments looks poorly managed, creating confusions as to whether the father–daughter relationship or that of Bob and Ariana is the primary focus. Whichever, the scene illustrates the tension that exists between an ideological meaning based on bare narrative functions, here the reunion of Pākehā father and half-Māori child, signifying the victory of the Pākehā patrilineal over the Māori matrilineal, and the gap between the powerful paternal function Old Ben represents in outline and the actual scrawny, dishevelled, alcoholic, possibly criminal (there is a suggestion he has sold muskets to the Mā ori) figure played by Stanley Knight, the actor Hayward praised as 'probably the greatest character actor we have produced in this country'.[35] As for the question of whether Ariana lives or dies, it is possible that Hayward deliberately chose ambiguity over certainty, avoiding the double bind whereby death reads too pessimistically, survival too facilely, thus still emphasizing the blending of the races of the epigraph, but realistically emphasizing doubts.

Modern times

Two social problem films: *On the Friendly Road* (1936); *To Love a Maori* (1972)

Hayward's career lasted in diminished form almost to the brink of the late 1970s renaissance. The documentaries made with his second wife, Ramai Hayward, after returning to New Zealand in 1957, reflected two strands of his output: his continuing interest in Māori life, no doubt increased by his marriage, and, in the three shorts made in China in 1957, his left-wing sympathies. Though the Chinese documentaries have no overt political content, the act of making them was an implicit expression of political imperatives. Gilbert Mair's letter to his Māori friends in the coda to *The Te Kooti Trail* reflected a dream, albeit paternalistic, of intertwined progress. The two features considered here were attempts to respond optimistically to the failures of aspects of the New Zealand dream: *On the Friendly Road* (1936) to the Depression's undermining of pioneer myths of egalitarianism and the better life; *To Love A Maori* (1972) to the problems of race in the city. There is a telling moment in the latter film, suggesting how far the realities of race in New Zealand have compromised the ideals generally held, when Tama's Aunt Mary (Ramai Hayward) suggests that New Zealand should have 'a law against racial discrimination like they have in Britain'.

On The Friendly Road

Hayward's first sound film did not appear till 1936, symptomatic of the difficulties of developing sound camera technology faced by the early New Zealand film-makers. *On The Friendly Road* emerged from more of a group ethos than Hayward's previous films: this 'New Zealand Film Guild' production only credited Hayward as photographer, with Auckland lawyer and lively minor literary figure Leonard P. Leary as director/producer, but there is no doubt that Hayward directed.

On The Friendly Road takes its title from the non-denominational radio church of early New Zealand commercial broadcasting, dominated by the Methodist minister Colin Scrimgeour, 'Uncle Scrim', who makes audio and occasional visual appearances in the radio talks and letter-answering sessions which form a vital part of the film's narrative. In the Depression, which hit New Zealand hard, and brought the first Labour government to power, Scrimgeour's socially oriented sermons were powerfully influential, his status as a religious minister giving him access to airways otherwise so tightly controlled that visitors such as the Social Credit leader Major Douglas and the Indian guru Krishnamurti were banned from them as too contentious.[36]

Part avuncular social preaching, part sentimental crime drama, part children's film, *On The Friendly Road* is set in a New Zealand more riven by socio-economic disparities than it believed itself to be, its road of life (the film's dominating metaphor) far from friendly without the good samaritanism Scrimgeour preached. It juxtaposes class extremes the new society denied having in the relationship between the wealthy Stevenson and the struggling McDermitt families. The undeserved imprisonment for theft of 'Mac' McDermitt (John Mackie) is not easily overcome as he is blackmailed by two escaped convicts (Arnold Goodwin, Harold Metcalfe). Stevenson (James Swan), a JP for whom McDermitt originally worked, hires him again, demonstrating a precarious charity that blows hot and cold, first of all dismissing him, then, pushed by his more sympathetic wife (Gladys Swan), rehiring the family as domestics. Blackmailed into helping the convicts commit a theft, McDermitt is in danger of being returned to jail. The theft introduces the Māori world, as with most of Hayward's films. McDermitt's children, Harry and Alex (Neville Goodwin, James Martin) find a greenstone mere (small club); Stevenson confiscates this, but has enough conscience, or desire for prestige, to return the ancestral treasure to the local iwi (tribal people). Pākehā and Māori worlds – already briefly joined in McDermitt's and his sons' charming little haka on finding the mere, and in a friendly encounter between 'Hori' (Wharepeia) and 'Old Bill' the swaggy (Stanley Knight) at the film's opening – come together in the ceremony where Stephenson receives a golden tiki (the object of the theft) as thanks from the tribe, a scene of gentle satire with the Europeans politely clapping Māori entertainments and the comedy of Hori's inept translation into English of the Chieftess's compliments, which make it appear scandalously that Stevenson is the literal rather than metaphorical father to many Māori children. In the film's conclusion, the McDermitt children defeat the convicts and – after various misunderstandings in which, first, McDermitt seems bound for jail again, then likewise the kindly swaggy Bill, who tries sacrificially to take his place – Stevenson is finally converted to social responsibility and the McDermitt family restored to their previous life. The broadcasts of 'Uncle Scrim' – one of which prefaces the film, another of which ends it ('may we so bear ourselves that when we reach our journey's end and turn to farewell our fellow travellers they will wave back to one whose memory will be cherished as long as they live') – enter the narrative first when McDermitt's wife (Jean Hamilton) writes to him and his radio appeal results in gifts to keep the family going, and then later when the McDermitt boys, discovering their father's difficulties, write a letter asking for advice, which he replies to on his programme. Unhappily travestied in Martin and Edwards' filmography, *On The Friendly Road*,[37] is a film of great charm and positive social commitment which unpretentiously embodies religion as practical charity, the figure of the elderly swaggy Bill echoing the religio-secular identifications of R.A.K. Mason – with whom twenty years later Hayward was to visit China – in his poem of the time 'On the Swag': 'Let the fruit be plucked / and the cake be iced, / the bed be snug / and the wine be spiced / in the old cove's nightcap: / for this is Christ.'

To Love a Maori

Early in *On The Friendly Road* 'Old Bill', the swaggy, chats with a Māori called 'Hori' (a name now avoided because of its stereotypical connotations). Bill asks the time, and Hori, inspecting the sky, replies very approximately. When Bill points out Hori's pocket watch, the Māori takes it out, but it has no hands and houses a spider. 'Pai Korry, I forget this is Saturday. This is the forty-hour-week watch.' At one level the comedy is questionable – 'Pai Korry' is linguistically as stereotypical as the name Hori; at another, taken more generously, it dramatizes unjudgementally Māori–Pākehā differences in registering the rhythms of time. The world of Hayward's first colour film, thirty-five years on, is very different, set in the anomic environment of rural Māori immigrants to the Pākehā city. Though the young interracial couple, Tama and Penny, visit Tama's parents on the East Coast, and various positives of the old lifestyle are shown, the future clearly lies in the city. Thus the film begins with the Auckland-bound exodus of three young Māori – Tina (Connie Rota) with nightclub singing ambitions, Tama (Val Irwin) headed for a skilled apprenticeship, and Riki (Rau Hotere), a typical early school-leaver, bound for difficulties. The accompanying song, 'Goodbye to my old marae, / The place I'll love till I die, / Where the elders have their say' expresses nostalgic regret, but leaving seems inevitable. Another song pleads with Tina, 'Go home, Maori girl, go home, / You're too young to drift and roam', and for her the city is disastrous as her naïveté leads to her being forced to become a ship girl, imprisoned and used sexually by the crew. But, though the film's most famous literary predecessor, Noel Hilliard's *Maori Girl* (1960), has a female centre, Hayward's film largely follows the two young men: Riki, flirting with crime before he ends up in the traditional Māori army career, and, most centrally, Tama, both at work and in his romance with, and later marriage to the middle-class Pākehā, Penny (Marie Searell). In the dance-drama of interracial romance at the university where the pair meet performing the leads, there is a scene in which young Polynesians try to pull him away from her and young whites her from him, prefiguring the prejudice they will encounter, especially from Penny's parents (Desmond Lock, Sybil Lock). Eventually the couple marry, but they find survival exhausting, with Tama tempted to throw in his apprenticeship, the key to his transcending the usual urban Māori fate of unskilled work. Penny gets a job at the well-known Crown Lynn potteries as a designer and incorporates her new-found interest in Māori art into commercial designs. *To Love a Maori* eventually stages an optimistic closure, the birth of a child reconciling Penny's parents to the marriage. However, the film, for all its optimism, seems unsure that one personal example of integration shows the future way. Tama's unprejudiced father (Toby Curtis) tells Penny that some elders fear intermarriage will swallow their people up. And when Penny's prejudiced father plays golf with a lawyer friend (Harold Kissin), the lawyer alludes to the Māori activism just beginning.' If we don't meet the needs of these people we'll end up by paying anyway'.

To Love a Maori is a lesser film than *Broken Barrier*, made over twenty years before it, but it does more than simply replicate it. Its love plot is more transgressive, a Pākehā girl and a Māori boy rather than the more usual white boy and Māori girl. Though this first feature to deal with urban Māori life revisits the old marae, it declines even to suggest the pastoral dream of return found in *Broken Barrier* and, more recently, in *Once Were Warriors* and *Broken English*. However, Hayward's imaginative drive is less than in his earlier work. The film, announcing itself as 'A Dramatic Documentary', credits a social worker's case histories, but its force either as fiction or documentary is fitful. At times it presents itself almost as naïve folk art: for example, the schoolbook-like mural of Māori life behind the credits, and naïve songs like the one that follows Riki to the army recruitment centre ('What can a joker do / When his life is all puckeroo?') or another associated with Penny ('People say I'm crazy, just a fool / To love a happy-go-lucky Maori'). At other times, it surprises with its understanding of an age far from the one in which Hayward made his major films, as when Penny's raunchy friend Deirdre (Pam Ferris) announces to the prejudiced mother that 'For years men have been romanticizing South Sea Island women, now it's our turn to discover the men', and the golfing lawyer, warning Penny's father of the cost of ignoring Māori needs, registers the beginnings of contemporary Māori activism. A telling detail in the integrationist dance-drama (attributed to a Māori choreographer) is that, rather than showing the elders of both races trying to separate the lovers, it has young people pulling them apart, suggesting that Hayward still had his ear to the ground.

Notes

1 Robert Sklar, *Landfall*, 25.2, June 1971: 147–53.
2 Sklar, 149.
3 Sklar, 147.
4 Sklar, 148; similarly, 153.
5 In England after the war, Hayward made two lost films, the feature *The Goodwin Sands* (Warner Brothers, 1947) and the documentary *The World Is Turning (Towards the Coloured People)* (MGM, 1947).
6 Printed in *New Zealand Listener*, 8 November 1940.
7 James Cowan, *The Adventures of Kimble Bent: A Story of Wild Life in the New Zealand Bush*, Whitcombe and Tombs Ltd, London, Wellington, etc, 1911. Reprinted by Capper Press, Christchurch, 1975.
8 James Cowan, *The New Zealand Wars: A History of the Maori Campaign and the Pioneering Period* (1922/1923: 2 vols), reprinted with Preface by Michael King, P.O.Hasselberg, Govt Printer, Wellington, 1983.
9 'The Defenders of Orakau', *Hero Stories of New Zealand*, 1935: Southern Reprints, New Zealand, 1996, 99–110.
10 Preface to *The New Zealand Wars*, x.
11 Michael King, *The Penguin History of New Zealand*, Penguin Books (NZ), Auckland, 2003, 518.
12 F.E. Maning, *Old New Zealand*, Whitcombe and Tombs Ltd, Christchurch, etc, 1930 [1868].
13 Minette Hillyer, 54–5.
14 Keith Sinclair, *A Destiny Apart: New Zealand's Search For National Identity*, Unwin Paperbacks/Port Nicholson Press, Wellington, 1986, 81.
15 For a marginally different synopsis, see Edwards, *A Chronology of New Zealand Cinema*, 28, and Hayward's generalizing statement – 'my subject was stories about experiments in rejuvenation by means of monkey glands', Hayward material, NZFA.
16 *Napier Daily Times*, 6 September 1928.
17 Hayward material, NZFA.
18 *Ibid*.
19 Peter Wollen, *Signs and Meanings in the Cinema*, Secker and Warburg, London, 1972.
20 Chris Watson, paper on Hayward's comedies, Australian and New Zealand History and Film Conference, 'National Cinemas: Sites of Remembrance', 1998, Hayward material, NZFA.

21 Hillyer, 77.
22 Cowan, *The New Zealand Wars*, I, 359.
23 Cowan, *The New Zealand Wars*, II, 319.
24 *The Sun*, Auckland, 11 November 1927.
25 Belich, *Making Peoples*, Penguin, London, 1996, 241–2.
26 Sklar, 152.
27 Martin and Edwards, 34.
28 *The Sun*, 11 November 1927. Internal Affairs censorship document, Hayward material, NZFA.
29 Hayward material, NZFA.
30 *The Dictionary of New Zealand Biography*, I, 260–7.
31 A.W. Reed, *Rewi's Last Stand: Based on the Film Scenario by Rudall C. Hayward*, A.H. and A.W. Reed, Dunedin and Wellington, 1939.
32 *The Dictionary of New Zealand Biography*, I, 260.
33 Russell Campbell, 'In Order That They May Become Civilized: Pakeha Ideology in *Rewi's Last Stand, Broken Barrier* and *Utu*', *Illusions* 1, 1986, 6.
34 *Ibid.*, 14, but the ambiguity is recognized later, 15.
35 Hayward material, NZFA.
36 R.J. Gregory, *Politics and Broadcasting: Before and Beyond the NZBC*, The Dunmore Press Ltd, Palmerston North, 1985, 102–3.
37 Martin and Edwards, 49.

4

Sustaining the dream: the age of O'Shea

***Broken Barrier* (1952); *Runaway* (1964); *Don't Let It Get You* (1966)**
John O'Shea (1920–2001) directed the only three features to be made in New Zealand in the more than thirty years between Hayward's *Rewi's Last Stand* (1940) and *To Love a Maori* (1972). His autobiography, *Don't Let it Get You* (1999), reveals a mind agile almost to incoherence; an admirer of Céline and Barry Crump, the macho yarn-spinning bestseller; a man of intense admirations, but also surprising antipathies (he despised Norman Kirk, the revered Labour Prime Minister of the early 1970s for his broadcasting policies); a serious cinephile with a memory filled with global cinema, but not above strategically doing down Rudall Hayward's art; a fierce critic of the New Zealand television policies which locked out independents like himself; an equally enthusiastic internationalist and nationalist; an always passionate advocate of both Pākehā and Māori identity, and a biculturality based on the idea that all New Zealanders, Polynesian and European, were immigrants and exiles. Trained as an historian, he left the university world to join Roger Mirams' and Alun Falconer's Pacific Films (founded in 1948) in 1950, and was associated with what, after the others left by 1957, became his company for the rest of his life (Figure 7).

The film world O'Shea entered was dominated by documentary, largely the government-sponsored National Film Unit, which O'Shea regarded ambivalently for its official links. Along with short sponsored and advertising films, O'Shea's work was predominantly, through necessity, in this genre. In his autobiography O'Shea is repeatedly unflattering about documentary, declaring that he had, before the making of *Broken Barrier*, become disillusioned with the 'dull wastes of the genre'.[1] But documentary left its mark on his features, particularly *Broken Barrier* with its sequences of cattle mustering, hui (Māori gathering), small-town dance, and forestry working, transcribing in

7. The second father of New Zealand film, John O'Shea, working at his Pacific Films in 1992. Photographer: Paul Estcourt.

lyrical factual detail whole ways of life. O'Shea records having only agreed with Roger Mirams to do a 'Māori film' if it was not documentary,[2] but nevertheless the documentary impulse remained an important part of the fiction. However, even though O'Shea's primary desire was for fiction films, circumstances dictated that he could, with extreme difficulty, make only three.

The documentary–fiction relationship in O'Shea's work is more complicated than creative fiction versus pedestrian documentary. The feature films often utilize documentary codes, while Pacific Films' documentaries often push beyond the conventional. Whether directed by O'Shea himself – or by his protégé, the brilliant Tony Williams – they consistently take interesting routes, tending, for instance, to dispense with an authoritative voice, often becoming a montage of voices and views – as in *Wellington in the 60s* (Williams, 1968) where numerous people, including the poet James K. Baxter, give very different views of the city, or *Take Three Passions* (Williams, 1972), a celebration of different obsessions which switches between rugby writer Terry McLean, musician Maxwell Fernie, and astronomer Peter Read. Even a filmlet advertising Edmonds Baking Powder, *Cookery Nook* (Mirams and O'Shea, 1955), turns into a lively fiction; dad and mum quarrel over whether she will make afternoon tea when the boss calls round or visit her mother, leaving dad to attempt the baking disastrously till his daughter's domestic science class rescues the day. Another documentary, produced by O'Shea, directed by Barry Barclay and written by James McNeish, *The Town That Lost a Miracle* (about Opo, the famous dolphin), is a fascinating mix of documentation, interview, metaphor and mythology. And as routine a subject as road safety, in *Keep Them Waiting* (Tony Williams, 1972), is handled with time reversals, when it is announced that 'in a film you can turn back the clock, the characters can have a second chance', and the scenario is restaged with the accident averted. A tendency that Pacific's documentaries shared with others through the late 1940s to 1960s was the introduction of limited elements of fiction. For instance, *Journey For Three* (Michael Forlong, NZFU, 1949), a short aimed at encouraging British immigrants and released theatrically in Britain, has aspects of a foreshortened fiction as it follows three new immigrants – Margaret Allen, Harry White and Cassie McLeod – as they settle into the pleasures and occasional disillusionments of their new life, with a blossoming romance between Margaret and Harry, initially the least adaptive to the informalities of New Zealand ways. Even the poetic scenic *Snows of Aorangi* (National Film Unit, 1955) dramatizes three characters: an American, a New Zealander and a Swiss guide. From a later perspective these films embody a frustrated urge towards fictionalization in an age where constraints against making feature-films were overwhelming. A different solution was found by Robert Steele, an Auckland film-maker of small-scale commercial films, in his remarkable *Indictment!* (1950), made for the Auckland City Mission's appeal for a home for the poverty-stricken aged, where a stylistic adapted from Film Noir infuses the documentary with unexpected force.

Don't Let It Get You (1966) was O'Shea's last feature as director. He was 46. He remained until his death in 2001 a central figure on the film scene, during the period of the flourishing of the industry of which his films had been the immediate precursors, not just as senior statesman, but as producer and/or writer of a number of films, among them the groundbreaking television series *Tangata Whenua* (1974), 'definitely the single most crucial television series ever in raising the consciousness of this country to see the existence of a Māori "map" of our land just as valid as the Pākehā "map"'.[3] His Pacific Films was responsible for the features *Pictures* (Michael Black, 1981), *Ngati* (Barry Barclay, 1988), *Sons for the Return Home* (Paul Maunder, 1979), *Leave All Fair* (John Reid, 1985) and Barclay's later film, the highly ambitious *Te Rua* (1991), so that he was a key figure supporting the emergence of Māori film-making. Not all these partnerships were particularly serene – he quarrelled with both Maunder and Barclay over final cuts – but it is a major production portfolio, reflecting his enduring interest in Māori, bicultural relations, and New Zealand subject matter, sometimes in the widest international contexts (French and English settings in *Leave All Fair*, Berlin in *Te Rua*, and German influences in the German co-productions he developed for *Among the Cinders* and *Te Rua*).

Broken Barrier (1952)

In Ronald Hugh Morrieson's novel *The Scarecrow* (1963), the young narrator Nick Poindexter and his mate Les often go to the local Klynham fleapit, to see serials with titles like *The King of Diamonds* and *The Fire God's Treasure*. In the film (Sam Pillsbury, 1982), the young characters attend an evening session rather than a children's matinee. Here, following a local newsreel, the boys exit, leaving the older Prudence and her friend Angela, as they whisper about boys, to watch, not an American or British film, but *Broken Barrier* (1952), in particular the scene where Tom and Rawi, during the roundup, lose their horses, and sink down together amorously until they are hidden by the tall grass. This meta-cinematic moment – sandwiched between threats on the characters from other members of the audience: the juvenile Lynch gang threatening the boys, and the psychopathic murderer, Salter, sitting behind the girls – pays homage to a landmark in New Zealand feature film-making. O'Shea claimed that *Broken Barrier* was locally successful, asserting rather vaguely that it 'played to record audiences around the countryside', less vaguely that it was 'Kerridge's box-office leader for a month'.[4] Thus it might actually have played in towns as small as fictional Klynham, as it did in Wairoa, near where it was made (*Wairoa Star*, 30 September 1952). Despite the ironic context of tawdry cinema, preoccupied audience and the distractions of suspense, the extract, though brief, is imposing. The brilliant black and white photography, the exquisite sense of nature, the great valley, the tall grass formed by the breeze into rich patterns and textures, and the epic sky impress themselves on the later viewer at least, who has, however, the advantage of seeing the film not as an anomaly, but from the perspective of 1982 and beyond, as one of the new film culture's foundational works.

No film from another age comes to a present audience without a history of meaning attached, and, as with Hayward's, those O'Shea's hold cannot be separated from the enormous difficulties of pre-1980s New Zealand feature-film making. There are also local meanings which translate with difficulty to external audiences. An instance is the dismissive *Monthly Film Bulletin* review during the film's minor UK release. 'After problem pictures concerning the colour bar from so many sources, this one from New Zealand can have little to offer, though it does present a picture of the extent to which prejudice persists in a country which has accepted racial equality as a principle'.[5] Metropolitanly conflating national differences, the review then contradictorily admits *Broken Barrier*'s specificity, which is New Zealand's positive self-image of race relations, demonstrating, against its own argument, that the film is not about an abstraction called race, but emerges from a particular situation which precedes more general patterns. Considered from a global perspective, O'Shea's and Hayward's films may only be a footnote, but in the history of local film they are icons of great potency, not easily available in all their fullness of meaning to outside audiences (Figure 8).

Discussing *Broken Barrier*, Laurence Simmons notes the American psychologist David Ausubel's *Landfall* article eight years after the film, challenging New Zealand's good race relations as deceptive, and providing a retrospective pointer to the film's earlier critique of optimistic

8. Original poster for O'Shea's groundbreaking race-relations romance *Broken Barrier* (1952), featuring Terence Bayler and Kay Ngārimu.

assumptions.⁶ O'Shea, writing much later, when biculturalism had replaced integration as the official creed, apologized for his film's sociopolitical naïveties, speaking of it as 'warmed by the dying embers of a sentiment that saw the Māoris as "noble savages"', and of its 'idyllic but not very convincing ending' with the couple returning to the Māori farm 'presumably in an attempt to break the racial barrier through solidarity with her Maori people'.⁷ The comment about 'noble savages' illuminates the initial Fordian low-angle shots of Māori characters against big skies, part of a romanticism that presents rural Māori as too untainted to be quite believable. O'Shea later noted Barry Barclay's 'furious urge ... to illuminate one of the riddles of Maori personality – violence and intellectual capacity, bent by colonialism, co-exist behind prison bars',⁸ but avoids such questions in his own films.

Nowadays a film would not use, as O'Shea's does, a Pākehā voiceover defining Māori. Nearly thirty years later the television series *Tangata Whenua* (1978), of which O'Shea was a major enabler, set the newer pattern of avoiding paternalistic tropes. But conditions have changed in the half-century since the film was made for an overwhelmingly Pākehā audience knowing little of Māori life, and *Broken Barrier* has to be seen in its historical context, where the narrator formed a bridge to an audience positioned differently from today's. O'Shea's integrationism may now look naïve, but was not ignoble in holding to the best of the philosophy whose last major articulation was the Hunn Report of 1960 (Jack Hunn being Secretary of Māori Affairs), which saw the necessity for Māori to adapt to European ways, but also demanded change of Europeans. Thus the 1962 Department of Māori Affairs pamphlet 'Integration of Maori and Pakeha', spoke of 'integration' as 'a dynamic process by which Maori and Pakeha are being drawn closer together, in the physical sense of the mingling of the two populations as well as the mental and cultural senses', into 'the making of a whole new culture by the combination and adaptation of two pre-existing cultures'.⁹ The problems with this ideal were, first, that Pā kehā saw little reason to change, so that integration meant, practically, one-way assimilation,¹⁰ and, second, that it underestimated Māori desires to preserve difference. *Broken Barrier* recognizes both problems in its vignettes of Pākehā racism and in Tom's disturbed reaction to Rawi's enwrapment in the hui, and is simultaneously both realistic in finding little possibility in 1952 of a prejudice-free Pākehā world, and idealistic (but simultaneously, in larger social terms covertly pessimistic) in finding the only path to integration in Tom's return to the Māori world, just as rural Māori are flooding into the cities. At the same time, it attempts to implement the unregarded aspects of the

Hunn Report's philosophy in having Tom, the Pākehā protagonist, change and move, however unlikely reverse integration might be as a prescription for white society.

In *Broken Barrier* Tom (Terence Bayler), a young freelance journalist researching his series 'I Lived with the Maoris', written for a 'colourful' overseas publication, wanders into an East Coast Māori farming community and meets Rawi (Kay Ngārimu), a Māori girl, back on holiday from her city nursing job. Her parents Alec (George Ormond) and Kiri (Mira Hape) – he mixed blood, she a full Māori – put him up and he works on Alec's successful farm. The young people begin a relationship which is observed by Kiri with uneasy sympathy, uneasy because, although she has brought Rawi up to compete successfully in the Pākehā world, she fears that marriage to a white man will take her away from her family. During the round-up the pair lose their horses and end up making love. Kiri, to test Tom's commitment, invites him to a hui, where he reacts negatively to Rawi's involvement in her tribal culture. At the western-style dance that follows, Tom behaves badly, showing off his possession of Rawi unpleasantly, provoking her anger. When she returns to work in a Wellington hospital, Tom eventually follows her and they resume their relationship. There are, however, major difficulties. Tom's prejudiced parents find the idea of their getting married horrifying, and Rawi reacts understandably badly to incidents of casual racism. Just as Tom's guilt about his articles reaches crisis point, she discovers his publisher's letter suggesting an article about cannibalism. Rawi breaks the relationship and returns home. Tom wanders off to the Kaingaroa Forest and works in the forestry industry where he becomes mates with a Māori worker, Johnny (Bill Merito), in whom he confides his problems. Johnny, who shares the film's integrationist philosophy, tells Tom that he should return to Rawi. In a forest fire Johnny sacrifices his life to save Tom, who is left with the memory of Johnny's act and advice. He returns to the village where Rawi now works as a nurse, and is reunited with her, the suggestion being that, at least for the present, Tom will integrate with the Māori community rather than the pair return to the city. This ending contrasts with that of the contemporaneous short fiction film *Aroha* (Michael Forlong, National Film Unit, 1952), which has some striking similarities to *Broken Barrier*. There the young Māori heroine, like Rawi, trains in the white world but returns to a largely self-segregated Māori society, seeking to combine modern practices with older values. The difference is that she chooses as future husband not her white suitor, but a Māori, whom she encourages to follow her own trajectory of study and return, and in doing so preserves rather than disassembles barriers.

Broken Barrier was made under conditions in which, because of the crudity of equipment ('two mute 35mm 200-foot-load Arriflex cameras'[11]), synchronized dialogue proved impossible. Instead there is a music soundtrack and, in the absence of dialogue, post-synchronized internal monologues over the action, by various of the characters, primarily Rawi, her mother Kiri, Tom, and most frequently the unseen commentator. So, after the beginning titles, the middle-aged paternal Pākehā voice generalizes, over images of Māori gathering kai moana (seafood), about the problems the Europeans' coming has caused. 'Though the Māoris live in peace with the Europeans, many of them try to keep up with the pace of the modern world. They're stranded, caught like fish out of water. All of them face barriers of misunderstanding and prejudice. Whenever two races live side by side there are problems. Here is the story of some Māoris and Europeans and this is what they think about it all.' (The 'some' here is rather modest and qualifies the inevitable sense that the film, the first made about contemporary race relations in New Zealand, is dealing in absolutes.) After concentrating on figures in the water, the camera centres on a middle-aged woman: 'My name is Kiri ...', who talks about her husband Alec, and her daughter, Rawi. From Kiri's point of view, Tom wanders onto the beach and she speculates about the possibility of Rawi falling in love with a white man as she watches Tom and Rawi making contact and Alec inviting Tom home. As they move to the house, the commentator talks about Māori hospitality': Yes, they're kindly and friendly people.'

This opening passage is a digest of the narrative's technique, moving between the words of the commentator (who might have been invented by Michael King as an earlier repository of those New Zealand virtues of tolerance, commonsense and goodheartedness claimed in the last paragraph of his *Penguin History of New Zealand*, if somewhat limited by well-meaning 1950s paternalism) and internal monologues by the main characters as the action continues around them. This happens with considerable flexibility, sometimes including moments that may be attributed to the characters' imaginations – as when Rawi, during the disastrous dinner party, envisages the roadworkers who are the only Māori Tom's parents ever see; or sequences where the characters act in ways that go beyond the monologuist/imaginer's knowledge, as when Kiri talks of her pride in the hospital accepting Rawi as a nurse rather than a Māori, with the scene showing her, while Kiri's monologue continues ('She's just a girl in love ... a girl in love with a white man'), placed between two doctors: one white and one Māori. Here, though, Rawi's fixed gaze at the Māori doctor, perhaps to be read as suggesting 'this is the kind of man, Māori and qualified, that in ordinary circumstances I would (should?) have married, and I would probably therefore have found life less difficult as a result', presumably exists outside Kiri's view.

Broken Barrier falls into four sections: the first two (i) East Coast idyll (ii) unidyllic Wellington, largely antithetical; then (iii) the relationship between Tom and his Māori friend Johnny, providing the eventual conditions for the short coda (iv), Tom's return to Rawi on the East Coast. While a warm transparency of desire for better racial relations dominates the film, its overarching affirmative/negative structure is complicated by more hesitant elements, clustering in the later parts. Largely speaking, the first section is lyrical: Māori foreshore life, the rhythms of farm work, the lovers' encounters. The problems that arise are overtly signalled: the bad faith of Tom's journalism, his ambivalence about Rawi's commitment to Māori culture; his rather coarse proprietorial behaviour at the dance, all endangering the lovers' relationship. But basically optimism dominates: Kiri's worries about the relationship are in no sense hostile, and a detail like the chicken Tom finds on his bed is comic rather than denigratory – after all, better a chook on one's bunk than the cockatiel Tom's pretentious sister improbably sports on her shoulder! By contrast, Wellington is a site of racism, even though the hospital where Rawi works is an egalitarian environment, where she is valued for her abilities. But away from it, we see a passing Pākehā woman's too curious scrutiny of Tom as he goes towards a dingy house, obviously known for Māori lodgers; Tom's family's humiliating disapproval of Rawi; Tom's female friend ignoring Rawi; another woman, in a powder room, meaningfully shifting her purse when the Māori girl stands by her. Early on, Kiri, watching Rawi's confidence when she first meets Tom, remarks significantly that she doesn't suffer from 'shyness' (the Māori term 'whakamā' that she suggests through the word can have connotations of feelings of inferiority to Pākehā), but now the narrator describes her as 'becoming conscious, too conscious, of her race'. In the Wellington sequence's one idyllic moment the couple watch the 1950 All Blacks v British Isles rugby test at Athletic Park, its significance underlined by the voiceover: 'A happy New Zealand crowd that makes footballers its gods. Here the only feeling the two races have for each other is pride. Brown skin or white makes no difference – there's no barrier here.'

In the third segment the narrative follows Tom, the logic being that the failing relationship is in no way Rawi's fault, and that it is Tom who must alter. This he does (like the Hunn pamphlet's idealized Pākehā), through his friendship with Johnny. Johnny's function is a simple one – perhaps too uncomplex, as O'Shea attributes to him a positive uncluttered simplicity: 'to his uncrowded mind the issue was a simple one' – that risks being found unreal. Whatever, Johnny's death confers a blessing on the interracial couple, while his friendship with Tom injects a rare bi-racial element into the Pākehā world of mateship (reworked comedically in Gary and Howard Morrison's pig hunt and the word game number 'Have You Ever Seen?' in *Don't Let It Get You*).

Within this simple, moving framework, a more oblique episode has Tom accompanying Johnny to Rotorua, here a deceptive, ambiguous site, claiming Māori authenticity, yet also the dubious epitome of colourful touristic New Zealand, not just the natural wonders of geysers and boiling mud, but of crowd-pleasing Māori spectacle on tap. 'Nature turns on a sideshow, and the Maoris join in' as a by now critical Tom puts it, reminding us of Grierson's strongly expressed feeling that 'I knew the Maoris of Rotorua were all right for what they were doing but that, I was sure, was not the true creature of Polynesia with a quality of grace and strange vitality'.[12] The early twentieth-century Young Māori Party had a major role in developing Rotorua tourism,[13] so it is over-simplified to see it as a Pākehā imposition. Belich's account reflects ambivalence about a place that can be seen both as commodified and as culturally preserving. Much of Tom and Johnny's visit visually resembles a celebratory 'scenic', but is complicated by Tom's uncelebratory meditations and by his meeting with Johnny's fiancée Mārama (Ata Ananu), a native Rotorua guide. As the Māori perform, Tom, scrutinizing the tourist watchers, thinks, 'Māoris in a showcase; no wonder they keep on treating most of them as if they should still be wearing grass skirts and making chisels out of shark bones. Bring in a few dollars; the Yanks lap it up.' This is clearly placed in antithesis to the earlier uncommodified hui, but less straightforward is Tom's meeting with Johnny's fiancée, where he is disconcertingly impressed by the Māori girl moving easily between native and modern costumes. The commentator notes, 'Somehow he didn't feel so bad about the articles he'd written', meaning, presumably, that Tom's guilt is eased by his perception of the fiancée's complicity in Māori commodification (or is it admirable adaptability?), and Johnny's lack of concern at it. If one constant throughout this subtle sequence is Tom's attaining more complex views of the other culture, another is that what he sees troubles the simpler binaries dominating the main plot (Māori innocence/Pākehā exploitation: Māori authenticity/Pākehā inauthenticity; indeed, the very concepts of a pure authenticity and inauthenticity) without, however, overtly undermining the idealization of the East Coast farm.

The ending's rhetoric is triply affirmative, with Kiri's statement 'they love one another and they will marry. No one can stop them. No one should try', bound both to the local and to the international, through two quotations, Kiri's 'Ka pū te ruha, ka hao te rangatahi' (the old net is cast aside, the new net goes fishing), spoken in Māori without subtitles, and the end graphic of the United Nations statement against racism. Again, within the overarchingly positive framework there are local details that repay attention. Rawi's mixed-race father, Alec, is not just any agricultural worker, but runs a large, successful farm: 'He's proud of it', the narrator says, 'and the sheep and cattle it carries'. As such, he is 'one of those fortunate Māoris who's held on to his land'. (This reference to Māori land dispossession is tangential, but there to be read.) It is implicitly important that the family Tom ends up in has this substantial holding, run as well as any Pākehā farm, since it not only shows a Māori farmer as a success, but that Tom, working for Alec, possibly eventually inheriting from him, is hardly 'going native' in any pejorative sense. However, as anything but a one-off exception, the ending has elements of the mythic. The problematics of Māori farming at the time are outlined by King and Belich.[14] Sir Āpirana Ngata's Native Land Reforms of 1928 arranged public loans designed to 'paint the map of New Zealand with Māori farmers'.[15] But by the late 1940s Māori farming (usually small scale) was failing to sustain a growing population, adding one more motivation for the rush to the cities. Alec is one of those exceptional farmers who, King mentions, 'did spectacularly well',[16] but clearly his farm stands out against the general pattern. It is also significant that Rawi is the product of an interracial marriage, giving her a head start in living between traditional Māori and European urban society and predisposing her towards marriage with a Pākehā. Would it be the same if Tom had wandered into a purely Māori rather than part Pākehā set-up? Does Rawi's being part white conceal the fact that prejudice may exist on the other side as well, that intermarriage may not have looked so desirable to many Māori not married to a part-white man as Kiri is? Did Rawi's part-whiteness (like Ariana's in the 1940 *Rewi*) make it easier for the early 1950s Pākehā audience to approve the marriage? These elements do not in any simple way undermine the film's lyricism, but they complicate it, making sure that its idealism does not lose contact with reality. Meditating the ending of Douglas Sirk's great 1950s melodrama *All That Heaven Allows*, with its socially rather than racially transgressive relationship between the bourgeois widow and her gardener, Laura Mulvey notes how the New England of the past (Walden and Thoreau), which Ron represents, and the socially prejudiced New England of the present 'can be reconciled only by Cary [Jane Wyman] moving, as it were, *into the dream*'. The ending of *Broken Barrier* observes the same pattern, though the movement is Tom's, but whereas, as Mulvey observes, in the American melodrama the dream is broken by Ron's accident,[17] here it is allowed to prevail, except for the kind of implicit doubts suggested above.

Runaway (1964)

In *Runaway* (1964), David Manning (Colin Broadley), caught up in the affluent lifestyle of the fast Auckland set, commits a minor fraud to keep up his sports car payments. Quarrelling with his father, the most literal of the patriarchal figures he encounters through the narrative (the rep threatening to reclaim his car; his boss; the businessman, Tom Morton; the Westland deer-culler Clarrie) when he asks for help, David embarks on an ambiguous, unresolved quest. Heading north, he stays in the rural Hokianga peninsula, wavering between Isobel Whararewa, a gentle Māori girl (Kiri Te Kanawa), and a predatory European, Laura Kossovich (the European starlet Nadja Regin), with the dark glasses, amorality and freedom symbolized by her white sports car that irresistibly conjure up the Italian art films of the period (Figure 9). After violently quarrelling with Laura, unable to commit himself to rural nativism with Isobel, and wanted by the police for his appropriation of Laura's car, David leaves. Hitching a ride, he quarrels with his temporary host, an aggressive businessman, Tom Morton (Gil Cornwall), who dies of a heart attack as they argue. Instead of reporting the death, David self-destructively hides the body. On the South Island ferry, he meets Diana (Deirdre McCarron), Morton's daughter, though David never knows this. He persuades her to come with him to his remembered childhood Westland. They stay in a hut used by a sinister deer-culler, Clarrie (played by the iconic bushman-author Barry Crump), who betrays them to the police. Pursued, the pair take off into the Franz Josef Glacier. When Diana is injured, David presses on alone, towards a certain (but undramatized) self-destruction.

Runaway is a work of high ambition made in a hard time, lacking adequate technological, artistic and economic resources, as well as the multiple infrastructural elements later available, so that the disjunction between desire and execution is irreparably present. But the desire is fascinatingly evident. *Runaway* is the first self-consciously modern feature to be made in New Zealand, crossing highly specific local elements with late 1950s/early 1960s European art film ambiguity, opacity, undeclared motivation and cultural and sexual angst. O'Shea took a print of Antonioni's *L'Avventura* (1959) on location, where 'he and

9. Conflict between David (Colin Broadley) and Laura (imported Bond girl Nadja Regin) in O'Shea's odyssey of alienation, *Runaway* (1964).

the crew watched it repeatedly with the intention of using it as a template for many of the ensuing scenes'.[18] Antonioni's film was one of a number of European art films that, through festival showings, impacted on New Zealand film circles at the beginning of the 1960s. Highly cineliterate, O'Shea was attracted by Antonioni's cinematic modernity. If *Runaway* does not much replicate the Italian director's placement of figures against architecture, it certainly is influenced by his treatment of figures in landscape: *L'Avventura*'s early scenes on the water find a satisfying metamorphosis in the Auckland beach sequences at *Runaway*'s beginning. Though certain of *Runaway*'s ambiguities were accidentally intensified by the problems described below, Antonioni's purposive ambiguity certainly interested O'Shea. Famously, in *L'Avventura* Anna's mysterious disappearance is never solved, a paradigm of art-film indeterminacy. Similar opacities surround David Manning's angst-ridden questing. Antonioni's treatment of the sexual also palimpsests onto O'Shea's preoccupations, despite *Runaway*'s generally inexplicit (censorship wary) coyness, and Antonioni's ornate choreography of lovers' faces and bodies is certainly echoed, with a landscaping inflection. Characters in both films grasp at sex as escape, before suffering disillusion, with the existential solitude that haunts Antonioni's characters playing into the antipodean solitude of the 'Man Alone' motif. Occasionally there is even a scene adapted from the original. In *L'Avventura*, Monica Vitti wanders round the bedroom, pausing at a mirror to make a series of comic faces. In *Runaway* Diana, alone in the hotel, makes a series of comic poses in the mirror, using her long hair to form a moustache, while she puts on a hat and transforms her lipstick into a cigar, her transformations enacting a playful assumption of maleness (not the effect with Monica Vitti). As in *L'Avventura*, the audience is left to form its own conclusions. Does Diana's routine suggest her desire to assume David's male role as quester, rather than her own as female understander? Does it emphasize the desire for changed identity running through the film? Or does its parodic hypermasculinity – bushy moustache, bush hat and phallic cigar – burlesque the almost hysterical masculine identity thematics surrounding David? No single meaning is underlined; possibly all three are relevant.

Viewing *L'Avventura* alongside *Runaway* is an interesting experience, with the later film not always eclipsed, visually at least, but perhaps the greatest difference is in the dialogue. Whereas Seymour Chatman notes how Antonioni 'dislikes textual redundancy' to the degree that 'He has virtually returned cinema to the predominance of the visual that it lost with the advent of sound',[19] O'Shea's film features very overt theme-summarizing dialogue, often to its detriment. Though this dialogue's opacity might key in to art film conventions, its over-overtness, its sometimes unfortunate banality, compare badly with the film's visual sophistications.

John Reynold's doctoral thesis on *Runaway* details the extraordinary difficulties O'Shea faced in making a bigger film than the relatively modest *Broken Barrier*, while lacking any industrial and cultural infrastructures. Actors doubled as crew, and occasionally crew as actors. The music was composed by the expatriate New Zealand composer Robin Maconie, then studying in Vienna, from 16mm copies of scenes flown across to him.[20] The British Director of Photography pulled out at the last moment. The shooting schedule was so tight that a scene where David proposed marriage to Isobel, delayed because of Kiri Te Kanawa's facial eczema, had to be abandoned altogether, leaving a hole in the narrative. And when the actress objected to a mild bedroom scene, O'Shea lacked the budget to replace her.[21] A chain of meta-dramatic scenes originally placed throughout the narrative only survives in the mysterious moment beginning the film where Diana speaks in some sort of actors' studio Desdemona's words to Othello ['The heavens forbid but that' omitted] 'our loves and comforts should increase / Even as our days do grow' (*Othello* 2.1.191–3). It is difficult to speculate what this signifies without its extended context. The original is Desdemona's reply to Othello's hyperbolic statement that 'if it were now to die / 'twere now to be most happy': in other words, that he has reached a summit of happiness that he may never equal. Desdemona's reply seems to assert a less extreme view of slowly growing affection and happiness. Its relation to O'Shea's narrative might be endlessly speculated, but what is unquestionable is that leaving the radically decontextualized moment in the film, especially in combination with the bravura optical effect of the dots of light reforming through focus pulling into Diana's face, allows it to be read – even emptied of narrative coherence, perhaps *because* emptied of it – as a pure sign of *Runaway*'s modernism. Whatever the production difficulties, the film's music is highly effective, and its photography (which Tony Williams and Michael Seresin took over at the shortest notice) is frequently beautiful. On the other hand, some of the enforced changes and resulting lacunae unquestionably have negative effects: like the extreme abbreviation of the material involving Isobel. Although it is still clear that David's dream of a prelapsarian interracial idyll recalling *Broken Barrier* fails, the treatment is too shorthand to bear the weight it should.

Despite such faults, *Runaway* has over the years accumulated meaning to itself, discourses as much connected with failure as success, a fate that can only happen with a certain kind of groundbreaking film at certain stages of cinematic history. A programme note to a retrospective showing emphasizes *Runaway*'s symbolic place in New Zealand cinema, asserting that 'the film's enduring impact is its manifest desire to synthesize and translate a head full of British and European cinema into the wide open spaces of New Zealand'.[22] In the end this symbolic aesthetic counter- negotiation (taking from Europe aesthetically while losing out to it politico-economically) may outweigh other meanings such as O'Shea's suggestion that it was an allegory of New Zealand's imminent loss of secure economic and cultural identity, resulting from Britain's commitment to the European Common Market, made 'in the wake' of his Pacific Films documentary *Food For Thought* (1962), which warned of this coming blow and speculated on its effects. There is an interesting review in the (UK) *Guardian* (26 August 1965) entitled 'Breakaway from Meat and

Rugby' in which F.A. Jones, by-lined as '12 years a New Zealand film critic' describes 'an important breakthrough in his country's movie industry'. Jones, after relaying O'Shea's allegory as the key to the film, discusses its failure at home: 'The reaction of discriminating cinema viewers was particularly difficult to understand. "Runaway" was, after all, made in a style thoroughly familiar to them after so many Continental importations. It might have been expected, at least, to invite their sympathetic criticism. But they thought it silly. They condemned the film's anti-hero, found the script weak, complained that the local settings were obtrusive'. He ends by suggesting that English audiences, rather than coming to 'the same conclusion' might 'take the view of a handful of New Zealanders who felt that their fellow countrymen, told the uncomfortable truth about themselves, not only refused to face it but reacted to it with revealing violence'. This hope was disappointed. The *Monthly Film Bulletin*, though recognizing 'some style (however conscious)', classed *Runaway* with American teenage problem films rather than European antecedents: 'In a vague way (too vague to mean anything to anybody) the script tries to embody the whole ethos of mixed-up kids as the screen has showed them over the past decade'.[23] The film's slim chances of minor recognition were made even smaller by the commercial pressures that changed its name to *Runaway Killer*, with a poster claiming 'He was a hungry young man in a hurry – his blood on fire'.

David's quest engages too many adjacent trajectories to be tied down to O'Shea's 'official' interpretation, and this plurality of meaning can be seen much more sympathetically than it was by the (British) *Kinematograph Weekly* reviewer who wrote that 'too many motives are stated but never fulfilled'.[24] Escaping from a succession of father figures, intertwined with successive females, seeking some kind of renovated identity in the remotest parts of the country, acting out his version of 'Man Alone', David's movements are too particular to yield convincingly to unmediated equations. Laura equals villainous Europe? Morton equals the self-satisfied New Zealand economy heading for a shock? Diana (in Jones's too heavy assertion) 'symbolizes human awareness'? The equations are not wholly without point, but too crude to carry conviction. It is interesting that Mrs Milligan, the Hokianga landlady, a lower-class Englishwoman, should be such an unflattering cameo to go with the European Laura Kossovich, but while they do not contradict O'Shea's over-stated intentions, they hardly clinch them. Rather, we should see O'Shea's allegory as another level of allusion and the historical events looming as an enlarging echo chamber into which multiple meanings sound.

To some degree sociological explanations closer at hand are more convincing. David's ennui is that of a generation brought up in the material comfort of the seemingly never-ending boom, the 'golden weather' of post-war New Zealand, sceptical of politics, but seeking some kind of protesting action, some sort of unconventional self-definition, even if self-destructive. If this risks substituting one reductive allegory for another, it is at least more concrete. One can point to a pattern of patriarchal figures with whom David is in conflict: his distant father, in whom codes of self-reliance have curdled into suburban body-and-mind-armoured rigidity; the crude, pragmatic Morton with his self-made man philosophy ('Just keep working hard like I have if you want a car like this'), who is also in conflict with a son; Clarrie, the 'Man Alone' deer-culler, the modern throwback to pioneer ancestors, whom isolation proves not to have refined, but turned more crude and sinister than the suburban prototypes; the unsympathetic males searching for David on the glacier ('The young fool. It's no more than he deserves').

Is David then in flight from the masculinity now so negatively written about in New Zealand cultural commentary? It is tempting to see his encounters with the narrative's women as prefiguring those calls for the feminizing of the New Zealand male historically just around the corner, but if we grant the film some prescience here, such intimations are fleeting, and the women too various (some too negatively drawn) to easily fit a pattern, particularly a redemptive one – Sandra (Doraine Green), the bored epitome of David's Auckland lifestyle; Isobel, who offers a simpler existence and a rapprochement with the Māori; Laura, who offers the dangerous allure of the European femme fatale; and Diana, who seems to mirror David's unsettledness, comes from the same businessman father background, travels restlessly, says she is an actress, sees herself without a home, but is anchored enough to keep her place in the mundane world (she is travelling to visit her mother when David meets her). Despite these women's narrative importance, David is almost always the centre of attention, with the camera more interested in Colin Broadley as primary specular object than them, most markedly as he sunbathes at the film's opening, and in an erotic scene where he is the one half undressed, rather than the fully clothed Nadja Regin.

Similarly, the Māori thematic is foregrounded, but too restrictedly to dominate. Here Isobel; her brother Joe, with whom David talks about the possibility of finding peace in the Hokianga; their churchgoing mother; Tana, from whom David at least temporarily takes Isobel; as well as Laura's and Morton's anti-Māori statements and behaviour, are all important, but disappear from the narrative when David heads south. The Māori, with a longer tenure of the land, is associated for the questing Pākehā with a version of 'home', a longer-standing relationship with the environment, but here it seems to be only one association among many, rather than the definitive solution, and the quest moves on, as if some answer lies in the extremes of New Zealand's less habited geography. This version of quest is deeply embedded in the literature O'Shea's generation grew up with, centred on displaced colonial children seeking rapprochement with a new environment, the task's difficulty expressed through the country's sometimes forbidding landscape forms, 'the 'savage forests' and 'gaunt hills' (from the semi-official poet laureate of landscape unease, Charles Brasch, in his 'The Silent Land').

Part of David's opaqueness consists in how, without doing anything lethal, he acts the part of a more serious criminal than he is. If David feels as guilty as he acts (in a curious moment, hiding, he watches a skulking surrogate clamber on board the night train in the Film Noir influenced Taihape Station sequence), what is he is guilty of? His undeserved material comfort? Colonization's displacement of the Māori? His patriarchal inheritance? Perhaps all of these, but the key incident seems to be Morton's death, for which David is not really responsible, since he could hardly guess that such robust philistinism hid a weak heart. Nevertheless, he treats it like a murder, hiding the body rather than reporting the death. Twice he visualizes Morton's face in the water, the second appearance so paralysing that he fails immediately to rescue Diana from drowning. David seems obscurely intent on condemning himself for parricide. At the same time he appears to be moving geographically and psychically back to his Westland childhood, which he speaks of both movingly and regressively: 'that's what Westland's like. Clear water off the mountains. Lakes surrounded by bush. Streams run down to the sea'. There is a strange moment on the Franz Josef glacier where Diana (perhaps David's surrogate in an act too maternally oriented for him to perform), bends down and kisses, or seems to drink from, a mound of snow that is definitively breast shaped.

What all this suggests is that meaning is overdetermined: that the quest is both concrete and vague, involving overlapping connotations, freedom, escape (as in Rim D. Paul's theme song 'Runaway, drift away like a bird. / Drift away, wing away like a bird'), evasion, guilt, flight from (or redefinition of) masculinity, search for the feminine and for origins, generational revolt, revolt against materialism and security, even O'Shea's allegorical perspectives, and meaning in a religious-existential sense, as when David kicks the deer skulls outside the Westland hut, asking 'Is this all I am?'. At the same time, David's drive for meaning (often literal in this proto-New-Zealand road movie where the hero says 'driving is like dreaming' and cars sometimes progress oneirically without noise) through minimalism and the shedding of urban comforts is sardonically inspected from time to time, not least by Joe Whararewa when, as David talks of settling down in the Hokianga, he says 'Nah, man, you like things too much'.

The film, though teasing the viewer with symbolic gestures – David's surname of Manning has New Zealand Everyman connotations as well as invoking F.E. Maning, with his famous account *Old New Zealand* (1863) – does not attempt to resolve its protagonist's enigma, a trait echoed in Clarrie's remark after he betrays David: 'I don't usually help the police; but this joker ...'. His sentence trails away, leaving completion for the viewer. To say this, though, is not to assert limitless ambiguity; its parameters are defined within the film and involve, whatever universals are involved, characteristically New Zealand problematics and connotations. Two examples of this. First, Clarrie is played by Barry Crump: of enormous local iconicity, familiar to just about every New Zealander at the time, he contained meanings unavailable outside the local scene, with his bestselling 'crew culture' yarns, nostalgic revivals of the myths of pioneering toughness and self-sufficiency. But in the film Clarrie turns out to be – long before revelations by acquaintances and wives exposed a blackness within Crump's real-life persona – a sardonically bleak portrait of the loner, sexually and otherwise threatening, the most archaic of the father figures turned betrayer. Second, the film's last moments are accompanied by impressive religious-sounding organ music as the camera cuts repeatedly between David stumbling slowly on and travelling aerial shots of the mountains he is disappearing into. Whatever else, in terms of triumph or disintegration, may be read into the sequence, it is a kind of sublime parody of the famous documentary *Snows of Aorangi* and those many mountain and skiing sequences in New Zealand touristic documentaries over the years, but here, without the comforting commentative voice and the pleasures of alpine sports, starkly severe and minatory.

Don't Let It Get You (1966)

O'Shea's last feature as director was *Don't Let It Get You* (1966), that extreme rarity: a New Zealand musical. It is difficult to think of predecessors, or, indeed, successors. Hayward's second *Rewi's Last Stand* had Ramai Te Miha performing two waiata (songs), but neither of them survived the British distributor's cuts. The three 1930s South

Island films *Down on The Farm, Phar Lap's Son?* and *The Wagon and The Star* all featured numbers. Later 1980s and 1990s films, following neo-Hollywood fashion, are often saturated with New Zealand pop songs, sometimes memorably – one thinks of Costa Botes' use of Dave Dobbyn's 'Language' in *Saving Grace* (1997), or Gaylene Preston's of Neil Finn's 'Not The Girl You Think You Are' and Don McGlashan's 'Anchor Me' in *Perfect Strangers* (2003). Florian Habicht's *Woodenhead* (2003) moves sometimes into a quasi-operatic mode, and there are extraordinary musical moments in *Heavenly Creatures*. The only other film, however, which centrally fulfils the conditions of the genre is Garth Maxwell's *When Love Comes* (1999), a backstage musical that I will consider in Chapter 6.

New Zealand popular music of the 1960s, which sold less than the British and American performers who dominated the hit parades, had a significant internal live performance presence. This scene was dominated by Māori and Polynesian performers, whose talent the film showcases – Eliza and Herma Keil, the Quin Tikis (who accompany Rim D. Paul in *Runaway*), Rim D. Paul himself, Gary Merito, the opera singer Kiri Te Kanawa, just beginning her rise to international fame, in a different mode, and the perennially popular Howard Morrison. These were joined by local white singers such as Lew Pryme and Gwynne Owen, and the newly successful Australian, Normie Rowe, who, with the Australian male and female romantic leads, gestured hopefully to the Australian market.

Shorn apparently of the important themes of the previous films, and without the interracial love story at the heart of *Broken Barrier* and on the margins of *Runaway, Don't Let It Get You* is the most relaxed of O'Shea's films – a pastoral like the one that Tom and Rawi briefly experience at the rugby, staging images of integration through the utopic mode of the musical. An aspiring drummer, Gary Wallace (played by himself) tries to get a job from the Māori entertainer Howard Morrison (also played by himself) in Sydney, the bigger apple where most New Zealand pop stars go, but Morrison is returning to New Zealand to promote a Rotorua pop festival. However he promises to help, and they fly to New Zealand together where Judy Beech (Carmen Duncan), a girl Gary has just met, is also heading with her snobbish mother (Alma Woods). If the film's romantic casting suggests Australian predominance, the narrative has Australians seeking out New Zealand, happily reversing the usual exodus. Morrison gets Gary an audition with the Māori group The Quin Tikis, which he fails when it is sabotaged by his rival, in drumming and love, William Broadhead (Harry Lavington). This slight narrative resolves with the lovers united, the hero taking his chance, and the festival a success, and with Gary's rival getting his come-uppance when Judy's dragonish mother fancies him. Gary's non-romantic quest for a place in the Polynesian band (a weightless version of the reverse integration of *Broken Barrier*), is, despite his initial setback, easy to achieve compared with the obstacles blocking the earlier films' protagonists. Centrally, as in any musical, there are multiple numbers, here shot with stylish ingenuity by Tony Williams, who had put in time in England and acquainted himself with Dick Lester's work in the Beatles musical *A Hard Day's Night* (1964). The numbers' excited motion, created through camera work and cutting in the absence of professional dancers, is constantly inventive, especially in the development of visual conceits from local material. Normie Rowe's number 'I'm Tellin' Ya Now', shucks off its early visual allusions to 'Sergeant Pepper' in favour of that New Zealand institution of yesteryear, uniformed marching girls, attaining autochthonous effects unlikely with the Beatles. Similarly, Gary musters sheep on his bicycle, turns his drumsticks into pan pipes as he leads the animals from the round-up, then relaxes with his sheepdog whose tongue he uses to wet the edges of a cigarette paper, and, most strikingly, there is Kiri Te Kanawa's singing of Rossini's 'Una Voce Poco Fa' inside a Māori meeting house, the most concentrated example of a repeated motif of Māori carvings benignly surveying the characters and performers (Figure 10).

A one-off event – with no native film musical tradition for it to follow – *Don't Let It Get You* is closer to the Dick Lester Beatles films than to the Hollywood template. *Don't Let It Get You* has more of a conventional love plot, but its importance is largely formal. Gary plays the drums but hardly sings or dances, and Judy is played by a straight actress (Carmen Duncan) who is only an audience to the numbers. As already suggested, *Don't Let It Get You* avoids the interracial sexual problems of the other two films. In this it might be seen as a laidback celebration following the two earlier problem dramas. However, lack of an interracial love plot does not mean lack of interracial thematics. As O'Shea himself wrote, integration has already been effortlessly achieved in the film's world – 'There is no reference at any stage to racial groups and integration is taken as a norm of life in New Zealand'[25] – as Pākehā, Māori and Polynesians mix as musicians, spectators and friends, if not as lovers. Howard Morrison becomes mates with Gary, helps him, takes an avuncular interest in his romance, and also is buddies with Normie Rowe. Gary, a Pākehā, is accepted into the Quin Tikis Polynesian band. In scenes where segregation of brown and white seems to be set up, expectation is undermined. The moment

10. Deliriously mixed whakapapas as rising opera diva, Kiri Te Kanawa, treats a bicultural children's audience to 'Una voce poco fa' in O'Shea's musical *Don't Let It Get You* (1966).

found in many touristic films of Pākehā spectators watching Māori kids diving for coins from the well known Puarenga stream bridge is pleasantly subverted when the internal audience watching the divers turns out to be more Māori than Pākehā. A moment of potential Pākehā privilege, as the performers fool about in the hotel pool, turns out not to be since Herma Keil and Kiri Te Kanawa share it too, with Kiri reversing the tourist/touristic spectacle roles by taking snaps of the Pākehās horsing around. Notably, the Māori-display elements of Rotorua, problematically viewed in *Broken Barrier*, are here presented as unproblematic, a carnival site, maybe removed from certain realities, but certainly not condemned, the past preserved through traditional Māori arts, and the present engaged with through pop.

Inasmuch as the content of many of the songs is, as with most popular music, sexual ('It Takes Two', 'She's the Girl I Need to Love', and so on), European/Polynesian fusion takes place on the broadest level, both brown and white singers singing love songs to mixed white and brown audiences. Where it does not happen is in the narrative's white-on-white love plots, and where the central character, at least in performing and entrepreneurial terms, Howard Morrison, is stably married with a Māori wife and children. (Even on stage his only female partner, briefly in 'Livin' and Lovin", is Māori.) Perhaps all this is so because the interracial love plot, though desired, is considered a melodramatic not comedic subject, arousing, in the earlier films, a complex of inhibitions, barriers not broken. At any rate, as if to counter its importance as racial index, the main plot between Gary and Judy is decidedly lightweight, especially in the performative terms essential to the musical. Judy has no performance role whatsoever, and though Gary is in various numbers, he is performatively restricted, mainly drumming and fooling about. What skills he has, like the engaging metamorphoses he puts his drumsticks through, are comic rather than romantic, and what in a sense is his big romantic number is given entirely through Howard Morrison. This, the number 'I'm Home', the moment in the film that most balances the evanescent love motifs of pop music with marriage, and which by surrogate dramatizes Gary's change from independence to commitment, begins with Morrison walking along the seashore alone; then has him on the floor with his kids playing with toy racing cars; then with his wife and children outdoors – images that precede and anchor domestically all the others – playing squash; clowning with Normie Rowe; being photographed sitting between Māori statues; talking to girl fans; conversing with a business partner; driving; being friendly backstage with fellow performers; on stage singing; horse riding for relaxation across the countryside; all to the lyrics 'No more worries / So glad to settle down / At home and relaxing / Now I have found / My friends all around me'. The point here is that as Gary is drawn further into Howard's orbit – almost immediately afterwards they go pig hunting, and then, not much later, he wakes the singer up, initiating Morrison's second version of 'Haere Mae' – it is natural, since Gary cannot sing his feelings adequately, that they should be sung by his mentor, the figure who ideally brings together the domestic and the public, business and entertainment, freedom and commitment.

It has been suggested that *Don't Let It Get You* critiques

> the idealism of the widely accepted myth of a common culture of the 1950s, with the image of New Zealand as a rural idyll and land of material opportunity, supported by traditional and shared laissez faire notions of 'God's own Country', 'she'll be right', 'A great place to bring up the kids', or that at least it reports its unease with the imperfect realization of such a project as well as the passing of its moment. Instead it

reflects ... that this pattern of cultural beliefs has undergone a structural change and is now threatened by a grittier account of New Zealand's social reality based in urbanization, suburban consumerism, geographical mobility, youth culture, the instrumentalization of patterns of friendship and social relations as well as the resistance of indigenous Māori culture to such social changes, all of which have produced, as we have become so profoundly aware, a culture founded in, and upon, alienation and violence.[26]

While the above accurately summarizes cultural changes, it symptomatically makes no attempt to show how such social trends are acted out in the film. There is obviously a wish that the film should show itself subversive by deconstructing the myths referred to, but in fact not a single one of these topoi is presented so as to generate unease. For instance, the car ('C'mon, get your car in gear, / C'mon, let's get out of here' as Lew Pryme sings) is presented as the means to a mobility leading to general happiness; consumerism – of which cars, the music industry, Caltex, Ringamops, Dulux paints and Black and Decker tools are part, the small endorsements scattered throughout a film that had to seek desperately for any kind of support – is presented as innocently desirable, part of the good life; urbanism and ruralism are idyllically bound together in the New Zealand suburban dream in the number devoted to Howard Morrison's home and public life; and the relation of Māori culture to the Rotorua festival is presented affirmatively (all those carved faces looking on presidingly). Further, the film actively denies (however mistakenly in terms of sociological accuracy following Johnny Devlin) the establishment of a separate musical youth culture. Thus the Rotorua festival audience is repeatedly defined as embracing all ages. The beginning of Normie Rowe's number 'I'm Tellin' Ya Now', finds him in a sharp, light-coloured suit and tie, hair half over his ears, but highly trained, like all the other performers disconnected from the wilder side of 1960s rock, flanked by his co-performers, reminiscent of 'Sergeant Pepper', while to the left are two boys in New Zealand holiday gear of checked shirts, shorts and short hair, and at the right are a family of two parents, slightly elderly looking so that they could even be grandparents, with two children, the older figures unambiguously interested in the performance. In Eliza Keil's roller-skating number 'It Takes Two for Kissin', at one point the singer puts a little girl skater on her knee, and turns the song momentarily from teenage to mother love. Later, in the auditorium an elderly male among the dancers happily raises his walking stick two-handed above his head, while, nearby, two little girls, brown and white, twist together. During the final number 'Don't Let It Get You', Morrison, moving among the audience, touches the face of a grandmother, lifting off her glasses. Clearly this is far from a portrait of a separating youth culture. Here as elsewhere, Morrison is pivotal, not only in terms of race, but of unsectored entertainment. This is, after all, the singer whose signature numbers were 'Granada', 'How Great Thou Art' and 'Po Karekare Ana'. While surrounded by younger rockers, he anchors the whole in general appeal. Notably the lyrics of his two big performance numbers, 'Livin' and Lovin'' and 'Don't Let It Get You', bridge the gap between teenaged and married romance ('Live for today, there is no other way, / You can't get love on credit / ... It only lasts for a day, / For a day, for a day', but also 'Hand in hand, in love without a care / ... Happiness for ever and nothing less'). Because of his domestically settled role within the film, these lyrics double as benedictions both to fleeting teenage passions and to 'happiness for ever', while Morrison, rather than the nominal hero and heroine, also resolves the further antitheses of mainstream pop and rock, Māori and Pākehā, rural and urban, sincerity and show.

The only places where the idyll is threatened are two moments which might briefly suggest a subversive racial subtext not visible elsewhere. In the first, Morrison drives into a Caltex service station and is greeted by a Pākehā attendant. Morrison's response, without varying his usual friendly, laidback manner, is to reply with a burst of Māori, so that most listeners, like the attendant, have no idea what he is saying, except for the one word 'Boron' (a well-known brand of motor oil). It is this word, taken up by the attendant, when he says that 'Boron' is the same in any language, that benignly comedicizes the moment, making Morrison's gesture, rather than the aggressive difference it might signify, a pleasant joke asserting racial harmony (we're all consumers, all drivers, all New Zealanders), and deflecting other possible divisive meanings (such as, despite a superficial similarity as consumers, we're very different, speakers of literally different languages, as I'm demonstrating now, since you don't understand a word that I'm saying, with the one exception). Similarly initiated and simultaneously defused is a second moment where Normie Rowe tries to ingratiate himself with Morrison's infant son, only for the child to reject him. Seeing this, Morrison goes through an ostentatious charade of friendliness with Rowe, shaking first the child's hand, then the singer's, trying to convince the infant to accept Rowe's handshake. But the child again refuses and starts to cry. Brown child rejects white adult handshake in spite of mainstream father's integratory blandishments? A sign of things to come? The failure of cross-cultural middlebrow taste, 'Ordinary Brown Entertainment', as Billy T. James joked about Morrison's OBE? But while the possibility is raised, to pursue it you would have to read obsessively against the grain of the scene's more amenable meanings: comedy based on the child's wilfulness, the adults' inability to deal with it, with everyone so relaxed that racial subversions are far from their minds, dissolving such implications away.

After the problematics of prejudice in *Broken Barrier* and the hero's self-destructiveness in *Runaway*, *Don't Let It Get You* relaxes in the utopian atmospheres of the musical, substituting for the earlier films' more riven macrocosms the idyllic microcosm of New Zealand entertainment mid-1960s style, in which – at least so it seems in the film – no social or economic barriers exist between Māori and European. Here Howard Morrison as Māori is the admired paradigm, singing star, ideal husband, father, and entrepreneur, and Kiri Te Kanawa can join whakapapas (genealogies) with Rossini as she sings 'Una Voce Poco Fa' in the meeting house. Of course in many respects this is a dream. However, it has some footings in reality: Kiri Te Kanawa did go on to become an international diva, and though the film hides the fact that 1960s local pop music was controlled by Pākehā entrepreneurs, still, as O'Shea reports, Morrison was a business partner in the film.[27] If, as might be felt with the presence of Afro-American performers in earlier Hollywood musicals, the implied interracial optimism enacted is deceptive, the situation of cameo performers like Lena Horne and the Nicholas Brothers being excluded from the narratives is not the position here, since Howard Morrison is actually the narrative's centre, emphasizing the difference (for all the local hypocrisies about racial matters) between the New Zealand and American racial situations. And if we still feel that the film's optimism is, in realist terms, extreme, we should remember that the musical is a genre defined by its utopic thrust, governed by definitions of the ideal in art which go back as far as Aristotle.

Influence

Reviewing Bieringa and Dennis's *Film in Aotearoa / New Zealand*, Lawrence McDonald wrote to the effect that the collection's desire to aureole New Zealand cinema with the light of two New Zealand modernists, Len Lye and Colin McCahon, neglected both the popular New Zealand cinema and the figure, John O'Shea, who was most crucial to 'the shape and course of film making within this country since the Second World War'.[28] McDonald argued 'that it is possible to construct' from O'Shea's three feature films, 'three loose lineage models' within which large numbers of later films can be grouped. Thus *Broken Barrier* 'inaugurates a lineage of post-war films that deal with the question of race relations' and which cross over different historical definitions of the problematic and its attempted solutions (integration, biculturalism, separatism); *Runaway* a lineage of 'quest for Pākehā-identity-film[s]' redefined by the writer as the 'quest-for-Pākehā male identity', which he sees crossing over from the earlier combination of Pākehā high art thematics with European art cinema into the popular counter-cultural influences of the new American cinema of the 1970s; and the musical *Don't Let It Get You* a more diffuse lineage of works using popular genres. If we accept the third category as very amorphous, though McDonald seems to be arguing a tighter category than all popular culture genre films, citing a 'line of not particularly well-known films' (unidentified) that 'inhabit / customize film genres in quite idiosyncratic ways', and that there may be a tendency to locate the quest-for-identity film too universally, the analysis holds and asserts O'Shea's film-making as crucial for the later period as well as his own.

Notes

1. John O'Shea, *Don't Let It Get You, Memories-Documents*, Victoria University Press, Wellington, 1999, 37.
2. O'Shea, *Don't Let It Get You*, 37.
3. Brian McDonnell, 'John O'Shea, the Father of New Zealand Film', *North and South*, October 1989, 86.
4. O'Shea, *Don't Let It Get You*, 42.
5. *Monthly Film Bulletin*, 19 (222), July 1952, 89.
6. Laurence Simmons, '*Broken Barrier*: Mimesis and Mimicry', *Landfall*, 185, 1993, 131.
7. O'Shea, *Don't Let It Get You*, 65.
8. O'Shea, *Don't Let It Get You*, 25.
9. *Speeches and Documents in New Zealand History*, ed. W. David McIntyre and W.J. Gardner, Clarendon Press, Oxford, 1971, 438–41.
10. King, *The Penguin History of New Zealand*, 480–1.
11. O'Shea, *Don't Let It Get You*, 38.
12. Reprinted in 'La Faccia di un neozelandese / The Face of a New Zealander', *Te Ao Marama: Il Mondo della Luce Cinema della Nuova Zelanda*, a cura di: Jonathan Dennis e Sergio Toffetti, Torino, 1989, 79–82.
13. Belich, *Paradise Reforged*, 204–5
14. King, *The Penguin History of New Zealand*, 336–7, 341–2, 467–71, and Belich, *Paradise Reforged*, 202–3.
15. M.P.K. Sorrenson, ed., *Na To Hoa Aroha: From Your Dear Friend: The*

Correspondence between Sir Apirana Ngata and Sir Peter Buck, 1925–50, 1986–87, vol. 2, 17.
16 King, *The Penguin History of New Zealand*, 471.
17 Laura Mulvey, 'Notes on Sirk and Melodrama', *Movie*, 25, 1977–78, 53–6.
18 John Reynolds, *Going Far?: John O'Shea's Runaway in the Context of His Attempt to Establish a Feature Film Industry in New Zealand* (PhD thesis, Auckland University, 2 vols, 2002), 1, 265.
19 Seymour Chatman, *Antonioni: or The Surface of the World*, University of California Press, Berkeley, 1985, 88–9.
20 Reynolds, I, 216, 302, 304.
21 Reynolds, I, 308–9.
22 Bill Gosden, Programme Note, 31st Wellington Film Festival.
23 *Monthly Film Bulletin*, 32 (377), June 1963, 94–5.
24 *Kinematograph Weekly*, 29 April 1965, 17.
25 O'Shea, *Don't Let It Get You*, 7.
26 Laurence Simmons, 'Don't Let it Get You: Livin' and Lovin' in New Zealand's First Film Musical', *Music in New Zealand*, 26, 1994, 24–7.
27 O'Shea, *Don't Let It Get You*, 70.
28 Lawrence McDonald, 'A Book Review of *Film in Aotearoa New Zealand* That Ended Up as an Essay on Film in Aotearoa New Zealand', *Illusions*, 21/22, 1993, 59–60.

5
Living white males: New Zealand cinema 1975–1985

The new industry: mapping the field

Strict divisions are almost always arbitrary, and the line between a period of initiation, centred around the institution of the New Zealand Film Commission but reaching back to Geoff Steven's *Test Pictures* (1973–1975), and a later era of development could be drawn in slightly different ways. For reasons set out below, 1985 is here chosen as the transitional date.

Murphy and Donaldson: 'the end of the beginning'

The year 1985 marked Geoff Murphy's last important film, *The Quiet Earth*. Roger Donaldson was Hollywood-bound by 1983, with Murphy following in 1988, drawing a line under the pair's direct input to the early industry. Murphy's and Donaldson's early films have a permanent canonical place not just for their temporal firstness, but for their mastery of popular cinematic form and complex thematic doubleness, inheriting the concerns of the previous era, but influenced by newer ones. Such doubleness, centred around representations of masculinity, though not to the exclusion of other concerns, also dominated many other films of this early period.

The feminization of New Zealand film

By 1985 the beginnings of a perceptible feminization of New Zealand film are observable, not only in subject matter and emphases, but in directing personnel, with Melanie Read's and Gaylene Preston's first features, *Trial Run* (1984) and *Mr Wrong* (1985). Even at its masculinist height, though, the cinema of the early industry was often highly sensitive to cultural changes.[1] These are, however, not only visible in the adventures and abjections of male protagonists, but in male directors working on female-oriented material of three kinds: (i) female biopics such as *Sylvia* (Michael Firth, 1985, about the novelist and educationist Sylvia Ashton-Warner), *Iris* (Tony Isaac, 1984, about the writer Robin Hyde [Iris Wilkinson][2]) and *Leave All Fair*, with its displaced refined quasi-biopic elements (John Reid, 1985, about Katherine Mansfield); (ii) films built around female protagonists such as the 'woman's picture' interracial romance *Other Halves* (John Laing, 1984), *Constance* (Bruce Morrison, 1984), *It's Lizzie to Those Close* (a.k.a. *A Woman of Good Character*, David Blyth, 1983), centred on a female pioneer immigrant, and *Vigil* (Vincent Ward, 1984), organized around a young girl's subjectivity; and (iii) more extensively, films with growingly less stereotyped portrayal of women than previously: *Solo* (Tony Williams, 1977) may be taken as a paradigm of this.

Establishment of industrial, generic, thematic and stylistic patterns

By 1985 the major generic, thematic and stylistic patterns of later film production had been established, or in some measure, prefigured, as discussed under the various headings that follow here.

End of the tax breaks, stabilization of production, off-shore elements, the low budget New Zealand film

By 1985 the short uncharacteristic boom period of tax loophole production with private-sector money was over, with production stabilized into (i) state subsidization (ii) a mixture of state funding and private-sector monies – either 'on-shore' or 'off-shore', including a few international co-productions, and (iii) exceptional films made wholly with private-sector investment. From 1973 to 1985 some 48 (figures will very slightly vary according to definitions of 'New Zealand' and 'feature') features were made, 46 of them between 1977 and 1985. Though there were fears that the tax break boom and bust would destroy the industry, it survived. At first attracted by the tax loopholes, but later by more permanent conditions of scenic variety and cheap technical skills and resources, 'off-shore' production – typical of New Zealand film's early days – became an established factor again (for example, *Dead Kids* [US, 1983]).

The low-budget patterns of the industry were established early. Leaving aside as exceptional the miniscule costs of *Angel Mine* (NZ$29,000) and *Test Pictures* (NZ$14,000), well under half the period's films cost less than NZ$1 million, and, indeed, over half of those under NZ$500,000 (at the lower end, *Squeeze* NZ$100,000 and *Middle Age Spread* NZ$120,000). The eleven films with budgets of over NZ$1 million ranged from NZ$1.2 (*Smash Palace*, *Heart of the Stag*) to

NZ$2.2 (*Came a Hot Friday*, *Wild Horses*, *Should I Be Good?*), with only three higher, *Utu* at NZ$3 million, while *Mesmerized*, NZ$5.6 million, and *Race for the Yankee Zephyr*, NZ$6 million, were films with overseas actors aimed outside the home market.[3]

The selling of New Zealand films

By 1985 most of the strategies, not only of New Zealand film production but of its literal and metaphorical selling, were established; in particular, the focus on foreign film festivals, with the returns of many New Zealand films depending on overseas distribution deals for theatrical and television showings and, increasingly, video release. Success overseas was also a home box-office stimulus. Particular landmarks were *Vigil*'s being the first New Zealand film chosen for official competition at Cannes, 1984, and *An Angel at My Table*'s Special Jury Prize at the Venice Film Festival, 1990. With the critical success of *Smash Palace*, *Utu*, *The Quiet Earth* and *Vigil*, 'New Zealand Cinema' became a known category, with seasons on television (BBC2 in the UK and ZDF in Germany in 1984) and at the National Film Theatre, London, in 1981, the Cinémathèque Française in 1983, and Washington in 1985. In this context New Zealand films became the subject of sophisticated international discourse in newspapers and journals, with Murphy and Donaldson much praised by the *New Yorker*'s film critic Pauline Kael, and *Vigil* written about in the UK, USA and Europe.

Directors and producers

(i) Directors

The early directors with 'alternative' affiliations (Steven and Maunder) eventually abandoned fiction feature making, illustrating the new industry's predictable retreat from experimental beginnings. Symptomatically David Blyth soon followed the surrealist influences of *Angel Mine* (1978) by moving into Horror films. A number of major directors went overseas: Donaldson and Murphy to the USA, and Tony Williams to Australia. The period also saw the beginnings of long-term journeyman careers by Sam Pillsbury, John Laing and Ian Mune, important, if not for many films of great achievement, as staple figures of a persevering industry, with occasional high points – Mune, for instance, with *Came A Hot Friday* and *The End of the Golden Weather*. Melanie Read importantly led the female incursion into feature film making, followed by Gaylene Preston at a higher level of achievement. Of other early male directors who stayed, John Reid directed an impressive small body of films, and Bruce Morrison made two, including the also impressive *Constance*. However, Vincent Ward, staying until 1988, stood apart, the first New Zealand film-maker to be recognized in art-house Europe.

(ii) Producers

In the absence of studios, producers have played a vital role. A number of major facilitators began in this period: John O'Shea moving from director to producer, John Maynard, particularly important (later with Bridget Ikin) in enabling auteurist and art cinema, Don Reynolds, Robin Laing beginning a long partnership with Gaylene Preston, and John Barnett and Larry Parr both associated with a wide range of films.

Actors and stars: 'Our Mary Pickfords, our Douglas Fairbanks, our Ramon Novarros'

Most visible to the public are, of course, actors. This early period, though it saw losses overseas, most obviously Sam Neill, marked the emergence of many film actors as cinematic acting became, if not in itself a sustaining local career, a contribution to a career in acting across the media, sometimes in combination with writing and/or directing, with work in the bigger nearby Australian television and film industries also possible. Lacking stars from the beginnings, New Zealand cinema is rich in character actors like Grant Tilly, Dorothy McKegg, John Bach, Marshall Napier, Judy McIntosh, Derek Hardwick and Wi Kuki Kā, all in films of this early period. The lack of local stars led film-makers to import overseas actors, hoping both to increase overseas sales, and attract local audiences, a strategy going back to *Runaway*, with, for instance, John Carradine in *The Scarecrow*, David Hemmings in *Beyond Reasonable Doubt*, and Cliff Robertson in *Shaker Run*, as well as many Australians who, like New Zealanders in Australia, have an easy entry into the sibling industry through similar speech and socio-kinetic patterns and broad cultural similarities.

Several factors militate against stardom in New Zealand cinema: the smallness of the population and production base, its films' limited overseas distribution, domestic actors' slight earning power, meaning an ordinariness of lifestyle unconducive to the institution of stardom, and a downbeat scepticism in the national psyche about the 'up yourself', 'skiting' aspects of self-projected iconicity. The 1950s fantasy of Juliet and Pauline in *Heavenly Creatures* is to go to Hollywood, not to be in John O'Shea's next film!

In pre-historic times (in New Zealand film terms): expatriates had achieved considerable film success: Winter Hall and Rupert Julian were major Hollywood silent actors, with Julian directing *The Phantom of the Opera* (1925), before *The Lord of the Rings* the best-known film directed by a New Zealander, though neither of these Hollywood practitioners was known as such. Nola Luxford had minor parts in nineteen Hollywood films (1920–1935)[4] before, like Bathie Stuart, making a career in broadcasting and publicity. In the 1930s, Ra Hould (Ronald Sinclair) became a minor Hollywood child star, still visible on nostalgia internet sites. These actors' careers predated any possibilities of full-time acting in New Zealand. Closer to the New Zealand scene were Vera James, 'a daughter of Dunedin', briefly famous as the lead in the Australian classic *A Girl of the Bush* (1921); Bathie Stuart, Kiwi McGill in *The Adventures of Algy*; and Dale Austen. An advertisement for *Algy* suggests that New Zealand was not immune to dreams of local stardom: 'You remember the excitement and hopes of Mr [Beaumont] Smith's screen tests … Our Mary Pickfords, our Douglas Fairbanks, our Ramon Novarros. Could New Zealand produce a man or woman star to take a high place in the world's ranks for screen talent?'[5] Dale Austen was briefly the most celebrated, the nearest to local stardom. A 'Miss New Zealand', she had small parts at MGM, before returning and starring in Hayward's *The Bush Cinderella*. 'The Sweetest Star in southern Skies',[6] with an egalitarian inflection 'Chosen by the People',[7] was the centre of the film's advertising campaign, with other advertisements claiming over 20,000 viewers in one week for the film 'Starring Dale Austen who combines Hollywood expertise and Technique with a Flawless Photographic Face'.[8] However, the cinematic moments of all three were short-lived: despite Hayward's attempts, there was no production base for local careers.[9]

Bruno Lawrence and Sam Neill

Writing about Bruno Lawrence, Andrew Spicer reworked the term 'actor-icon' from an obscure article about Hollywood stars to describe major actors in small national cinemas such as New Zealand's.[10] It was clearly the attached words 'an amalgamation of cultural impulses' that motivated Spicer's reinvention of this terminology,[11] to characterize actors who, with their limited circulation, cannot be called stars, yet are of great cultural significance nationally. New Zealand cinema is, then, a cinema without stars, of iconic actors whose effectiveness depends largely on their ability to literally embody the very local complexities of the culture as it is lived.

I will return for a moment to Lawrence, the pre-eminent screen actor of this early period, and briefly compare him with its other major figure. Sam Neill's middle-classness and more malleable command of different accents and styles allowed him access to international films, while Lawrence's more pronounced (literally so in his 'broad' rather than refined accent) demotic New Zealandness, meant a more restricted Australasian career, though one eliciting more intense home audience reactions. This was partly the result of Neill's lesser commitment to home films (only three in nearly thirty years), but also, importantly, the result of Lawrence's earthier, working man's persona. More will be said in passing about Lawrence below. Neill, the subject of much journalism but little analysis, is intensely interesting in his representations of other sides of New Zealand maleness than Lawrence's. On the one hand, he is the contemporary development of idealizations of the male New Zealander, such as found in David Bruce, with his combination of physicality and intellectuality, in Jane Mander's *The Story of a New Zealand River*, or the quietly self-possessed New Zealand soldiers John Mulgan so admiringly recorded in *Report from Experience*. Yet he is often hiddenly stress fractured, doubtful, with a nervous edge to his handsomeness, a frayed undertone to his charm, both the good patriarch (avuncular in *The Dish* [Australia, 2000]) and the intensely flawed one (Alisdair Stewart in *The Piano*).

A brief meditation on landscape in the New Zealand cinema
Between 1973 and 1985, the early identification of New Zealand cinema with landscape is repeatedly reestablished; whether in the Milford or Marlborough Sounds of *Rangi's Catch* and *The Lost Tribe*, the Hawke's Bay of *Utu*, the western-like North Island central plateau in *Wild Horses*, or the Coromandel bush of *Sleeping Dogs*, to give only a few examples. Many of these locations, like *The Lord of the Rings*', are hardly the habitat of many New Zealanders (they are spectacular holiday sites to them as much as to tourists); yet they recur cinematically, articulating a bond between landscape and population, asserting meanings beyond the merely decorative 'calendar' views of 'Monsieur Cedric', who transforms photos into gaudy oil paintings for his clientele in *Pictures* (Michael Black, 1981). A sense of the pressures of landscape in the New Zealand experience can be gained in Janet Frame's novel, *A State of Siege* – the source of one of Vincent Ward's early films – with its intense rendering of changes in the protagonist's psyche when she moves from the south to the near subtropical north.[12]

One instance of landscape taking on extensive meanings despite being few people's habitat is Central Otago, recently important in *In*

My Father's Den (Brad McGann, 2004) and *Fifty Ways of Saying Fabulous* (Stewart Main, 2005). In *Den* and the earlier *Heart of the Stag* (Michael Firth, 1984, set in the King Country, though the hero remembers his 'Central' upbringing), the same iconic poem is quoted: James K. Baxter's 'High Country Weather' ('... Upon the upland road / Ride easy, stranger, / Surrender to the sky your heart of anger'), carrying formidable psychic resonances – solitude, pioneering origins, and the man (or woman) alone drifting among the elements, part of a Pākehā 'geomentality' or 'psychogeography' still highly significant. Such bondings take on different significances at different historical points, though these 'geomentalities'[13] are often palimpsested complicatedly one on another: for example (i) Visions of exoticism in the earliest cinema, in particular the mudpools and geysers of Rotorua. (ii) The 'New Zealand Sublime', mountain spectacle, as recapitulated in those opening aerial perspective shots of the Southern Alps in *The Two Towers*. (iii) Vistas reminiscing pioneer ruggedness, acted out in period films like *Utu* and *Pictures*, where in similar scenes terrifyingly flimsy rope ladders are the only way up impossibly precipitous cliff faces, or in contemporary films, imprinted by past action on the landscape, as in *Pork Pie*'s shots of the train traversing the spindliest viaducts over enormous gorges. (iv) More accommodating landscapes suggesting a secular settler covenant glimpsed in Hayward's historical films especially: not so much in overtly ideological moments like Ropata's and Morgan's viewing of Waikato pastureland in *Rewi 2*, as in unofficial moments of men at ease in largely unspoiled environments. (v) Minatory landscapes suggesting hostility to settlers unhabituated to a new environment, that thematic so stressed by the 1930s–1950s nationalist school of poetry, like the gaunt wind-blasted valley in *Vigil*, or the opening of *Utu* with its army fort looking vulnerable in a misty, unreceptive terrain. (vi) A depressing variant found in the self-inflicted scarring of unidyllic slash and burn landscapes like the surrounds of Stewart's house in *The Piano* and the unfinished, careless rawness of small towns in *Wild Man, Skin Deep, Beyond Reasonable Doubt, Bad Blood* and *Smash Palace*. (vii) The Māori 'geomentality' of the tangata whenua (people of the land), which fascinated both early film-makers like Markey with his Aotearoa full of haunted burial caves, and settler culture with its lack of ancestral bodies in the earth. This increases in films of the mid-1980s and then constitutes an important part of Māori films in the late 1980s (think, for instance, of Kura showing Awatea the hill on which her grandmother lived in *Mauri*). (vii) An ecological undertext, evident in the typical landscape orientation of some later films, that elides contemporary

Pākehā and traditional Māori attitudes to the land.

Erena Le Heron has listed New Zealand cinema's primary generic landscape sites as (i) pasture and countryside; (ii) 'The bush'; (iii) rivers, mountains and beaches; (iv) cities (with the suburbs a subcategory); and (v) travel between spaces.[14] Though her small film sample lacks historical depth, she does identify the main sites, as well as the obvious scenic rationale of New Zealand films' not uncommon 'road movie' structure. While the significances of 'the bush' and mountains, both within settler and traditional Māori ideologies, is obvious enough, a named but neglected site is the beach, which takes multiple significances from the facts (a) that for New Zealanders living more than a short distance from the sea is rare; (b) that the sea shore inevitably suggests New Zealand's isolation, from before the first Polynesian immigrations to the present of incoming and outgoing journeys; (c) that it has strong associations with the relaxed outdoor life that is an ideal for most New Zealanders; and (d) that it has as important a place in Māori as in Pākehā life, as witness the Kai Moana (seafood) gathering beginning *Broken Barrier*, the constant seascapes in *Ngati*, *Mauri* and *Te Rua*, as well as recent controversy over ownership of the foreshore, as symbolically loaded a place as any in both Pākehā and Māori perceptions. Landscape's importance in New Zealand cinema is evidenced by the way that even very urban films introduce landscapes and beachscapes. This is not just brand-marking in a cinema partly sold on scenery, but a deeply internalized identification. For instance, Maxwell's *When Love Comes* (1998) ends by bringing all its highly urban characters to a Northland beach; it is a literal homecoming for the singer Katie Kepa (Rena Owen), but that sense spreads metaphorically to the others. Narbey's *The Footstep Man* (1992) is largely set in an urban postproduction studio, but even the hero's suicide attempt takes place at the beach, the film's second sequence has him driving along it and then through bush landscapes to the city, and later there is another beach sequence where Sam and Vida go to record wave sounds. Even the film-within-the-film – 'Monsieur Henri', being a New Zealand production, although set in Paris – includes a scene where Toulouse-Lautrec and friends picnic on a beach. Equally, John Reid's *The Last Tattoo* (1994), which cultivates many aspects of urban Film Noir, finds ways of staging important sequences in two beachside situations.

Le Heron, however, marginalizes urban and, even more, suburban 'psycho-geography'. The labelling of Australia as perhaps 'the first suburban nation'[15] is almost equally true of New Zealand with its similarly high rate of suburbanization. In a few early contemporary films

– for example *Middle Age Spread* (John Reid, 1979) and *Angel Mine* (1978) with its Masport motor mower operating and DB-beer-drinking Bergmanian Death – the suburbs are satirically observed, but this is exceptional. Even when, as in *Constance*, much of the film's subject matter is complacent suburban restrictiveness, the suburbs are seldom seen, however ironizing the social context, as other than the good place of a life more spacious than old world cities allow, with their easy access to country and beach an invitation to an outdoors lifestyle situated between urban and rural, keeping links both with the pioneering past and with the more extreme natural phenomena celebrated in the cinema. Though Preston's *Ruby and Rata* (1991) has its quota of critique, its opening shots of the typical green Auckland suburb of Mount Albert embody that casual sense of promise (however compromised) the suburbs often suggest in the background of New Zealand films.

In many later films, Auckland and to a lesser degree Wellington (to an overseas eye looking, with their harbour settings, still very nature dominated as metropolises) are implicitly celebrated. It may be a villain in *Zilch!* (Richard Riddiford, 1989) who explicitly declares Auckland to be a great Pacific city, but the metro-aesthetics of the evening traffic streaming off the harbour bridge in shots binding metropolis, engineering and natural vistas, suggest that this is true, as do views of the city back from the harbour (with Wellington, too), and shots of the Auckland skyline dominated by the casino tower in later films. There are, of course, opposing treatments of the city, most famously the juxtaposition of the clichéd touristic New Zealand landscape poster with the South Auckland sprawl at the beginning of *Once Were Warriors* (Lee Tamahori, 1994), as well as the nocturnal noir worlds of the horror and crime genres, and films like *Stickmen* (Hamish Rothwell, 2000) and *I'll Make You Happy* (Athena Tsoulis, 2000) with its Karangahape Road sex world, which tend to cut out daylight views, though the latter has a scene near the end where Siggy and her father scatter her mother's ashes over an idyllic vista looking across the North Shore to the city, again demonstrating the presence of landscape even in the most urban films.

Predominant genres

Contemporary New Zealand film, like other postclassical cinemas, exhibits loosenings of generic structures, resulting in the mixing of genres, subgenres and overarching modes. However, the extent of this may be exaggerated by twin tendencies to overstress (a) the stability of classical film genres, and (b) the comparative generic diffuseness of contemporary cinema, and contemporary New Zealand cinema in particular. There is no doubt that cross-generic categories often ask to be invoked – as, say, for *Goodbye Pork Pie*'s comedy-adventure, crossed by the elastic road and buddy (or mateship) subgenres, and a local inflection of the amorphous international modern quest narrative, in the 'Pākehā pilgrimage' or 'quest for Pākehā identity' film.[16] However, whatever differentiating formulations are made, they tend to modify and/or combine clearly visible generic or modal categories, as listed here:

The action-adventure/action-thriller, a staple of most commercial cinemas, is frequent early on, with exploitation of the landscape an important element: For example, *The Race for The Yankee Zephyr* (David Hemmings, 1981), *Battletruck* (Harley Cokliss, 1982), *Wild Horses* (Derek Morton, 1984), *Shaker Run* (Bruce Morrison, 1985), and in historical costume in the big tax-loophole-budgeted *Savage Islands* (Felix Fairfax, 1982). **Horror**, later to become a niche genre for New Zealand film-makers, first appears with David Blyth's derivative *Death Warmed Up* (1984), and cross-generically in *The Scarecrow* (Sam Pillsbury, 1982), *Mr Wrong* and *Trial Run*. **Crime** – primarily represented by *Beyond Reasonable Doubt* (John Laing, 1980), *Bad Blood* (Mike Newell, 1981) and *The Lost Tribe* (Laing, 1985) – exhibits a number of tendencies: factually based social critique with *Beyond Reasonable Doubt*; documentary impulses in *Beyond Reasonable Doubt* and the 'Mr Asia' material of *Should I Be Good?* (Grahame J. McLean, 1985); and emphases on a metropolitan milieu mostly new to the local cinema in *Should I Be Good?* and *Restless* (Denis Lewiston, 1985), and on psychodrama in *The Lost Tribe* and *Trespasses* (Peter Sharp, 1984). **The biopic** appears early on, with *Sylvia, Iris, Pictures* and, tangentially, *Leave All Fair* (John Reid, 1985), with their counter-masculine bias towards the female artist. In the New Zealand context, because of an apparent unwillingness to dramatize groups in conflict with society, the traditional 'Social Problem Film' with its attack on institutions and aim of arousing indignation, tends to take the form of films dramatizing unarticulated social strata, the **social revelation film**, with implicit arguments for comprehension rather than ignorance, exemplified in *Sons for the Return Home* (Paul Maunder, 1979, Samoans in New Zealand), *Squeeze* (Richard Turner, 1980, homosexual lifestyles) and *Kingpin* (Mike Walker, 1985, remand school drama with racial focus). **Melodrama**, increasingly important in the 1990s, has a male inflection in *Smash Palace* (Roger Donaldson, 1981), and female ones in *Constance* (Bruce Morrison, 1984) and *Other Halves* (John Laing,

1984), a **woman's film** narrative of a thirty-something woman's relationship with a Polynesian street boy half her age. Among more marginal tendencies, only one **science fiction** film appeared, though a major work – Murphy's *The Quiet Earth* (1985) – while the **children's film** had a minor presence in the early *Rangi's Catch* (Michael Forlong, 1971) and *The Silent One* (Yvonne McKay, 1984). The relative infrequency of the historical costume film, so popular in 'new wave' Australian cinema, is notable, making *Pictures* and *Utu* exceptional, despite the former's proximity to, and the latter's central placement in, the most characteristic and intrinsically native of all New Zealand genres, the **New Zealand Wars film**. *Utu* has no successor until Ward's *River Queen* (2006), though, as argued in chapter 6, other inhibiting factors than cost in a cash-straitened cinema, connected with arguments over the representation of Māori, played a part. The only other pioneer period films were the low-budget, small-cast productions *Wild Man* (Geoff Murphy, 1979) and *It's Lizzie to Those Close* (David Blyth, 1983). Another non-economic reason for the rarity of period films may have been to avoid unfavourable comparison with the 'AFC' historical films so successful in the contemporary Australian cinema. While a selection of eleven significant films of the period are foregrounded later in this chapter, two genres or modes, the most significant not emphasized above, Comedy and the Art film, are discussed immediately below.

Early comedy

Wild Man, Geoff Murphy, 1977; *Skin Deep,* Geoff Steven, 1978; *Middle Age Spread,* John Reid, 1979; *Carry Me Back,* John Reid, 1982; *Came a Hot Friday,* Ian Mune, 1984; *Second Time Lucky,* Michael Anderson, 1984; *Pallet on the Floor,* Lynton Butler, 1986.

The comic mode in New Zealand film inherits traditions of local humorous writing, examples of which, going back to the mid-nineteenth century, are collected in J.C. Reid's anthology *The Kiwi Laughs*.[17] Definitions of the basic historical features of Australian comedy[18] turn out, unsurprisingly, to be largely applicable to New Zealand: a picture emerges of a frontier society's somewhat roughhouse humour, reflecting the values of a predominantly male society, often without much female leavening in its earliest periods, irreverent, anti-authoritarian, targeting pomposity and privilege, egalitarian and crude – the comedy of a 'crew culture', to use James Belich's term for the semi-nomadic workers living in the mainly male groups of colonial expansionist days.[19]

Reid's anthology emphasized these deep-rooted topoi: (i) comedy expressing dislike of old world servitude, and satirizing social pretensions; (ii) comedy of New Zealand's both inferior and superior self-image as regards the larger cultures Britain, America and Australia; (iii) comedy of male experience, often sexual, and anti-romantic; (iv) the crew-culture tradition of the tall tale; (v) tales of conmen tormenting authorities, as in John A Lee's 'Shiner Slattery' stories, one of which Roger Donaldson filmed early in his career; (vi) comedy deriving from laconic, hard-bitten, male narration; and lastly, very much in the old mainstream, (vii) comedy of race, inevitably Pākehā observing Māori. To these Reid added instances of (viii) modern female, and (ix) urbane metropolitan wit. Later publication should have included (x) some of Frank Sargeson's anti-puritan comedy, and would have faced (xi) traditions of comic obscenity, derived from the demotic oral, much evident in recent New Zealand film.

These are the local comic traditions inherited by contemporary New Zealand cinema, many still influential, though the new industry took off as some had become outmoded, particularly satire of social climbing, since society is now viewed (perhaps complacently) as too egalitarian for that to flourish and satire of the pseudo-aristocratic has given way to satire of bourgeois lifestyles (as in *Middle Age Spread*). Comedy of New Zealand/British relations has declined as distance grows from origins, though satire of 'poms' is still a shorthand way of reinforcing New Zealand identity. The most important casualty of progress has been racially based humour at its crudest, with stereotypes like the 'dumb Māori' now unacceptable. The newly sensitive area of bicultural comedy threatened to be so constrained by political correctness as to become oppressive, but the great Māori comedian Billy T. James – able to reverse the Pākehā gaze as well as rework, from inside, older-style Māori based comedy – loosened up this area with his knowing manipulation of older stereotypes, underlining that how something is said may be as crucial as what is said, and that comedy's role is to expose and negotiate rather than wholly deny.

The new industry's first comedies were made: *Wild Man* (Geoff Murphy, 1977), the extended sketch spin-off of the Blerta TV show, centred like *Came a Hot Friday* (Ian Mune, 1985) on the adventures of confidence men; Geoff Steven's one mainstream film, the small-town satire *Skin Deep* (1978); John Reid's *Middle Age Spread* (1979); Reid's *Carry Me Back* (1982); and the first two of three films based on Ronald Hugh Morrieson's comic-grotesque small-town novels, *The Scarecrow* (1982), and *Came A Hot Friday* (1984). Apart from *Middle Age Spread*, these films cultivated traditional local humour's laconic, rural and masculinist modes, though with a complex mixture of fond nostalgia and critical forward-looking sensibilities that parallels Murphy's and Donaldson's films. They tend to be set in the past and in small towns: the Klynham of *The Scarecrow*, the Tainuia of *Hot Friday*, the Marlborough farm in *Carry Me Back*, the Carlton of *Skin Deep*, thus allowing for the recreation of a half-caressed, half-satirized past (*Hot Friday*, *The Scarecrow*) or a present clinging to the past (*Carry Me Back*, *Skin Deep*). Like Murphy's and Donaldson's films, they also take much of their interest and complexity from their implicit dramatizing of times in change and modes of masculinity in decline. *Middle Age Spread*, contemporary and urban, is the exception to the rural bias, its not too disruptive satire of the professional middle classes looking forward to the more urban subjects of the middle 1980s on. While most of these films' comedy is laconic, that of *Middle Age Spread* (based on Roger Hall's play) is hugely talkative, its targets education, politics, the New Zealander abroad or dreaming of abroad, and suburban snobberies (fondu parties, personally labelled wine bottles), social climbing, and cultural malaise.

Three films – *Carry Me Back*, *Came a Hot Friday* and *Skin Deep*, the first two minor comic masterpieces – are bound together in their cultivation of 'Old Comedy'. The voiceover of *Came a Hot Friday* gives its setting as 1949, but the others' contemporary settings present a world psychically tied to a past 'when men were men and sheilas were their mothers' as *Carry Me Back*'s epigraph jokes. The males of the 'Carlton Progressive Association' in *Skin Deep*, though, see themselves as inhabitants of an altering world, with their project to raise NZ$20,000 for modernizing the town to be eventually handed over to an advertising company to persuade city businesses to move there. This project is linked to the hiring of Sandra Ray (Deryn Cooper), an Auckland masseuse, to update the town's gym by offering massages, the two plots linked by the large penile shape dominating the town's main street, on which the growing sum collected is marked. (As a sign of double-edged masculinist thematics it is only challenged by the moment in *Pork Pie*, in the rock'n'roll montage on board the train, where Gerry swings Shirl off her feet and they end up posed with his face fronting her pudenda, a kind of Judith and Holofernes reversed). But 'progressive' is ironic, since despite the rebarbative Sandra's reluctance to move into the 'extras or sextras or whatever' one of the characters asks about, her presence causes problems – a policeman puritanically interrupts a handjob ('you must be desperate' has been Sandra's hardly encouraging comment), the men generally regress to prurient childishness, and Phil (Grant Tilly) falls mooncalfishly in love with her, begging her to accompany him in his flight from his puritanical wife. However, even a film as satirically oriented as *Skin Deep* is not wholly describable in such terms: if some of its 'Old' New Zealand aspects are satirically treated, others are nostalgically invoked: indoor rugby training, the scrum machine, the local fete's wood chopping contest, even Phil's shrewish wife's lament for past certainties having their point when compared with the implied vision of even worse things in store for the town if the advertising campaign takes off.

In *Carry Me Back*, two brothers, Arthur (Grant Tilly), the older, and Jimmy (Kelly Johnson) live on the family's remote Marlborough farm, tyrannized by their father, 'TK' (Derek Hardwick), who puts them down by calling them 'sheilas' (girls). When they visit Wellington for a Ranfurly Shield challenge, the patriarch dies, leaving a will gifting the farm to the Rugby Union unless he is buried on his estate, a situation forcing the sons into various adventures as they illicitly smuggle the corpse homewards to avoid losing the farm. Again, like the Murphy and Donaldson films, *Carry Me Back* is suspended between old and new. The males' naïveté is exposed in Wellington as they encounter both a stripper dressed in All Black rugby gear gyrating to a souped-up version of 'God Defend New Zealand' and an uninviting masseuse reminiscent of Sandra in *Skin Deep*. Then the 'man alone' mythos is parodied in the curious subplot involving the jail breaker 'Old Mac' (based on George Wilder), who is revealed, in contradiction to his folk-hero reputation, as a puny oldster, wearily begging the police to reincarcerate him. Throughout the journey the father's corpse undergoes various posthumous humiliations, punishments for his regressive patriarchalism, the corpse of 'the bastard', 'the old bugger', finally ending up enthroned on the outdoors dunny (lavatory), trousers round his ankles. The younger son, Jimmy, gets attached to a girl (Joanne Mildenhall: nameless, but then this is 'Old Comedy'), who will bring female influence to the future, while TK's grotesque but feisty sister in law, Auntie Bird (Dorothy McKegg), wrongfully excluded from part-ownership of the farm by TK, is reinstated into a newly formed post-TK family. The film, like the others, looks at the old both critically and nostalgically, so that the farm is allowed to stand, in the newer world, if not for most suburban New Zealanders' way of life, then as a symbol of a desired independence, working for oneself rather than others (the latter the terrible fate Arthur threatens Jimmy with if they fail to get TK home), a necessary pioneer-invoking dream in a society as highly corporatized as anywhere in the world. The title, 'Carry Me Back', refers to the father's command, but also invokes a geographical and psychic return to the heartland, a return, though, that is not a simple regression, but a renegotiation of past weaknesses and virtues, with their modern equivalents.

Came a Hot Friday, based on Ronald Hugh Morrieson's novel (1964), is structured around the picaresque adventures of the confidence men Wesley Pennington (Peter Bland) and his younger offsider Cyril (Philip Gordon), who descend on small towns to work a horse-racing scam on (illegal) bookies. Its ambivalent moral structure is announced with the vocal epigraph that 'It is 1949, the privations of war are behind us, there is money to be made', followed by shots of a crowd transported with greed, rushing the totalizator. Similar crowds gather at Sel Bishop's woolshed/gambling emporium, and in the film's catastrophe, the 'Tainuia Kid' (Billy T. James), thinking – reasonably, given the mores on show elsewhere – that the taniwha (monster) he believes inhabits the river will only be influenced by money, tosses everyone's ill-gotten gains into the river. 'I think of us as wearing the mantle of avenging angels dispensing a kind of wild justice' is the opulently rhetorical Wesley's way of justifying his and Cyril's actions against the bookies and gambling entrepreneurs. The rhetoric is wholly opportunistic, but they have that appeal of witty tricksters (from Volpone to Curnow's Sir George Mandragora in *The Overseas Expert*[20]) who, rather than seducing innocents, invite dormant frailties to flower. The small town of Tainuia may have its relative innocents – like Don's father (Bruce Allpress), the crusty, sterling old Anzac clumping on his wooden leg, and Esmerelda 'the dusky maiden' (Marise Wipani, softened from the easy commercial traveller's lay of the less benign source) – but even Don (Michael Lawrence), the wonderfully average local Kiwi boy, is lastingly ripe for temptation. This is shown when, despite having won the lovely Esmerelda, his gaze at the Anzac Day ceremony ending the film still follows the conmen longingly as they leave, while Dinah (Erna Larsen) – despite still being honeymoon hot with Dick (Philip Holder), the local car salesman – is Wesley's for the taking in the stockpen that even his quotations from *Romeo and Juliet* hardly transform into a salubrious locus of love. Approaching the less venial end of the scale, Norm Cray, the town bookie (Don Selwyn, the least sympathetic of the three Māori characters), in his growingly psychotic attempts to exact revenge on the conmen, provides a bridge to the darkest of the characters, the gambling entrepreneur and murderer Sel Bishop (Marshall Napier). These, and others like Morrie (Michael Morrissey), Don's darker version, the weak young man pushed by debt into arson and accidental murder by Sel, outdo even *The Scarecrow*'s memorable cluster of small town down and outs – Ned's father, DK (Des Kelly); uncle, Athol Cudby (Bruce Allpress) the classic 'bludger'; and Charlie Dabney (Jonathan Hardy), the town undertaker; and the younger contenders: the pedantic constable, and the hoons (larrikins) of the Lynch gang – as the most precious repository of older New Zealand stereotypes on film. They are crowned by the celebrated comedian Billy T. James's Tui Purano, the 'Tainuia Kid', a heroically culturally confused Māori under the impression that he is a Mexican bandido or sheriff (depending on the circumstances). This extraordinary creation (via Morrieson's original) is a hyperbolization of sociological actuality, since, as variously attested, Māori youth of previous generations were known for wearing cowboy costume. Blythe quotes a memo from the Attorney General in 1936 worrying about 'Maori boys [who] dress and act the part of the characters displayed, who are usually heroes of the wild west films',[21] a later instance being Kingi in *Mark II* with his Clint Eastwood poncho and hat.

The adaptation of Morrieson's earlier novel *The Scarecrow* (1963) is centrally comic in its portrait of small town life, and male adolescent rites of passage, but, with the sex murderer Salter's (John Carradine) presence, it is also verges on the horror film. Though softening them, it preserves elements of the source's darker interests, in the voyeuristic fascination held by the protagonists (the narrator Ned [Jonathan Smith] and his friend Les [Daniel McLaren]) for the sex murders, even if deleting the book's implicit masturbation orgy, and largely displacing Ned's incestuous interest in his sexually flowering sister onto Les's puppy love. The boys' sexual trajectory, despite being surrounded by perversity, is happily resolved in their meeting with the 'hard case' twins, a happiness expressed in traditional deflating male narrator's terms when, contemplating the mystery of what 'it' is like, Ned quotes his older brother, 'It's like bluebirds flyin outta ya bum'.

The third Morrieson adaptation, *Pallet on the Floor* (Lynton Butler), adapted from the writer's grimmest novel, though not released till 1986, dates from 1983. Morrieson's novels are all dark, but this is the most extreme, its setting the freezing works (that historical foundation of the New Zealand good life), where many of the characters are employed. If the novel's message on the fellmongery door – 'So you were in Belsen, huh?', fails to make the film, the peephole through which sadistic voyeurs watch the lambs being slaughtered, does (just), and though in a weakening omission the central character Sam (Peter McCauley) becomes much blander without his prototype's nervously ingested seconal, mogadon, anatensol and sleeping draughts, drink plays the same role for the characters, dulling the grimness of their work. 'Let us drink until the horrors come, lest sober we go mad'. *Friday* and *The Scarecrow* have central scenes of conflagration, but such intimations of Hades are hardly necessary in *Pallet*'s world, where even the most sympathetic characters commit three murders and a manslaughter, albeit of malevolent characters. *Pallet*'s interestingly muddied colour spectrum – as if pursuing the title's potential pun, pallet/bed: artist's palette on the floor – creates a dull, floorbound range of tones that matches the grim surroundings, in which the pigeons flying overhead are less symbols of freedom than scavengers circling the slaughterhouse. Some of the film's comedy comes from the lugubiously witty Basil Foster Beaumont (Bruce Spence), the English 'remittance man without a remittance', called by one of the villainous Voot brothers (Marshall Napier, John Bach) 'that long stream of pommy piss', but who, like Wes in *Friday*, has, even in decline, the traditional English upper-class advantages of loquacious wit over the colonials. Basil eventually knowingly kills himself driving the blackmailing Breens to their deaths. In the source McGee, dying from cancer, did this – his imminent death giving plausibility to the sacrifice, whereas with Basil the logic is the old-world character enabling the new-world ones. It is Basil, too, who persuades Sam, married to the Māori Sue (Jillian O'Brien), to escape the rat race by living with her in her pā, something he has previously seen as a shameful return to 'the mat', the optimistic racial ending securing the film's inconstant comic trajectory.

The art or experimental film

Test Pictures, Geoff Steven, 1975; *Landfall*, Paul Maunder, 1977; *Angel Mine*, David Blyth, 1979; *Strata*, Geoff Steven, 1983; *Vigil*, Vincent Ward, 1984; *Leave All Fair*, John Reid, 1985

Though a persistent rhetoric asserts New Zealand film-making's originality, the art or experimental film, the obvious site of difference, is rare. A leader of the modernist abstract film movement, Len Lye, was a New Zealander, but made his short films overseas, and could not be said to have impinged in any way on New Zealand feature film making.

The first three of the films above, emerging from an alternative, anti-Hollywood ethos, were made in extreme low-budget circumstances before the more conservative parameters of post-1977 feature-film funding were solidified. Of the directors involved, Steven and Maunder left the feature-film scene, Blyth joined the mainstream, while for Reid *Leave All Fair* was an untypical project. Of these figures only Ward (see chapter 7) with *Vigil*, and later *The Navigator*, carried on the original art/experimental impulse, though Ward's greater talent differed from the others not just in its emotive and mythic tendencies, but in his prodigious imagination's demands for larger-scale budgets, eventually satisfied only in international co-production and Hollywood.

Different though the films listed are, they all foreground formal self-consciousness and pervasive ambiguity, downplay classical causality, and display marked subjective and expressive aspects. *Landfall* and *Test Pictures* are films at present almost impossible to see, marking the way in which, though important when made, their influence lapsed. The provocative suburban surrealism of *Angel Mine* was similarly largely issueless. *Test Pictures*, like *Landfall*, cultivated a characteristic 1970s drop-out alternative lifestyle narrative. A review by Karl Mutch stressed the film's jettisoning of the original script and evolution into a series of episodic moments (the film's subtitle is *Eleven Vignettes from a Relationship*), its interest in texture rather than classical narrative, its (natural noise) soundtrack, and its formal experiments – mentioning a five-minute *temps mort* sequence with two panning shots foregrounded.[22] Steven's later film *Strata*'s narrative experiments follow two different actions, which, though geographically proximate, only intersect late on. In one, a geologist working in a forbidding (untouristic) volcanic region is interviewed by a writer accompanied by a photographer; in the other, characters refusing to be interned in a government security centre wander in terrain adjacent to the first action. The hostile landscape, with many long shots situating the humans as small and vulnerable, binds together both 'plot' areas, while the interviewer's and photographer's activities emphasize self-reflexiveness, with the geologist Victor's musings about the mind and the geological strata which give their title to the film suggesting further cryptic significances. Blyth's *Angel Mine*, influenced by surrealist film texts, was more scandalous, with a definite element of *épater le bourgeois*. Reid's film is a psychologically oriented *Kammerfilm* (intimate chamber film), in which Katherine Mansfield (Jane Birkin), while central, is already more than twenty years dead, appearing only spectrally in the minds of her husband, John Middleton Murry (John Gielgud), visiting France for the publication of her *Journals*, and a New Zealander, Marie Taylor (also Jane Birkin), who discovers her famous 'leave all fair' letter (asking Murry not to publish unfinished work, which he has disobeyed); thus the film becomes an internalized battle for possession of the great writer. Both *Leave All Fair* and *Angel Mine*, though otherwise wholly unlike, play with doppelgangers, switches between fantasy and reality, and psychic projections. The major film of the group, Ward's *Vigil* develops an emphasis on subjectivity, to a degree unknown in New Zealand film, filtering all its events through the young girl Toss's consciousness, traumatized by the death of her father (Figure 11).

11. Ethan (Frank Whitten) and Toss (Fiona Kay), enigmatic against a forbidding landscape in Vincent Ward's *Vigil* (1984), the first New Zealand production to gain art-film applause overseas.

Murphy and Donaldson
Butch and Sundance

Murphy and Donaldson are distinctly different film-makers, but nevertheless shared tendencies that impacted heavily on the New Zealand film scene. Seen through the prism of Geoff Steven's documentary on the sometimes rawly masculinist beginnings of the new industry, *Cowboys of Culture* (1991), they were briefly the male odd couple, the Butch and Sundance, at the centre of early activity.

First, both were basically American in their sensibilities, attuned to Hollywood rather than British or European film. The European art film which influenced more peripheral contemporaries like Geoff Steven, Paul Maunder and, briefly, David Blyth, passed them by, except as it was domesticized into Hollywood post-studio modes. *Temps mort* has limited attractions for action addicts. This factor was important for local success, where Hollywood was always the dominant comparison, and later eased their transitions to Los Angeles.

Second, both were intuitive practitioners in tune with dominant audience tastes, uninterested in radically questioning modes or in seeking alternative models. Though Murphy was allied with the anarchic entertainment group Blerta, and through that with elements of the counter-culture which influenced his work,[23] this sat comfortably with the Hollywood post-studio genres, especially the road movie familiar to many of their audience through films like *Easy Rider* (1969). For both directors, one suspects, politics was anti-authoritarian gesture, preferably Jack Nicholson's in *Five Easy Pieces* (1970) or *One Flew Over the Cuckoo's Nest* (1975).

Third, this distance from theory and the avant garde was true of both in ways reaching wider than the cinema. Though both made films capable of vividly articulating meanings and contradictions beyond their overt ideologies, both were basically populist conservatives, with, especially in Murphy's case, an anarchic inflection. This is nowhere clearer than in their inclination to the masculine, even macho. Women are generally minor, ambivalent presences in their films, something soon to provoke criticism of 'boys' own stories', but it is a tribute to both directors' insight that their masculinist sympathies never simply stood unchallenged; indeed, that their films of sometimes seemingly regressive last-gasp saloon male assertion, the climacteric of the dominantly masculinist culture from which they emerged, were also films of social crisis, responsive to the stirrings of change which they intuited. Tied to, in many ways celebrating, older values, they also diagnosed their insufficiencies.

Fourth, despite their eventual departures for Hollywood, the two directors also shared an unashamed, uninhibited New Zealandness, though Donaldson was originally an Australian. In this they had the luck to be in the right place at the right time. Only fifteen years before *Sleeping Dogs*, O'Shea's *Runaway* was, it is claimed, partly redubbed because it was feared New Zealand audiences and critics would react negatively to screen characters with local accents. It is unclear whether this is more than a myth – Leo Pilcher, Ramai Te Miha, Stanley Knight and others all employ New Zealand accents in Hayward's sound films, and New Zealand accents are unhidden in *Broken Barrier* and *Don't Let It Get You* – but it is certainly true that a negative self-consciousness about local performers affected *Runaway*'s reception. By the time of *Sleeping Dogs* and *Pork Pie*, nearly twenty years of television had accustomed audiences to New Zealanders on screen (if not often in fictions), and the conditions of receptiveness for local cinematic expression were in place. One of both directors' achievements was their foregrounding of the local demotic. This came to them through a long tradition in which literary art had mixed lower with more elevated registers in a line of demotic prose from Frank Anthony to Frank Sargeson to Barry Crump, to be transmogrified into the exhilarating release on screen of the dialect of the white and many of the brown tribe(s) as Gerry in *Pork Pie* greets the pump attendant with 'G'day, where's your dunny?' (compare this with the poet Allen Curnow's 'how sad the dunny / And the things you drew on the wall'), or Te Wheke talks of the army chasing him as 'run [ning] around like a chook with its head chopped off'. They were also able to utilize a new generation of actors, mostly, at the beginning, male – especially Bruno Lawrence, Sam Neill (in *Sleeping Dogs*), Kelly Johnson and Tony Barry – providing audiences with the spectacle of distinct New Zealandness on screen, 'the gesturality and morphology of the body' in Susan Hayward's phrase, whose 'gestural codes', she argues, 'even more than the narrative codes, are deeply rooted in a nation's culture'.[24] (Apropos of which, this author once recognized a silent Buddhist monk as a New Zealander by a typical facial grimace which, if Ray L. Birwhistell, the proponent of the codification of facial semiotics, had worked on New Zealand rather than American material, he would have classed among the many facial expressions in use in New Zealand daily life).[25] It has been remarked that 'British stars, like those of other indigenous cinemas, give things to home audiences that Hollywood luminaries cannot – reflections of the known and close at hand, typologies of the contingent, intimate dramatizations of local myths and realities'.[26] What is true here is equally true of New Zealand, though we are talking of performers and character actors rather than stars in the usual usage.

Man Alone and men together

It is hard to find a discussion of New Zealand culture in which John Mulgan's novel *Man Alone* (1939)[27] does not figure as the primary rendition of one of Pākehā culture's persistent thematics: the male figure who, by accident or design, leaves society for the bush and solitude. It should be noted that the novel is much more ambivalent than is usually remembered, a classic case of more popular versions of the myth simplifying its most complex statement.

In Mulgan's novel, Johnson, an immigrant Englishman, drifts uncommitedly through pre-Depression and Depression New Zealand. Eventually at the Depression's height he works for a dairy farmer, Stebbing, but things deteriorate when Stebbing's young Māori wife pushes him into an affair, resulting in a confrontation with the farmer in which Johnson accidentally kills him. Johnson escapes into the bush and survives in dreadful conditions, tramping to eventual safety, a boat passage out of the country. Notably in this most celebrated version of the myth, extreme solitude is not chosen, but forced on the hero, and the bush is a site of privation and danger, endured rather than celebrated. What is also seldom recalled is that Johnson, the uncommitted loner, ends the book going to Spain to fight for the Republic, acknowledging the necessity of bonding and political action. Not unexpectedly, in many popular versions, such as the bestselling yarns of Barry Crump (for example, *A Good Keen Man*, 1960), such elements as Johnson's eventual political, though highly undoctrinaire, engagement, the taint of criminality, the manhunt, and the bush as enemy are omitted for a hard but not debilitating simple life, reminiscent of pioneer existence, of hunting and self-sufficiency, and of freedom from social demands, women, bureaucracy and family responsibilities.

The thematic (past its apogee and beginning to be criticized as with Clarrie in *Runaway*) exists in different manifestations in these early films, from something akin to Mulgan's gaunt complexity to more pleasing superficial shapes, flattering for quiescent, apolitical, highly bureaucratized, predominantly urban New Zealanders. Though they usually replace political critique with a more generalized anti-authoritarianism, they tend to retain elements of the pursued criminal and the manhunt (already seen in *Runaway*), either in serious (*Sleeping Dogs*, *Smash Palace*, Mike Newell's *Bad Blood*), or comedic terms (most obviously *Goodbye Pork Pie*, and parodied in 'Old Mac' in John Reid's *Carry Me Back*, 1982). Smith leaves his family to live alone in *Sleeping Dogs*, and, on the run in Coromandel, is hunted down by the security forces. Al in *Smash Palace* takes off to a hut in the bush with his little daughter, searched for by the police. *Pork Pie*'s odd couple, finally reduced to John alone, is pursued all the way by police and, eventually, sharpshooters. In *Utu*, Williamson (Bruno Lawrence), his wife killed, rides alone searching for vengeance on Te Wheke, who, in his Macbeth-like difference from his followers, is also a (Māori) version of the 'man alone'. The most extreme of these figures, Stanley Graham, in *Bad Blood*, after killing various townspeople and policemen, takes to the wilderness, where he is hunted to death by the police and army.

These protagonists are largely womanless, at least for much of the narratives: Stanley and his wife are separated when he goes on the run; Smith in *Sleeping Dogs* leaves his wife and children; for much of *Pork Pie*, Gerry and John are on their own; Zac is an Eveless Adam at the beginning and end of *The Quiet Earth*; the brothers in *Carry Me Back* – though this changes a bit – are also womanless; so too in any permanent sense are the itinerant conmen, Wes and Cyril, in *Came a Hot Friday*.

Actually, few of these figures are literally men alone, as that thematic is joined to a second great Australasian motif, that of mateship. This also recalls pioneer days, where significant numbers of males lived in the wholly masculine worlds of the 'crew cultures' (ships crews, labouring and construction gangs, and so on), where strong homosocial bonds were necessary and idealized.[28] The films' pattern of paired males is often embodied in couples constituted in difference rather than similarity, giving rise to possibilities of fracture. Smith and Bullen in *Sleeping Dogs* are the most extreme example, acting out mateship in extremis, despite deep-seated differences. In *Pork Pie*, Gerry (young, promiscuous, thoughtless) and John (ageing, more meditative) exhibit considerable differences beneath their anti-authoritarian affinities (Figure 12). In *Smash Palace*, Al's and Ray's mateship cannot survive Ray's relationship with Al's wife (though Smith and Bullen draw closer in a similar situation), but it still binds them together in a sardonic sense, quite literally through the wire noose attached to Al's rifle at the end. In *The Quiet Earth*, where Zac and Api are divided by racial history as well as desire for Joanne (Figure 13), their differences are so great that no bonding occurs. Patterns of differences of age and temperament are also found with the conmen Wes and Cyril in *Came a Hot Friday* and the two brothers in *Carry Me Back*. These allow the

12. Antic roadies at historical turning point. John (Tony Barry, right) and Gerry (Kelly Johnson) hitting the tarmac in Geoff Murphy's *Goodbye Pork Pie* (1981).

dramatic interest of temperamental clashes, as in a marriage or love relationship, while also presenting, through the wider spectrum of two individuals' characteristics, a more extended portrait of masculine traits.

Cut me like a bastard, Geoff

Both Murphy and Donaldson were deeply influenced by contemporary Hollywood practice. The question of style in their early New Zealand films is of central importance in that, given their main audience's identification of cinema with Hollywood, their films needed to demonstrate they could stand comparison with the internalized model. In Donaldson's *Sleeping Dogs* certain sequences demonstrate this, especially the moments of kinetic action, the shooting of the police by government agents, the motel poolside massacre of the American specials, the brutal police charge in which Bullen and Gloria are caught up, Smith being chased pell mell through Queen Street crowds. There are others – like the helicopters flying low over New Zealand bush, with echoes of Vietnam footage, or the mid-air shot of jet fighters employed against the resistance – which, while narratively expendable, are absolutely essential in asserting the film's ability to match its models. Murphy's three early films all begin with consciously virtuosic shots: in *Pork Pie* and *Utu*, complicated long single-shot openings, whose fluidity and multiple setups state equality of expertise irrespective of their content; and in *The Quiet Earth*, where the opposite, the long static shot of the Pacific sun rising, bespeaks an equal confidence. A cut early in *Pork Pie* can hardly have failed to affect audiences in the way suggested, when Gerry, having gutted Leslie Morris's lost wallet for driving licence and money, tosses it away into streetside offscreen space only for an immediate cut to complete its trajectory by landing it, transformed now into Les Morris's driving licence, on the car rental desk. Seen now, the cut still suggests infectious confidence, and was for many viewers the first time that the Hollywood style was not an external negative comparison but a successfully internalized mode. The other part of the equation is that what the style worked on with such panache was intensely local material, like the sequence in *Sleeping Dogs* where Bullen and Smith escape penned in a sheep truck. Here the codes of the action film combine suspense and comedy with a phenomenon familiar to every driver on New Zealand roads, the ubiquity of trucks carrying sheep destined for the slaughterhouse, with the added ironies of the fact that the escapees look bound for it too.

Goodbye Pork Pie, hello LA

Both Murphy and Donaldson left New Zealand to pursue Hollywood careers: Donaldson after only two features, Murphy after four. Murphy, although the greater talent in terms of early contemporary New Zealand cinema, has been only moderately successful, his status as director of follow-ups, rather than the originals, revealing. Donaldson has achieved a greater penetration of the mainstream, to become a major commercial director. Like Murphy, within the Hollywood system, Donaldson ceded his earlier dual role as writer–director for that of director of others' screenplays, suggesting less personal work. While Murphy retained more connections with New Zealand cinema, carrying out second-unit direction on *The Lord of the Rings*, Donaldson's film-making connections seemed to be shrinking to disappearance after the Pacific-oriented transitional work *The Bounty* (1984), and the tiny homage in *No Way Out* (1987), where a fragment of the action takes place at the New Zealand embassy in Washington's Waitangi Day party. However, both film-makers have recently made films again in New Zealand: Murphy, the conspiracy thriller *Spooked* (2004) and Donaldson *The World's Fastest Indian* (2005), the latter a big home box-office success, the former attracting few viewers.

The films

Sleeping Dogs, Roger Donaldson, 1977; *Goodbye Pork Pie*, Geoff Murphy, 1980; *Smash Palace*, Roger Donaldson, 1982; *Utu*, Geoff Murphy, 1983; *The Quiet Earth*, Geoff Murphy, 1985

Sleeping Dogs

Roger Donaldson's *Sleeping Dogs* has the unrepeatable distinction of being the first 1970s New Zealand feature to prove a major box-office attraction, thereby enabling the rapid developments that followed. Grossing as much as its cost, however, it still left its makers in the red. As an argument for government underwriting of a potential film industry, its influence was threefold: it proved (i) that large audiences would watch a New Zealand film; (ii) that there was the talent to make such films; but (iii) that without institutional support the economics of sustained film-making in a small market could not be mastered. Undoubtedly, the film accelerated the inauguration of the Film Commission (1977/1978).

Sleeping Dogs was well timed, and the decision to adapt *Smith's Dream* (1971) by the New Zealand novelist C.K. Stead,[29] which had already created a considerable stir, was a strategic one, bringing the film publicity and prestige from its source. The film, like Stead's novel, visualizes a dystopian near future in which New Zealand has become a rightwing American client dictatorship under emergency regulations. Stead's novel exploited a sense of trauma deriving from Britain's imminent joining of the European Common Market, much closer in 1971 than in *Runaway* (1964), and joined it to a scenario of collapsed markets, foot and mouth epidemics, and fears of expanding communism in South East Asia. Between the novel and the film a further destabilization had occurred: the 'oil shock' of 1973, quadrupling the country's petrol bill. This is no doubt reflected in the epigraph to Murphy's *Pork Pie*, with its backward glance to a time when 'petrol stations were always open and gas less than a buck a gallon'. In Donaldson's film 'out of gas' signs are prominent in the TV news broadcast that sets the political scene at the film's opening.

Donaldson's film follows Stead's narrative, though with important differences, discussed below. Smith (Sam Neill) separates from his wife Gloria (Nevan Rowe) because of her affair with a teacher Bullen (Ian Mune), and, leaving his children behind, heads north, oblivious of politics. Living a 'man alone' life, he is arrested for supposed espionage. Imprisoned in Auckland, he is told by an old school acquaintance, Jesperson (Clyde Scott), now high in the security forces, that he will be shot unless he makes a false confession. Smith escapes and, from necessity rather than conviction, becomes implicated with the resistance. He reluctantly aids a massacre of American special forces, and has no option but to move closer to the rebels, where he finds that Bullen and his wife have become resistance fighters. Smith's anger at Bullen's affair with Gloria eventually subsides, and, though Smith never agrees with Bullen's commitment to political struggle, the pair, as they are hunted down, become a classic mateship duo, especially after Gloria is killed. When Bullen is desperately wounded, Smith all but carries him through a desperate bush trek, at the end of which they are gunned down by their military pursuers, headed by Jesperson.

While maintaining its basic trajectory, Donaldson's adaptation ruthlessly excises much of Stead's original. There is no attempt to find a cinematic equivalent for its complex narrator figure with his meditations on how 'we' New Zealanders became complicit with a non-democratic government and on the violence on both sides that has ensued. The fact that Bullen and Gloria have joined the communists is also deleted, with Donaldson choosing to keep the politics vaguer. Also dropped is Smith's meeting with Volkner, the Prime Minister, whose rhetoric is a brilliant inflection of New Zealand racial myths: the

Māori ascending to supremacy among the Polynesians because of the cooler latitudes they now inhabit, and the Pākehā to supremacy over the original inhabitants of the British Isles because of the perfect mixture of Celt and Anglo Saxon achieved in New Zealand but never in their original home. The dream that gives the novel its title is omitted too, a delicate, somewhat mysterious evocation of a New Zealand pastoral – the beach, the sea, fading summer, and a girl. The new title, with its inevitable context of the proverbial 'Let sleeping dogs lie', presumably functions ironically and warningly: the sleeping dogs are the latent tendencies that socio-political hard times may unleash, with the implied imperative reflecting easygoing apolitical tendencies in New Zealanders who would regard the film's scenario as impossible. Donaldson is quoted as saying:

> I think Sleeping Dogs has something important to say. Civil liberties are declining fast in many parts of the world. Although they don't all suffer from events as violent as those in the movie, there have been plenty of indications in the last few years that New Zealand is becoming a constricted democracy. If Sleeping Dogs has a lesson, it is that we should be aware of giving anyone too much power in the belief that he [or she] won't abuse it.[30]

This 'official' version is certainly part of the film's meaning. Audiences saw a plausible scenario of an economically pressured New Zealand succumbing to rightwing extremism and American intervention, albeit at the government's request. In the sadistic figure of Colonel Willoughby (Warren Oates), there was an ogre whose political violence and cynicism were shocking. In a defying of the overbearing superpower, Willoughby and his men are shot up by the local resistance in a Rotorua motel. But just as exciting was the spectacle of New Zealanders acting machiavellianly, as where the masked specials shoot their own police to create an exploitable incident, with one of them executing the others to hide the evidence, or where the resistance acts as callously as the enemy when Bullen leaves the wounded Dudley (Ian Watkin) to die, or they betray Smith to get him away from Gut Island. Such moments played against myths of essential New Zealand decency and political innocence – the subversion of which, though shocking, was also exciting – suggested an overdue joining of the larger corrupt world.

However, there is a sense, abetted by the dropping of the source's more concrete political allusions for a more generalized populist anti-authoritarianism, that some of the film's deeper meanings are played out in parallel to, rather than by, such thematics, in two prototypical New Zealand cultural directions.

Country music (also important in *Smash Palace*),[31] in one of its most traditional forms celebrating the 'ramblin' man', dominates the soundtrack in two important areas of the film: Smith's drive north, and the narrative's ending, where, as Smith falls, shot, the song 'Let Sleeping Dogs Lie' begins. The first song celebrates, with touches of regret, Smith's cutting himself loose from his domestic troubles, culminating in 'Don't look back . . . Keep on amovin', baby'. This is followed briefly by the jukebox song in Dudley's store, lamenting the singer's exile down south working for 'Fifty five dollars a day / For planting trees on the Auckland highway' and wishing return to the paternal farm – a wish that seems to contradict the previous lyrics by returning to rather than escaping the domestic, but actually harmonizes with their desired movement from urban to pastoral, with the son's dreams of return to the paternal site foreshadowing *Smash Palace*. The third song accompanies the brutal killing of Smith with seemingly optimistic open road lyrics ('The time for regrets is done, / And the black clouds rollin' in from the south, / Well, they seem to be drivin' me on'). If we look for a meaning less facile than covering the film's ending with a generalized feel-good aura, what emerges is the underscoring of the film's two most powerful subtexts: the 'man alone', combined with *men* alone; in other words, the film's other classical antipodean motif of mateship. In the opening scene Smith leaves his wife and two children in emotional but opaque circumstances, only explained later – he has chosen to go rather than compete with Bullen for her. Though later moments remind us that Smith misses them, the sequence driving north suggests the predominance of other feelings, expressed when he stops to look at a crepuscular view of Gut Island and beats a rapid ecstatic fist tattoo on the car top, as if to assert that he has found what he wants: isolation from men, from women and from a complicated world. While there is a lot in Stead which this follows – for the writer has explicated elsewhere his novel's close relation, even to the point of conscious rewriting, to Mulgan's famous work[32] – what there is not is the motif of mateship. In the novel, Smith's interaction with Bullen is comparatively slight. In the film's long last part, however, Smith and Bullen are constantly together as an isolated couple. Gloria's death leads to a kind of reconciliation; indeed, by the end she seems almost to exist as a median term bringing the two men together, to a point where their political disagreements become immaterial. Their interchanges become more minimal, phatic, composed of tough masculine banter in which the meaning lies beneath the laconic surface: 'We did it, boy, we did it!'; 'Brilliant revolution! Two guys shitting themselves in the bush!'; 'We're here, Bull, they couldn't bloody stop us'; '*Bullen* (wounded): Why don't you just piss off. Gloria'd never know.

Smith: Yeah, but I would. *Bullen*: Sorry, Smithy.' Elsewhere their interchanges become almost hysterical with homosocial intensity, as when Smith insists to Bullen, 'I won't leave you, Bull, I won't leave you here', suggesting a transference of emotions invested in woman to the more dependable terrain of masculine camaraderie.

Another area of profound ambivalence centres round Smith's involvement with the resistance. Perhaps one of the key factors in the film's success lay in the fuzziness of its politics and Smith's degree of involvement with them, thus allowing film and audience to have it both ways: on the one hand, Smith fights against the enemy; on the other, he preserves his representative apolitical stance, his wariness of commitment, his typical pragmatic New Zealand dislike of the ideological ('*Dudley*: I didn't think you were one of us. *Smith*: I'm not. I never was'). This, whatever Donaldson jettisons of Stead's original, is at one with the deeper source in Mulgan, where Johnson's eventual commitment to the Spanish war is decidedly unideological, making Smith a combination of the man alone, crossed with mild inflections of the counter-culture protester ('all you soldier boys and boy scouts'), and the man of action crossed with the average New Zealander's wariness of politics.

Goodbye Pork Pie

Goodbye Pork Pie, made on a budget of about NZ$320,000, took $1.2 million on first release and another NZ$300,00 on re-release a few months later, and then had 1.5 million viewers (50 per cent of the population over five) on its first television showing. These were phenomenal figures. Murphy's account credits the film's extraordinary success to its energy, its 'culturally accurate' wit, and to its last-gasp optimistic feel at a time (1980–1981) when 'there was a definite feeling that things were changing for the worse. We were coming to the end of the age of innocence'.[33] The specific instance he gives is Māori protest, so it is significant that, apart from the baffled authority figure of the Māori policeman in Kaitaia (Don Selwyn), the film is without Māori characters (though when John finds Gerry having his breakdown he holds a tokotoko, a carved ceremonial walking stick, which he finds lying around). Although the film achieved many overseas sales, these were never large, and 'it was never to be a hit anywhere else'. In Murphy's view the cultural specificity that made it so popular in New Zealand limited its appeal elsewhere. 'The heroes behaved and spoke in a manner that suggested New Zealand was the only place on earth. It was a celebration of New Zealandness'.[34]

The film's title derived rather recondítely from Murphy's jazz enthusiasms. The words 'Goodbye Pork Pie' are John's valediction to Gerry when he leaves him, perhaps dead, and drives on to Invercargill, Pork Pie being the words on Gerry's T-shirt and cap, later stencilled on their yellow mini. The precise reference is to Charlie Mingus's composition in memory of Lester Young, a jazz musician famous for his pork-pie hat, hence its title 'Goodbye Pork Pie Hat', from which the film's comes.[35] (The film's opening music echoes it distantly.) For most viewers the title's rhyming, slangy opaqueness functions similarly to a phrase like 'See ya later, alligator', suggesting a hip casualness, a quirky anti-authoritarianism. But another less immediately obvious sense is one of elegy; even without the precise referent of Lester Young's death music, the film's title is still 'Goodbye' to someone or something, suggesting a framing melancholy, atmospheres of loss, surrounding the often frantic action. But if elegy, elegy for what? For the times when gas was less than a buck a gallon of the epigraph? For the politically innocent times Murphy referred to as ending? For youth? For freedom from officialdom and bureaucracy? For freedom without responsibility? Most particularly perhaps for the freedoms of a certain kind of maleness, inhibited by a now changing, more divided and less gender specific society? For the endangered myths of mateship and man, or men, alone? Part of the film's complexity is that all these seem, in an unpretentious, casual way, to be suggested.

Derived from Hollywood road and buddy movies, but transmuted into terms that pleased local audiences, the narrative is very basic, with incident dominating over plot. In Kaitaia in the far north, Gerry (Kelly Johnson) – young, independent, promiscuous – chooses the road rather than the employment agency. Left with the driving licence dropped by a female he has tried to pick up, he adapts her name, Leslie Morris, to Les Morris (an initiating statement of masculine primacies) to hire the small yellow mini synonymous with the film, the first of his various name changes and identity switches. In a parallel action in Auckland, to which Gerry is heading, John (Tony Barry) – older, more experienced, more confined – is left by his long-term lover, Sue (Shirley Gruar), seemingly frustrated by his refusal of commitment. She flies to Invercargill to stay with her sister. John phones her to tell her he is coming to see her. The two men's parallel narratives converge in Auckland, where they meet in an anti-authoritarian situation involving the subversion of a traffic policeman, and set out on a journey only given direction by John's desire to get to Invercargill, New Zealand's southernmost city. Almost immediately the couple becomes a trio as they pick up Shirl (Claire Oberman), who has sex with Gerry. Heading south, they have multiple brushes with authority, as the police pursue what becomes known as 'The Blondini Gang', after Gerry's calling himself Groucho Blondini, a name conflating the anarchic Groucho of the Marx Brothers and Blondin the great French tightrope walker. (Gerry first asserts his Blondini identity while precariously standing on the rail of the inter-island ferry, emblematizing the outlaws' constant balancing act, their existence on the edge.) When Shirl is arrested for shoplifting, they continue without her into the South Island. Darker undercurrents multiply. Gerry reveals a growing paranoia. A deranged product of the drug counter-culture, Snout (John Bach), imposes on them disturbingly and then betrays them. Eventually, during a police chase, Gerry is injured, perhaps fatally (the film does not resolve this). John goes on alone, evading a hugely armed police blockade (prompted by Snout's lie that the gang is armed) that turns into a shooting party. In a car now in flames, he reaches Sue's sister's house, where Sue welcomes him and they make love. Another massive armed squad surrounds the house demanding his surrender. John walks out, insouciantly naked, to be arrested and presumably sent to prison, but with Sue reconciled to him.

Pork Pie resists summary: something true of works of art generally, but particularly so where so much depends on casual atmospheres and allusions not easily translatable to outside audiences, as well as the more kinetic excitements of the road movie, in a different way resisting intellectualization. Nevertheless, major structures govern the film's loose 'joshing' and 'riffing' progress – to borrow the terms that Pauline Kael, writing on *Utu*, used to describe Murphy as a director[36] – visible both in broader sequences and in microcosmic shots. For instance, early on there is a shot of John walking with suitcase towards the camera in the bus station, near deserted in the early morning. As he advances, a teenager glides along on roller skates, first behind him, then passing him, then progressing in front of him, scattering into flight pigeons on the pedestrian pathway, a multifaceted image that associates John first of all with the freewheeling teenager, then with the grounded pigeons taking to the air. At the same time it is clear that John is not a teenager, that he is not going to rollerskate to Invercargill, or fly like the pigeon, so that the fleeting moment as well as its atmospheres encapsulates one of the narrative's larger and more ambivalent structures.

The male couple (trio with Shirl, then couple again, then John alone) are like Bonnie and Clyde without the violence, their criminality softened to the most minor crimes. Gerry keeps the money in Leslie Morris's wallet; they twice trick service-station attendants into filling the car up, only to do a runner; they purchase dope from Mulvaney

(Bruno Lawrence) and smoke it a lot (though not doing harder drugs); they drive through a give way sign, crash red lights and generally drive dangerously; Shirl is arrested for shoplifting; and they evade chasing policemen continuously. In a background broadcast their crimes are reported as comically minor – 'stowing away on the inter-island ferry', 'possible appropriation of railway property'. Their transgressions give them a touch of the outlaw, but evade real-life consequences The most serious injury (apart from Gerry's) is a chasing traffic cop's broken leg, but here Gerry and John phone his colleagues for help before escaping. The crimes are ones that teenagers, or the teenagers dormant in adult viewers, might commit.

The film is one long motorized flight from pursuing authority, marked out by specific encounters: Gerry and the Māori policeman in Kaitaia; John's frustrated attempt to get past the airport security man to follow Sue (less likely to be so sympathetically viewed post-9/11); John trying to tease information out of a bus-station official; and then the encounter in which John and Gerry meet, when a fourth uniformed authority figure, the traffic cop, stops Gerry for not wearing his seat-belt, and is defeated by the support John gives his (untruthful) denials. Later, a motorcycle cop is escaped when the trio drive into the auto graveyard (reworked in *Smash Palace*); multiple policemen positioned to stop the escapees boarding the inter-island ferry are evaded; another cop chasing them, ends up in the river, on to the cops John escapes after Gerry has fallen off the car. The fetching insolence, simultaneously childish and liberating, of these encounters is caught in the early seat-belt scene. When Gerry gets out of the mini as the policeman approaches, he leans back, hands in his jacket pockets, against the car, while John, intervening, places his suitcase on the ground and uses it as a footrest to stand with an equally needling casualness. The dialogue catches the scene's irresponsibly pre-adult attractions ('*Cop*: What's yer name? *Gerry*: Les Morris. What's yours? *Cop*: Watch it. (to John) Yours? *Gerry*: (to John) Watchit –Yours. Funny name. *John*: Must be a Pom. *Cop*: Name? *John*: Smith ... Sir.') Similarly the ending's male-oriented double entendres (the police's command to John in bed with Sue to come out with his weapon; his reply that he's coming) have the same anti-authoritarian, very specifically youthful male aura.

However, it is hard not to see, especially with Gerry badly injured, possibly worse, a darkening of tone from about halfway through the film. Rifts develop between the male couple, with Gerry's behaviour growing more extreme, his shifts of identity more bizarre, while John's difference and part-alienation from Gerry (in part, it seems, arising from shame at accepting a crude bet that Gerry would 'be hanging out of' Shirl by the time they reach Wanganui) is dramatized as he seeks moments of solitary meditation. John also makes repeated variations on the phrase 'You're getting paranoid, Gerry'. The fumes of dope smoking, signalling counter-cultural liberations, give way to darker intimations. Both John and even the manically active Gerry have strange lapses where energy and invention splutter down to nothing. After racing to catch the ferry along a train platform, Gerry suddenly stops dead, and when Shirl asks 'What's wrong, Blondini?', replies 'I'm Gerry Austin'. He recovers his Blondini nerve, but later, going missing, is found by John sitting uncharacteristically alone, murmuring 'I'm gonna die', then shouting 'We're gonna crap out'. John's disquisition to him on the small causing the large – the atom bomb needing TNT, the TNT needing explosives, explosives needing a little detonator, a detonator working from a torch battery – appears designed to convince an existentially stricken Gerry that he is not totally insignificant behind the façade of his disguises. John suffers a comparable moment. Almost at journey's end, as he sees the Invercargill cemetery roadblock, he stops, slumps exhausted, apparently defeated, and it is only the sharpshooter's shots that galvanize him. Snout (John Bach), the unhinged hippie and Blondini Gang groupie, is a wholly negative variant of Gerry, even superstitiously attached to the car flags that have talismanic meaning for his hero. Affirmation of the protagonists' counter-cultural inclinations gives way, via Snout, to critique, or at least ambivalence. When John drives into the police trap, a youngish anti-establishment figure needles a young marksman with the questions 'First kill, asshole?' and 'Ya gonna splutter his brains all over the car, son?' and eventually frightens, with his 'Ready, aim [and very loud] FIRE', the novice into a barrage of shots which luckily hit the car rather than John. This happens where the audience is clearly positioned to be with John; indeed, as John drives away, he is surrounded admiringly by an on-screen audience, doubling for the off-screen one, who contrive to delay pursuit. Compare this with the other surrogate audience, at the end, who applaud when John appears naked. But, contradicting this, the shooting turns their outlaw identification back on the audience as the mocker's tirade turns out to be not only self-indulgent but also nearly fatal. Up to a point, you can see this as a synecdoche of the film's trajectory – the running down of the wild impulses that start the journey, the loss of confidence and energy, the sense that time, whether chronological or cultural, is running out on the heroes (as indeed it does for the cinematic outlaws in *Bonnie and Clyde, Butch Cassidy and the Sundance Kid* and *The Wild Bunch*, three films that Murphy's broadly alludes to).

Though the film centres on the male couple, John's ultimate goal is reconciliation with Sue, while for a significant part of their journey he and Gerry are accompanied by Shirl. Further, a trail of largely unprepossessing females is also scattered through the film. Leslie Morris is a 'snotty bitch'; Sue's sister is unpleasantly uptight; a girl Gerry sleeps with, 'that bitch I screwed in Auckland', steals his money; Ian Watkin, driving the yellow mini the police confuse with the gang's, has an all but invisible wife, submerged beneath squalling children; a girl at a party in Wellington gets her Marx Brothers mixed up as she calls Gerry 'Harpo' and makes him an offer that coincides with, or even provokes, his vomiting. The trio's Christchurch mini-tour takes in a local celebrity, 'the Wizard', a well-known public raver, who continues the largely misogynistic emphasis with his vision of wives spending husbands' hard-earned money and the fall of man heralding the rise of woman. Perhaps this is all too much, a tipping over from male-centredness into parody and critique. Two later instances support this. In the couple of the traffic cop, who drives into the river chasing the heroes, and his girlfriend, who falls in with his combining of sex with his authoritarian role in a scenario in which she has to offer herself in order to escape a ticket, it is the male who comes off worst, and Snout's catatonic woman, reduced to absolute speechlessness, parodies the counter-culture's less-than-progressive role for women. Actually, most of the male characters encountered, particularly the law enforcers, Snout, and Ian Watkin as the overweight family-harassed suburban father, hardly amount to a phalanx of desirable masculinity to set up against the women The heroes' problem seems to be that the women are apprehended as part of the forces of authority, their sexual attraction dragging the heroes into a domesticity they are trying to escape (but not wholly so with John, whose journey to freedom is paradoxically aimed at the recovery of a not too domesticated domesticity, while even Gerry after Shirl leaves seems to – fatally? –soften and begin to miss her). Shirl disappears from the narrative when she is arrested, ironically for a bigger crime than the men ever commit, along with her clutter of contradictory 'female' attributes – independent yet conventional, sexually voracious yet prudish, free spirited yet domestic, garrulously good-hearted but airheaded. Ludicrous though she often is, she has an energy that makes her more than a butt of male jokes, that suggests, with the non-closure of her disappearance, that she may reappear in other, perhaps less put-downable guises in later films. Sue, on the other hand, is more simply drawn: there are multiple indications that her walking out on John is aimed to get from him the commitment he has been unable to give, at least until the closing moments. Once his epic journey with its implicit wordless declarations ends, she seems happy to embrace him without change, though John has shown signs of internal reordering that suggest growing commitment – which the film ends by trying to mask, in its slightly deceptive ending of masculine fantasies of the sexy, all-forgiving, all-obliging female greeting her hero.

Smash Palace

A slowly panning long shot across a pre-dawn mountain landscape finds car headlights. A series of shots in the lightening dawn alternate between the car travelling on an empty road and the unknown driver's perspective. Eventually, the car unaccountably wanders across the road and crashes. Narratively, the scene introduces Al (Bruno Lawrence), his wife Jacqui (Anna Jemison), daughter Georgy (Greer Robson), and 'Smash Palace' itself, through Ray's phone call reporting the crash. But, unexplained, de-individualized – we never see the driver, never know if the accident was fatal – it also functions as a prefiguring metaphor for the narrative's emotional smash-ups, while suggesting through its opaqueness something of the inscrutability of Al's self-destructive trajectory. The connection is consolidated by the dissolve from the wreck to a close-up of Al and Jacqui standing happily in front of a racing car, revealed to be a photograph of better times as the camera descends to the phone ringing by the bed. Notably, the division of shots in the crash sequence – four of them from an objective viewpoint, with the car driving towards a fixed roadside camera position, three of them pinned to the unseen driver's subjective view of the road ahead – reproduces in miniature the film's larger subjective–objective tension, dividing the viewer between identification with the disintegrating male hero and a more detached critical view of him, abetted by the film's lesser but still real invitations to identify with his wife and child.

Living in a small central North Island town, Al Shaw runs a car wreck business, inherited from his father, with his French wife Jacqui. Only their young daughter, Georgy, seems to hold them together. Jacqui's nationality sets up European/antipodean differences on top of manifest others. Al spends his time restoring cars and getting his racing car ready for competition, while Jacqui, for all her efficiency in keeping the business's paperwork going, longs to move and unavailingly tries to push Al into selling up. Tensions flare, to the point of violence, and eventually Jacqui gets involved with Al's best mate, one of the town's policemen, Ray (Keith Aberdein). Al, more fixated on contact with Georgy than reconciling with his wife, becomes more violently demanding, a situation that escalates after Jacqui takes out an order effectively separating him from his daughter. Al eventually cracks (Figure 14). Abducting Georgy, he goes bush with her, staging their deaths by pushing his van into the river, hoping for a few weeks together before the idyll ends. But Georgy falls sick, and when he demands medicine from a pharmacy at gunpoint, he is recognized. Taking the shop girl hostage, he holes up with her and Georgy in Smash Palace, surrounded by armed police. Jacqui tries to reason with him, even telling him (we cannot know if this is true) that she still loves him and will go with him to Australia to start again, presumably after his prison sentence. Al shows no interest, but lets Georgy go in return for Ray coming in. When Ray arrives, Al traps him with a wire noose attached to his gun, then drives out with Ray hostage, shadowed by the massed sharpshooters. He parks on the railway line, where earlier in the film he frightened Jacqui by stopping the car momentarily. A train bears down, seemingly about to crash into them. Al, however, knows it will switch tracks at the last moment and miss them. Ray emotes 'You fuckin' bastard', while Al laughs hysterically as the film ends.

If *Goodbye Pork Pie* is a New Zealand inflection of the American buddy and road movies, *Smash Palace* is a local variant on full-blown male melodrama, crossed with the marriage-break, child-custody struggle narrative found contemporaneously in American films like *Kramer versus Kramer* (Benton, 1979) and *Shoot The Moon* (Parker, 1982). The subgenre of male melodrama has been defined as having two basic formulations: a positive one in which a troubled protagonist eventually graduates to the social roles and obligations of manhood, and a tragic variant in which a hero, of great potential, resists the roles and obligations he inherits, but in doing so is caught in his own contradictions and destroys himself in the process.[37] Gilliat's *The Rake's Progress* (1946) and Rafelson's *Five Easy Pieces* (1970) are representative British and American prototypes of the latter, starring Rex Harrison and Jack Nicholson respectively, two undoubtedly charismatic heroes, who reject their patriarchal inheritance, without, however, abandoning many of its attitudes, especially in personal life. Al compares very revealingly with them. Both Vivian and Bobby, while resisting their social destiny, exert their powers both on the cinema audiences and the film's internal audiences, in particular the women characters, fascinated by their non-commitment and mobility. Notably restless, resisting literal geographical, as well as social and marital placement, assailed by historical pressures rendering them growingly redundant, they remain perversely heroic in their refusal to conform.

Living white males 149

13. Requiem for a heroic fuckwit: Al (Bruno Lawrence) in a grotesque variant of the bonds of homosocial mateship with Ray (Keith Aberdein) in Roger Donaldson's male melodrama, *Smash Palace* (1982).

With Vivian these pressures are primarily those of class changes signalling the end of the privileged position that underwrote his lifestyle. With Bobby, as with many of Jack Nicholson's key roles, the pressures are socio-sexual: the decline of an automatic male hegemony which he resists, particularly in his attachment to redneck culture, which, given his complex make-up, he at the same time despises. Both heroes, in finding no place for their talents, are tragic, examples of masculine potential wasted; but in their refusal of the mediocre, their commitment to the self and its demands, their assertions of a threatened masculinity, they are more charismatic than the lesser figures around them.

In some respects Al is similar to Vivian and Bobby – like theirs, his destruction is self-imposed and in some sense deserved, yet because of the waste of powers involved, something to be mourned. In other respects, inflected by the particulars of New Zealand history and society, he is fascinatingly different. First, through Bruno Lawrence's presence, Al is redolent of a virility that broods over the narrative, but unlike Vivian and Robert he exhibits no interest in women. When Tiny, the older worker at Smash Palace, suggests that he should find another woman, Al replies 'The only lady I'm interested in happens to be seven years old'. A lingering manifestation of the hero's charisma for women in the narrative is preserved in Jacqui's attempts to keep the hopeless marriage going (noticeably, she touches Al a number of times, whereas Al never touches her), and in her later telling Al during the siege that she still loves him, which could be true, if increasingly unlikely. The one sexual intimacy between Al and Jacqui – though intimacy is hardly the word – comes after a physical fight when he has intercourse with her as she lies on the bed weeping. The scene, much debated by early New Zealand feminist critics, has been called a rape, for instance by Helen Martin,[38] which it is surely not, since Jacqui makes no protest, physical or verbal, but it is nonetheless ugly, one-sided, and rather pathetic too in dramatizing Al's implicit crude belief that sex is all that Jacqui misses.

Is it the film's intuitive realization that the mythic New Zealand male ought to be so portrayed, stunned by the difficulties of heterosexual relationships? Jacqui is attractive and intelligent, but Al tells Ray that he is not even sure he wants to try to do anything about their crumbling relationship, elsewhere talking about marriage as being like 'The Golden Kiwi' lottery. The only time he shows even minimal closeness is when he calls her to look at Georgy snorkelling in the bath, but significantly it is the daughter who mediates this brief closeness. Unlike Vivian and Bobby and their analogues, Al makes no escape to other women, instead closing in on himself and a masculinized world excluding women, other than his daughter, mainly centred around his archetypically laconic relationship with Ray.

While both Vivian and Bobby flee fatherhood, Al not only has a daughter, but embraces fatherhood at the expense of any other roles with females. Eschewing women, embracing paternity, Al displays another difference in that, whereas Vivian and Bobby revolt against their fathers, Al is unambivalently attached to his, seemingly planning to remain for ever in the car salvage business that his dead father founded, and where the presence of the grey-haired Tiny, the older worker, is a constant reminder of his presence. This attachment to the paternal site also means that unlike the other two, Al, except for his car racing, is connected with stasis, refusing to countenance Jacqui's desire to move to the city, and even his car racing has overtones of stasis in its repetitively circular laps. 'Smash Palace', first seen in an overhead shot, spreading over seemingly unending acres, as Al's place of definition collects symbolic properties to itself, suggesting not only broken relationships but a fracturing maleness, that the image, if not always the film's sympathies, suggests as regressive, an ossuary of masculinity in retreat.

Al's attachment to his daughter Georgy, characterized in tender moments like their bedtime word game, is one of the film's most moving elements. Even when, half-crazed, he interrupts Jacqui's, Ray's and Georgy's takeaway at gunpoint, Al remembers to include teddy when ordering Georgy to the van, and his improvisation of a birthday tea in the bush cabin with candles on a pie, party hats made out of newspaper, and a present of a knife just like his own (it is, of course, his own), a touching inflection of antipodean do-it-yourself ingenuity, creates powerful sympathies which sustain identification with him throughout. However, his devotion to Georgy has more questionable characteristics. When Georgy rides back to Smash Palace in Ray's police car, Al, driving ahead, watches the pair through his side mirror, very darkly, as if resenting the child's interest in any one else. Another scene, where she pedals her miniature racing car past bath time, shows Jacqui, as she yells at her to come in, pushed into the crew culture's view of the wife–mother as denying and disciplining parent (the other side of the archetype of 'Mother, pal and sweetheart' celebrated by the ancient country singer at the small town social), enforcing social conformities, which is generally how Al sees her (complaining about her making him speak with the mayor and her 'hoity toity ways'). It is also clear that Al's closeness to his daughter, loving though it is, is highly male-oriented, seemingly designed to turn the female into a clone of himself (sitting in the racing car's cockpit, racing her miniature car, helping him with his car tools, going rabbit shooting – though she is pleased that her shot misses), a tendency underlined by his occasional masculinizing of the females' names to 'Jack' and 'George'. Another overriding suggestion is that instead of a dual relationship with his wife and daughter, he has replaced the former with the latter, a relationship with burdens of care, but with a female at her least demanding, most adoring, with none of the complexities of maturity and equality demanded of him. In two fleeting moments of subjective entry into Al's mind when he is in the prison cell, Al thinks of Jacqui twice, but significantly only at his father's funeral, and then when giving birth to Georgy (in graphic medical film footage). In the first fragment, Al shields a pregnant Jacqui from view with his jacket as she urinates among the gravestones, in the second the bloodied child emerges, both moments not only placing Jacqui as secondary to the father and daughter, but associating her with extreme images of bodily process – pissing, shouting with pain, a bloody birth chamber – all of which suggests a fear of female impingement, which Jacqui's elegance and refinement, as embodied in the little shrine to femininity with its miniature vase of flowers she keeps amidst the masculine clutter of Smash Palace, can do little to diminish. However, students of mine have read both scenes more positively, finding Al's sheltering of Jacqui with his jacket a close and chivalrous gesture, suggesting positive things about their past, and his presence in the childbearing scene unexpected and positive. Perhaps the two views co-exist.

The film, we are not allowed to forget, is not just Al's tragedy, but Jacqui's and Georgy's, its ending centred on the numbed child's observation of the siege from behind the backseat window of the car, as when earlier she responds panickingly to her parents' fighting, switching her torch on and off in shocked reflex. Unlike some of the female characters in the new industry's films, Jacqui suggests complexity, possessing an autonomy of depiction outside Al's view of her in a series of scenes: looking pensively in the bathroom mirror after returning from the party, teaching French at school, letting loose with exaggerated playfulness her rather hysterically pent-up sexiness in scenes with Ray, with the narrative emphases never suggesting, even where she reacts angrily, occasionally spitefully, that the impasse is her fault. However, Al is the centre, raising the question why audiences (female as well as male, 'progressive' as well as 'conservative' in gender politics), might remain attached to him despite his violence and descent into near madness? Jacqui tells him at the end that she still loves him, that they can start again in Australia, though she may be just trying to quieten him. If the possibility that Jacqui may be telling the truth seems even remotely desirable, it is presumably because Al embodies virtues that draw the audience to him, and complicate feminist readings of the film, since they exist so interdependently with his vices. Even if we see him as the man regressively resisting feminizing demands (repeating/varying John's question and gesturing in *Pork Pie*, 'You want me to dance for you?' with 'You want I should juggle for you?), fighting for male centrality in the family and elsewhere, prosecuting an unarticulated, viscerally felt ideological rearguard action, he still (as Bruno Lawrence plays him) suggests not inconsiderable virtues, especially in his national and historical context. Thus he is his own man, independent, physical, practical, laconic, un-selfpitying, anti-authoritarian, humorous (freeing Rose, he reminds her that she still has time for her hair appointment): all qualities that New Zealanders like to think of themselves as possessing. Even at his most frightening, there are rough delicacies – as when he apologizes to Rose ('I'm sorry. I didn't mean to get you into this mess. I don't know what the hell I'm doing'), or self-deflating pungencies as he says to Ray in a situation where events have escalated beyond control 'You're a fuckwit, Ray, and I'm a fuckwit'.

There is a key scene where Al, trapped by the policeman Frank and his cronies and, forcibly stripped down to bare buttocks, is brutally beaten in front of a vengeful audience of both men and women. Frank believes (clearly wrongly given Al's lack of interest in women) that Al has slept with his girlfriend – an accusation Al seems happy not to rebut since it so obviously riles his enemy – so that the obvious motivation for the beating up is sexual jealousy. The scene, however, with its violent, mocking internal audience, much larger than one would expect, surely not all policemen in mufti, with women as well as men gloatingly spectating (can Al really have alienated so many?) seems motivated by more than this, seems a revenge for the incident (reminiscent of many in *Pork Pie*) where Al out-speeds a pursuing cop, which, unremarkable in itself, embodies Al's laconic anti-authoritarianism, provoking an extreme reaction from those flouted. Frank, whatever his other motives, explicitly administers the beating as the power of the disregarded law. Whereas the internal audiences in *Pork Pie* applaud John, this one is bent on punishment, and the moment where the hero's buttocks are stripped, rhyming with his removal of Jacqui's pants in their unmutual sex scene, suggest that the punishment enacted may be for that as well. However, the scene's dynamics, the mob attacking the single individual, presumably shifts the cinema audience's sympathies to Al. This moment, in which Al is the largely innocent victim, not only encapsulates dramatically a tension that runs through much New Zealand cinema of this period, between anti-authoritarianism and conformity, but also – more emotively than logically – suggests him as the main plot's victim as well. Here it is pertinent to remember that not only *Smash Palace*, but *Sleeping Dogs*, *Goodbye Pork Pie* and *Bad Blood* end with protagonists surrounded by armed policemen: Smith and Bullen hunted down by the security forces in *Sleeping Dogs*, and John surrounded in Sue's sister's house in *Pork Pie*. These moments stage in hyperbolic terms the clash of conformity with non-conformity (though that non-conformity has conservative, even regressive elements) and, in a displaced way, the besieging of masculinist culture.

Stripped forcibly and humiliatingly here, Al voluntarily strips himself naked in a confrontation with Jacqui and Ray. This full-frontal nakedness, varied in two other moments in *The Quiet Earth*, particularly associated with Lawrence as an actor, plays a performative subtext, suggesting the actor's stripping away of protective coverings. But at the same time, Al's baring of himself to Jacqui and Ray has a calculating theatricality that parallels the more baroque, more comically ornate roles of Jack Nicholson in the American cinema through the

1970s and 1980s. Both actors in different ways encapsulate a maleness under pressure, flawed and self-tormenting in its refusal to abandon aspects of a deeply felt masculinity without struggle, but charismatic enough to make audiences (even many female audiences) feel that though they may want change, there is much they want preserved.

Utu

The original print of *Utu* (1983) begins like David Lean's epics *Lawrence of Arabia* (1962) and *Doctor Zhivago* (1965) with an orchestral overture over an imageless screen. This sonic trope asserts a grandeur that risks, only to override, accusations of the grandiose, announcing the category 'epic', a viewing event claiming significance enough for a prelude taking up nearly two minutes of potential image time. It also boldly announces comparison with the international epics above, in ambition if not budget.

As suggested by Pauline Kael's *New Yorker* review, which brought the film and Murphy to an international attention that his later career largely disappointed, this was an epic crossed by 'a deracinated kind of hip lyricism', more febrile, less monumental than its predecessors.[39] The influences suggested by Kael and others – Kurosawa's *Throne of Blood*, which also shares an intertextuality with *Macbeth*, Rocha's *Antonio das Mortes*, and revisionist and 'Vietnam' westerns such as *Soldier Blue* (Nelson, 1974) and *Little Big Man* (Penn, 1970) – testify to the film's range, extended further in the ferocity of the fighting, the numerous past/present parallels introduced through conscious anachronisms, the critical inspection of colonialism, and in characteristic moments of grotesque destabilizing humour – for example, when one of Te Wheke's followers dips his head in a flour bag and pretends to be a Pākehā, or when Te Wheke's men launch a piano out of the upstairs window while their leader quietly chuckles over a copy of *Macbeth*.

While the Vietnam westerns' influence is immediately visible in the cavalry attack on Te Wheke's village, *Utu*'s narrative can, from a local perspective, most fundamentally be seen as rewriting its native predecessors – Hayward's New Zealand epics *The Te Kooti Trail* and the two versions of *Rewi's Last Stand* – in a kind of respectfully disrespectful deconstruction. Like the earlier films, *Utu* seeks a rapprochement of the warring indigenous and settler populations, though by the 1980s the integrationist ideal of 'the slowly blending New Zealanders' (the second *Rewi*'s epigraph) was in crisis, with not wholly implausible scenarios of impending racial violence leading to government action, most notably retrospective powers for the Waitangi Tribunal

(1985) and official-language status for Māori (1987). The later film, facing different circumstances, is hyper-aware of growing polarizations, Māori activism, and even separatism. Speaking from the pulpit of a hidden army that could muster 20,000 men on the streets of Auckland in an hour, Te Wheke obviously addresses the present as much as the past. In the second *Rewi's Last Stand*, when the whites leave the Morgans' mission, the Māori there are briefly presented as unreadable, their language untranslated into subtitles, though their facial mokos, their rifles and an axe being whetted, all suggest the minatory. In *Utu* the church scene – centred on Te Wheke's murder of the Reverend Johns – with its almost wholly Māori congregation, is a more prolonged, subtler version of such unreadability, a motif present throughout the film, for instance when Williamson (Bruno Lawrence) calls out to Wiremu (Wi Kuki Kā), 'How do we know you're not one of them?' [that is, Te Wheke's men], and Wiremu replies 'You don't'. As the congregation, dressed in Victorian Sunday best, sit impassively while the Reverend rails against the forces of darkness, the camera dwells on two males whose opaque looks raise possibilities that they know of Te Wheke's plans. Even when Te Wheke decapitates the Reverend and preaches with the severed head in front of him, the congregation's reaction is inscrutable. Here, if Te Wheke's violence is associated beyond its historical context with feared extremes of 1980s Māori radicalism, the degree to which it has caught hold of the congregation/population is left disturbingly unclear.

Any gesture to bicultural ideals taking over from an integrationism discredited as effectively meaning Pākehā domination, needed to avoid simplistic assertions, and the film was careful with its rhetoric of rapprochement as it rewrote Hayward for the present. (Figure 15) Like Te Kooti, the fictional Te Wheke – no longer the shadowy figure of *The Te Kooti Trail* but moved into the foreground, his conversion to violence against the settlers the central material of the film's first phase – begins a campaign of utu (revenge) instigated by an apparent military blunder which leaves his village destroyed and relatives massacred. Still wearing elements of his lance corporal's uniform – he has been fighting as a kūpapa on the Pākehā side – he takes to the bush with a small guerrilla force. The army pursuing him, making the narrative a loose reworking of much of the central action of *The Te Kooti Trail*, is at this late date in the wars no longer British but a mixture of colonial troops and Māori kūpapa (fighting tribal enemies under white command; like Lieutenant Gilbert Mair's Arawa Flying Column in *The Te Kooti Trail*). It is, however, commanded by Colonel Elliot (Tim Elliot), a British officer against whom Te Wheke has sworn particular utu, as bearing responsibility for the massacre, presumably remaining to keep some British overlooking of the action. Elliot – conservative, arrogant, racist and rather too patly homosexual to boot (we see him in bed with a young Māori servant) – contrasts with the younger officer Captain Scott (Kelly Johnson): New Zealand born, like Mair in *The Te Kooti Trail* and Ropata in *Rewi 2* a Māori speaker, and forward looking in his desire both to apply guerrilla fighting methods and to make friendships with the kūpapa. The celebration of the colonial as distinct from British forces in Hayward's portrayal of characters like Mair and Jackson and the famous Von Tempsky (in *Rewi 1*) is here given a further emphasis as, in a move which has been criticized for its untruthfulness, the British 'outsider' is made more racist than the colonials,[40] whereas there is evidence that the reverse was the opposite, though in fact Cowan provided a precedent when he blamed 'the Imperials' for various lapses from military discipline.[41] When Scott asks Wiremu which side he is on, Wiremu's reply is 'The same side as you, sir, I was born here too', constructing a rhetorical resolution of local enmities against an interloping third party (over the historical evidence that later Māori traditionally appealed to the British Crown over the heads of the settlers).

14. Director Geoff Murphy, the key figure of the early post-1977 industry, on set with kūpapa soldiers in his reworking of Hayward's New Zealand Wars epics, *Utu* (1983).

A third Pākehā, Williamson, wavers in his sanity after his wife is killed in Te Wheke's raid on his farmhouse, and also pursues Te Wheke, for personal utu, independent of the army. Hayward staged intimate Pākehā/Māori relations in all three of his films – most obviously the love plot in *Rewi 2*, the cosy interracial marriage in *The Te Kooti Trail*, and the homosocial bond between Mair and Taranahi in the latter – but in *The Te Kooti Trail* Mair's kūpapa are, except for Taranahi, faceless. *Utu*, however, foregrounds relations between kūpapa and whites, Scott with both Henare (Faenza Reuben) – who decides to join Te Wheke, but is killed before he can – and Wiremu, eventually revealed as Te Wheke's brother. The three pursuing whites, and the brothers Te Wheke on opposite sides, are joined by two Māori female characters: Matu (Merata Mita), whose wounded cousin is killed by Te Wheke when he slows the retreat, and Kura (Tania Bristowe), who has relationships with both Scott and Henare, and, having escaped execution by the army, becomes another of Te Wheke's victims when he mistakenly thinks she has betrayed him. Again *Utu* reworks the tradition it inherits: Kura may, like Ariana, Peti and Monika, eventually be a victim, but she is a character reconceived through 1980s feminism. Wiremu, played with Wi Kuki Kā's mixture of opaqueness and thoughtful gravitas, is impressively bicultural, in a way only hinted at in Hayward, with his command of French and his prowess at chess (reminiscent of Jimmy Tutaki reading Conrad in Devanny's *The Butcher Shop*), leaving, nonetheless, his command of Māori ritual and knowledge undiminished. These things seem to run in the family, judging by his brother's interest in *Macbeth*: in terms of modern parallels perhaps the brothers make us think of the emerging Māori graduates and intellectuals of the 1980s. At any rate, Wiremu is constructed very differently from the friendly but limited portraits of Māori biculturality in Hayward. While various of the characters – Scott and Henare (with Scott actually visiting his dead friend's tangi [funeral]), Scott and Wiremu, Williamson and Horace – form cross-cultural relationships, the difficulty of these is stressed, lightly in the scene where Scott and Henare contrast Māori and Pākehā bewilderment at each others' senses of humour, more seriously when Scott's visit to Henare's tangi is disapproved of by most of the Māori there.

Finally captured, Te Wheke stands trial with Scott in charge. At the guilty verdict, Matu, Williamson and Scott himself claim the right of personal utu in shooting him. At this moment Wiremu reveals himself as Te Wheke's brother and, as the only one present without personal motives, takes the role of executioner upon himself. This he does with Te Wheke's compliance, with utu now taking on its various other extended meanings of balance, compensation and reciprocation, with the ending, as Martin Blythe explicates it, suggesting a future of workable race relations, in which the blood sacrifice of various of the main characters blesses the future. For this to happen the two most extreme characters blocking reconciliation – representative of Pākehā racism and its obverse Māori extremism – are both 'executed' by Wiremu, Elliot the victim of purposeful 'friendly fire'.[42] This ending is comparable, for all its great difference of detail, to *The Te Kooti Trail*'s coda, where Mair writes his letter to the Arawa, except that, first, the situation is much more fraught in 1983 than in 1927, with the Māori no longer 'the smallest race' of the earlier film, but a growing, more politically assertive population with their own forms of intolerance matching Pākehā racism; and, second, that one of the main terms is reversed: it is no longer the Pākehā who is seen as the central figure (Mair at the end of *The Te Kooti Trail*, the Pākehā who loves Māori) but Wiremu, the Māori wholly at home in two cultures who is the paradigm: the Māori who loves Pākehā. What is also significant is that though the film has an interracial sexual relationship between Scott and Kura, it never assumes centrality, as if the film is conscious that the older narrative pattern of personal interracial sexual love as the fulcrum of interracial relations is insufficient and that a less private kind of symbolizing is needed.

Though some local critiques objected to the film's breaking of its careful historical reconstruction with blatant anachronisms, this is a deliberate strategy aimed at dramatizing past–present parallels. For instance, Te Wheke's extraordinary hairstyle and bricolage of clothing, shared by his followers, crosses late 1970s/early 1980s street-gang garb with the film's historical period, and even his receiving the full facial moko after declaring war on the Pākehā has a contemporary subtext of the urban revival of the moko as a mark of ethnicity and even threat. More unobtrusively dependent on audience inference is Wiremu's quizzical look when Scott, talking about his innovative Commando tactics, recommends them by saying that the Boers used them to repress the natives, a moment which crosses the past with recent memories of the anti-apartheid protests against the 1981 Springbok rugby tour, two years before the film.

Murphy's art tends to slightly camouflage its intelligence behind the more obvious characteristics of his method – the liking for fights, explosions (both compellingly handled in *Utu*), crude jokes (Gerry vomiting / cut to ketchup poured on fried eggs in *Goodbye Pork Pie*), a hard-to-shift sexism (the completely gratuitous shot up Lisa Eilbacher's skirt in *Never Say Die*), the assumption of a slightly hulking 'Good on yer, Mate' persona. But *Utu* is a film which deeply understands its place in New Zealand cinema, aspiring as it does to be the modern, ironic but respectful rewriting of Hayward's primary epics. Think, for instance, of the implications of that 'world upside down' shot through the Victorian photographer's lens near the later film's beginning. Murphy and his co-writer Keith Aberdein were also familiar with Hayward's source, James Cowan, even his less-known works. In one transmuted incident, Lieutenant Scott (Kelly Johnson) and his Māori soldier friend Henare (Faenza Reuben), enjoying a fishing expedition, joke about contrasting Māori and Pākehā senses of humour. Scott relates, as a Māori instance, an anecdote about Māori taking a British camp, where, finding a barrel of salted pork, they dig up two soldiers from fresh graves, mince them up and put the human flesh in the barrel, leaving it for the British reoccupiers to eat unknowingly. In taking this from Cowan's *Kimble Bent*,[43] the screenwriters acknowledge the tradition of Cowan and Hayward, but at a tangent, asserting through it their interest in the grotesque but revealing marginal, and also ensuring that the film's serious liberalism is not confused with ultra-cleansed pieties. They joke about cannibalism, a subject embarrassing to anxious white liberals, and in doing this the film announces that its sensitivity to cultural issues is not to be confused with the shallows of political ultra-correctness.

The second Cowan-derived incident is Wiremu's shooting of his brother, the final act of the film, the sacrificial killing that closes the cycle of utu. This derives directly from one of Cowan's later sketches.[44] In Cowan's account the murderer Wi Heretaunga is captured and an immediate 'log court-martial' is held. Like Te Wheke, Wi shows no fear of his captors. 'Wi sat by the fire warming himself. He taunted the gravediggers and boasted of the defeats his tribe had inflicted on the Arawa people in the olden days', spitting at the officer in charge and ostentatiously smoking. Various of his Māori enemies volunteer to shoot him for utu, just as Williamson, Matu and Scott do in the film. However, his nephew argues that if an Arawa shoots him it may cause tribal fighting, and that he himself, of high rank in the Urewera and Tuhoe tribes, should commit the act, just as Williamson, Scott and Matu press their claims, but give way to Wiremu. But the parallel is even more extended. In Cowan's anecdote the weapon the nephew uses is Mair's Westley-Richards Snider, given to him by a Scottish nobleman. Early in *Utu* Scott lays great emphasis on his rifle, a repeating Spencer Carbine, a weapon of great potency, gifted to him by an English aristocrat whose son he saved from drowning, and this is the weapon Wiremu shoot his brother with. This tracing of a source is not pedantic; it illustrates the screenwriters' ingenious search in the byways of New Zealand history, *Utu*'s intricate connection with both Hayward and Cowan, and finally the creative metamorphosis the anecdote, striking enough in the original, undergoes in the film. In the source the nephew says to his prisoner 'But for me you would have been slain by those plebeian people the Arawa'. But in Murphy's expansion interaction between prisoner and executioner goes far beyond hierarchical pride. The gun in Wiremu's ritual becomes a weapon fit to kill the tragic figure of Te Wheke, who – in the fierceness, but at times thoughtfulness and even humorousness, of Anzac Wallace's portrayal – constantly outspans the limits that ideologically over-sensitive criticism, concentrating on his savagery and inclined to overlook subtleties of performative effects, finds in his portrayal, justifying the tragic protagonist parallels drawn between him and Macbeth. 'This weapon is imbued with spirit. There is no greater gun in existence', Wiremu says, handing it for inspection to Te Wheke, by now the acceding victim-celebrant.

Discussing *Utu*, Roger Horrocks noted its failure to be comprehensively 'national', though coming closer to it than any other film.[45] In that his remark had the context of the newer heterogeneity of post-1970s New Zealand society, it is less a critique of faults in 'the remarkable *Utu*' than a recognition of the impossibility of any film successfully fulfilling the role it aspired to. Nevertheless, his point that 'ultimately the film attempted too much – even New Zealanders found it overloaded', could be expressed differently, and more positively. *Utu* remains a constantly rewatchable, renewable film precisely because of its ambitious 'overloading', because it mobilizes so many modes, so many competing discourses – historical re-creation, contemporary subtext, a 'parody' of Hayward that is both reverend and subversive. It is well known, as Horrocks notes and Gaylene Preston's documentary *The Making of Utu* (1982) demonstrates, that the film-making process encompassed sometimes enriching debate between Pākehā and Māori cast and crew, one of the factors producing a plurality which combines many of the fascinations of an open text with the satisfactions of more directly assimilable popular generic art.

The Quiet Earth

Murphy's last major film was *The Quiet Earth* (1985), adapted from Craig Harrison's novel.[46] A science-fiction narrative reflecting New Zealand's growing 1980s anti-nuclear feeling, the film's *donnée* is a secret American enterprise (echoing *Sleeping Dogs*' American presence), in which New Zealand is a junior, unconsulted partner, which misfires traumatically, wiping out the world's population, except for a very few who survive because they die from other causes at the precise moment of the disaster – Zac (Bruno Lawrence) committing suicide out of guilt at his scientific irresponsibility, Joanne (Alison Routledge) electrocuted by her hairdryer, and Api (for Āpirana, Peter Smith) drowned in a fight. The film's science may be imprecise but, clearly, atmospheres and relationships are more important than the science which enables them. So, while the action takes place suspensefully against the threatening recurrence of 'the effect', the film uses its dystopian premise to explore particularly New Zealand thematics, in a New Zealand now totally isolated rather than just distant from the rest of the globe, but not from its own history, which the survivors carry with them: another more literal version of what Murphy claimed about *Pork Pie*, that it proceeded as if New Zealand was 'the only place on earth'. Here the impressive telephoto lens filming of the Pacific sunrise opening the film has double connotations: on the one hand, a sinister resemblance to images of nuclear explosions, on the other, intimations of new dawns, new beginnings.

The first 35 minutes of *The Quiet Earth* is a tour de force of solo acting by Bruno Lawrence, seemingly the only human alive in New Zealand, maybe on earth. It is perfect casting, for Lawrence, the most celebrated New Zealand film actor on native terrain, made his reputation as the epitome of the populist New Zealand everyman: classless, demotic, more rough than cultured, but often with hidden sensitivities, and with a range capable of playing the guilt-stricken scientist Zac Hobson. This beginning – and, indeed, the ending, where Zac is translated to the beaches of a new world, a kind of cloned alternative universe New Zealand – acts out a hyperbolic literalization of the 'man alone' which the actor so often plays or alludes to, here a disoriented local Adam, an identification later reiterated in the mysterious sequence when, about to shoot himself, Zac is seemingly reborn, rising naked out of the sea. After his initial explorations of an eerily deserted Auckland, he passes through a series of metamorphoses in the enactment of his lonely freedom. Wearing a police hat, he drives a police car around the streets, enacting and/or parodying authority as he tannoys bureaucratic messages to the empty air; then, wearing the same police hat, he saunters down an empty rain-swept city street playing a saxophone; then he tours a huge shopping mall eating the best food and trying on the best clothes; he shifts, then, to a huge house redolent of colonial days, at one point carrying a large model moa off as a souvenir. We presumably take two points here: that the moa famously became extinct – a precursor, perhaps, of later human extinction – and that Zac, as the old-style 'white boss', as Api later aggressively calls him, is an endangered species. In the mall, images of the male as child, man and scientist are conflated in Zac's boy-like playing with a model train set, immediately succeeded by the fulfilment of the small boy's ambition of driving a real train – part innocent fantasy, but part dream of power and control through technology: 'playing God' as Joanne later puts it.

Other moments in the succeeding sequences are equally meaningful. Zac plays schizophrenic snooker with his split self, suggesting both a lostness without mateship and a critique of male competitiveness, since it is not enough, apparently, for Zac to play by himself: he needs the aggressive fulfilment of defeating a rival. When the film cuts to his new bedroom we notice there a female mannequin lifted from the shopping mall, seen previously accompanying him in the driver's cabin of the train, and whose slight oldfashionedness, encapsulated in her white ball dress, offers clues to regressive aspects of Zac's psyche. He moves to a wardrobe full of female garments, pressing one to his face, as if enveloping himself in the feminine. A cut finds him in front of a mirror, dressed in a woman's slip, a remarkable sight given Lawrence's persona of brooding virile male heterosexuality. Watching a work video of an American official telling New Zealanders that 'it is your country's duty' to support the research that has caused the disaster, a moment echoed in Ward's *The Navigator*, Zac blasts the TV set with his gun, and, announcing that it is time for him to 'take over', feverishly arranges a *son et lumière* in which images of Hitler, the Pope, the Queen and other figures of power form an audience which he addresses in Neronic purple toga from the balcony of the colonial residence. These moments present a concentrated paradigm of the whole sequence: the film-maker's and Lawrence's ability to suggest a destructive impulse for power, and, simultaneously, a self-aware condemnation of his propensities – for the point about Zac is that, though in one sense he is the film's fall guy, Governor Hobson (Zac's surname name recalls the colony's first Governor) getting his post-colonial comeuppance, critique never wholly banishes sympathy. In an unforgettable image Zac in his female slip walks on (given the Adamic circumstances, the aptly named) Eden Park, Auckland's premiere sports ground, its rugby goalposts still standing, surveyed by empty stands. In the last sequences of his absolute solitude, Zac, by now unhinged, invades the cathedral and shoots up Christ on the cross, before, as he destroys large amounts of the alternative deity of technology, whispering 'And now I am God'. So empowered, he embarks on an orgy of midtown destruction in a huge tractor, but stops in his tracks when he runs over a baby carriage. Though the carriage proves to be empty, his

15. The allegorical white male/white woman/Māori triangle at the centre of the later part of Murphy's *The Quiet Earth* (1985): left to right, Api (Pete Smith), Joanne (Alison Routledge) and Zac (Bruno Lawrence).

act's implications seem to drive him to suicide. As he puts the gun barrel in his mouth, he is distracted by an explosion. In the virtuosic moment mentioned above, he rises from the sea, and runs along the beach, presumably understood to have rejected both godlike fantasies and suicide. He has certainly decided to live, since, recalling Adam as the first gardener, he visits a gardening centre, emerging with multiple gardening tools. It is in the next shot, as he sits at his computer, that Joanne (Alison Routledge) enters and his man-aloneness – at least as a literal state – ends.

This long sequence is cunningly constructed, not least in the way the absence of dialogue is compensated for by multiple monologic substitutes – Zac talking to himself, to an imagined double in the snooker game, broadcasting messages and listening to the playback, talking to the computer, to his boss Perrin's corpse, reacting to the American video, orating as Emperor to his audience of effigies, and so on. It is also elaborately constructed thematically to exhibit Zac as Every (Pākehā) man passing through a series of episodes revealing the (representative) structures of his psyche, as he teeters on the edge of insanity, a range of extreme positions exposing both his authoritarianism and his conscience-stricken realization of it. The other foregrounded motif is Zac's wearing of female dress. Is this simply a response to his being absolutely deprived of the feminine? Does it connote the Man Alone's narcissism: the taking of himself as psychic lover? Might it, in line with his assumption of godlike powers, suggest the desire to turn himself into some sort of hermaphroditic deity? Does it, in a more socially bound way, suggest the rejection of a hyper-phallic trajectory and a taking on of feminine elements alongside the masculine? The film, too rightly jealous of the power of its images to dissipate them through reductive explanation, leaves them undeciphered, but we may well feel that there is an over-determination at work in which the various meanings suggested above all intersect.

The Quiet Earth's second part is shaped around Zac's discovery that he is not alone, but has inherited New Zealand with two other survivors: a young woman, Joanne, and a Māori, Api. The allegorical dimension is hard to miss: previously dominant white male encounters in radically changed circumstances the previously subdominant portions of the population, woman and Māori. As Zac and Joanne dance to Api's piano playing, when they are staying at Api's marae, Joanne asks him to sing another song. They follow Api in singing a version of 'Auld Lang Syne' in which, significantly, the 'should' in 'Should old acquaintance be forgot' is replaced by the imperative 'Let', changing the meaning of the famous words from a plea to preserve past relations to something paraphrasable as 'Forget the past structure of relationships in this new future-present'. In Harrison's interesting but incoherent novel Zac's relationship with Api is prominent, ending in warfare in which Jack (Zac's prototype) kills him, but Joanne is wholly the film's invention. In the novel both Api and Jack (Zac) are much more unhinged: Api having committed atrocities in Vietnam, and Jack full of murderous impulses. In the film, material is more economically and significantly deployed around primary themes. Even the low-budget special effects representing the tremors of the looming repetition of 'the effect' occur in ways that create a metaphoric relation between the catastrophe and the tensions faced by Zac (the social world shaken up, its structures loosened). In one case tremors occur as Zac contemplates a reproduction of Ingres' painting 'Le Bain Turc', full of naked odalisques owned by an unseen sultan. In another it is the carved Māori heads in Api's marae that shudder minatorily as if to register racial, as the earlier had enacted sexual, disturbances. The first phase of the film's second part is thus dominated by a couple (Zac and Joanne), the second by a triangle (Zac, Joanne and Api). Api's arrival disrupts Zac and Joanne's love affair and creates sexual and symbolic tensions, struggle for dominance, struggle for the woman (whom it has been suggested might be seen as the body of a contested New Zealand).[47] In one sequence, Zac, convinced that they must hurry north, instructs Api that they must abandon their temporary home in his marae. Delivered with a certain condescension, this leads to Api's outburst ('Honky, haven't you noticed things have changed around here. The White Boss went with the rest of them. There's just you and me now'). Though Joanne condemns both men for the apparently male presumption of playing God, Zac has obviously been the more culpable, and though she talks of caring for all three of them, it is Api she turns to sexually. After a brief explosion of anger directed at Api, Zac's resentment turns to philosophical acceptance, taking on shades of the semi-mystical feeling the other two are inclined to, when he tells Joanne that he has imagined that Api and she are his special guardians and that he feels that she and Api have known each other in the past.

Faced with evidence of an imminent further catastrophe, Zac commits suicide by driving an explosives laden truck into the research centre in an attempt to pre-empt it. After the explosion we see him, this time fully clothed, on the beach in what is another universe (clear from the overlooking Saturn-like planet). We presumably infer that his explosion has caused, rather than prevented, a new effect, which, as in the first instance, because Zac dies as it happens, displaces him to a parallel world. This ending raises but does not answer associated questions. Has Zac saved the lives of Api and Joanne so that they can become the bicultural Adam and Eve of a new dispensation, removing himself, incorrigibly committed to older ways, from the equation? Or has he extinguished the other two (who were not dying at the moment of the effect) and, by accident, or even, perhaps by design, destroyed them and saved himself?

Though in precis the film might appear a rather foursquare allegory in which the new order replaces the old, as experienced it is much more complex than that. If Zac is presented as highly flawed, at the same time, invested with Bruno Lawrence's charisma, he is more compelling than the other two. Conversely, Joanne and Api, and their relationship, are presented in such a way that it is made difficult to see them, despite their symbolic status, as superior to Zac. Joanne is played by the china-doll-like Alison Routledge, whose immature looks form a major part of her persona. Though she criticizes both male characters for 'playing God' in a recognizably 1980s feminist accusation, the psychobabble she shares with her predecessor Shirl in *Pork Pie* makes it hard to take her seriously at times, just as her super-aggressive driving and dangerous shooting off of a rifle to end a quarrel between the men somewhat undermines her moral position as whole-earth peacemaker. And her parodically feminine 'death' through her hairdryer accident hardly adds to her gravitas. Api likewise does not quite fit the positive mould the film looks to have designed for him. Though his war crimes in the novel have no place in the film, he retains an aura of violence from his eruption into the narrative, all black leather, balaclava and weapons, despite other elements that plot him as positive: like his Māori religious beliefs, which conflict with Zac's rationalism, but are more appealing to Joanne, as suggested when she watches him chanting at his mother's grave. It certainly is a feature of Murphy's films that he finds it difficult to draw women to be taken seriously on the intellectual plane, which might account for some of the more blatant contradictions in Joanne: feminist and airhead. Whatever the cause of the contradictions in Joanne and Api, their existence, alongside Zac's, turn the film from a simple allegory into a complex meditation on the faults as well as virtues of the three characters and the larger constituencies they represent.

Six important films

Solo, Tony Williams, 1977; *Bad Blood*, Mike Newell, 1982; *Heart of the Stag*, Michael Firth, 1984; *Constance*, Bruce Morrison, 1984; *Trial Run*, Melanie Read, 1984; *Mr Wrong*, Gaylene Preston, 1985

Bad Blood

While overseas film-makers have made significant films within the contemporary Australian cinema, so much so that O'Regan can say that their non-Australian imaginings became 'ours',[48] this is hardly so in the New Zealand cinema. To compare Nicolas Roeg's *Walkabout*, or *The Overlanders* (Harry Watt) with Ken Annakin's *The Seekers* (1954), or David Hemmings' *Race for the Yankee Zephyr* (1982) is to compare films of different orders of achievement. Earlier works such as Beaumont Smith's *The Adventures of Algy* and Pauli's *Under the Southern Cross* could be said to be imaginatively 'ours', at least for the minority who have seen them, but the only later foreign-directed film of which that claim could be made – apart from Alan Clayton's *Old Scores* (1991) and, perhaps, Gordon's *Her Majesty* (2004, see part 6) – is Mike Newell's *Bad Blood*.

Newell, whose later work includes *Four Weddings and a Funeral* and *Donnie Brasco*, made *Bad Blood* as a Southern Pictures (Southern Television, UK)/Film Commission co-production. With an all New Zealand cast (apart from the Australians Jack Thompson and Carol Burns) and an expatriate writer, *Bad Blood* is based on one of the great true-life crimes of New Zealand folk memory: the killing of twelve policemen and civilians by a farmer, Stan Graham, in the small West Coast town of Koiterangi, resulting in his being shot to death after a huge twelve-day manhunt. Lawrence Jones has outlined the largely sympathetic response to Graham as folk hero-villain, in a ballad 'The Hero of the Coast', three minor novels, a television documentary (1974) and Howard Willis's book on which the film was based. Jones saw this recycling embodying a change in the 'Man Alone' motif, from early to later uses where he [the Man Alone] was 'not a hero affirming society's values and dreams, but rather a victim of the puritan and narrowly materialistic society ... a society whose fears were made manifest by the depression'.[49]

In the line of films constituting a 'cinema of unease', *Bad Blood* occupies a paramount place. Jones's comment – that when the mob burn down the Grahams' house as the band plays 'Keep the Home Fires Burning', 'All the resentment against puritanical, conformist, provincial New Zealand that lies behind so much of the literature of the 1930s and 1940s is provoked',[50] identifies a primary strain in the film, where even the West Coast climate, cloud-shrouded hills and constant rain seems a metaphor for the oppressive social scene. The war background seems to release frustration in a near paroxysm of excitement in a strange scene where Stan and his wife, accompanied by their children, do night-time shooting practice, dancing and singing to 'Ten Green Bottles', as if the bottles represented not just German soldiers, but targets nearer home. While generally emotion is held in check – as in the gruelling moment where one of the townsmen, Les North (Martyn Sanderson), reads out to the pub the letter from his now dead son – with Stan it constantly threatens to explode, as the family's financial situation worsens with mortgage difficulties and the refusal of the dairy to take their cream. Their house, in the opening shots, and Stan himself, especially in the cattle market scene, are viewed through imprisoning structures, the chicken pen in the first instance, then the stockades at the cattle auction. Mateship, almost sacramentally affirmed in the letter, may exist for Les's son and his soldier comrades, but the only person to offer Stan sympathy is the policeman Besty (Dennis Lill), sympathy that Stan is too distrustful to accept, and ironically it is Besty's job to confiscate Stan's rifle, the incident which pushes him beyond recall.

Stan's crazed rampage is not justified, but he both indicts the crude world that surrounds him and exhibits curdled gentleness lacking elsewhere, as where he tenderly looks after one of his cows, and when he tracks a deer, only for his gun to be revealed as unloaded. Despite the exorcizing communal violence that burns down the Graham house,

Les North, sensitized by the loss of his son, tells a reporter, with inflections again of R.A.K. Mason's 'On the Swag', that 'If he [Stan] turned up for a feed I'd give it to him. He'd leave my place with a bellyful of warm tucker' and repeats the mythical message supposedly sent by 'Go balls' (Goebbels) to Lord Haw Haw: 'tell Stan if he can hold the South Island I'll send one more joker to take the North', adding 'Only trouble is they can't find a single bugger with the guts to deliver it'. As Stan is transported to die in hospital, ironically shot by a callow youngster, the same Kelly Johnson previously associated with non-conformity in Murphy's films, an anonymous woman gives him a blanket and hot-water bottle, a moment of pity, that provides a small counterpoint to the scene of the town dancing to 'Pack Up Your Troubles' and 'You are My Sunshine' while the Graham house burns and the band callously plays 'Keep the Home Fires Burning'.

Solo

Bad Blood can be seen as the culmination of the darkest meanings latent in the Murphy and Donaldson films – the grimmest version of the man alone and failing mateship, the bloodiest version of the struggle of conformity and non-conformity. *Solo*, released in 1977, takes very different directions. Directed by Tony Williams, the inventive maker of short films for O'Shea's Pacific Films, it had nothing like *Sleeping Dogs*' box-office impact, but might be seen in the long term as almost as influential in its own way, not only in its differences from the films of the 'cowboys of culture' (Geoff Steven's felicitous epithet for the dominant male film-makers of the period), but in its initiation of the tradition of the small-budget individual commercial cinema project – a discernable line running through to the present. Less formally innovative than Williams's shorter films, *Solo* cultivates a quieter, less conspicuous alternative route to the mainstream, using several of its prominent thematics – for example, the road movie (given an aerial perspective in the beautiful flying sequences), and man-, and woman-, alone motifs – inflecting the period's dominant male-centred tendencies with a three-way split in empathies between Paul (Vincent Gil), Judy (Lisa Peers), and Paul's vulnerable teenage son, Billy (Perry Armstrong); both the opening and closing perspectives of the film are situated with Judy, and equal weight is given to all the characters' dilemmas in their searchings for both love and independence, with Judy's need for the latter breaking the romantic relationship before it is really established. Thus the film's title, referring to Paul's son Billy's learning to fly, provides a more extensive metaphor for getting by on one's own. In his unfulfilled hopes, Paul becomes that very rare figure in the local cinema of the male feminized by love – needy and vulnerable. Typical of the film's well-crafted eccentricities is the role played by the philosophical Jules Catweazle (Martyn Sanderson), who enjoys a self-imposed isolation at the top of a lookout tower surveying the forests he and Paul in his plane have to watch over for forest fires, and whose chosen solitariness gives him detached insight into questions of human bonding and isolation. The male relationships so prevalent in the dominant films have only a subdued echo in Paul's and Billy's father–son dependencies and battles in a film which concentrates also on the complex of relationships between the hero and Judy, and between Judy and Billy. The ending with the hitchhiking heroine caught between tears and laughter, regret and relief in her movement towards freedom and solitude, is typically subtle. Williams's feature film making career came to a premature virtual halt, so that he has made only one other feature, the horror film *Next of Kin* (1982) set in Australia. His career as the maker of some of the best-known advertisements on New Zealand TV has been spectacularly successful, keeping him in public and filmic consciousness; although, for all the miniature pleasures of that work, it is impossible not to regret the loss the feature film suffered.

Heart of The Stag

Heart of the Stag and an interesting lesser work of the same year, *Trespasses* (Peter Sharp, 1984), both organize their narratives around a masculinity split into rival male figures – one a literal patriarch, the other younger, battling for an abused young female. In *Heart of the Stag* the literal father figure is Robert Jackson (Terence Cooper), a wealthy farmer, exuding primordial power, who forces his daughter Cathy (Mary Regan) into an incestuous relationship, which is endangered by the arrival of Peter Daley (Bruno Lawrence) a peripatetic drifter of some education, offered a temporary farm job by Jackson. In *Trespasses* the literal father is Fred Wells (Patrick McGoohan), a religious zealot, growingly more obsessive since his wife's death; the younger male, Stan Gubbins (Frank Whitten), the sexually predatory 'guru' of a commune; the female, Katie (Emma Piper), Fred's daughter, who, trying to escape her father's control, experiments with commune life, but ends up raped by the 'guru'. *Trespasses*, despite being pulled in contradictory directions – formulaic detection and psychodrama[51] – is a bleakly engrossing work, which ends with the father, having killed the abusive 'son', then, attempting to sacrifice the errant daughter, a catastrophe prevented, so that the film ends with him persuaded by her to give himself up. Here the father–son stand-off is seen as the clash of negatives, between males guilty of polarized authoritarianisms that victimize the daughter. In *Heart of The Stag* the battle between two figures of potent masculinity resolves itself, in the father's death, into the qualified optimism of the victory of the sensitized version of the traditional male that Bruno Lawrence embodies here: man alone, but not impervious to domesticity. This confrontation is far more complex than that in *Trespasses*, with fugitive half-resemblances (both know good wine from ordinary, both read) between the two figures. When Daley is invited for dinner, he, Jackson and Cathy can all quote from Baxter's poem 'High Country Weather', the father's comment not being a simple dismissal of the poetry that forms a bond between the stranger and his daughter, but the highly informed if reductive 'Baxter, sound classical background gone soft'. Male hardness becomes rampant in Jackson's obsession with killing the stag which becomes a floating signifier in the film, of maleness, of himself, even, fluidly, of the daughter and women. At a shearers' party Daley and Jackson compete in a raucous masculine contest of imitating the stag's call, though Jackson clearly wins. Daley's taking part in the game asserts a male potency, but he dissociates himself from the hunting that obsesses the father. Daley's courting of Cathy takes place in an environment turned high gothic by the incest and presence of Jackson's stroke-ridden wife, aware of her sexual replacement by the daughter. Cathy, drawn to Daley, puts herself in his way, but, traumatized, constantly retreats, her mixed desire and fear registered in gestures that assert then retreat from her femininity, so that Daley's role becomes that of protector rather than lover. In the film's climactic moments when he persuades her to leave with him, they are followed by Jackson intent on shooting him. As Daley makes his stag call, the great creature appears and impales Jackson, leaving him and Cathy implicitly to attempt a normal relationship in which the male will clearly be required to exercise tender reparative patience.

Constance

Constance looks forward (like the biopics *Iris* and *Sylvia*) to the more female-centred psychodramas of the later period. In one sense it was unlucky in that, though generally considered finely made, it was targeted by the newly active local feminist criticism. A piece by Jo Seton attacked its supposedly patriarchal power-play behind the façade of the Woman's Film, rescuing it for the radical female viewer with an 'against the grain' reading.[52] However, this says nothing that might not be attributed to the film's project, were it not for the dogma that the film's male director must blame the heroine – a view oddly denying the subversive possibilities of the 1940s Hollywood Woman's Film.

Constance, set in middle-class suburban Auckland in the 1940s, deals with a young woman's entrapment by a restrictive society offering her little scope for achievement, and her simultaneous beguilement by Hollywood, so that it is a key work (alongside the later *Crush* and *Snakeskin*) through which to trace local film-making's self-consciousness about American film culture. An ambitious psychodrama, it often eschews low-key realism in tracing its heroine's decline into madness. It begins with a fantasy scene set in The Civic, Auckland's great art deco movie palace, in which, accompanied by the Wurlitzer, a literally golden girl, covered in gold foil and all but naked, parades on stage surrounded by female dancers, watched by the fantasizing heroine in the audience, who then sees herself on another mental screen as a child sitting applying grown-up make-up, and dancing with her father. The narrative of Constance (Donogh Rees) thus begins in the cinema which so dominates her imagination, with moments of fantasy and memory attached to the film she is watching: *Gilda* (1946), starring Rita Hayworth at her most glamorous. Elsewhere she does her party piece, dressed in green and scarlet, with a long-stemmed cigarette holder, miming to Marlene Dietrich singing 'Falling in Love Again'. In her bedroom there is a compelling photograph resembling a movie still from *Gilda* in which, deep in the photographic field, she looks at the silhouette of a man with his back to the camera in the foreground, as if this faceless projection might be the solution to her dreams. Fulfilment through men alone is portrayed as powerfully dominating her psyche through her relationship with her father (Martin Vaughan) and the repeated marginalization of the mother (Judie Douglass) by the daughter–father dyad. But even when she meets men apparently capable of rescuing her from humdrum jobs (teacher and librarian), their promise is deceptive: Erroll (Graham Harvey), the son of a socialite, proves to be wholly dominated by his mother; the seemingly more sensitive and independent Richard (Mark Wignall), is ultimately as conventional as his parents; and Simon Malyon (Shane Briant), a New Zealander who has made it in Hollywood as a glamour photographer and who seems about to provide photographic as well as romantic fulfilment to Constance's dreams, rapes her in his photographic studio, an act of symbolic plenitude as well as traumatic consequences. Part of Seton's complaint was the absence of positive females to offer Constance an alternative trajectory (her sensible friend, Noeline [Hester Joyce], ends up marrying a plumber), but melodramas of entrapment tend to offer few positive role models, and, anyway, part of the problem, the film suggests, is their lack in the society portrayed. With even her father revealed as less successful than she imagines, Constance is repeatedly disappointed by men and her affairs of the heart end circularly with her briefly dating, and perhaps sleeping with, her father's elderly friend (Donald Macdonald). The film ends with Constance – now mentally ill – inviting a crowd of lowlife drinkers from a city hotel into her home, where, as she performs her Dietrich impression again, they appear as an admiring audience of characters from her life.

Sex changes: trial runs with Mr Wrongs

It is fitting to end discussion of a period dominated by a male-centred cinema with two precursors of change: Melanie Read's *Trial Run* and Gaylene Preston's *Mr Wrong*. Though these were not actually the first female-directed features – the precursor was Yvonne MacKay's *The Silent One* (1984) – they were the first reflecting a period of conscious challenge to male dominance of the industry. Read's career wound down and she moved away, but not before directing two feature films, as well as TV work, for example the innovative series *Marching Girls* (1988). Uneven in output – the TV film *The Minders* (1985), with its otherworld female protectors helping earthly women resist male sexual violence, defies parody – she was still a talented, outspoken presence. Gaylene Preston, working through the 1980s to the present, would become one of the country's pre-eminent directors, much of whose later feature and documentary work continued to use female-centred narratives.

Significantly, both chose thriller formats for their first features, the point being that audience knowledge of the genre's often exaggerated gender roles could be subverted with clearly understood effect, without didactic alienation of mainstream audiences. The critique of American and British thrillers (among which *Psycho* was invested with abject primacy), was also aimed at New Zealand film-makers with their 'boys' stories' and 'boys' games'. While some feminist theory proselytized the severities of a cinema and audience weaned off cinematic pleasure (the seductive sugar coating to the pill of patriarchal representation), both directors were content to harness the pleasures of suspense, while attempting to inflect them critically.

Trial Run

Rosemary Edmonds (Annie Whittle), *Trial Run*'s protagonist, is an aggressive stereotype of the new New Zealand woman – writer/photographer, ecologist, wife, mother of two, and even part-time middle-distance athlete (taking her inspiration from the distance runner

Allison, Roe glimpsed on television near the film's beginning). She accepts a commission to undertake a study of penguins at a nearby beach, which demands full-time attendance, requiring her temporarily to leave her family, except for their occasional visits, thus setting up the woman-in-jeopardy situation. Mysterious, threatening events endured by Rosemary structure the suspense narrative. The film's hermeneutic (who is responsible and why?) brings various suspects into view: Mr West; Rosemary's surly, distant neighbour (Martyn Sanderson), whose vicious dog, echoing his master's misogyny, menaces her and the penguins; another distant neighbour, a middle-aged woman; Rosmary's too-obliging-to-be-true husband, Michael (Stephen Tozer); her best friend Frances (Judith Gibson), a tough-minded feminist, but seemingly sleeping with Michael. The surprise revelation, keeping culpability within the family, but avoiding the over-predictability of the husband as villain, deflects guilt onto the secondary male, Rosemary's son, James (Christopher Broun), a computer-addicted control freak who has obsessively adopted the sadistic authority of the male athletic coach over his mother's body by organizing her training regime.

The thriller plot is constructed less for the erotics of suspense than for feminist thematics as its protagonist, capably transcending traditional heroines' weaknesses, resists her son's opposition to her absence, criticizes her husband's favouring James over his daughter, and remains calm in the presence of Mr West's mistreated wife's ghost and the unnerving incidents victimizing her. Occasionally Read's propagandistic tendencies create inadvertent comedy as sex-based judgements are transferred from the human societal realm to the animal kingdom, where West's dog parallels male wickedness to women in his attempt to kill a female penguin and her brood. Overnight at the beach, Frances sleeps in Rosemary's bed, though there is no suggestion of sexual intent, except inasmuch as the brief depiction of two women in the same bed may have constituted for some audiences a suggestion of lesbianism in tune with Read's criticisms in interview of 'heterosexism'.[53] This may in part explain the harshnesses of the final shot, where, after James has been accidentally knocked down by the family's car, her husband and daughter kneel by him, while Rosemary and Frances stand together apart. Other unresolved elements beside the seeming adultery surround Michael whose apparently unending obligingness as husband leaves the viewer unsure whether he is to be approved of as embodying the new man's acceptance of propitiating secondariness (the view Read put forward in interview with Alison Maclean), or whether the text contradicts the author's statements by suggesting a female satire of his weakness, or an exposure of the new man's insincerity.

Finally, there is the revelation that the son's terror campaign results from his obsessive desire to have the mother achieve a personal record running time, by forcing her to run for her life for help to the distant telephone box. What unresolvedly hangs around the explanation given is the (unspoken) suggestion that the boy's sadistic control may be a punishment devised for his mother's abandonment of the family. This gains unexpected support from the montage of family photos passing through Rosemary's mind as she photographs her penguin family, suggesting feelings of guilt. Read's comments on the ending, made defensively to female criticisms of her insensitivity to mother–son bonds, invoke the idea of an 'allegory' of 'what was known to be a universal truth at the time, which is that the rapist is nine times out of ten someone you know and more so someone who's close to you', and finish with a dismissive remark that 'there was still all that sensitivity about the feminist movement and women with sons'.[54] Does this mean that the son's actions are an 'allegory' for those of husbands/rapists? If so, the 'allegory' is less interesting than the unallegorized text, which for all its crudities, constituted with Preston's more refined film, an important moment in New Zealand film.

Mr Wrong

Read said she was 'fucked off with *Psycho*',[55] but it is *Mr Wrong* that invokes it intertextually, quoting the slicing windscreen wipers of Marion's car as Meg (Heather Bolton) drives towards her parents; Marion's pulling over and falling asleep, the second time with Meg not woken by a policeman but by her mother; and invoking but denying the notorious shower scene by having the rather homely Meg (Heather Bolton) – cast with teacherly overtones, like the slightly gaunt Annie Whittle, not to provoke the 'male gaze' or female envy – washing stockings and underwear in a very quotidian way before undressing ordinarily to take a bath or shower. Though the film generates its own suspense as its heroine is stalked by the killer, the three quotations from *Psycho* all come to nothing, as if to say that this film will take a different route from Hitchcock's.

Trial Run employs the supernatural very briefly, but *Mr Wrong* organizes itself around a narrative-long supernatural metaphor. Meg buys a second-hand Jaguar that once belonged to a young murdered woman, Mary Carmichael (Perry Piercy). Like the car in *Christine* (Carpenter, 1983) the Jag is an uncanny object in which Meg not only hears sound traces of Mary's murder, but meets both Mary and her murderer 'Mr Wrong' (David Letch), and which prevents on Mary's behalf Meg selling it when uncanny events and the young psychopath frighten her. Escaping from her flat, which 'Mr Wrong' has invaded, Meg finds herself being strangled by him in the car. Escaping, she is seemingly pursued by the car, which, however, bypasses her, carrying the frantic murderer to a fiery death. In the film's last moments Meg and the ghostly Mary Carmichael exchange a sisterly smile.

Like *Trial Run*, *Mr Wrong* uses its thriller plot as a hyperbole of the more mundane matters found in its interstices. In her life more ordinary Meg not only has to deal with her beautiful but numbingly conventional flatmate, Samantha (Margaret Umbers), but also with both Samantha's unpleasant boyfriends: Martin (Don Linke), who declares himself 'disgusted' with the woman's self-defence TV programme Meg watches, and Bruce (Gary Stalker), who treats Meg like a servant, and, frustrated by Samantha's absence, sexually assaults her, from which she is accidentally rescued by Wayne Wright's (Danny Mulheron) arrival. Unlike the smarmy car salesman, Clive (Philip Gordon), and Mr Whitehorn (Michael Haigh), Meg's middle-aged gay boss, whose misinterpretation of Meg's asking him home with her is comically vain, this amiable 'Mr Right', is treated gently, if a little comically, as the narrative keeps him at bay, refusing the expected relationship between him and Meg in a marginalization of romance, so that the final calling of a name, catching of an eye, and reciprocal smile are reserved for Meg and Mary.

Trial Run is one of those films whose primary fascination resides in its containing so many markers of its time, so that even its flaws are peculiarly representative of the skirmishes of the moments before women moved into the new cinema's mainstream. *Mr Wrong*, from the same time, survives better partly because as a major film-maker's work (with a marker of Preston's auteurship being the complex transmutations between the single red-rose gifts associated with 'Mr Wrong' and 'the Man' in *Perfect Strangers* nearly twenty years later) its didacticism is more humorously aware than Read's. Nevertheless, the two, taken together as in their almost simultaneous appearance, marked a major historical shift, and showed the way to later female directors, now a defining part of the New Zealand film scene.

Notes

1 See Russell Campbell, 'Smith & Co: The Cinematic Redefinition of Pakeha Male Identity', *Illusions* 7, 1987, 19–26, and 'Dismembering the Kiwi Bloke: Representations of Masculinity in *Braindead*, *Desperate Remedies*

and *The Piano*', *Illusions* 24, 1995, 2–9. See also Jock Philllips, *A Man's Country? The Image of the Pakeha Male: A History*, Penguin (NZ), Auckland, rev. ed., 1996.

2 Ambiguities exist as to whether a number of films, including *Iris*, should be classified as feature or television films, especially after videotape release further blurred original distinctions.

3 Figures from Martin and Edwards.

4 Information from 'Nola Luxford', www.imdb.com (accessed 12 April 2007).

5 Advertisement (Strand cinema) for *The Adventures of Algy*, 11 September 1925. *The Adventures of Algy* material, NZFA.

6 Advertisement (Strand cinema), 1 September 1928, Hayward material, NZFA.

7 *The New Zealand Film Pioneer*, vol. 1, no. 1, Hayward material, NZFA.

8 Advertisement (Strand cinema), Hayward material, NZFA.

9 Both Dale Austen and Vera James showed no great desire to pursue their film careers either in Hollywood or Australia, retiring into domestic life, an attitude interpretable either as admirably levelheaded or disappointingly unambitious.

10 Andrew Spicer, *Masculinity, Performance and the New Zealand Films of Bruno Lawrence*, Kakapo Books, Nottingham, 2000.

11 Will Holtzman, 'Towards an Actor-Icon Theory', *Journal of Popular Film* 4 (1), 1975, 71–80.

12 Janet Frame, *A State of Siege*, George Braziller, New York, 1966.

13 Terminology borrowed from Hong-key Yoon, 'Maori Identity and Maori Geomentality', *Geography and National Identity*, Blackwell, Oxford, 1994: 293–310.

14 Erena Le Heron, 'Placing Geographical Imagination in Film: New Zealand Filmmakers' Use of Landscape', *New Zealand Geographer* 60 (1) 2004, 60–6.

15 Donald Horne, *The Lucky Country*, Penguin, Harmondsworth, 1961, 25.

16 See Blythe, 130 ff; also Lawrence McDonald, 'A Book Review of Film in Aotearoa New Zealand That Ended Up as an Essay on Film in Aotearoa New Zealand', *Illusions* 21/22, 1993, 58–62.

17 J.C. Reid, ed., *The Kiwi Laughs, An Anthology of New Zealand Prose Humour*, A.H. and A.W. Reed, Wellington, 1961.

18 Geoff Mayer, 'Comedy', *The New Australian Cinema*, ed. Scott Murray, Hamish Hamilton, London, 1980, 45–59.

19 James Belich, *Making Peoples*, Penguin, London, 2001, 424–36.

20 Allen Curnow, *The Overseas Expert*, in *Four Plays by Allen Curnow*, A.H. and A.W. Reed, Wellington, 1972.

21 Blythe, 19–20

22 Karl Mutch, 'Testing Pictures', *Alternative Cinema*, 11 (2 & 3), 1983, 31–3.

23 Reid Perkins, 'Fun and Games: The Influence of the Counterculture in the Films of Geoff Murphy', *Illusions* 2, 1996, 15–23. See also Jonathan

Rayner, *Cinema Journeys of the Man Alone: The New Zealand and American Films of Geoff Murphy*, Kakapo Books, Nottingham, 1999.
24 Susan Hayward, *French National Cinema*, Routledge, London, 1993, 12.
25 Ray L. Birdwhistell, *Kinesics and Context: Essays on Body Motion Communication*, Penguin, Harmondsworth, 1973.
26 Bruce Babington, Introduction, *British Stars and Stardom*, Manchester University Press, Manchester, 2001, 10.
27 John Mulgan, *Man Alone*, Paul's Book Arcade Ltd, Hamilton, 1960 [1939].
28 James Belich, *Making Peoples*, 432–6.
29 C.K. Stead, *Smith's Dream*, New House Publishers, Auckland, 1993 [1971].
30 Interview with Donaldson, *Sleeping Dogs* material, NZFA.
31 The point develops one in Martin and Edwards, 64.
32 C.K. Stead, 'John Mulgan: A Question of Identity', *The Glass Case: Essays in New Zealand Literature*, Auckland University Press, Auckland, 1981, 66–98.
33 Geoff Murphy, 'The End of the Beginning', Bieringa and Dennis, 146.
34 Murphy, 146.
35 Thanks to John Saunders for his jazz expertise.
36 Pauline Kael, *New Yorker*, 15 October 1984.
37 Marcia Landy, *British Genres: Cinema and Society 1930–60*, Princeton University Press, Princeton, New Jersey, 1991, 282–3.
38 Martin and Edwards, 78.
39 Kael, *ibid.*
40 Nicholas Reid, *A Decade of New Zealand Films: 'Sleeping Dogs' to 'Came A Hot Friday'*, John McIndoe Ltd, Dunedin, 1986, 85.
41 Cowan, *The New Zealand Wars*, 1, 400.
42 Blythe, 246, 248.
43 Cowan, *The Adventures of Kimble Bent*, 197–8.
44 James Cowan, 'A Bush Court Martial', *Tales of the Maori Bush*, 1934: A.H. & A.W. Reed, Wellington, Auckland, Sydney, 2nd edition, 1966, 55–9.
45 Horrocks, 'New Zealand Cinema: Cultures, Policies, Films', 133–4.
46 Craig Harrison, *The Quiet Earth*, Hodder and Stoughton, Auckland and Sydney, 1981.
47 Blythe, 201.
48 O'Regan, *Australian National Cinema*, 46.
49 Lawrence Jones, 'Stanley Graham and the Several Faces of Man Alone', *Barbed Wire and Mirrors: Essays on New Zealand Prose*, University of Otago Press, Dunedin, 1987, 311.
50 *Ibid.*, 311.
51 Martin and Edwards, 96.
52 Jo Seton, 'Glamour and Romance: The Patriarchal Feminine in *Constance*', *Illusions*, 4, 1987, 17–22.
53 '*Trial Run*: Alison Maclean Interviews Melanie Read', *Alternative Cinema*, 11 (4), 1983–1984, 14.

54 Deborah Shepard, *Reframing: A History of New Zealand Film Women*, HarperCollins (NZ), Auckland, 2000, 107–8.
55 *Ibid.*, 107.

6

'World famous in New Zealand': contemporary cinema 1986–2005

Cinema and society 1986–2005

The contemporary New Zealand film industry is the product of a time marking a watershed with an older New Zealand dominated by subsidies and state intervention, economic stability, high levels of social security, a seeming absence of racial problems, and the extreme homogeneity of a British- and Irish-derived settler population, as well as privileged by seemingly divinely ordained high standards of living.

The major shifts of the 1980s that left their imprint on cultural production were: (i) the continuing adjustments caused by the necessities in New Zealand of economic, political and cultural redefinition following the Common Market; (ii) the growing impact of the electronic 'global village', bringing New Zealand into closer proximity with the centres; (iii) changes in the wake of feminism; (iv) changes in Pākehā–Māori relations; (v) the lasting alteration to traditional socio-economic patterns and expectations caused by the massive deregulation and privatization of the mid-1980s to mid-1990s; and (vi) changes involving multicultural immigration from the late 1980s.

While (i) and (ii) are too obvious to need commentary here, (iii)–(vi) benefit from introductory notations of the ways in which they interacted with the cinema.

(iii) *Changes in the wake of feminism*. In the twenty years since *Trial Run* and *Mr Wrong*, female directors have played a major role. From no female-directed features before 1984 to getting on for one in five since is a significant change, especially given the dominant critical status of Campion, Caro, Jeffs, Preston and Mita, making New Zealand cinema's reputation for female directors far from illusory. In *The Footstep Man* (Leon Narbey, 1992), it is presented as unremarkable that the director of the film-within-the-film should be a woman. True, there is a minor crisis when Vida, the director, makes Sam dismiss Jake, but the dismissal (if not getting Sam to do it) is justified, making it more a reminder of past than of present battles. The decision taken here not to treat female-directed films as a separate category stems from the perception that following 1985 they are parts of, not exceptions to, the mainstream. A further point (warning against too simple treatments of New Zealand's socio-sexual history) is that, although this new prominence owed much to feminist activity, it is, in the longer perspective, the reactivation of a long tradition of female artistic accomplishment – embodied in writers such as Katherine Mansfield, Jean Devanny and Jane Mander as well as the poets Blanche Baughan and Mary Ursula Bethell – even if marginalized by a later dominant literary masculinism.[1]

(iv) *Changes in Pākehā–Māori relations*. These, examined interacting with cinema below, were the culmination of post-war processes, especially the movement of rural Māori into the cities, ending the virtual urban/rural segregation of the races. Old problems, previously hidden, were magnified – Māori unemployment, lowest job status, health problems, educational failure, cultural displacement, crime, and white racism in circumstances of closer coexistence. The urban drift's more galvanizing consequences were the land protests; the second Māori cultural renaissance; a contemporary rhetoric of indigenous separatism (politically impossible, but effective in speeding government action); the reparative machinery of the Waitangi Tribunal; the elevation of Māori to an official language and active support for Te Reo (Māori language); and major changes in the state's attitude to the relations of its two founding populations.

(v) *Changes from the New Right*. From 1984 into the mid-1990s, New Zealand society underwent decisive metamorphoses based on market liberalization, dismantling of state intervention, monetary policies overridingly prioritizing price stability, deregulation and deunionization of the labour market and workforce, and cutting of state spending and social services. These 'five fundamentals'[2] turned one of the most protected socio-economic systems in the developed world to one of the least. Jane Kelsey has noted the social costs of their implementation, resulting in a society dominated by 'corporate entrepreneurs, consultants and technocrats', a switch from production to speculation that helped produce the stock market boom and crash, the sale of government services 'to private owners whose driving force was profit', and a major increase in poverty.[3]

In 1998 Roger Horrocks noted how little the lasting traumatic social impact of 'New Right' economics had found cinematic expression.[4] This view has not been much challenged by later films, though, with hindsight, the medieval Cumbrians' meeting with the Auckland foundry workers facing redundancy in *The Navigator* and *Desperate*

Remedies' ambivalent viewing of a fantastical colonial New Zealand through the prism of the 1980s–1990s free market take on significance, alongside Preston's *Ruby and Rata* and *Bread and Roses*, which Horrocks cited as exceptions. Predominantly, though, New Zealand films, when not ignoring such matters, display a satirically tinged acceptance (as in *Stickmen*'s 'rebirthing' redundancy clinic, *Zilch!*'s 'Money is Energy' seminar and *User Friendly*'s antic chase for profits). At an institutional rather than narrative level, though, as the critic implied, the changes were registered in production ideologies, inflecting an industry originating from the old interventionist order, more towards dominantly economic imperatives than might otherwise have been the case.[5]

One of Horrocks's exceptions is Richard Riddiford's comedy-thriller *Zilch!* (1989), the only film foregrounding Auckland as the 'City of Sales' and dynamo of the share-buying mania behind the 'Black Tuesday' 1987 and 'Black Monday' 1989 New Zealand stock market collapses, and also the spectacular frauds such as Equiticorp Holding's NZ$67-million debacle, a new metropolitan ethos crystallized in David Grant's cameo: 'Never again would Rod Petrovic, executive chairman of the soon-to-collapse Euro-National Corporation, stand tall with fellow entrepreneurs at Auckland's fashionable Hotel de Brett wearing T-shirts emblazoned with the message "We run this town."'[6] *Zilch!*'s conspiracy narrative is based on Auckland's growth requiring an alternative cross-harbour route to the existing bridge, a competition won by the corrupt Gary Hyde's 'Infacorp', the name (like 'Megacorp' in *Send a Gorilla* and 'Conspec' in *Ruby and Rata*) mimicking an actual one. Hyde (Roy Billing), suppressing unfavourable structural analyses, gains the contract for his tunnel by filming a key official's perverse activities with a call girl, Anna (Lucy Sheehan). Her sexual association with the protagonist ensures that a whole lifestyle is implicated, not entirely excluding the hero and heroine: Sam (Michael Mizrahi), a telephone operator whose voyeuristic eavesdropping alerts him to the conspiracy, is hardly an idealistic figure fighting corruption. For all his opposition to property 'development', he is a rather dysfunctional, apolitical figure. The film's insistence on a wider critique is seen in the way the hero's mate, Curtis, with his pre-1980s socialist values, appears comically quaint – so that even though the narrative punishes the worst entrepreneurial excesses, it does so in a social context of unregulated privatization of the moral as well as economic sphere. This engaging, intelligent film is also notable for its wittily Hitchcockian finale at Kelly Tarleton's Waterworld, where the hero escapes by swimming past sharks out into the harbour – sharks in their double sense encapsulating the film's financial predators. Geoff Murphy's first New Zealand feature for more than twenty years, *Spooked* (2004) takes up material from this period, though in updating it into a twenty-first-century present (referencing Osama Bin Laden) the film, though skilfully made, loses much of the particularity *Zilch!* has in abundance.

(vi) *Multiculturalism*. New Zealand's traditional homogeneity included various minorities, but only in small numbers. TK's prejudice against foreigners in *Carry Me Back* is expressed in his putdown 'Lived here all your life have you?' addressed not only to a Greek taxi driver but even to an English ferry steward. In the late years of the twentieth century, New Zealand redefined itself by taking in a wide geographical and racial range of immigrants, with South East Asian immigration favoured as aiding Asian markets, and possessing entrepreneurship helpful to the country's economy, though these changes were not wholly approved, being viewed by some Pākehā as diluting indigenous settler distinctiveness, and by some Māori as seriously endangering the Māori position in a bicultural state.

The primarily metropolitan multicultural population also includes the longer-standing immigration of Pacific Islanders, now constituting a fast increasing 5 per cent of the whole. This is the context behind two Samoan-oriented films, the early *Sons for the Return Home* (Paul Maunder, 1979) and *Flying Fox in a Freedom Tree* (Martyn Sanderson, 1990), though it may also be that Samoan specifics (later asserted in the hit comedy *Sione's Wedding*: Chris Graham, 2006) were earlier used as a screen for portraying racial relations in harsher terms than the usual Pākehā–Māori representations.

Recently there have been films foregrounding multicultural thematics: *Illustrious Energy* (Leon Narbey, 1988), *Broken English* (Gregor Nicholas, 1997) and *Gupta Versus Gordon* (Jitendra Pal, 2003), with its Indian diaspora thematic paralleling better-known British films, while *Memory and Desire* (Niki Caro, 1998), discussed as melodrama below, unexpectedly distilled the context of new economic, cultural and touristic relations, unthinkable thirty years previously, between New Zealand and Japan (with Japan now a huge investor in the country's economy) in wholly unpredictable ways.

Illustrious Energy

Narbey's film combines the historical Chinese presence in the nineteenth-century Otago gold rushes with an interest in the new multiculturalism. Increasing Chinese immigration led to a Prime Ministerial apology at Chinese New Year 2002 for the old poll tax Chinese had to pay to enter New Zealand (and Australia and Canada) and other indignities suffered by the small local population, such as not being allowed to bring in family. *Illustrious Energy*'s milieu is a harsh hyperbole of the early difficulties of the majority culture, with its remoteness figured in the commitment of the Chinese characters to a homeland to which they send money for half-forgotten dependents, and to which they dream of returning, a reality for most of them only in a posthumous journey on a 'corpse ship',[7] something alluded to in the film's beginning as Chan and Kim exhume a relative's bones for that purpose. But the lot of the Chinese is even harder because of prejudice, exemplified in Hayward's *My Lady of the Cave*, where an intensely stereotyped Chinese, his pidgin rendered in intertitle – 'Polis, polis, alleee chance gone, I no hang' – throws himself over a cliff to the comment, 'Huh, that'll save the hangman's job – been dodging the police for knifing a gumdigger'.

In *Illustrious Energy*, Chan (Shaun Bo) and his old father-in-law Kim (Harry Ip) live in this limbo, while their colleague Wong (Peter Chin) achieves unusual integration, marrying a Scottish wife and having children. But Wong's life is exceptional, as shown by the virulent sinophobia vented on Chan on his visit to town. Exceptionally, two white characters exhibit more tolerance: the local Chinese church minister – who, though shocked by Chen's resistance to Christianity, enjoys their speculative conversations – and a surveyor – who, despite his prejudiced partner, makes friendly contact and, with his theodolite, acts as a surrogate for the film director in the multicultural age. This future is glimpsed when Chen is accepted into an Australian travelling circus, with the troupe's genial white boss presiding over a microcosm of multiculturality, a harbinger of the future, but only possible in the narrative's present in the carnival world. Attracted to an unconventional young Chinese woman, Miss Li (Geeling) who insists that she is Australian not Chinese, Chen enjoys a night of love with her, but has to leave because of his obligation to Kim. Freed by Kim's death, but unable to find the money the old man has hidden, Chen makes his solitary way across the landscape, a figure born too early to fit in (an updated version of the 'Dally' (Dalmatian) in Sargeson's famous story 'The Making of a New Zealander').

Broken English
Broken English is, in comparison, inferior, but still with multiple interests, not least when the Māori hero, Eddy (Julian Arahanga), and Croatian heroine, Nina (Aleksandra Vujcic), walk on an Auckland roof top amidst clustered satellite dishes, their romance thus placed

against the technological apparatus of the border-dissolving village's intersection with the nation state, the latter, however, not rendered unmeaningful, but on the contrary intensely meaningful to those seeking New Zealand as a haven from war-torn former Yugoslavia or Asia's overpopulation. *Broken English*, its title doubly referring to new immigrants' speech and later history's inflection of the original settlers, brings two kinds of transshiftings into relation, one internal (Eddie's movement into the city where his tree, representing his 'whakapapa', maintains a fragile transplanted growth), the other external (Croats, successors to New Zealand's older 'Dalmatian' population, and Chinese illegal immigrants caught up in the fake marriage for residence business, moving to Auckland).

The Croat daughter marrying a Māori has older precedents as well in patterns of intermarriage between Dalmatians and Māori in the far north.[8] However, Nina's father (Rade Serbedzija), almost erotically possessive of his daughters (underlined when Nina struggles to remember the word 'whakapapa' – 'fuck a what?'), violently opposes their relationship. The narrative, though ending with the couple united, suggests that new identities may not be easily attained. The Croatian men live in an enclave dominated by harshly patriarchal codes and ethnic hatreds. The windscreen wipers of the car driving through the war-broken city in the opening shots suggest a wiping away of the past, but the image is contradicted elsewhere, with Nina's brother, Darko (Marton Csokas), rather than responding to change, helping the father imprison his sister, who eventually has to break with her family in order to make her new life.

A multicoloured freeze-framed wedding photo features the Samoan minister, Māori, other Samoans, the Chinese, the Croatian heroine, and the odd Pākehā, but such urban complexity gives way to a lushly romanticized finale in which the interracial couple walk their child along a northern beach far from the urban complexities that dominate the film.

Intrinsic developments

Production and budgets

The period 1986–2005, predictably, given the industry's relative simplicity and centralization, has been marked by no major changes, but, rather, by moderately sustained small-scale production (roughly 125 films in 20 years as distinct from about 45 in the 10 years 1975–1985), only the emergence of digital features in the early 2000s substantially increasing the number of films made, though not the number gaining mainstream exhibition. Outside of the extremes of Jackson's vastly financed CGI productions and cheap digitals at the other end of the spectrum, films remained low budget, many until recently still being made at mid-1980s costs – at the lower end *Via Satellite* (1998; NZ$1.45 million), *Rain* (2001; NZ$2.1 million) and *Stickmen* (2000; NZ$2 million); in the middle, *Memory and Desire* (1997; NZ$3.3 million) and *50 Ways of Saying Fabulous* (2005; approximately NZ$3 million); at the higher end only *In My Father's Den* (2004; over NZ$7 million) and *Whale Rider* (2002; approximately NZ$10 million) – both off-shore funded – doubling the more expensive 1980s levels, and only the more substantially off-shore funded *River Queen* (2006) and *Perfect Creature* (2007), though final figures are unavailable at the time of writing, in excess of NZ$15 million.[9]

Co-production, foreign funding

A way of increasing budgets, or at least spreading costs, is international co-production, either through official national agreements (as with Britain, Canada and Australia), or with individual overseas companies or institutions, as in New Zealand's minor history of co-production with German institutions, *The Piano*'s French funding and the English company Portman's part funding in the late 1990s of the low-budget films *Via Satellite*, *Scarfies*, *Jubilee*, *Stickmen* and *Snakeskin*. While those five were almost wholly New Zealand acted and all locally directed, co-production often means overseas stars – as in *The Piano*, *In My Father's Den* and *River Queen* – and, occasionally, directors, with implications both positive and negative for local film-making.

Increasing off-shore production

The period also witnessed major growth in off-shore productions, with US telemovies and series dominating numerically, the most celebrated being the series *Xena: Warrior Princess* (1995–2001) and *Hercules: The Legendary Journeys* (1995–1999) with its feature spin-offs. Among theatrical films *The Last Samurai* (Edward Zwick, US, 2003) and *The Lion, the Witch and The Wardrobe* (the expatriate Andrew Adamson, US, 2005) have been the most prominent. Some of these, particularly *Xena* and *Hercules* and its spin-offs, brought local actors to international cult attention, though this was exceptional, as are the major production and technical roles for locals in Jackson's later US-financed films.

The selling of New Zealand movies 2: 1986–2005

The Festival Circuit continued to be the primary site for foreign sales. Representatively *ON FILM* (September 2002) noted appearances of

Whale Rider at the Toronto and San Sebastian international festivals, the premiering of *Toy Love* at the Hamburg Film Festival, and *Tongan Ninja*'s appearance at the Hawaian Film Festival. Awards, however specialized the festivals – like those for Fantasy Film in Puchon and Tokyo, at which *The Price of Milk* won prizes – bring prestige and, in many cases, increase home as well as overseas audiences. The diffusion of target overseas audiences today is illustrated by the 1999 sales projections for Christine Parker's *Channelling Baby*: (in thousands of NZ$) UK: 150; German speaking: 175; French speaking: 120; Canadian: 100; Scandinavia and Netherlands: 20 each; Korea: 20; and the US: –very speculatively – 300, though these figures proved highly optimistic.[10]

Accompanying this diffusion has been a greater change: the proliferation of new modes of viewing. At first minor theatrical release in Britain, the US and Europe was the target, with the possibility of terrestrial television sales, but home video soon became a rapidly expanding market, joined by cable and satellite TV, and now the phenomenally expanding DVD market, up to NZ$100 million sales in 2004, with 47 per cent of New Zealand homes possessing DVD players.[11] The growing predominance of home viewing sales, even before the DVD boom, was illustrated by Justice Doogue's at first sight puzzling 1996 local court ruling that Ward's *The Navigator* was not a feature film.[12] This proved to be neither a quarrel with World Archivists' definitions, nor a reactionary aesthetic judgement, but a close following of the 1976 Income Tax Act, which ruled that 'a feature film must derive the majority of its revenue from cinema release, so it did not qualify as a feature film under the act', thus underlining the long growing predominance of home-oriented outlets.

Directors and producers

The increase in female directors has already been noted, with Campion pre-eminent, but with Caro and Jeffs also becoming internationally known figures. Their success has led to work in the UK and US. While the duration of the latter two's expatriatism is not yet clear (Campion now identifies herself as an Australian film-maker), all three illustrate the continuing lure of the major production centres, which also took away Ward, Tamahori and Maclean in the 1990s. Ward, Campion and Jackson (discussed in chapter 7) were the towering figures of the period, defining New Zealand film positively to overseas audiences However, at the local level, the picture has negative aspects hidden by the euphoria often surrounding New Zealand film. John Reid, Costa Botes, Peter Wells, Richard Riddiford, Stewart Main, Garth Maxwell,

Merata Mita, Barry Barclay and Leon Narbey – whatever their achievements in documentary, television or other fields (for example, for Narbey, as cinematographer) – have found the feature industry less supportive than they should have. Of the most talented figures only Gaylene Preston has managed the feature productivity that might be expected, but that still amounts to only four features, and the feature-length documentary *War Stories*, in twenty years. Of lesser film makers, Pillsbury (like Blyth and Laing also working in America), Mune, Laing (working for the Bradley US audience and grasping cheap digital opportunities with *The Shirt*) and Dale Bradley, mostly making films for American markets, managed the considerable feat of continuing productivity. The recent appearance of newer talent creates optimism, but does not outweigh the industry's failure to sustain experienced ability. Producers remained vitally important in the system, with John Barnett, Larry Parr (through various financial disasters) and Don Reynolds active long term, though Maynard and Ikin, significantly, found the 1990s inhospitable to artistic ambitions and concentrated on Australia. While at the grandest level Jackson and Fran Walsh were among the producers of *The Lord of the Rings*, despite its American provenance, more minor figures proliferated, a creative instance being Fiona Copland, Harry Sinclair's producer. Not wholly positive in its implications has been the indefatigable activity of Grant and Dale Bradley, by far the most prolific local producers, with Grant Bradley claiming 20 productions (18 of them New Zealand), a few partly locally aimed, but the majority bypassing theatrical release anywhere and aimed at US and international satellite, cable and DVD sales. Examples of these include *Kiwi Safari* (Dale Bradley, 1998) and *Terror Peak* (Dale Bradley, 2003), with their minor American stars against highly coloured New Zealand backdrops of kiwi rustlers, exploding volcanoes and ancient supernaturally appearing kuia (female elders); or, more usually, films where New Zealand is disguised as the US in what may be called 'left-hand-drive cinema' after the necessary adjustments of vehicles and driving codes required in such metamorphoses: for example *Cupid's Prey* (Dale Bradley, 2003), *No One Can Hear You* (John Laing, 2001); and non-Bradley instances such as *The Frighteners* (Peter Jackson, 1996), *Heaven* (Scott Reynolds, 1998) and *Shearer's Breakfast*, a.k.a. *When Strangers Appear* (Scott Reynolds, 2001).

Actors and stars 2: 1986–2005

Though most of the earlier period's characteristics prevail, some newer patterns are observable: (i) the emergence of younger protagonist actors following lower audience age demographics, such as Dean

O'Gorman, Danielle Cormack, Kevin Smith, Karl Urban and Kate Elliott; (ii) some of the more publicized female figures being either children (Anna Paquin, Keisha Castle-Hughes) or adolescents (Emily Barclay [*In My Father's Den*] and Alicia Fulford-Wyzbicki [*Rain*]), as discussed in relation to child- and adolescent-centred films below; (iii) a foregrounding of Māori, Islander and mixed Polynesian/Pākehā actors, with several reaching 'demi-star' status, such as Temuera Morrison, Cliff Curtis, Rena Owen and Kevin Smith; (iv) the new phenomenon of local actors (for example Morrison, Curtis, Karl Urban) commuting between New Zealand careers and minor Hollywood parts; and (v) these, among others like Rena Owen and Danielle Cormack, becoming well known enough to have their own web pages and fan sites. Curtis', Lawrence Makoara's and Owen's websites highly accent their Māoriness, which functions as a useful 'glocal' difference, even if the overseas parts it leads to tend to a more generalized 'otherness'.

Even at four million, New Zealand's population is too small to support a star system, though enough for local celebrity. Expanding celebrity journalism has pushed the typical New Zealand 'picture personality' closer to the 'star' with whom on-screen and off-screen life are conflated,[13] so that, despite the same cultural constraints operating as earlier, there now exist local 'demi-stars', whose images circulate, albeit limitedly, in muted celebrity discourse. Three contemporary actors – Danielle Cormack, Karl Urban and Kevin Smith – figure characteristically in a typical British-derived, antipodeanly inflected, star as 'anti-star' discourse constructed through (i) their socio-economic ordinariness, (ii) scepticism of their own glamour, (iii) their propensity to talk articulately about film-making, and (iv) their part-resistance to the self-promotion involved in stardom. Thus articles emphasize Cormack's 'westie nest' (West Auckland house) 'in Auckland's sprawling working-class suburbs', and her frugality, have her responding to the invocation of Botticelli with 'Most of the time I look more like Bob Marley than a Botticelli', quote her sardonic view of the average New Zealand film, and her sceptical view of self-projection: 'It would be interesting to know whether these people that do that can actually spend a whole day by themselves'.[14] Karl Urban says that he does not like being a household name, and then – as reconstructed Pākehā male, bearing the whole of crew culture history on his shoulders – confesses 'I don't think I had any real concept of what a relationship was. To me, going to the movies was just foreplay, for my ultimate goal, which was to get into a girl's pants. And I just look back and cringe ... I really wish I could go back to all those people and apologize for what I was then'.[15] Like the other two, the late Kevin Smith exhibited connections with ordinariness, and, publicized as 'New Zealand's sexiest man', was at pains to distance himself from his 'himbo' image: reminded that he wept in *Channelling Baby*, he replied with the irony of 'Yeah, so after every take I went down to the pub and hit someone just to show I was still a man'; he also asserted, without irony, his embarrassment at playing an All Black in *Jubilee* – 'I would have been mortified if an All Black had come and caught me wearing the gear. A handful of men have *earned* that'.[16] Smith, like Urban, thus performed off- as well as on-screen fascinating post-feminist inflections of traditional New Zealand masculinity.

The films: genres, major types and pre-eminent modes

Earlier slightly deflationary remarks in chapter 5 on the New Zealand cinema's tendencies to generic mixing also apply to the later period. With films influenced by multiculturalism and the 'new right' (with different generic manifestations) already treated, this account covers traditional genres and modes as the recognizable bases for inflection-recombination, then proceeds to three areas of particular interest: horror, child-centred narratives, and the art film, followed by longer sections on wider categories (like the latter two, containing very disparate films): comedy, melodrama/psychodrama, and the multigeneric double category 'two-culture film-making and Māori-made films'.

Action-adventure/action thriller: in a genre where local versions tend to the highly formulaic, a few films stand out for degrees of inventiveness. *The Grasscutter* (Mune, 1988), *Never Say Die* (Murphy, 1985), *Zilch!* (examined earlier), *The Last Tattoo* (Reid, 1994: see the **war film**) and *Spooked* (Murphy, 2004) all imported socio-political material into their action – local civic corruption in *Zilch!*, New Zealand/American relations in *The Last Tattoo*'s setting in the Second World War, Irish sectarian conflicts reaching out to Dunedin in *The Grasscutter*, international arms-selling conspiracies in *Spooked*, South African/New Zealand relations before apartheid's collapse in *Never Say Die*. *Bridge to Nowhere* (Mune, 1986) inflects the genre differently: a teenage jeopardy narrative spasmodically interesting for its antipodean lost-in-the-bush plot, and for Bruno Lawrence as a figure of rural nemesis. The rest are largely formulaic, falling predominantly into the two categories noted with the Bradleys: action films with New Zealand settings like *Kiwi Safari*, *Terror Peak* and *The Vector File* (Eliot Christopher, NZ/Germany, 2002) and 'left-hand drive' films with New Zealand standing in for the US – such as *No*

One Can Hear You (John Laing, 2001) and *Shearer's Breakfast* (Scott Reynolds, NZ/Australia/US, 2001) – with only *Heaven* (Scott Reynolds, US/NZ, 2001) narratively and stylistically ambitious. **The biopic** continued its female emphasis, with Campion's *An Angel At My Table* (1990, based on the novelist Janet Frame, see chapter 7) and Preston's *Bread and Roses* (1993; also originally made for TV), a major work for the centenary of women's suffrage about the local politician Sonja Davies; Roger Donaldson's *The World's Fastest Indian* (2005), was the resolutely male exception in a cinema curiously lacking in male biopics, its subject an elderly Southlander who broke a world speed record. **The musical:** *Don't Let It Get You*'s only clear successor is Garth Maxwell's *When Love Comes* (1998, see **Melodrama**, p. 208), though Jackson's *Heavenly Creatures*' generic potpourri includes major musical elements. **Romance/the woman's film:** like romantic comedy, romantic melodrama (only present in the early contemporary period in *Other Halves*, though before that with *My Lady of the Cave*, *The Bush Cinderella* and *Broken Barrier*) has been infrequent in New Zealand cinema, though the pattern is broken by a cluster of films, starting in the early 1990s: *Crush* (Alison Maclean, 1992), *Heavenly Creatures* (1994), *Memory and Desire* (Niki Caro, 1997), *Channelling Baby* (Christine Parker, 1999), *Perfect Strangers* (Gaylene Preston, 2003) and, most famously, *The Piano* (Jane Campion, 1993). A much more conventional film, crossing romance, family, and New Zealand scenery is *Wild Blue* (Dale G Bradley, 2000). **War:** despite warfare's great importance in both the Māori and the Pākehā mythos and the existence of a distinct genre of **New Zealand Wars films**, there are few war films with later settings, although the Second World War is still close enough for the *New Zealand at War* television series (1995) to have had great impact, as did Gaylene Preston's memorable feature-length documentary about New Zealand women from the same period, *War Stories Our Mothers Never Told Us* (1995). Both, as documentaries using newsreel footage, escape the genre's demands of staging battlefield action on restricted budgets, a problem for *Chunuk Bair* (Dale Bradley, 1991), New Zealand's Gallipoli film, where lack of spectacle compared with the Australian equivalent *Gallipoli* (Weir, 1981) creates almost inevitable feelings of restriction. Both of the other instances of the genre escape such demands in different ways: Larry Parr's *A Soldier's Tale* (1991) is set behind the lines, its violence small scale and personal, while John Reid's *The Last Tattoo* (1995) – creatively mixing historical reconstruction (the US army in New Zealand in 1942–1943), film noir and political commentary – is, though surrounded by the Pacific war, a home-front film, its only military action war games on a beach. Analysed by this author elsewhere, it is one of the most interesting films of the 1990s.[17] Elsewhere, the importance of declining actual and increasingly inherited family memories of the period are marshalled by other home-front films: *Bad Blood* and *Absent Without Leave* (John Laing, 1993). **Crime**: distinguished from various thriller formats by concentration on the criminal or investigative processes, the crime film is a minor genre in the New Zealand cinema, its most distinguished later example – *Heavenly Creatures*, with its true-crime base – bursting generic boundaries. The few other examples fall into the categories of a curious subtype of teenage revenge on criminal quasi-bad-parent figures – *Dangerous Orphans* (John Laing, 1986) and elements of *Queen City Rocker* (Bruce Morrison, 1986) – or psychodrama – *For Good* (Stuart McKenzie, 2003), *Orphans and Angels* (Christobal Araus Lobos, 2001) and *The Waiting Place* (Harold Brodie, 2003). *Fracture* (Larry Parr, 2004) adapts the novel *Crime Story* by Maurice Gee efficiently but limitedly, compared with McGann's adaptation of another Gee novel, *In My Father's Den* (2004). *Scarfies* (Robert Sarkies, 1999), reworking the British film *Shallow Grave*, differentiates itself from its source in its student setting and local Dunedin atmospheres. All these films centre on accidental criminals, underlining New Zealand film's ideologically suggestive retreat from narratives of organized crime, making John Laing's digital *The Shirt* (2000) exceptional, an inventively grotesque tragicomedy of a minor drug criminal, cultivating wittily knowing references, especially in the hero-villain Marty's ever-present mother, to 1930s and 1940s Hollywood prototypes.

Horror

Bad Taste, Peter Jackson, 1988; *The Returning*, John Day, 1990; *Anagram*, Gerben Cath, 1991; *Grampire*, David Blyth, 1991; *Braindead*, Peter Jackson, 1992; *The Frighteners*, Peter Jackson, 1996; *The Ugly*, Scott Reynolds, 1997; *The Irrefutable Truth about Demons*, Glenn Standring, 2000; *The Locals*, Greg Page, 2000; *Kung Fu Vampire Killers*, Phil Davison, 2002

Horror became an unexpected growth area following Jackson's *Bad Taste* and *Brain Dead*, the comic-abject visceral excesses of which made them cult successes, discovering a profitable international niche for New Zealand films. Indeed, Standring's *The Irrefutable Truth About Demons* has been among the most profitable New Zealand productions, through its major US deal with Blockbuster Video. Among minor instances, *The Ugly* efficiently developed its female-psychiatrist-meets-charismatic-serial-killer outlines, while *Grampire* was a children's mock-horror film and *Anagram* an adults' one. Neither these nor the accomplished *The Irrefutable Truth About Demons* make use of Māori motifs, though *The Locals* transposes the 'tangata whenua' to a settler context, in which a sinister zone of the Waikato is haunted by white farmer undead rather than Māori ancestors. Though tied to a banal teenage-jeopardy narrative, *The Locals* has an acute visual sense that creates eerie nocturnal landscapes, spasmodically generating an indigenous Pākehā sense of the *unheimlich*. The city-centred *The Irrefutable Truth About Demons* develops a classically 'fantastic' narrative hovering between supernatural and rationalistic explanations. Harry (Karl Urban), an anthropology lecturer dedicated to exposing religious cults, has war declared on him by a self-proclaimed demon for his blasphemy against the satanic-spiritual realm. The frightening consequences combine traditional interstitial monstrosities (given a local twist in their revival of immemorial New Zealand childhood fears of wetas, large cockroach-like insects) and blasphemies (Harry's girlfriend crucified) with the flotsam and jetsam of city nightlife. Harry's (apparently demonic) lawyer girlfriend and the police psychiatrists doubt his story because of his drug-taking, interpreting it as marijuana-induced paranoia, thus creating the instability of 'the fantastic'. Like Jackson's films in their play with New Zealand stereotypes and 'Kiwiana', *Demons* and, spasmodically, *The Locals* combine international appeal with local reflections, the latter at least present in the cheap digital *Kung Fu Vampire Killers* with its Dunedin-based narrative derived from a local nineteenth-century Chinese presence. This 'return of the repressed' provokes the question whether the more interesting local horror films enact, alongside primordial fears, specifically local meanings – for example, in *The Truth About Demons*, the old masculinist unease with the female, and a very secular culture's punishment for absent spirituality. Among films with Māori content considered below, motifs of malign sacredness intersect the horror film with other genres (such as the 'tapu' house in *Among the Cinders* and the boys' reaction to the sacred mountain and the tapu burial ground in *Mark II*). Apropos of this, it may be noted that contemporary Māori sensibilities tend to be more receptive to the supernatural than sceptical Pākehā ones, and that one of the successes of Māori Television was *Mataku* (2002), a series of ghost dramas.

Child-centred/rites of adolescent passage films

***The Scarecrow*, Sam Pillsbury, 1982; *Vigil*, Vincent Ward, 1984; *Kingpin*, Mike Walker, 1985; *Mark II*, John Anderson, 1986; *Dangerous Orphans*,**

John Laing, 1987; *Starlight Hotel*, Sam Pillsbury, 1987; *Ngati*, Barry Barclay, 1987; *Among the Cinders*, Rolf Haedrich, 1987; *The Navigator*, Vincent Ward, 1988; *Mauri*, Merata Mita, 1988; *An Angel at My Table*, Jane Campion, 1990; *The End of the Golden Weather*, Ian Mune, 1991; *Alex*, Megan Simpson, 1992; *Crush*, Alison Mclean, 1992; *Jack Be Nimble*, Garth Maxwell, 1993; *Map of the Human Heart*, Vincent Ward, 1993; *Heavenly Creatures*, Peter Jackson, 1994; *The Whole of the Moon*, Ian Mune, 1996; *Flight of the Albatross*, Werner Mayer, 1996; *Rain*, Caroline Jeffs, 2000; *Whale Rider*, Niki Caro, 2003; *Her Majesty*, Mark J. Gordon, 2005; *Fifty Ways of Saying Fabulous*, Stewart Main, 2005

New Zealand narratives persistently depict children or adolescents passing through rites of passage. Indeed, an adaptation of Ian Cross's novel, *The God Boy* (Murray Reece, 1976) – in which a Catholic boy remembers his parents' fraught marriage, ending in the mother's killing of the father – was New Zealand's first feature-length television film. Frequently found, the pre-adult protagonist is central to many of the local cinema's major works, among them *Vigil*, *An Angel at My Table*, *The Navigator*, *Rain*, *Heavenly Creatures* and *Whale Rider*.

Vincent Ward has suggested that 'maybe we are attracted to the [childhood] theme because New Zealand is so remote that when we venture into the world we do so as innocents'.[18] This psychic figuring of national smallness and vulnerability might occasionally seem regressive, as in the near-hysteria accompanying Anna Paquin's and Keisha Castle-Hughes' Academy Award and nomination for *The Piano* and *Whale Rider*. Within it, the female child plays out meanings connected with a traditionally masculinist society's feminization; the Māori child suggests both vulnerability to change and the optimism of increasing cultural assurance and birth rates, while the male Pākehā child struggles either with the complexities of attaining masculinity or against an imaginatively restrictive society. Geoff (Stephen Fulford), in *The End of the Golden Weather*, epitomizes the latter, the burgeoning artist in a world too practical for aesthetics. The narrative centres on Geoff's encounter with the fantasies of the mentally unstable Firpo (Stephen Papps) of becoming an Olympic athlete. Firpo's humiliation brings Geoff knowledge of the world's irreparability, putting the simplistic 'God's Own Country' optimism of the Reverend Thirle (Ray Henwood) in perspective. Importantly, however, accommodation is made between proto-artist and unartistic world through the reaffirmed bond between the son (snubnosed, freckled, in many aspects the product of his world, not its opposite) and Paul Gittins's slightly puritanical, but kindly New Zealand patriarch, whose repressed aesthetic, anarchic sides are released in the high-spirited fantasy of his mad-doctor holiday routines. A female version of the child artist's struggle is found in Jane Campion's version of Janet Frame's autobiography, *An Angel at My Table* (1990).

Among films with adolescent Pākehā protagonists moving towards mature masculinity or femininity are *Among The Cinders*, *Fifty Ways of Saying Fabulous* (with its revisionist homosexual variant) and *Alex* (with its schoolgirl swimmer heroine trying to make the New Zealand 1960 Olympics team, whose teenage problems culminate with her boyfriend's death). Often it is the encounter with death, with Geoff's experience of Firpo's abjection equivalent to the discovery of mortality (as distinct from more formulaic fatalities in the films noted at the end of this account) that sets these films apart from more superficial versions – for instance, the deaths of family and friends in *An Angel at My Table*, *Among the Cinders*, *Vigil*, *Rain*, *Ngati*, *Mauri* and *Map of the Human Heart*, the beached totemic whales in *Whale Rider*, and the teenagers' cancer in *The Whole of the Moon*. *Mark II* involves no deaths, but the Polynesian boys' road trip brings darker knowledge of problems of racial prejudice and the inequalities of the social system. More conventional children's films are also found: the pleasant early racially mixed *Rangi's Catch*, *The Silent One*, *Worzel Gummidge Down Under* (1986, repackaged from TV for film release) and the recent Bradley-produced *Treasure Island Kids* trilogy. Films aimed largely at a teenage audience include *Alex*, *Secrets*, *Bonjour Timothy* (a comedy playing clever variations on the growing up gap between teenage boys and more quickly maturing girls), the affecting *The Whole of the Moon* (with its cancer-striken teenagers), and the more conventional *Queen City Rocker* and *Dangerous Orphans* (thriller-gangster inflection) and *Bridge to Nowhere* (teenpic thriller-horror inflection).

The art film 2: 1986–2005

The art or experimental feature's short life circa 1975–1979 has already been noted. Its continued absence post-1986 – with Ward's *The Navigator* (1988) a lonely exception with its bracing high-art difficulties (epitomized in that opening sequence of Griffin's trance with its delayed establishing shots, alternation of monochrome and colour, and unexplained, though memorably vivid images) – has a double context: first, the internalized local division between experimental short film and large audience-friendly feature production, and, second, the older European art cinema's giving way to an international 'art house' cinema effecting complex compromises worldwide between art film and popular modes. The latter is particularly important as regards Ward's and Campion's later careers and those being developed by Caro (via *Whale Rider*'s greater stylistic conservatism), Jeffs, McGann and Maclean. As is noted below, melodrama/psychodrama has been the generic site where art film impulses have generally found a home (as demonstrated in such films as *Jack Be Nimble*, *Memory and Desire*, *The Piano* and *The Footstep Man*).

The immediate product of the new cheap digital technology has been an interesting but narrow range of films (such as *Shifter*) based on a hyper-realism particularly suited to miniscule budgets. Placed against both this and mainstream practice, Florian Habicht's *Woodenhead* (2003) is fascinatingly different, extending aesthetic experiment usually confined to the experimental short film to feature length.

Made in almost cottage-industry circumstances, though with considerably more resources (NZ$30,000) than *Shifter*, the differences that make *Woodenhead* unique among local films, and which have generated much international interest, can only be sketched here. Reversing usual audio-visual procedures, the whole soundtrack (not just the music) was pre-recorded as an eccentric sonic narrative before filming. This reversal's aesthetic spin-offs were, first, the soundtrack's elevation to much more than mere support for the images; second, Habicht's combining, in a way only associated with musicals in mainstream cinema, ideal sonic with ideal physical presence (if a Diane-Arbus-like category of the ideal pathetic-grotesque is admitted); and, third, developed from this, the film's systematically imperfect lip-synching, constantly adding to the off-key atmospheres generated through landscape, costume, characterization, acting styles and divergences from classical shooting. This sonic regime, which the characters fail to master, is a constantly activated trope for other misalignments in a world of misconstructions, misalliances, broken hearts and unfulfilled quests – 'The world is a difficult place', as the heroine Plum says. It is also a strangely invented place, another version of Ward's argument that the old-world material of *The Navigator* is as much the European-derived New Zealander's heritage as the European's.[19] Subtitled 'a Grimm musical Fairytale' it creates a world (a stylized and hyperbolic contraction of the director's Germano-New Zealand autobiographical situation) of New Zealand landscapes and characters seen through a prism of minatory fairytale. Here, Gert, the town's dustman (acted by Nicholas Butler, voiced by Steve Abel), is commanded by his employer, Hugo (Warwick Broadhead), to take his daughter Plum (Teresa Peters/Mardi Potter) to meet her unseen groom, resulting in a journey reminiscent of Hansel and Gretel, in which the childlike lovers have (somewhat grotesque) sexual relations, but are eventually separated. In a narrative dominated by the grotesque, devious and derelict – with the image of the town dump paramount –

Plum's brutish businessman father, Hugo, Hugo's wicked servant, Goerdel (Tony Bishop/Lutz Halbhuhner) and the escaped circus strongman Gustav (Matthew Sutherland), grotesquely laid low by love, are all given their moments of centrality and abject empathy. The film's circus allusions (culminating in the Chinese ringmaster [Henry Lee] who meets Gert on the beach and fails to persuade him to join the troupe) constitute not just a vision of life as tragic vaudeville, which the marionette-like Gert is too naïve or noble to accept as he chooses to return to solitary life by the dump, but a set of cinematic references different from any others activated in the New Zealand art film – an antic expressionism, the Eisensteinian 'attractions' of circus acts signalling alternatives to realism.

Later comedy: 1986–2003

Footrot Flats, Murray Ball, 1986; *Bad Taste*, Peter Jackson, 1986; *Pallet on the Floor*, Lynton Butler, 1986; *Send a Gorilla*, Melanie Read, 1988; *Zilch!*, Richard Riddiford, 1989; *Meet the Feebles*, Peter Jackson, 1990; *User Friendly*, Gregor Nicholas, 1990; *Ruby and Rata*, Gaylene Preston, 1990; *Old Scores*, Alan Clayton, 1991; *Braindead*, Peter Jackson, 1992; *Cops and Robbers*, Murray Reece, 1994; *Jack Brown, Genius*, Tony Hiles, 1994; *Bonjour Timothy*, Wayne Tourell, 1995; *Chicken*, Grant LaHood, 1996; *Topless Women Talk About Their Lives*, Harry Sinclair, 1997; *Via Satellite*, Anthony McCarten, 1998; *I'll Make You Happy*, Athena Tsoulis, 1999; *Magik and Rose*, Vanessa Alexander, 1999; *Hopeless*, Stephen Hickey, 1999; *The Price of Milk*, Harry Sinclair, 1999; *Savage Honeymoon*, Mark Beesley, 2000; *Jubilee*, Michael Hurst, 2000; *Toy Love*, Harry Sinclair, 2001; *Kombi Nation*, Grant LaHood, 2002; *Tongan Ninja*, Jason Stutter, 2002; *Stickmen*, Hamish Rothwell, 2003; *This Is Not a Love Story*, Keith Hill, 2003

At least as regards quantity, comedy has a major presence in recent New Zealand cinema, a product partly of policies favouring commercial 'feel good' films.[20] This account separates social from romantic and sex comedy, though boundaries blur. Surveying earlier comedy, another division was made between 'old' and 'new' comedy, with *Middle Age Spread* pivotal. That binary no longer dominates, with most later comedy contemporary and urban. Nevertheless, 'old' comedy's roots reach deep, the return to its stable knownness, often under the cloak of satire, allowing the recuperation of semi-atavistic pleasures. Tellingly, the age's paramount comedians – John Clarke (Fred Dagg), Ginette MacDonald (Lynn of Tawa), Billy T. James and the Topp Twins – all specialize(d) in self-conscious 'old comedy' stereotypes. Three films alluding to 'old comedy' are the popular cartoon feature *Footrot Flats*, with its loving satire of 'down on the farm', *Old Scores* and *Jubilee*.

Old Scores

In *Footrot Flats*, Wal dreams of scoring against the Lions and the French. Later, in *Tongan Ninja*, the hero, Sione, dreams of playing alongside Tana Umaga, the All Black centre. Contemporary sophistication knowingly refers to critiques of homosocial old New Zealand when the villain asks why he doesn't dream of girls, speculating that he may be 'a 'omo'. Sport's pre-eminence for New Zealanders may come under sporadic attack, but still remains a staple of life, even though life has grown more complex. At TK's funeral in *Carry Me Back* the rugby official envisages TK passing the ball on to his sons, but it is a pass into a different world. *Old Scores* (Alan Clayton, 1991), a Welsh/New Zealand co-production, coinciding with the 1991 Rugby World Cup, uses both societies' passion for rugby to meditate on similarities and differences, old cultures and new cultures, and white whakapapas (genealogies).

A dying touch judge's confession that he gave a winning test match try illicitly 'for Wales', twenty-five years before, catalyses the narrative, with the bi-national agreement to replay the game in Cardiff, with the original teams. This situation of middle-aged heroes taking the field again both reinforces and, simultaneously, distances the national obsession, since, for all the players, life has become more complicated than a game of two halves.

The contest's preparations assemble, on the New Zealand side, the most splendid cast of male cultural stereotypes since *Came a Hot Friday*, headed by the Coach, 'Acid' Aitken (Martyn Sanderson), a compendium of the old Pākehā male's shortcomings: militaristic, obsessive, single minded, shrewd, a more genially comedic version of the coach, Tupper, in the scriptwriter Greg McGee's more trenchantly satiric play, *Foreskin's Lament*. This is balanced by Celtic deviousness, particularly encapsulated in the Welsh comic actor Windsor Davis's President of the Welsh Rugby Union.

Some of the film's intricacies arise from the complication that Bleddyn Morgan (Robert Pugh), after winning the original match for Wales, emigrated to New Zealand because of amorous disappointments and, rejecting the land of his fathers, married a New Zealander. Within the parallel actions of the teams' preparations emerges a thematic of shared origins as well as differences rare in a contemporary cinema tending to assert New Zealandness almost parthenogenetically, so that between this populist film and the high art of *The Navigator*, with its medieval Cumbrians visiting their descendants, there is a curious bond in reverse. Here the white ancestors make themselves felt. Bleddyn, the new New Zealander, refusing to play for

Wales, is won over by his grandfather singing 'Land of Our Fathers'. In Wales, his wife Ngaire (Alison Bruce), charmed by older-world traditions, finds herself cheering against her own team, or, rather, for the past within the present, a past that in the official celebration of Māoriness and the beginnings of the multicultural revolution had begun to seem to many Pākehā undervalued. The project of this pleasant comedy is that one should cheer for both new and old, with the game drawn, when the All Black conversion that could win it is unknowingly made with the ancient Welsh heirloom of a ball cunningly introduced into play, which, dying of an expired bladder, ends up sitting on the crossbar, a neat emblem of the film's double allegiances.

Jubilee

Jubilee (Michael Hurst, 2000) in many ways returns to older small-town comedy, its running joke of Billy and his mates urinating on the pub wall (and suffering intimate shocks when its owner electrifies their unofficial urinal) the oldest style of New Zealand male humour (though in 2000 it might constitute mock punishment for the characters' atavism). A voiceover by Billy (Cliff Curtis) introduces Waimatua as New Zealand's kūmara (sweet potato) capital, the town's name later explained as meaning 'the source', these self-consciousnesses underwritten by the narrative's organization around the town school's seventy-fifth anniversary, and Billy's attempts to organize the celebrations. This anniversary theme, with Waimatua a ramshackle microcosm of the bicultural nation, asks if there is more to celebrate than Denis Glover's sardonic 1940 centennial poem found ('In the year of centennial splendours / There were fireworks and decorated cars / And pungas drooping from the verandahs / But no one remembered our failures'). Biculturality is amusingly articulated through the marriage of the Māori Billy and his Pākehā wife Pauly (Theresa Healey), and the town's integrated world of Pākehās and (mainly) Māori, allowing both familiar stereotypes and their subversion, with Māori characters knowledgeably wine tasting and Pauly burning down the cottage to avoid the dreaded visit of her mother-in-law, in a politically incorrect comic denial of the benefits of the Māori extended family so often used to criticize Pākehā atomism. It continues in the rejection of the commandeering of the jubilee by the overbearing Pākehā schoolmaster, Mr Crawford (Stephen Tozer), which brings about Billy's initially disastrous, but eventually triumphant, succession. The film's most interesting elements lie in its relaxed take on a New Zealand seen as an ambivalent mix of Māori and Pākehā elements, the Māori ones identified as genial, and people- and community-centred, but inefficient to the point where Pauly, exasperated with Billy, is tempted by the return of her first love, the former All Black captain Max Seddon (Kevin Smith), almost fleeing with him to Auckland at the height of the celebrations, before duty and affection recall her as the film celebrates the marriage's permanence and Billy's final success, although, contradicting what may have been thought too overt a binary, Kevin Smith's Pā kehā-Polynesian features prevent a simple bicultural/monocultural choice at the end. The most significant bicultural comedy was Billy T. James', on television. But his late sitcom *The Billy T. James Show*'s (1989/1990) incorporation of contentious material into an interracial family comedy, was less successful. By softening its comedicizing of conservative-radical conflict over race matters, *Jubilee* gives pleasure, but less ambitiously.

Other social comedies

Much 1990s social comedy takes a determinedly contemporary urban turn, attempting a playful, satiric registering of the instabilities of New Zealand society: for example, the job held by Billy (William Brandt) as virtual farmer, conducting sheepshearing exhibitions for Japanese tourists in *User Friendly*, or the same film's villainness, Miranda (Judith Gibson), when told that the Tokabaruan Pacific Islanders miss their pillaged dog goddess, replying 'Who cares what they want?' just a year before the 'cultural properties' concerns of *Te Rua*. *Cops and Robbers, User Friendly, Chicken, Jack Brown, Genius* and *Zilch!* parallel to a small and timid degree, with their often black comedy of an economically and morally unregulated society, Jackson's horror-comedies *Bad Taste* and *Brain Dead*, and the grossout wit of *Meet the Feebles*, though without anything like their relentless nerve. Another group of films centres on families or surrogate families, *Via Satellite* (working-class family), *I'll Make You Happy* (Karangahape Road prostitutes) and *Savage Honeymoon* (Auckland West Coast biker family), managing to retain kinds of unity under the pressure of the fracturing of social myths of equality and cohesion. The key social comedy of the period, *Ruby and Rata*, manages, though with unassuming rather than frenetically grotesque strategies, to intertwine aspects of both sets of films.

Ruby and Rata

Gaylene Preston's *Ruby and Rata*, like much of the director's work, combines social concern, female protagonists, subversive wit and generous sympathies. It brings into relationship the octogenarian Ruby (Yvonne Lawley) – Pākehā, middle class, anglophile – and Rata

Cawley (Vanessa Rare), a single-parent Māori street girl, tugging her psychologically endangered child, Willy (Lee Mete-Kingi) through a peripatetic no-address life of minor benefit frauds and fly-by-night exits. Their lives intersect when Rata, impersonating a financial executive, arrives as Ruby's prospective tenant, installing herself before Ruby registers her racial and underclass undesirableness. War breaks out, with Ruby drawing Willy into her control as her errand-running 'slave', by exploiting the child's mistaking her for a witch. As Willy, to Rata's exasperation, comes to love the old woman, Rata's deteriorating relations with the social services put her in danger of losing custody. As she faces prosecution for benefit fraud and Ruby is hospitalized, a temporary utopian solution is found for everyone: so that she can continue to live at home, Ruby gifts her property to Willy, allusively meaningful in the light of the new retrospective Treaty of Waitangi claims.

Ruby and Rata redresses the absence from the cinema of the consequences of the cutbacks of the mid-1980s on, with the odd couple both victims of the new State Owned Enterprises order – Ruby facing the Golden Sunset Eventide retirement home, Rata at the bottom of the economic heap, and Willy, speechless for much of the narrative, victimized by her peripatetically chaotic lifestyle. It also brings the corporate culture into view through Ruby's pretence of an executive position at Conspec ('con' to cheat, 'spec' to speculate), within whose gleaming building she works as a cleaner. Rata's 'Apocalypse' song lyrics make variations on the dominant bureaucratic ethos: 'Fill me out a form, make me sign on the dotted line, / It doesn't make a difference to your world, but it does to mine ... And you can't tell me what to do, / You just want me to be like you'.

The film's major characters are constantly implicated in deceptive language, pretences and impersonations.[21] In a microcosm of such effects, Rata assumes the language of financial expertise to intimidate Ruby's nephew, the aspiring yuppie, Buckle (Simon Barnett), while, showing her the flat, Buckle adopts estate agent's terminology, which Rata knowingly deconstructs. Rata mimics social-service jargon to 'tickle' her welfare officer; disguised as pregnant, she tries to claim benefits. Buckle takes in her band with his assumed managerial expertise, demanding, with unconscious irony, that they should perform 'with a little more integrity'. Neither Ruby nor Rata is idealized: Ruby's deceits, snobbery, authoritarianism, selfishness and tinges of racism match Rata's asocial individualist concerns (Rata sleeps with Buckle only while she thinks he has access to his father's money). But the characters' deceptions are understandable, even necessary, strategies for survival in the world they inhabit.

Like all Preston's features, *Ruby and Rata* prioritizes female experience, but pivotal to the narrative is Willy, the delinquent boy, who is eventually gifted a two-generation female family, rather than a mostly absentee mother, thus making the relationship between Willy and Ruby central. Culturally poor, Rata has inherited nothing either from her original culture, or, except for street savvy, from the dominant one. Though she loves Willy, her mothering is deficient, with little to pass on to him, wholly taken up as she is with surviving. Ruby's world may be quaintly passé, a curious amalgam of imperial England, old New Zealand and the mystic East, but it is redolent with meaning and emotion. Her prayers may be sentimental, but they invoke values beyond the uncaring social milieu's. Ruby's history, however eccentrically, provides a map of the human heart for Willy. The film's wariness of easy sentiment will not let the characters wholly escape the age's ethos; the final settlement is 'a business arrangement', a house for mother and son, in return for enabling Ruby's continued independence, but a 'business arrangement', inflected by more caring elements, that both reflects and transcends its environment.

Sex comedy/romantic comedy

Jack (Paul Newman): Are you very modern in New Zealand?

Barbara (Jean Simmons): Oh people fall in and out of love here too, yes. (*Until They Sail*)

Monica (to Nick): I just missed ya. Ya old bastard. (*Arriving Tuesday*)

In New Zealand's cinema, romantic comedy runs a poor second to sex comedy, satire and deconstructed romance. Several factors explain this: first, strong early traditions of deflationary masculinist comedy militated against the genre; second, in the 1980s, feminist views of masculine culpability were equally as inhibiting to romance. Recent US television comedy influences have purveyed a humour of confusion in the sexual sphere, impinging on a cinema without Hollywood's or Britain's traditions of affirmative couple comedy. The lack of such models and the niche-market targeting of younger audiences through immature even dorkish protagonists (as in *Hopeless*) have been as influential lately, perhaps, as what can be generalized about unromantic national characteristics. The title of *This is Not a Love Story* thus underlines a tendency in New Zealand cinema. There the squirmingly gauche Belinda (Sarah Smuts Kennedy), finds her inconstant object of desire in a TV actor, whose comic character has to metamorphose into a Christian in order to gain a new audience niche, suggesting a parallel between the risible oddity of Christianity in a secular society and the misprisions of romantic love. Even Emily Dickinson, when quoted, adds to the scepticism: 'We outgrow love like other things / And put it in a drawer'. Vanessa Alexander's *Magik and Rose*, despite its double romantic resolution, is more about the individual women's problems and their odd couple bonding. Even in *Arriving Tuesday* (1984), the romantic comedy of Nick and Monica's fraught relationship (complicated by their encounter with Rawere Paratene's Rick), is more a means of exploring mid-1980s Pākehā attitudes to bicultural New Zealand than to romance itself. Even *The Price of Milk*, treated below as the apex of local romantic comedy, shares similar deflectionary characteristics.

Send a Gorilla

As the last film emerging from the early period of difficult female breakthroughs into the industry, Melanie Read's *Send a Gorilla* (1988), propelled by an aggressive feminism verging on retributive misandry, also fits this dominant pattern of unromantic romantic comedy. Often thought a complete failure, it is more interesting than that. Slapdash and approximate though some of its sequences are, it has any amount of verve and colour – literally so in its bright, deliberately unmasculine palette, emblematized by the pink Fiat Bambino which announces a garish girls-versus-boys competition with *Pork Pie*'s yellow mini – and ambitious aspirations towards an opera-like aesthetic.

In its crowded narrative, three Wellington girls working for a novelty telegram company – Clare (Carmel McGlone), fighting her ex-husband for custody of her son, Joy (Katherine McRae), training as an opera singer (which motivates some vivid operatic moments), and Vicki (Perry Piercy), who begins the film by literally throwing her unfaithful boyfriend out – carry out a relentless schedule of delivering messages on the commercialized festival of Romantic Love, Saint Valentine's Day. Their performative telegram deliveries structure the narrative, along with the progress of Clare's custody case, Joy's singing ambitions, and Vicki's progression from anger (attacking Lisa, who slept with her boyfriend) to finding love again, though in keeping with the film's satiric and anti-romantic tone her falling for a fireman is too clichéd to be for a moment serious.

The telegram scenarios vary, but are generally characterized by the remark 'It's a Revenge Telegram: always a favourite of mine'. Saint Valentine's Day seems less a festival of love than a saturnalia of false consciousness. Elsewhere, though, complexity infiltrates the satire, whether by conscious design or otherwise, with recipients turning on the deliverers, while, in reported offscreen incidents, telegrams find the wrong targets, with Clare admitting, 'I've just delivered a Valentine to a man whose wife died five days ago'. At times the heroines act as grotesquely as the male comic monsters they skewer. For instance Vicky's abuse of Lisa ('you smell of breastfeeding'), suggesting almost pathological disgust with female reproduction, is cited as disturbing by Ann Hardy.[22] More creatively complex is what Hardy analyses with reference to Jungian psychology, the shadow implications of the gorillagram suit which Clare, vying with Vicki as the angriest of the trio, wears, as an unconscious expression of her rage. *Send a Gorilla* swings between punitive scenarios – at a men's club a huge penis-shaped pink mousse is destroyed – moments of self-inspection, comic invention, social critique and colourful celebration in the delivery of a telegram (Habanera-style) to a Japanese soprano, and the final operatic street number. Its faults prefigure those of spasmodically inventive but ill-disciplined 'social' comedies like *Cops and Robbers*, *Chicken* and *User Friendly*, and its rancour makes romance impossible, but its energy and invention provide compensations.

Stickmen

Publicity for the metro-glamorous *Stickmen* exploited some small resemblance to a popular contemporary British crime film – '*Lock Stock and Two Smoking Barrels* meet Courtenay Place', asserted one piece of publicity[23] – though the resemblance is lesser than *Scarfies*' to *Shallow Grave*. However, in both cases the New Zealand versions achieve original inflections, mixing their 'deliberately international, unerringly commercial style with an idiosyncratic New Zealand sensibility'.[24]

Stickmen's primary interest is announced by a barrage of verbal and visual phallic puns: cues, balls, balls in pockets, Jack and Karen's hyperbolic intercourse intercut with the opening's pub pool game. Though the male pool-playing trio intersect with the margins of the underworld, *Stickmen* is never a crime film, but about masculinity, spurred on by British 'new laddism' translated into New Zealand metropolitan terms. As a response, much layered in irony, to perceptions of female societal predominance, it presents unregenerate males wholly untouched (except for sexual needs) by femininity, but divides them into the unreally cool Polynesian superstud, John (Robbie Magasiva) – endlessly sexually engaged with Karen (Simone Kessel), whose name he studiously cannot recall – and the two genial 'poor white' losers, Wayne (Scott Willis) and Thomas (Paolo Rotono) – both ditched by bored girlfriends, with Thomas only rescued from his relational ineptitude by the initiative-taking claim on him by Sara (Ann Nordhaus). At one point Thomas relates to Jack a story about a depressive building a device to hold his genitals while he cuts them off, an abysmal counterpoint to the film's phallic celebrations. Of the three heroes, only Jack is employed in any mainstream sense: Thomas attends female-led seminars reinterpreting redundancy as 'birthing', and Wayne's only work is chauffeuring call girls, his only half-possibility of relationship eventually with a call girl traumatized by a client falling asleep on top of her.

In the pool tournament, the 'heroes' chart a victorious but difficult progress between extremes, defeating a gay bar team (despite the distractions of TV monitors showing anal intercourse), then a team of catholic priests, in their way provoking equally difficult reactions, only to face semi-final defeat at the hands of 'Bastinado', whose minatory title is a front for Karen and Sara, needing the prize money for their London OE (overseas experience). Sara, however, throws the game for love of Thomas, and the boys win the final. In the narrative's one love relationship, Sara's devotion to Thomas involves no idealization ('You're a man of simple wants', she says after he orders instant coffee in a coffee bar), suggesting the heterosexual woman's need to shop resignedly downmarket. *Stickmen* cleverly has its cake and eats it, simultaneously sharp and fuzzy in its update on metropolitan sexuality, presenting images of male independence and sexual power, centred around Jack, but contradicting these with the socially impotent Thomas and Wayne, and allowing a female ironic gaze, as well as comic castration in the girls' appropriation of the phallic pool-playing gear.

Harry Sinclair, Topless Women Talk About Their Lives *(1997),* The Price of Milk *(1999),* Toy Love *(2001)*

Sinclair's three features are New Zealand cinema's sole instance of sustained attention to sex and romantic comedy, with *The Price of Milk* swerving from his usual sex comedy to romance. The ingratiating cleverness of several early shorts suggested what the features confirm, that Sinclair is one of contemporary New Zealand cinema's distinctive presences, particularly well known – a trait both applauded and criticized – for his improvisatory techniques. Characteristic attachments to the self-reflexive and the meta-cinematic figure in the home-movie-like beginning of *Topless Women Talk About Their Lives*, where the German tourist asks Liz (Danielle Cormack) and Pru (Willa O'Neill) if they are on the beach used for *The Piano*, a question which amusingly contrasts Sinclair's small-scale improvisatory art with New Zealand's most famous melodrama, and the girls' fooling with the heavier resonances of the Holly Hunter/Anna Paquin dyad. In *The Price of Milk*, meta-cinematic self consciousness is equally pervasive in the film's fairytale ambiance and gently surreal images: the bath in the paddock (Figure 16), the agoraphobic dog in the box, and the painterly philosophical allusion to Magritte's *La Condition humaine*, provided by the easel-like window and its view from Rob and Lucinda's house.

The two sex comedies, *Topless Women* and *Toy Love*, follow the chaotic relationships of Auckland twenty-somethings, displaying a knowing anti-romantic resistance to last-minute amorous epiphanies. In *Topless Women*, though Liz's (Danielle Cormack) baby is born, her vagrant relationships result in no commitments. Though *Toy Love* ends with the coupling of Ben (Dean O'Gorman) and Chlo (Kate Elliot), its site is an Air New Zealand jet's toilet, under the curious psychological condition of being observed by Chlo's toy cat, Frank, and only made possible by Chlo's perceiving Ben as 'unavailable' (her condition for sexual excitement) because he is narcissistically in love with

16. The unconventionally sited bathing arrangements of Lucinda (Danielle Cormack) catch the oneiric, mildly surrealistic ambiance of Harry Sinclair's *The Price of Milk* (2000).

himself. When Ben does fall in love with Chlo (or with her condition of ungraspableness), he is uncharacteristically impelled to utter the word 'love', but knows he must not. His solution, after an initial scenario in which they role-play a bored middle-aged couple for 'our first fuck', is to impersonate young honeymooners, allowing him, under the cover of irony, to say the unutterable. In contrast, the word 'fuck' is endlessly uttered, its ubiquity as a sign of sex rather than romantic comedy underlined when Ben meets Jim's daughter – a pre-pubescent child, disturbingly aware of her stepfather's adulteries – who in her distress vainly attempts to utter the 'f –f– f' word, but is one of the few characters in the two films unable to break down constraints against it. This literal child, like the films' other children and infants, ironically emphasizes the older characters' long-lasting childishness, most literally enacted by Chlo, who, after sex with Ben, disappears into a cubbyhole to gorge herself on 'Cocopops'. Sinclair's unchanging preoccupation with his post-adolescents may sometimes appear a juvenilely regressive trait. It might, however, be more profoundly interpreted as a fascination with characters who hyperbolically embody the instabilities of desire with which he is fascinated, and which his films suggest are psychically ineradicable.

In *The Price of Milk*, Rob (Karl Urban) and Lucinda (Danielle Cormack) live happily on their dairy farm, until Lucinda's sudden fear that Rob has tired of her prompts her to follow advice from her girlfriend Drusophila (Willa O'Neill) that quarrelling revives passion, leading her to swap his herd in order to recover their mysteriously stolen quilt, an act which breaks up their relationship, and leads to Rob marrying the manipulative Drusophila, before true love prevails.

Full of delicate dreamscape dawn and dusk ambiances, *The Price of Milk's* contemporary fairytale mysteriously softens harsh actualities. One violent reality transformed is the worryingly high national road-death toll. In *The Price of Milk*, potentially fatal accidents continually contrive to be harmless: Lucinda, driving carelessly, knocks over the Māori grandmother, without harming her; as the girls smoke dope in an upturned car, Lucinda comments 'I always take that corner too fast'; after offscreen crash sounds, Bernie (Michael Lawrence) appears, saying unconcernedly, 'tricky corner that one'. After Drusophila crashes her car, Bernie's small truck is revealed sitting on top of it, explained by his 'Sorry about that, I wasn't concentrating'. Immediately, from the sky, a detached caravan falls to earth.

A second metamorphosis softens the everyday cruelty of animal farming. New Zealand town dwellers have often been shocked by farmers' treatment of working dogs. In *It's Lizzie To Those Close* the farmer's son brutally shoots Lizzie's dog; the gaunt farmer in *Arriving Tuesday* commits the same act. In *The Price of Milk*, Rob's dog, Nigel, is a neurotic agoraphobic, self-encased in a cardboard box. When Bernie compliments Rob as too nice a guy to have him put down, he implies that most farmers would. As the title suggests, Rob's cows are central, their whole apparent meaning their yield in conjunction with market rates.[25] Like any modern farmer, Rob, rather than naming his cows, numbers them with instrumental efficiency. Yet, with tender improbability, he greets each one as if by name – '18, how are ya? ... 39, good to see ya'. (How would he tell them they were bound for the freezing works after their fifth calfless lactations?) In preparation for Lucinda's wedding, the Hindu Bhanas, owners of the local store, array the cows in colourful paints and finery, honouring their sacred role of producing milk and ghee.

A third sector of transmuted anxiety (perhaps making conscious ludic variations on Mita's 'white neurotic cinema') lies in the film's Māori who, in a way slightly reminiscent of *The Piano*, but more self-consciously, function as an unpredictable fairylike population surrounding the Pākehās' oneiric terrain of wishes and dreams. Again, minatory phenomena, whilst playfully transmogrified, do not completely vanish (the difference between anodyne and complex pastoral), but unpredictably veer between charm and comic threat. Even the nephews' bizarre addiction to golf fits this pattern, reflecting not just the game's popularity among Māori and the successes of Michael Campbell (the Māori winner of the US Open), but, in an oblique transmutation, the well-remembered Bastion Point protest (1997–1998, the subject of Merata Mita's documentary) over tribal land converted into a golf course. The opening's visual equivalence between quilt and landscape ('country crumpled like an unmade bed' in Denis Glover's poem 'The Search'), begins a playful reworking of the disturbance to Pākehā life of Māori land claims, though with a touch of anxiety in the transmutations preventing total relaxation: for example, the grandmother's complaints of feeling 'cold', her mass appropriation of quilts, her remark on returning Lucinda's quilt that she might ask for it back, and the nephews (in an antic version of Waitangi Tribunal awards) building a huge power station to warm her.

What of the romantic plot's connection with this interwoven material? In Rob's and Lucinda's vicissitudes, instabilities are internally generated, by, presumably, Lucinda's fears of love's evanescence. Just as the minatory aspects of Māori land claims, the road toll and farming's brutal nature are caressed into a half-fairytale world, so the central (usually unspoken) problem of romantic narratives, the instability of desire – the subject of Sinclair's sex comedies – is filtered through the idealities of romantic love and the film's dreamlike palette: its greens and blues, its dawn and dusk shadings, and sari-bright colours against the hills, mutedly psychedelic especially in combination with Danielle Cormack's Rapunzel-like corn-coloured hair, the faint drugginess of the visuals itself a refinement of the soft-drug-taking almost obligatory in New Zealand films. The film also deploys an unexpected sonic-emotive background of late Russian romantic music from works like Liadov's *The Enchanted Lake* and Rimsky-Korsakov's *Scheherezade*, interacting with hyperbolic love conceits, Lucinda's tears filling her bath, the fridge leaking lactic oceans. The film shares, perhaps unconsciously, with its companion pieces a Schopenhauerian view of love, in which the comedy of the lovers' frenzies are ironized by their causes in the reproductive instinct whose consequences they try to avoid.[26] *Topless Women* begins with the doctor telling Liz that forgetting her abortion appointment means she wants the child, and ends with the infant's birth in a vet's clinic, surrounded by animal spectators. With the film synchronized with Cormack's real-life pregnancy, her swollen stomach is displayed throughout, oiled in one scene, in another providing a momentary *trompe l'oeil* as in a beachscape it appears momentarily to be a sand dune. In *The Price of Milk* such physicality is refined away into the unconscious mechanisms spurring on Lucinda's obsessive collecting of baby shoes, stored in the womb of her suitcase, rising mysteriously to the surface of the (enchanted) lake where Drusophila has thrown them, and then in the film's last lines overtly linked to the couple's lovemaking.

Melodrama/psychodrama

Crush, Alison Maclean, 1992; *The Footstep Man*, Leon Narbey, 1992; *Desperate Remedies*, Peter Wells and Stewart Main, 1993; *Jack Be Nimble*, Garth Maxwell, 1993; *The Piano*, Jane Campion, 1993; *Heavenly Creatures*, Peter Jackson, 1994; *Broken English*, Gregor Nicholas, 1996; *Saving Grace*, Costa Botes, 1997; *Memory and Desire*, Niki Caro, 1997; *When Love Comes*, Garth Maxwell, 1998; *Channelling Baby*, Christine Parker, 1999; *Rain*, Christine Jeffs, 2001; *The Waiting Place*, Christobal Araus Lobos, 2001; *Perfect Strangers*, Gaylene Preston, 2003; *Orphans and Angels*, Harold Brodie, 2003; *In My Father's Den*, Brad McGann, 2004

> 'c comme **collision** / r comme **revolte** / u comme **urgence** / s comme **sexe** / h comme **haine**' (French poster for *Crush*, 1992)

The category 'melodrama' here embraces both 'family melodrama' and 'the woman's film' as well as common usages attached to a trans-generic mode, whether melodramas of 'action' or 'passion'.[27] Recent instances of the last are *The Waiting Place* and *Orphans and Angels*, both characterized by psychically extreme situations, like the former's in which one of the escaped murderers hiding in the abandoned mental hospital eventually rapes the other under the illusion that he is the wife he murdered, then offers him/her a knife to kill him. 'Psychodrama' might be the preferred New Zealand category, used by Roger Horrocks, for films prioritizing intense mental states and conflicts.[28] Narratives described by either term pursue reversals, recognitions, highly wrought 'situations', often 'the greatest possible intensity of feeling' and 'a demonstrative and often hyperbolic aesthetic'.[29] For instance, Costa Botes' *Saving Grace* certainly embodies a highly wrought 'situation', involving a Māori carpenter (Jim Moriarty), who, like Johannes in Dreyer's *Ordet*, claims to be the Christ, and a street girl (Kirsty Hamilton), whose need to believe impels her to nail gun him to his cross. Botes' film eventually takes a more secular turn than Dreyer's, leaving no doubt that Gerald is deluded, but its aim is less a case study of delusion than an exploration of desires for transcendence.

Thomas Elsaesser's analysis of film melodrama aesthetics, 'Tales of Sound and Fury', defines 'the appeal to a reality of the psyche' through discontinuity, fissure, coincidence, dynamic expressive codes of *mise-en-scène* and music, 'sublimation of dramatic conflict into décor, colour, gesture, and composition of frame', and the way 'melos is given to "drama" by means of lighting, montage, visual rhythm, décor, style of acting, music'.[30] Such definitions are particularly interesting for a cinema where dominant forms of 'classical' realism were challenged by a concentration of films between 1992 and 1994: *Crush* (1992), *The Footstep Man* (1992), *Desperate Remedies* (1993), *The Piano* (1993), *Jack Be Nimble* (1993) and *Heavenly Creatures* (1994). Not just *The Piano*, but all these films embraced marginalized melodramatic modes. As regards 'a demonstrative and often hyperbolic aesthetic' (which stylistically reticent psychodramas like *Saving Grace* and *The Lunatics' Ball* hardly approach), consider *Crush*'s jabbingly insistent uses of reds in décor, costume, and *mise-en-scène*, as well as the orange- reddish filtered colouring of the bubbling mud in the long opening shot, an unashamedly unmodulated trope of underground passions (sex, hate, revolt) against which the acid lime green of the titles clash with immediate dissonance (collison, urgency), and also Alison Maclean's estranging uses of the most banally colourful touristic-cinematic counters of New Zealandness – thermal Rotorua, but shot in winter, television images of the All Blacks hakaing before a test match, Māori women poi dancing, all displayed as if in the distorting mirror of the electric toaster's surface which Lane offers Colin to view the results of the haircut she has given him. As regards discontinuity, fissure, coincidence, take *Channelling Baby*'s enacting of the last in the fateful geometries of Geoff, returning to attempt a reconciliation with Bunnie, walking past their house where both his and the audience's perspectives are blocked, leading to his (and the audience's) misinterpretation of Bunnie shouting 'I know you're there, you stay away from me, you hear', words seen later by the audience (via Cassandra's narration, where a different angle unblocks the scene) as aimed at the obsessed child, not Geoff, whom Bunnie (being blind) does not know is there.

However, this counter-tradition has been, with the exceptions of *Heavenly Creatures* and *The Piano*, unpopular at the box office and with many critics, as recently demonstrated in the generally obtuse reception given to Preston's *Perfect Strangers*. Reviewing that film, this author interpreted the moment in *Memory and Desire* where Joel Tobeck's nameless young New Zealander attacks a party of surfies mocking the Japanese heroine's ecstatic grieving dance, as an allegory of frustration at, and even punishment of, local audiences' insensitivity to the mode.[31] The more positive recent receptions of *Rain* and *In My Father's Den* may contradict the trend; however, they contain relatively little aesthetically disconcerting for audiences. *Heavenly Creatures*, of course, had its subject's notoriety to help it, as well as the dynamic, often comic, attractions of the girls' fantasies. Also, *The Piano* particularly appealed to female audiences everywhere, not least in New Zealand.

Poles of melodrama: two films by Garth Maxwell (i) *Jack Be Nimble*
If a single New Zealand film most embodies Elsaesser's categories it might be Garth Maxwell's *Jack Be Nimble* (1993), one of the few works, in a cinema where 'classical' subordination of aesthetic densities to narrative smoothness is the norm, in which colour, design, sound and juxtaposition of image dominate. The dark fairytale-alluding narrative centres on two children, Jack and Dora (played as adolescents and adults by Alexis Arquette and Sarah Smuts Kennedy), abandoned by their mentally ailing mother (Tricia Phillips) and their brutally uncaring father (Paul Minifie), and losing each other when they are separately adopted: Jack by grotesquely cruel farmers, Clarrie (Tony Barry) and Bernice (Elizabeth Hawthorne), and their four sinister daughters, a condensation of cultural critiques of the farm as synecdoche for older New Zealand as a fount of cruelty, philistinism and violence, in their vendetta against Jack and Dora, beyond reveng-

ing their parents' murders, implacable to-the-death pursuer-destroyers of difference and sensitivity.

Jack murders his unspeakable step-parents with a hypnosis-inducing machine cobbled together out of bric-a-brac as in an adolescent's dream of revenge on a hostile world. United with his psychically empowered sister, though resenting her relationship with her lover and fellow psychic Teddy (Bruno Lawrence), Jack sets out with Dora to find their biological parents, a quest culminating in Jack also murdering their biological father with his machine. But as Jack passes beyond the pale, he and Dora are pursued by the malevolent sisters, farm-truck-driving Eumenides, who eventually slaughter both Jack and Teddy, before Dora destroys them with her telekinetic powers. In the film's coda, Dora, pregnant with Teddy's child, whom she addresses in her womb as Jack's reincarnation, is reunited with her natural mother.

Stated barely, the narrative seems glaringly excessive, but its flaws are minor. Within its dreamlike movements, images of startling power abound, holding remarkable condensations of meaning. In one sequence, intercutting between the separated children, little Dora hesitates to cut her birthday cake decorated with an idyllic farmyard inhabited by tiny animals, including a marzipan pig, while little Jack, dragged out by his sisters, is forced to watch a sadistic Clarrie butchering a real pig. As Jack looks aghast at the strung-up carcass, a close-up of its blood dripping into a bucket turns one drop into a blood-red birthday cake for Dora. Another sequence estranges that local backyard icon, the revolving clothesline (by way of Blyth's *Angel Mine*) as the mother's breakdown is figured by her face's engulfment by a sheet blowing on the line, while another, as if animated, attacks her. The narrative's positive elements cluster around the marigolds in Teddy's garden, some of which he picks and places in a vase when Dora first enters his house, and about which he recites a poem, actions and words repeated by Dora's restored mother in the film's last moments. Patterns of yellow and orange deriving from them abound, from the opening title sequence's flash-panning of orange light through black foliage shapes, to the ginger cat Jack's school friend lets him hold, to the orange and black tree design in Dora's bedroom, to their part in the memorable composition created by Dora lying down with her great weight of dark hair spread around her face, full of yellow and orange flowers, an image disrupted by the shocking cut to Jack's agonized, bloodied, upside-down face as he is dragged away by the dreadful sisters, the juxtaposed images creating a rush of concentrated heavenly/hellish meanings that it is hard to imagine not exciting any viewer alive to cinema's visuality.

Poles of melodrama: two films by Garth Maxwell (ii) *When Love Comes*

Of the mainstream genres the most conducive to the intense play of aesthetic signifiers are melodrama and the musical, combined by Maxwell in his second feature. However, not all melodrama is as extreme as *Jack Be Nimble*; indeed, films where moments of excess punctuate relatively realistic texts are more common (for example, Sirk's American melodramas), just as in the backstage musical, the stage numbers are moments of utopian enactment that intersect with, but do not wholly take over, the narrative. *When Love Comes* is a backstage drama, foregrounding sometimes painful material, a melodramatic musical like *New York, New York*, in which, if one thinks of Richard Dyer's five categories of utopic peformance, 'intensity', which paradoxically may embody painful emotions in a celebratory genre, predominates.[32]

The narrative follows the interactions and couplings of six characters connected to the commercial music scene – two young lesbians, Sally (Sophie Hawthorne), a singer, and Fig (Nancy Brunning), a drummer, beginning their careers; Mark (Dean O'Gorman), their brilliant, unstable lyricist, torn between promiscuity and fidelity; his older lover, Stephen (Simon Prast), and Katie Keen (Rena Owen), a vocalist who has made it in America, but returned home to try to surmount a career crisis, and visit her old friend, Stephen, followed out by her American manager/lover Eddy (Simon Westaway). After various complications, the three couples are together at the film's end, two of them, Katie and Eddy (though it is true to say that their heterosexual relationship is underdone in comparison with the homosexual ones), and Simon and Mark contrasting in their knowledge of love's and life's vicissitudes with Sally and Fig, hardly touched by experience. The film's treatment of what Mark calls 'the love thing' is emblematized in all its meaningful absurdity by Steven's gaudy paperback, Cherie La Fontaine's *Love's Furious Raptures*, with the hyperbolic heterosexuality of its cover cleverly referencing the pre-polymorphous era's homosexual artist's dependence on camp.[33] *When Love Comes* approaches the homosexual milieu very differently from the straightforward realism of *Squeeze* and the camp pyrotechnics of *Desperate Remedies*. Here the camp is more verbal than visual, the realism constantly inflected by highly wrought images (such as the recurring green-lit playground swing), and theatricality, as in Fig's and Sally's overt presentation of the action. Celebrating a more polymorphous era, the film preserves, through its older characters' reminiscences, past as well as present social history in Steven's reminiscences of the 'brilliant period' of coming out: 'Maybe it wasn't so brilliant. Where did all that getting in touch with your anus get me?' Something more of the film's many layered tone – emotive, theatrical, camp, moving – is caught in Katie's reminiscence of her small-town beginnings: 'Oh, baby, if you'd seen me. Hot pants with this flicky sort of Carly Simon hairdo, oh, and my shoulder bag nicked from "Sensations" in Kaitaia ... Baby, I was news'.

When Love Comes, as a musical, combines literal *melos* with its non-musical extensions. Its three big songs enact extremes of emotional experience, from Mark's celebration of love's masochistic abjection ('Suck the hand, the hand that bleeds you / Bleed the one that needs you'), to his elegy for lost love ('In another year when we are dust, / When the big waves have rolled through, / Perhaps there'll be another me, / Waiting for another you'), to the infectious optimism of Katie's old hit ('A Brand New Start'). During Sally's performance of 'Suck the Hand', screeched almost ferally, Mark, shot from estranging angles, staggers out of control with drink and drugs, fellates a dreadlocked stranger, and returns to feed Fig and Sally hallucinogens, the drug-clouded momentary strangeness of the scene being that they are seated in front of themselves still performing. Mark's lyric, dedicated to Steven, 'In another year' is sung by Sally in a studio, its half-regretful, half-hopeful plangencies listened to by Fig, Mark and Katie, and assisted by Katie as session singer. Whereas most musicals show audiences deindividualized into rapt unanimity, this number individualizes their responses, particularly Mark's as he remembers looking at Steven through his window, and Katie's, perhaps thinking about lost love, but also wondering whether helping Sally means calling time on her own career. The third number, 'A Brand New Start', is first heard played diegetically as Steven demonstrates to Mark how important Katie has been, with his dancing to the recording happily catching the fleeting utopian potentialities of popular music. Floating extra-diegetically over the film's end, the song presides over all the characters with its lyrics of emotional renewal, which, however, within their optimism, reflect all the characters' fracturedness between competing drives for individual assertion and coupledness ('I know I can do it on my own / I know I can get there all alone / All I'm looking for is a guy / Who's ready for my kind of love ... my sweet embrace, my certain heart, / No more mistakes, a brand new start').

The Footstep Man: psychodrama and metadrama

In the New Zealand cinema, where art films are scarce, melodrama/psychodrama has provided a home for elements of the mode, not only by its foregrounding of the aesthetic, but in its self-reflexive tendencies, reminding us, paradoxically in the most emotional of genres, of the processes of artistic manufacture, sometimes through highly wrought artifice, and sometimes through allusion to artworks. Think of 'the Man' playing 'Madam Butterfly' and reciting Dennis Glover's love poem in *Perfect Strangers*; of Bunnie's piano-tuner vocation in *Channelling Baby*; of the author–critic situation and Lane's quoting of Colin McCahon on the landscape in *Crush*; of *When Love Comes*' music-industry setting; of *Desperate Remedies*' use of *La forza del destino* and the quoting of Hardy's first novel in its title; of *Heavenly Creatures*' heroines' obsessions with Mario Lanza, film and opera; of *Rain*'s motif of photography; of the role of poems, photographs, books and paintings in *In My Father's Den*; and, of course, of Ada's piano and the *Bluebeard* play in *The Piano*.

Leon Narbey's meta-filmic *The Footstep Man* has relations both with Truffaut's film about film-making, *La Nuit américaine* (1973), and Woody Allen's intersecting of on- and offscreen worlds, *The Purple Rose of Cairo* (1985). It is a mark of Narbey's ambition that his film combines both situations. The protagonist, Sam (Steven Grives), a 'footstep man' or 'foley artist ' (that is, a sound-effects technician), identifies with the heroine Mireille's drowning herself at the end of the film he is working on because of his own attempted suicide by drowning after his wife left him, taking their daughter. His identification with Mireille (Jennifer Ward-Lealand), is so strong that she appears to him in dreams, speaks to him from the film, and he even dreams himself into the fictional brothel where she works.

As Sam works on the film, enough of it is shown for its major situation to be clear. *Monsieur Henri* is, though a New Zealand production with New Zealand actors, set in nineteenth-century Paris. In it, a model and lover of Toulouse-Lautrec (Michael Hurst), the prostitute Mireille, decides to emigrate to Argentina, but, before she leaves, learns that she has syphilis. As the film ends, she drowns herself, a situation so fraught for Sam that he tries to influence the director, the archly named Vida Brevis (Rosey Jones), to change the ending to reflect the hope he feels after his own *Piano*-like survival. Vida, whose equally personal response to the film is coloured by her sister's suicide, asserts directorial authority, refusing to reprieve Mireille.

As the 'Foley Man', Sam literally walks in the characters' shoes to create their footsteps, either dragging his foot on the treadmill for Toulouse-Lautrec's limp, or clattering along in Mireille's high heels. At one point he torturedly mimics his own emotions to provide Lucy's gasps as she lies dying of syphilis. With Vida also rewatching Mireille's suicide, the film's psychodrama revolves around the film-makers' identification with the characters whose lives they control. Vida not only wants the film to mirror her despair at her sibling's suicide, but also takes personally the question she asks about Mireille's sexual relationships with Marcelle and Henri: whether she can love as well as be loved? (There are suggestions that Vida, like Mireille, is bisexual, though *The Footstep Man*'s financial problems resulted in the part of Vida's female lover Lyndi being cut merely to a phone call).[34] Sam has complex relationships with both central fictional figures, mirroring Henri's reluctantly helping Mireille to leave in his own attempts to accept his wife's departure, desiring Mireille, who sleeps with him when she visits him in a dream, and reading her actions at the narrative's end as mirroring his own. The relationship, perhaps temporary, between Sam and Vida that ends the film, smiled on by a spectral Mireille, is paralleled by Vida's agreement with Sam that Mireille should not drown herself, though this happy ending, it is clear, has its own fragility, since in Sam's and Vida's discussion about the historical basis of the narrative it is made clear that Mireille still has syphilis, and will die in Argentina (see *Channelling Baby*'s and *The Piano*'s double endings).

Camp fires: *Desperate Remedies*

Peter Wells (the co-director with Stewart Main of *Desperate Remedies*) has characterized the culture he grew up in as 'tacitly, on occasion expressly, opposed to imagination, to the power of sensibility'.[35] Though a homosexual artist, Wells made no attempt to disguise his dislike of the conventional linearity in Turner's groundbreaking homosexual-milieu film *Squeeze*.[36] Wells' finest short films *The Mighty Civic* (1989), a celebration of Auckland's great art deco picture palace, and *The Newest City on the Globe: Rebuilding Napier in the 1930s* (1985), a paean to the city's Santa Barbara art deco metamorphosis after the 1931 earthquake, in a less hectic way than his feature film embody processes of imagination and transformation, the opposite of stolid realism, pushing the documentary so influential in New Zealand cinema in oneiric directions: 'the enchanted castle, The Civic, where everything ordinary was left behind'; 'not Napier as it is, but as it seems to be'.

Desperate Remedies sacrifices the rhythmic crescendos amidst surface realism that characterize most melodramas to a wholesale *gesamtkunstwerk*-like artifice, defended in Wells' proselytizing accompaniments to the film[37] as an aesthetic based on homosexual camp reactions to 1940s women's films and melodramas. With its subversively fantastic Victorian setting, the film's title echoes the name of Thomas Hardy's first (sensation) novel, and its heroine Dorothea Brooke, George Eliot's heroine of *Middlemarch*. The triple quest faced by Dorothea (Jennifer Ward-Lealand) is to make money through her dressmaking business; to rescue her opium-addict sister, Rose (Kiri Mills), from the predatory control of Fraser (Cliff Curtis, a Māori who in the film's historical fantasy has entry to Pākehā society), by bribing Fraser to disappear; and to pay someone else to marry Rose and care for her child, while she continues her lesbian relationship with her young employee Anne (Lisa Chappell). Dorothea's choice for Rose's husband is Lawrence Hayes (Kevin Smith), an impoverished fellow immigrant who falls in love with Dorothea, a feeling she seems to reciprocate. In the finale, both Hayes and Fraser return to the 'town called Hope', Rose and her child having died of typhus – Fraser to extort money, Lawrence to claim Dorothea, now in a marriage of convenience to a corrupt politician, William Poyser (Michael Hurst). Finally, in a spectacularly amoral denouement, Anne shoots Fraser (the scene enacted with typical inventiveness as if on an opera house stage watched by Dorothea in the audience), freeing Dorothea from his demands, and escapes unapprehended. Dorothy leaves Poyser, and tells Lawrence that her heart has chosen Anne. The narrative ends with the lesbian couple at the prow of a departing ship, an image reworking the solitary presence of the sexually ambiguous Greta Garbo in *Queen Christina* (Mamoulian, 1932).

The film, if sometimes in an arch and self-congratulatory way (subliminal anal intercourse, the camera's game of peekaboo with Kevin Smith's penis in the men's washroom), is distinguished by unruly subversion of almost every cliché of conventional colonial history. Headed by a rat scampering down a ship's rope, the pioneers head for the city, quick cash, and sex of all kinds, as distinct from the sturdily moral official version of a film like *One Hundred Crowded Years*.

Desperate Remedies is an extraordinary example of the unyielding pursuit of style in the mostly realist New Zealand cinema. Filmed in quintessential studio stage conditions in an Auckland warehouse, it is one local film that absolutely refuses the siren call of landscape. If the lubricious element is always eye-catching – mokod buttocks, Cliff Curtis' nipple ring, the enormous black codpiece suspended from Kevin Smith's braces, women wearing below the waist only the skeletons to support nonexistent gowns – there is also the film's creation of design plenitude from meagre resources by way of paint, metalwork, gauzes and lighting. In many moments these flaunt their process of metamorphosis, like the wonderfully composed *mise-en-scène* of the opium den with addicts curled up in hammocks like caterpillars, overtly European until yellow lights translate their faces to a chinesified hue, far more satisfactory in the film's artifice-celebrating terms than hiring Chinese extras in the first place.

For all its extraordinary difference, *Desperate Remedies* might seem a little passé, a last-gasp celebration of an aesthetic dependent on suppression and marginalization, its male homosexual content displaced onto prettified surrogate lesbians, though somewhat subverted by the camera's lack of carnal interest in their impeccably tasteful embraces, and its flaunted interest in the bodies of Cliff Curtis and Kevin Smith. Indeed, even Dorothea seems so sexually moved by Lawrence that her ultimate choice of Anne seems purely theoretical. Even those, however, to whom two hours of unadulterated camp aesthetics and erotic decodings might eventually seem too much of a good thing might applaud the film's local uniqueness.

Four versions of the woman's film

In 1984, an attempt at a revised woman's film – sardonic, unerotic, determinedly unromantic – was made in *Trial Run* and *Mr Wrong*, via a revised thriller form, its only links to the classic 1940s woman's picture through allusions to the persecuted female cycle, though with no rescuing good male in sight.[38] The 1990s saw, surprisingly, a major local reinvention of the woman's film, marked by exactly the excess, intensity and romantic yearning the earlier films were intensely suspicious of, taking place, in complex motions both with and against the grain of the feminist theorizing that was the film-makers' implicit – and, with Maclean and Preston, explicit, immediate formative context. Of *The Piano*, and the four films examined here, only *Crush* is determinedly without a hint of transcendence, its meeting point with the others being all the films' centring on female protagonists playing out narratives of female desire.

Crush

Released the year before *The Piano*, Maclean's film takes a very different route: instead of a mute Scottish heroine arriving in New Zealand, a garrulous American femme fatale; instead of the search for love and a reconstructed male, female sexuality as a medium of promiscuous power; instead of the imprisonment of hyper-patriarchal marriage, internalized imprisonments by instabilities of desire; instead of a symbiotic mother–daughter bond, a father–daughter bond fractured by desire for the same sexual object; instead of sea shore and ocean mirroring forest, the weird incongruities of a steam-wreathed modern part-urban Rotorua; instead of powerful identificatory devices, constant movements between distance and empathy in its inter-culturally resonant narrative of the destabilizing impact of the American visitor Lane (Marcia Gay Harden) on the novelist Colin Iseman (Wiliam Zappa), his daughter Angela (Caitlin Bosley), and Christine (Donogh Rees) the literary critic, and probably her lover, whom she almost kills in the car crash at the film's beginning. While the brain-damaged, hospitalized Christina acts out abysmal articulations of the other characters' passions and vulnerabilities, Lane at least metaphorically seduces Angela, Colin's daughter, then abandons her for the father, leading to the catastrophe, in which Angela nurses Christina back to partial recovery and understanding of Lane's abandoning her after the crash, provoking her to push Lane to her exemplary touristic death from a scenic platform.

Maclean's celebrated earlier short films *Taunt* (1982) and *The Kitchen Sink* (1989) centre opaquely on sexual interchanges and confusions, unstable power relations, psychological violence, and the narrow line separating desire and revulsion. These, less abstractly, also dominate *Crush*, where the enigmatic title (like the French poster) jams together contradictory elements, the soft connotations of having a 'crush' on someone, with the related psychic violence of erotic vulnerability, crushing and being crushed. Maclean's films were clearly affected by her early involvement with feminist film theory's interest in gender destabilization, but spurn its often moralistic–didactic emphases, disregarding any call for female role models in a fascination with unstable movements between masculine and feminine, dominance and enslavement, sadism and masochism. In *Crush*, destabilization of gender characteristics becomes a master trope for other instabilities, a process initiated by implications (characteristically never quite pinned down) of a lesbian relationship between Christine and Lane and furthered by Lane's combination of gaudily coloured miniskirted femininity and masculine gesture, by Angela's cropped, androgynous appearance, with Lane's pretending to mistake her for a boy, by Angela's later feminine transformation through the red dress Lane gives her; and by the metamorphosis of Colin's sensitive 'new man' face into Barthesian femininity as he weeps, undone by desire, in the sickly green light of his word processor (though, later, when Lane, who has previously completely dominated him, suddenly loses control, he quickly asserts power over her, another example of the shifts of dominance the narrative cultivates).

Crush radically replaces the 'mythemes' of the traditional woman's film – woman waiting, passively suffering, hoping, suspended between duty and desire, self and family –with images of women as active, even predatory, agents, but, if escaping from control by one set of forces, prey to others, simultaneously both victims and victimizers.

Channelling Baby

By contrast, *Channelling Baby* overtly alludes to 1940s and 1950s melodramas, the director stating that 'it was inspired by the old "woman's pictures" – melodramas you watched on TV in black and white ... and with all the devices they used like fate and chance and coincidence, and the passions running high, but I wanted to rework that'.[39] This reworking takes over, unlike *Crush*, traditional woman's picture 'mythemes' like the mother–daughter bond, the afflicted woman (Bunnie's blindness) and transcendent but ill-fated love. Formed out of intense relation to the cinema, its other, unspoken, reworking is of the Japanese art film *Rashomon* (Kurosawa, 1950), perhaps the cinema's most celebrated instance of multiple, partial and untrustworthy narration, structured around four different versions of the same incident – the rape or seduction of a woman by a bandit, and the killing, or suicide, of her husband – given by the participants, the bandit, the woman, the husband (posthumously via a medium) and a witness.

Channelling Baby, set at the cusp of the 1960s and 1970s, juxtaposes the hippie era and New Zealand's Vietnam involvement, with Geoff (Kevin Smith), bound for the war, and Bunnie (Danielle Cormack), protesting at the troops' going, confronting each other. Later, Bunnie, looking at an eclipse of the sun with unprotected eyes, is blinded. The narrative shifts into the present, where Bunnie, a younger woman, Cassandra (Amber Sainsbury), and her brother Tony (Joel Tobeck) wait in opaque circumstances for Geoff's arrival. The exact circumstances of this meeting and how Cassandra and her brother know Bunnie and Geoff are only revealed later in a narrative structured between flashbacks and the present gathering. Four flashback narratives – Bunnie's, Geoff's, Cassandra's then Tony's – recount Geoff and Bunnie's marriage and its break-up with the death of their child 'Baby', all returning to a tense present, escalating into violence in which the overwrought Bunnie shoots Geoff. Limited vision dominates all the narratives, literalized in Bunnie's blindness: Bunnie believing that the war- traumatized Geoff has killed 'Baby'; Geoff, that she has; Cassandra, driven by hatred of her liberal middle-class family, fantasizing a 'family romance' in which she herself is 'Baby', that is Bunnie's daughter, not her parents'; Tony, dominated by his older sister's fantasy, half-believing that he has rescued Baby/Cassandra from near death.

The film is full of heightened tropes: Bunnie blindfolding Geoff as she shaves him, then having sex with him – one partner literally blind, the other blindfolded; Bunnie accidentally hypersensitizing Tony, the little boy next door, by getting him to read her a manual on relationships with chapters like 'To Know Him is to Love Him'; the young Tony watching through orange tinted glasses a television game show where a boy sings in front of the 'wheel of fortune'. Conflating *Rashomon*'s testimonies from the dead husband and the independent witness, *Channelling Baby* closes with Baby herself addressing both Bunnie and Geoff from beyond the grave ('so here's how I remember it'), as well as the audience ('I bet you thought I wouldn't show up'), and giving the most objective view of the events ('No one's fault') as she unravels the final occluded elements: the child dying of a genetic weakness, Bunnie finding her cold, taking her into the sun to warm her, Geoff thinking she has killed her, Tony fantasizing that he has rescued her, and so on. However, while Baby's testimony is clearly the truth, it has its own wish-fulfilments, presenting a final scene contradicting the pair dying on the floor (Bunnie somewhat obscurely has also been mortally injured while fatally wounding Geoff), in which the couple are seated outside by a pool, gravely coming to terms with Baby's death, but then smiling and laughing, with Geoff crowning 'Queen Bunnie' with a daisy chain. A helicopter flies overhead into the afternoon sky, a reminder of the horrors of Vietnam, but heard by Geoff now without trauma, an image of healing which reworks the ambiguity of Hollywood melodrama's sometimes happy endings: both a false wish-fulfilment and an utopian urge's striving for transcendence, for what might have been.

Memory and Desire: 'the female sublime'

An imagined New Zealand film, shot at home but set in nineteenth-century France, *Monsieur Henri*'s oddity pales beside the real-life strangeness of Niki Caro's *Memory and Desire*, a New Zealand film in which the main actors are Japanese, and New Zealanders background figures in their own country, glimpsed at the edges of Japanese tourists' defamiliarizing perspectives (Figure 17). Apparently the director and producer even discussed having the film's dialogue in Japanese.[40] Had this happened, the English subtitles demanded would have given the film the most indubitable marker in the public mind of the art film, foreign language and subtitles. But even though it retreated from this extreme, it was too deviant to win substantial audiences in New Zealand, though it did gain awards and some critical esteem.

17. Sayo (Yuri Kinugawa) sitting at the global signpost suggests a near allegory of a 'glocal' New Zealand cinema in a transnational age in *Memory and Desire* (Niki Caro, 1997).

Memory and Desire, derived from a short story by the author/director Peter Wells, was based on a reported episode in which a Japanese woman was discovered inhabiting a cave on Stewart Island in circumstances never clarified after she was hurriedly returned to Japan.[41] Wells' narrative, followed by Caro, fills the blank at the anecdote's centre with a narrative of *amour fou*: Sayo's return to and refusal to leave her cave-shrine near where her husband Keiji drowned, until the New Zealand and Japanese authorities forcibly repatriate her. If the female centrality of the story is occasionally confused by Wells' homosexual overlay of Sayo's attempts to overcome her husband's impotence, the film with its female director indubitably places female and heterosexual desire at its centre. *Memory and Desire* has been little analysed, but the title of Jane Sayles' article, 'The Gendered Sublime in *Memory and Desire*', distinguishing a female sublime from the masculine, proposes intriguing pathways.[42] Her 'female sublime' suggests the heroine's intensity, sacrifice and excess (all hyperbolic versions of women's film 'mythemes') not as a subject for critique, but as creating astonishment at her refusal to accept loss and dimming memory, her refusal to allow mourning, as in the Freudian view, to reach its eventual, natural end.[43] Certainly Sayo's trajectory is never presented in a critical or ironic light, never seen as imposed by belief systems or social forces; in fact, the opposite, since her behaviour upsets expectations equally in New Zealand and in Tokyo. If it stems from psychic processes more expected of the female than the male, and is further distanced from the New Zealand quotidian in being attributed to an oriental 'other', interestingly the New Zealand spectator surrogate introduced into the film is male, the (wholly speechless) part of the local fisherman (Joel Tobeck), drawn fascinatedly to the heroine as if to some inarticulable revelation of meaning.

Perfect Strangers

Romantic sexual melodrama/psychodrama seems an unlikely mode for Gaylene Preston, indubitably one of the major contemporary New Zealand film-makers, whose work, in which documentary claims a place equal to fiction, is dominated by social and communal priorities, and who typically presents herself as a communal artist, secondarizing elaborate aesthetic aims ('I like the story to lead ... if you're saying what a great shot then you're withdrawing from the characters, you're coming out of the film').[44] Though unfailingly vivacious, her earlier films display – albeit for always coherent purposes – a slightly brisk marginalization of the erotic, as in *Mr Wrong*, *Ruby and Rata* and (after her early romantic flings) in *Bread and Roses*, where Sonja's commitment to social progress depends upon a marriage in which friendship and work seem almost to rule out sexuality. *Perfect Strangers* is, in the light of all this, surprising, having elements of a kind of 'return of the repressed'. Mel (Rachael Blake) – independent, sexually aggressive, stuck in a dead end job, nursing (beneath her apparently invulnerable surface) weaknesses and resentments over a failed past relationship – gets herself picked up seemingly for casual sex by a handsome, ruggedly elegant nameless man (Sam Neill), who takes her prisoner on his boat, to a beach on a deserted West Coast island owned in fact by his mundane opposite, the uncouth bushman type Jeff, who Mel once had a brief affair with and rejected (Joel Tobeck). Treated by the stranger with extreme romanticism, given beautiful clothes to wear, a bath surrounded by candles, serenaded by Madame Butterfly on the stereo, she is nevertheless a prisoner of an unbalanced romantic idealist who becomes dangerously angry at her casual sexual attitudes, the opposite of the romantic commitment he desires. Trying to escape, she accidentally stabs him, but in the days before he dies, as she tries to keep him alive, his extreme of devotion and infallible knowledge of her psychic wounds awaken dormant longings for absolute love and commitment, so that when he dies she keeps his body frozen in a huge deep freeze, communing with him and fantasizing his presence in her bed. When the boorish but still desiring Jeff turns up and discovers the corpse, Mel ensures his silence by convincing him that she wants to marry him. The narrative ends at their wedding where, as the bridal couple dance, a spectral Sam Neill, seen only by Mel, also dances with her.

Thinking of *Memory and Desire*, it is difficult not to be struck by the curious, central resemblance which binds together two films as unalike as it and *Perfect Strangers*. Both, for all their great and obvious differences, enact the same situation: a woman's refusal to accept the ordinary consequences of the death of her husband or lover, and consequent entry into a state where she brings him back to life again, living with him in solitude, making love with him. Remarkably, both films also use the actor Joel Tobeck in a crucial third-party role, though his uncouth character in Preston's film is very different from *Memory and Desire*'s sensitized figure, raising the question whether the coincidence is accidental, or whether Preston, the later film-maker, grasped the relation of her film to Caro's, simultaneously solidifying and undermining it, by her use of the same actor. If one interprets *Perfect Strangers* simply through Preston's slightly blunt artistic credo and the marginalization of romantic desire in her other features, one might see it simply as a cautionary tale, warning against the perils of the narcissistic myths of romantic love; however, if read in the light of such moments in her previous films as the documentary *War Stories*' first narrative, Pamela Quill's romance and marriage (interrupted by his death in war) to the airman who resembles Marlon Brando, which transcends the other more mundane stories, or Ruby's perhaps invented memory of a similar past in *Ruby and Rata*, then Mel's surrender to reawakened childhood needs for a surrogate parental figure to endlessly forgive and love her looks less wholly definable in blackly comic didactic terms. *Perfect Strangers'* achievement depends on its extreme ambivalence, the acting out of a fantasy built into the human being's primary narcissism, in which everyone is a put-upon prince or princess looking for romantic redemption, drawing the audience into its seductions, while, at the same time, in a way quite distinct from the grave tenor of *Memory and Desire*, cultivating pronounced elements of absurdity and grotesque comedy at its centre.[45]

Two-culture film-making and Māori-made films: 1981–2005
(i) Selves and others

[*Rangi's Catch*, Michael Forlong, 1971; *To Love a Maori*, Rudall Hayward, 1972;] *Pictures*, Michael Black, 1981; *Utu*, Geoff Murphy, 1983; *Came a Hot Friday*, Ian Mune, 1984; *Other Halves*, John Laing, 1984; *The Lost Tribe*, John Laing, 1985; *The Quiet Earth*, Geoff Murphy, 1985; *Kingpin*, Mike Walker, 1985; *Sylvia*, Michael Firth, 1985; *Pallet on the Floor*, Lynton Butler, 1986; *Arriving Tuesday*, Richard Riddiford, 1986; *Mark II*, John Anderson, 1986; *The Lie of the Land*, Grahame J. McLean, 1987; *Among the Cinders*, Rolf Haedrich, 1987; *Never Say Die*, Geoff Murphy, 1988; *Ruby and Rata*, Gaylene Preston, 1990; *The Returning*, John Day, 1990; *Broken English*, Gregor Nicholas, 1996; *Flight of the Albatross*, Werner Meyer, 1996; *Crooked Earth*, Sam Pillsbury, 1999; *Jubilee*, Michael Hurst, 2000; *Whale Rider*, Niki Caro, 2003; *Her Majesty*, Mark J. Gordon, 2005

Contemporary New Zealand film's thirty years span a period of greater change in Pākehā–Māori relations than any since the colony's founding. The only overview of these changes' interaction with mainstream cinema, at least up to 1987, is in Martin Blythe's *Naming The Other*. The categories structuring his account are, understandably, given the period's political-cultural vicissitudes and the greater number of films produced, more amorphous than those for earlier periods, but nonetheless articulate underlying tendencies. Of these, the 'Politics of Repression' points to films withdrawing from the complexity of Māori phenomena, with *The Lost Tribe* seen as a paradigm; the 'Politics of Blame', to films self-enacting Pākehā guilt, and the 'Politics of Irony' to films (approved by the critic) in which Māori and Pākehā essentialisms are broken down into more complex bicultural – even multicultural – projections.[46] Subverting such polarizing simplifications as a cinema of uninterrupted progress or regress, of Pākehā inauthenticity or Māori authenticity, Blythe presents a riven terrain bisected by different, conflicting conceptions of nation and culture, competing essentialisms, pluralisms and relativisms, including the newer forces of multiculturalism and post-modernism. If the much fictionalized nineteenth-century photographers in *Pictures* (Michael Black, 1981), the Burton brothers, double as contemporary film-makers, then the colonial audience's absolute preference for Alfred's (Kevin J. Wilson) picturesque over Walter's (Peter Vere-Jones) verismic New Zealand Wars photographs indicts the local cinema's complacencies. However, the 1980s–1990s situation was complicated by other inhibiting factors, most influentially culturally separatist assertions that only Māori could and should depict Māori. Further, with the appearance from 1987 of Māori-directed films, there was an added inhibiting sense that indigenous filmmakers had cornered 'authenticity' in this area, though like any other 'authenticity', that of the various Māori-made films has its limitations.

Films in which cultural interaction is central are the New Zealand Wars period films *Pictures* and *Utu*; two Polynesian youth films, *Kingpin* (the young offenders subgenre) and *Mark II* (a lively road movie); the biopic *Sylvia* (based on Sylvia Ashton Warner's rural schoolteaching experiences with Māori children); two romantic narratives, *Other Halves'* 'woman's picture' relationship between an older middle-class Pākehā woman and a sixteen-year-old Māori streetboy, and Riddiford's romantic comedy *Arriving Tuesday*'s mixed-race triangle; the unruly comic text, *Came a Hot Friday*; and the Pākehā rites-of passage narrative, *Among the Cinders*, along with films considered under other headings, like *The Quiet Earth*, *Ruby and Rata*, *Crooked Earth* and *Broken English*. Increasingly apparent across all these is the disappearance of the most obvious paternalistic figurings of the 'Māori as problem' discourse. Also observable are films reversing the 'problem' element to some degree, interrogating the Pākehā through Māori presence, as in *Pictures*, *Utu*, *The Quiet Earth*, *Mark II* and *Arriving Tuesday*. Traces of this reversal mark another set of (minor) films, where traditional Māori religio-psychological concepts such as tapu (sacred, restricted), mākutu (curse) and mate Māori (Māori [psychological] sickness) are employed: *The Lie of the Land*, *The Returning*, *Among the Cinders* and *Flight of the Albatross*. Such uses – following those of poets like Fairburn in his 'Tapu' and Baxter's invocation of 'Hine nui te po', the Māori Goddess of Death, in 'East Coast Journey' – familiarly assert white indigenous specificity through Māori iconography, but also impart to the different narratives psychological retribution for land alienation, ecological concern and a critique of European ultra-rationalism (none of which, though, depends on literal belief in the concepts invoked).

A brief overview of the present situation shows contradictory processes of widening and narrowing, the former seen in the status of Rena Owen, Temuera Morrison and Cliff Curtis as 'demi-stars' of the mainstream cinema. Simultaneously, though, a curious contradictory process is observable: the reinvention of the 'Māoriland' romance, in which all but segregated Māori worlds are produced, but in contemporary settings, paralleling tendencies in Māori television drama, in which the European world is, if not entirely expelled, then extremely peripheral. If there are benefits in either, in the marginalizing of dominant European voices and the foregrounding of Māori, it is also difficult not to see in both retreat from complex actualities. Two major productions, Whale Rider and Crooked Earth, exhibit this development.

Crooked Earth

Crooked Earth (Sam Pillsbury, 1999) is a near all-Māori narrative, with the only whites momentarily foregrounded – a racist police chief, a drug-dealing gangster and the government minister arriving to seal a forestry deal with the tribe – all unpleasant, with even the shopkeeper the hero at one point defends, unappealingly craven.

The updated contemporary 'western' narrative is a classic face-off between two Māori brothers, the Bastions (a name invoking the 1977–1978 land protest): Will/Wiremu (Temuera Morrison), the older, returning from many years in the army, and Kahu (Lawrence Makoare), the younger, whose anti-colonialist rhetoric has gained him community charisma. The brothers meet at the funeral of their father, who has brokered a government deal over moneys from the use of tribal forests, leading to the question of who will take up the greenstone patu (weapon) of power: Wiremu – moderate, sceptical, entitled to it, unwilling – or Kahu, whose extremist position, vividly articulated ('Having fucked us over for 400 years the bastards want us to roll over so they can shove it up our arses for the next 100 years'), descends into criminality and murder, with his political movement funded by a marijuana factory producing dope sold to ruthless gangsters who execute rivals with his knowledge.

The narrative moves to a confrontation between the brothers on a mountain Kahu has taken possession of. Having burned the marijuana factory, Will attempts to persuade Kahu to leave with his followers. Misapprehensions lead to a shootout in which Will kills Kahu in self-defence. However, assuming leadership, Will reveals himself won over by Kahu's view (if not his methods) – not so far as to burn the forests, but far enough to use the threat to pressure a better deal. At the end, paralleling Whale Rider's motif of female succession, he tells his daughter, Ripeka (Jaime Passier-Armstrong), that she will one day take over from him, thus reconciling, like Whale Rider, Māori culture and feminism.

Unlike *Whale Rider*, with its timeless contemporaneity, *Crooked Earth* is specifically placed after the Tainui (1995) and Ngāi Tahu (1998) reparatory settlements, cited by Marama (Nancy Brunning), the schoolteacher, giving Wiremu a history lesson. Framing statements announce that 'Māori leaders forced the government to honour the broken treaty, and the long battle for justice began', and that 'By the end of the twentieth century Māori leaders had successfully regained hundreds of millions of dollars in land and assets wrongly taken from them. Hundreds more claims are expected to be settled over the next decade'.

Successful at the home box office (300,000 admissions), the film generated some unease for its exploitation of contradictory points of view. Kahu's drug harvest harms Māori teenagers and he is directly or indirectly responsible for several killings. Repeatedly, though, circumstances partly exculpate him, preserving his captivating aura, not least in his vivid rhetoric: 'Farmers, fuck, Will, dying in spite of the deregulated, knowledge driven, every shithead for himself New Zealand free market.' Similarly, despite indications that he is a power-hungry megalomaniac, the moment when, alone, overlooking the forests, he recites the prayer 'Let the calm be widespread, the sea be like greenstone...' suggests higher motives. *Crooked Earth* expertly exploits conflicting feelings in the air – Māori demands as justified? As unjustified? Violence as justified? Unjustified? If one posits, as it might be the makers did, prototypes of a Māori and Pākehā spectator, what is gained for either by reducing the wider frame of New Zealand to a scatter of vicious or unlikeable Pākehā and enacting the issues almost wholly through Māori? For the Māori spectator, the benefits, it might have been surmised, are that Pākehā are marginalized into baleful versions of Māori peripherality in many mainstream films, and threatening multicultural complexities are shelved; while for Pākehā the benefits may be an escape from the accusations (or self-accusations) of condescending paternalism almost inevitably aroused by white characters in bicultural dramas involving moral questions, and a more relaxed watching of the issues being fought out by Māori (no longer labelled 'hostile' and 'kūpapa'). The situation is rather different in *Whale Rider*.

Whale Rider

Whale Rider is one of New Zealand film's greatest successes, with home box-office takings only second to *Once Were Warriors*', and major business overseas.[47] As with *Once Were Warriors* and *The Piano*, success propels the film into a good object realm almost beyond criticism, creating analytic difficulties. Among the subtextual readings attachable to its finale of the restored waka (canoe) moving across the ocean (reminiscing the original Polynesian voyages of discovery) is an allegory of the New Zealand cinema, penetrating overseas markets into the new millennium with its combination of Māori 'glocalism' and feminism's most appealing face. The effect the film aroused is indisputable: 'As the Canadian audience leapt to its feet to clap through the credits ... a choked up Sam Neill struggled to speak. "This is a film from the heart", he told the world premiere crowd at Toronto's Cumberland 3 theatre, "And my response is from the heart". He was crying, Niki was crying, we all cried', says writer Witi Ihimaera. 'In a world which thinks it knows everything and has seen everything, *Whale Rider* and Niki's fantastic direction took us to a place where we could rediscover the innocence in ourselves'.[48] Rather than dismissing this salinity, in which the film has floated like its whales, it is more useful to examine the tears' cause in the quadruple triumph of the small – played out in the enmeshed indigenous, feminist, national and industrial themes – as well perhaps as relief at the film's swimming past the ethnic-cultural divide through its Pākehā writer-director, undermining the polarizing position that only Māori could or should tell Māori stories.

With all these fleets of extra-textual riders, what does this charming, well-acted film actually do? It is, of course, based on Witi Ihimaera's novella,[49] in which the adoring relationship of a young Māori girl, Kahu, with her grandfather causes suffering because his obsession with finding a new leader to secure his tribe's future can only patriarchally focus on males, leading him to block her access to the knowledge reserved for boys. Finally, her supernormal empathy with whales, culminating in her reenactment of the tribal ancestor Paikea's mythical whaleback journey, convinces her grandfather that she is the chosen one. The novella's brevity leaves space for many felicitous inventions (including the restored waka), which successfully resist being made secondary to the literary text. Here omissions are as revealing as additions, the magical realism reduced, the passages from the whales' viewpoints deleted, conservatively pushing the film towards an only slightly mystically inflected realism, and deleting harsh material such as the (Māori) scavengers chain-sawing a still-living whale's jawbone. The film, though set in the present, erases historical markers present in the novella, such as the Waitangi Tribunal settlements and Koro's involvement in Māori politics, also omitting the narrator's experiences of racism in Papua New Guinea. Though Anna, the German wife of Rawiri (Cliff Curtis) – the German-funded film's invention – turns up (mutely) at the end, the film's community is strangely self-contained, so that when the whales are stranded, the source's 'navy personnel ... and members of Greenpeace, Project Jonah, and Friends of the Earth also', are nowhere in sight as Māori alone tend the creatures.

Paradoxically, though, it is this expulsion of whiteness that allows its implicit return. The director's DVD commentary revealingly interprets details of this Māori world as epitomes of undifferentiated New Zealandness, with Koro fixing his outboard motor, and everyone's emotional reserve when Paikea (Keisha Castle-Hughes) leaves her grandparents, representative of the culture at large. The house in which Koro (Rāwiri Paratene) and Nanny Flower (Vicky Haughton) live doubles every Māori item with a Pākehā one (most tellingly, and often in shot, a kowhai blossom dish towel with New Zealand printed on it). One key to the film's extraordinary success is, then, its readability in terms of both the indigenous community and the larger society, ultimately possible because societal tensions and complexities have disappeared with the all but complete removal of whites, leaving both the ills and the hopes of the community undefined to the point where they can carry almost any positive community, national and indeed international desires (all the vaguer since the lifestyle portrayed is so idyllic that it is hard to see how it could be better). The German wife is the exception to the film's segregation, but her presence provides an isolated explicit surrogate for the Pākehā viewer and a guarantee that the indigenous community is not, as it might logically seem to be, blocked to non-Māori. Apropos of this, while the heroine's name change from Kahu to Paikea, identical with the ancestral whale rider's, has the benefit of simplicity, its significant subterranean spin-off is the quasi-homonymity established between the words Paikea and Pākehā. Another alteration the film makes is to modify the original's greater insistence on hierarchy, aristocracy and the leader in line with the more democratic demands of modern society.

Light of a kind is shed on *Whale Rider* by *Her Majesty*, a surprising American film, made on location with an all-local cast, in which a twelve-year-old Pākehā girl, obsessed by the young Queen Elizabeth II's 1953–1954 royal tour, achieves her heart's desire of getting her home town on the royal itinerary, while also defying the town's and especially her vicious brother Stewart's prejudice against the old Māori woman Mata Hira (Vicky Haughton of *Whale Rider*), to whom the Queen returns her grandfather's spear, declaring the battered kuia a true New Zealander. The later film shadows the earlier, its nostalgia for a more secure past paralleling *Whale Rider*'s; as does its heralding of a more independent future as the heroine bids the Queen farewell;

as does its girl protagonist, embodying the best of her race, pursuing her destiny despite opposition; just as its *Back to the Future* reparative action, showing history as it should have been, parallels Paikea's push through the past towards a better future; all achieved with a stylistic conservatism easier for Gordon to achieve than the Caro of *Memory and Desire*. A film of calculated charm and sentiment, *Her Majesty* also parallels *Whale Rider*'s dependence on the same qualities, and the appeal and limitations of its (much reciprocated) desire to be loved.

Two-culture film-making and Māori-made films: 1981–2005.
(ii) Māori film-making

Ngati, Barry Barclay, 1987; *Mauri*, Merata Mita, 1988; *Te Rua*, Barry Barclay, 1991; *Once Were Warriors*, Lee Tamahori, 1994; *Te Tangata Whai Rawa O Weniti/The Māori Merchant of Venice*, Don C. Selwyn, 2002

The appearance of *Ngati* in 1987 – the first Māori-directed feature, closely followed by *Mauri* in 1988 – was a key moment in New Zealand film history. Barry Barclay memorably asserted the desire for self-representation by asking the majority to 'Imagine a whole culture not to be able to talk about your land in your own way. Imagine if you were born in London or Copenhagen, and the only – and I mean only – images of yourself were scripted and shot by people from Algeria or Tamil Nadu and transmitted simply to capture good ratings among their own viewers'.[50] These exaggerated reversals of perspective (clearly Māori and Pākehā are not as geographically separate as Copenhagen and Tamil Nadu, and most Māori share more culturally with Pākehā than Londoners with Algerians), belong to a moment (1992) which now seems deceptively distant because of the swiftness with which Māori and Māoritanga (Māori culture) have become integral parts of the media: significant films have been made, and the ground has been laid for future film and TV production, even if, around 2003–2005, some backlash against special Māori funding occurred. At the same time, past difficulties should not be erased – those first Māori-directed features only emerged ten years into the new post-1977 order through arduous pioneering in the face of majority culture apathy, even hostility – nor the different problems minimized facing Māori film-makers at present in manoeuvring between demands for effectively monocultural films, and for films reflecting the realities of the wider society, as well as negotiating the various pressures of realism, idealism, sentiment and analysis: inwardness, outwardness, self and other.

Ngati and Mauri

Ngati ('Tribe': Barclay, 1987) and *Mauri* ('Life Force': Mita, 1988), for all their proximity and similarities, are very different films: *Ngati*'s slow-paced serenity is reminiscent of classical Hollywood's small-town communalism, while *Mauri* is structured by melodrama's psychic violence. They are, however, linked by their retrospective settings: *Ngati*, circa 1948, *Mauri* later, in the 1950s, in tiny settlements, allowing the celebration of traditional communities without provoking accusations of overidealizing the present. The communities differ, though. *Ngati*'s Kapua is integrated, predominantly Māori, but with Pākehā closely bound in, while *Mauri*'s is wholly Māori, except for the Semmens, the white owners of the biggest farm, gained by the father in questionable circumstances. His son, Steve (James Heyward), is willing to integrate, by marrying Ramiri (Susan D. Ramiri Paul), and returning the land to Māori ownership through his wife, in spite of the grotesque racism of his father (Geoff Murphy). *Mauri*'s greater aggressiveness of relations is immediately prefigured when Willie Rapana (Willie Rāna), making a toll call, reacts angrily to the operator's mispronunciation of his name. It shares *Ngati*'s pastoral idyll only intermittently, as when the elderly Kura (the Māori Rights activist, Eva Rickard) and Hemi (Sonny Waru) are with their granddaughter, Awatea (Rangimarie Delamere), and in the communal festivities at Steve and Ramiri's wedding, though even these are punctuated by minatory moments.

Both narratives implicitly balance on the edge of change, the breakup of rural communities through exodus to the city. In both the process is already under way. The more saturatedly nostalgic *Ngati* alludes to the Māori Battalion's post-war return, but omits reference to the difficulties experienced by veterans returning from overseas experience to traditional life (reportedly more pronounced in Tama Poata's original screenplay).[51] The city-dwelling Sally (Connie Pewhairangi) regrets returning to Kapua, where she finds herself fighting the elders' conservatism, not least that of her father, Iwi (Wi Kuki Kā). *Mauri* records the same emigration of youth, but with worse consequences. Willie Rapana's gang life results in his assassination, and both Rewi Rapanas (the hero, Anzac Wallace, and the dead man he impersonates) have years before gone urban, running into criminal trouble. *Ngati* is more nostalgic, with historical forces on hold at the film's end, but *Mauri* has within it potential criminality, neurosis and violence, and its wholly positive characters, the grandparents, are old, and Awatea, very young: figures of the past and future, not so much the troubled present (Figure 18). Merata Mita, the director, who defined the white film industry as 'neurot-

18. A pastoral moment amidst the angst of cultural displacement in Merita Mita's *Mauri* (1988): right to left, Awatea (Rangimarie Delamere) and her grandparents Kara and Hemi (Eva Rickard and Sonny Waru).

ic', highlights the demented older Semmens' (Geoff Murphy) racial neurosis, but her film also suggests more internalized problematics. In *Ngati*, the leukaemia suffered by Ropata (Oliver Jones) is an unavoidable mystery that has to be borne. In *Mauri*, however, the sickness is a kind of mate Māori (Māori psychological sickness). This – encapsulated when Anzac Wallace, inevitably carrying resonances of Te Wheke in *Utu*, howls his agony to the camera – is seen to have fundamental causes in the wider context of land loss and cultural displacement. Mita herself argued that 'the story is really a parable about the schizophrenic existence of so many Maori in Pākehā society',[52] but this is exacerbated by the younger men's attraction to gangs, something the film temporizes ambivalently about, with Kara sentimentally seeing Willie's gang as the extension of the 'strays' he kindheartedly collected as a child, while the audience see him brutally murdered. Though an uncaring Pākehā world is signalled through old Semmens, and the visiting government Minister whose community consulation is an arrogant sham (compare this with a similar scene with *Ngati*'s white freezing-works owners), there are subterranean intimations of internally generated as well as externally imposed problems. Just before surrendering, Rewi has momentary visions of distant, hakaing warriors, suggesting (whether Mita intends it or not) the unresolved modern problematics of a warrior culture in transition. Mita's 'identity, resolution, survival' mantra characterizing Māori cinema can only be applied to her film in a complex, unresolved way, at least as regards the first category, where another schizophrenia is visible in the question of whether Māori culture is typified by the gentle Kura and Hemi, or by those warriors who appear to Rewi in extremis.

In *Ngati* the mixed community unites to keep the works going. In the romance plot the young Australian doctor Greg (Ross Girven), originally racially prejudiced (at least against 'abos'), will return to marry Jenny Bennett (Judy McIntosh), the schoolteacher, daughter of the liberal Pā kehā Dr Bennett and his wife (Norman Fletcher and Alice Fraser), and even discovers himself, untraumatically, to be half-Māori. Individual desire and communal feeling blend almost seamlessly. Sally, the city-dwelling Māori daughter, frustrated by resistance to change, decides to stay, indeed is the most forceful speaker at the meeting which decides to buy the works. Tradition and progress meet when her father commends the young as the voices of the future. Even Iwi's ageing wife's pregnancy (seen earlier by Sally as irresponsible) is celebrated in Dr Bennett's hopes of seeing 'a bouncing mokapuna' (grandchild), with its implication of a rising Māori birthrate countering Ropata's death. The competition for the body of Ropata between the Māori tohunga (expert; here, spiritual healer) – Uncle Eru (Tuta Ngarimu Tamati) – and Doctor Bennett, with his western medicine, ends in a draw, since Ropata's leukaemia can only be alleviated, not cured, in 1948, though by 1987, the film's date, western medicine was increasingly successful in treating childhood leukemia. But by 1987 the tohunga was a figure of cultural affirmation, more metaphorical than literal, the disasters of Māori medicine in past influenza and TB epidemics forgotten, and his place as a cultural signifier of 'Māori knowledge' pre-eminent.

Mauri's narrative, like its aesthetics (flashbacks, near-subliminal memory shots, a more jagged mixing of modes than in *Ngati*) is multi-layered and ambiguous. Narrative unfoldings reveal that Rewi Rapana (Anzac Wallace), his real name only uncovered late on, moved to the city and got involved in a bungled robbery. Escaping by car, he gave a lift to another Māori, a Rewi Rapana, returning home after many years. In a crash the passenger is killed. Pushing the car with the body inside it over a cliff, the protagonist assumed the passenger's identity and returned to Rewi Rapana's village where (somewhat implausibly) his impersonation is accepted. Guilt at his impiety as well as fear of arrest, makes him reject the love of Ramiri, who marries Steve Semmens instead. As the police close in, Rewi seeks advice from Kara, who instructs him in the traditional penance required. With Rewi having to further expiate his act to Pākehā law and with the aged Kara dying, things seem to end with little hope. However, the flight of the white heron (kōtuku), a recurrent symbol, amalgamated with the child Awatea's imagining of Kara's soul flying to Hawaiki, as well as Ramiri having given birth to Rewi's child, allows optimism centred around the next Māori generation to be affirmed.

Te Rua

Barclay's ambitious *Te Rua* ('The Storehouse', 1991) had a troubled history. Its narrative of Māori activists repossessing from a Berlin museum ancestral wooden heads stolen a century earlier from their coastal village ran into disagreements between the director and the producer, O'Shea. A residue of short-circuited exposition does not, though, cause sufficient incoherence to justify neglect of an aesthetically intense, inventive film, both in New Zealand, where it hardly surfaced, and overseas, meaning, despite festival showings, that the most complex Māori-made film to date, the most far reaching in its interfacing of tradition with modernity, the local with the transnational, has been little seen anywhere.

Te Rua's narrative of mana tūturu (spiritual guardianship) – bringing into view demands by indigenous populations for the return of artefacts collected at the height of European imperialism – involves many characters representing four far-flung sectors, very different from the more homogeneous worlds of *Ngati* and *Mauri*: (i) the rural Uritoto Māori; (ii) sympathetic Pākehā New Zealanders – Rewi's colleague, Hamish (Stuart Devenie), and ex-mistress, Fiona (Donna Akersten); (iii) characters, both third world and European, in Berlin – Filipinos, an African diplomat, a Turkish *gastarbeiter*; and an aid organization's employees; (iv) senior Berlin museum staff caught up in the crisis. Set in complicated relation/opposition, these groups are also differentiated internally. The Uritoto Māori range from characters who have presumably never left their land, like the ancient Nanny Matai (Nissie Herewini), to cosmopolitan figures like Rewi Marangai (Wi Kuki Kā), a patent lawyer living in Berlin, and his performance-poet nephew, Peter Huaka (Peter Kā). There are also divisions between the more radical aid-agency workers and their boss, whose economically dominated views obtusely marginalize culture's importance. Within the museum, too, there are divisions, between the troubled, sympathetic Professor Beiderstedt (Gunter Meissner) and his less responsive successor Dr Sättler (Walter Kreye).

At the narrative's centre, Wi Kuki Kā's Rewi is the most complex representative of the communal Uritoto protagonist, reworking a German-speaking, contemporary version of his French speaking cosmopolite in *Utu*. Following the opening beach sequence, close-ups of the ancestors' heads with light playing across their eyes, making them seem sentient and demanding, summon an impeccably europeanized Rewi from drowsing in his chic Berlin apartment. With the activists' arrival, he belatedly commits himself to leading them, organizing a reciprocal unilateral 'guardianship' of European treasures, provoking a police siege and, ultimately, his own imprisonment, but not before the return of the taonga is agreed. Half-mirroring Rewi in complexity is the retiring museum director, Professor Biederstedt (Gunter Meisner), who eventually realizes that though much of his life's meaning has been in collecting, he is happier giving the objects back.

The third-world characters have an important role, not just in aiding the statues' return, but rather poignantly, considering the film's New Zealand failure, in dramatizing the applause of 'third-world' audiences for 'fourth-world' (in other words, indigenous inhabitants of settler nations) artists.[53] These audiences may be formal, like that at Peter Huaka's Third World Poetry Festival performance, serendipitously present, like the Africans watching the siege from their tenements, or single characters, like the Professor's Turkish help (with her song answering Peter Huaka's chant to the ancestors) or the African diplomat who helps persuade the Professor. Together they comprise a more appreciative audience than local ones – as when the poetry audience spontaneously chant 'Ugda Poy Ugh Cha Cha' during Peter Huaka's performance of Apirana Taylor's fable,[54] and the multicultural onlookers party to Dalvanius's androgynously sweet 'I'll Be There for You' in tribute to the Māori. Such moments are touchingly inspirational, and yet also a little dreamily regressive in their displacement of the difficulties of winning over local audiences.

Te Rua enacts the new Māori intellectual's/artist's 'glocal' position, steeped in both indigeneity and internationalism, inhabiting both the literal and global villages. Even the Uritoto villagers have a grasp of media politics – as where Rewi's daughter, Helen (Vanessa Rare), tells reporters that they, not the media, will control news releases about Nanny's hunger strike. The film, after all, borders on the age of Māori TV, and Rewi demonstrates awareness of global electronic contraction when, during the Berlin stand-off, he demands a computer. Though urban New Zealand is all but absent from the film, two of the characters are Pākehā, both drawn to Māoriness: Hamish, Rewi's partner, gets involved in the museum battle; Fiona (Donna Akersten), Rewi's ex-lover, speaks Māori; while Hannah (Maria Fitzi), Peter Huaka's German girlfriend, is also a convert. Though there might be elements of self-sustaining narcissism in the way 'white arse' – Peter's epithet – is irresistibly drawn to Māori men, both Rewi and Peter seem drawn to white women as well (if Peter's relationship with Hannah is more than strategic). Here and elsewhere, the film looks both outward and inward, with at least some Māori desiring the further world, and parts of the further world embracing (sometimes literally) the indigenous. Barclay, a bi-racial and cosmopolitan intellectual, the New Zealand film-maker most given to introspective commentary on his own work, spends much of his book *Our Own Image* debating the priorities of 'talking in' to the Māori community and/or 'talking out' to the Pākehā audience.[55] *Te Rua* enacts an interesting balance of the two, with more 'talking out' than much of Barclay's theorizing might suggest, dispensing with *Ngati*'s Pākehā semi-protagonists, but, through Hamish's partnership with Rewi, suggesting an attenuated second, bicultural rather than monocultural plotline. Here, as if to assure viewers that the film's perspective includes New Zealand, not just a tribal Aotearoa, Hamish and Rewi legally protect computer developments originating in New Zealand against European commercial predators, along with other material suggesting a New Zealand, as well as tribal consciousness: for example, the long-term expatriate Hamish paralleling Rewi's return home, and Fiona explaining to Hannah that white sympathizers can help but finally must stand aside while Māori act.

Moving between tribal pastoral and European metropolis, *Te Rua* is also stylistically mobile, marshalling multifarious effects, suggesting oneirically the psychic forces the tribal statues are credited with; staging certain moments like a quasi-musical, and even occasionally recalling Brechtian modes. Many other moments – despite the easy caricature of Dr Sättler's pronunciation 'May-oris' – unsettle the most straightforward readings: for instance, the Māori author of a book on cultural properties, Dr Waru (Dalvanius) has a not unreasonable dislike of Peter, whose sudden possession while eating traditional fermented corn with his girlfriend suggests narcissistic exhibitionism; Fiona's sharp no-nonsense reply to Rewi's taunt that as a Pākehā she has no roots; Rewi's peaceful confrontation with the brother of the man who is living with his wife, which admits to histories of Māori violence; and others, all with a part in making *Te Rua* the most complex product of the new Māori cinema.

Once Were Warriors

Te Rua's complete commercial failure contrasts strikingly with the success of *Once Were Warriors*, the first film to gross more than NZ$6 million at home, beating even *Jurassic Park*).[56] It also had great impact overseas, becoming one of the best-known New Zealand films internationally. Its source is the first novel of the Jake Heke trilogy by the Māori writer Alan Duff, a controversial figure, reviled by some Māori for arguing – as the chief of Beth's tribe, Te Tupaea, does in the novel (a view cut out of the film) – 'Nor was the Chief into blaming people, the Pākehā, the system, the anything for the obvious Maori problems: you know, our drop in standards just in general'.[57] Apirana Taylor, giving some sense of the passions book and film aroused, wrongly called Duff a writer of 'no status', without mana, 'simply a literary kupapa – a product of European publishing', one of the 'modern kupapa enemies of Maori social, cultural and physical advancement and independence', claiming that 'To demoralise, to undermine Maori confidence ... is the primary objective of *Once Were Warriors* – both book and film'.[58]

The novel's style – sometimes brutal, mixing slang and demotic obscenity in its rendition of underclass speech and thought patterns, but with constantly accompanying intellectual grace notes creating a choric authorial voice which stands both close to and at a distance from the characters – finds impressive extensions throughout Tamahori's film, previewed by the harsh titles, reminiscent of agit prop posters with their uncompromising reds and blacks, colours of threat as well as of traditional Māori art, which announce the film's often minatory colour design, cutting out, wherever possible, greens, blues and pastels. It is also a film with an unrelentingly graphic presentation of Jake's violent life as bar-room strongman and husband, with extraordinarily intense performances, by Temuera Morrison and Rena Owen, and highly significant in bringing two Māori actors not just to coterie appreciation but to national and even international attention (Figure 19). This domestic violence – male brutalization of women, women's acceptance of it as the norm, and its effect on children – is a major part of the novel, but its movement to the absolute centre, where it becomes *the* rather than *a* theme of the film, banishable by an act of female heroism, is bought at a cost.

The film, paradoxically in view of its harshly real violence, softens Duff's original. An important white figure, Gordon Trambert – whose family's middle-class lifestyle holds yearning meanings for Beth and especially Grace (Mamaengaroa Kerr-Bell), who hangs herself from a tree on the Trambert property – is wholly deleted, rendering the film a

19. No indigenous pastoral here, but urban disintegration and violence in Lee Tamahori's version of Alan Duff's controversial novel: Jake (Temuera Morrison) and Beth (Rena Owen) in *Once Were Warriors* (1994).

(dystopic) version of the all-Māori world of *Whale Rider*, with hardly a white except for a few authority figures to be seen, thus removing the novel's insistent comparisons of white (and even immigrant Chinese) success with Māori failure. The switch of site from small town to a tough South Auckland suburb, creating visual parallels with the Los Angeles of gang films (rappers and bodybuilders are immediately introduced as Beth walks home at the beginning), proved to be a canny decision as regards the film's overseas reception, but sacrificed local realities (in which there simply had to be a greater white presence).

While many effects of the feminization of New Zealand film discussed in chapter 5 have been beneficial, *Once Were Warriors* displays them more questionably. Robin Scholes, the producer, explained the decision to dispense with Alan Duff's screenplay. 'Why? ... Because Alan had reached a point where he couldn't be a woman. [!!] He was a good scriptwriter, but ultimately whenever he wrote a scene Jake would come in and dominate the scene. So we had to get a woman [another Maori writer, Riwia Brown] who could turn it around and even then it was tough'.[59] Beth is a central consciousness in the novel, and her trajectory (eventually throwing Jake out because she believes he drunkenly raped his daughter, and at the novel's end doing community work supporting Chief Te Tupeia's philosophy of Māori 'self-help') is twinned in importance with Jake's, but the film's rousing 'feel good' climax – with Beth presiding over the violent nemesis Jake hands out to Uncle Bully (Cliff Curtis), the film's rapist, before leaving him – clouds with (unintentional) ambiguity her flight from violence. The film opts for female strength – and the return to the traditional rural marae that Hayward's characters farewelled in *To Love A Māori* – over wider complexity, also deleting the death of Nig (Julian Arahanga) in a gang war. Spared, Nig eats with the family, the difference between his violent escape route and Boogie (Taungaroa Emile) learning of interior warriordom over external violence from Mr Bennett (George Henare) in the borstal, minimized in the cause of an image of the good mother and family unity to just the difference between wearing your 'look' (that is, 'tats') outside or inside. Another internal censoring erased Beth getting drunk in the bar as she tries to get Jake to leave to continue the visit to Boogie and then sharing the picnic she has prepared with the boozers, clearly because the incidents showed the heroine less ideally than desired. In a further cleansing, the ambiguity that hangs over the identity of Grace's rapist – until the second volume of the trilogy, when he is cleared, it seems that it may have been Jake – is completely removed, the material of possible incest being presumably viewed as too traumatic, and the guilt placed on Bully.

These choices are often in conflict with the film's great forcefulness at other levels, inspired as other of its inventions are – the sequence utilizing the current local hit song 'What's the Time, Mr Wolf?' as the family, for once precariously united, drives along to visit Boogie, before Jake inevitably stops for a beer, with predictable consequences; the playing-out of Mr Bennett's interaction with Boogie in the borstal, only implicit in the source; and the brilliant combination of visual and sonic meanings in the film's opening image, where a pastoral New Zealand scene, full of touristic promise, is revealed as a poster overlooking a motorway and urban desolation, the images accompanied by a complex of sounds, traffic noise, fierce electric guitar riffs, Tūtānekai's flute and the primitive, wordless vocal murmur associated with ancient warriors and Jake's rages. The points made above do not underappreciate the film's stylistic dynamism and kinetic force, rare in local films, and the salutary frightening realism of its domestic violence. They do, though, underline the pertinence of the minority dissenting view expressed by several local critics.[60]

For all its backings-off, though, the film was a truly major event, an occurrence of national importance, giving rise to debates and controversies in a way few films do, particularly about domestic and other violence, not only in its known Polynesian manifestations, but in its more hidden or unadmitted white ones. Its unfortunate sequel, *What Becomes of the Brokenhearted?* (Ian Mune, 1999, though with Duff credited as screenwriter) turned the equally distinguished second novel of the trilogy's complex meditations on violence into a confused action film, besides which *Warriors'* forcefulness is unerring.

Te Tangata Whai Rawa O Weniti/The Maori Merchant of Venice

The *Māori Merchant of Venice* (Don C. Selwyn, 2000) differs substantially from these other films. Adapted from a translation of Shakespeare into a highly expressive Māori (te reo kōhatu) part of its rationale is to display the language's resources. This helps explain its stately pace, which has more than verbal effects, allowing emphasis on a highly aestheticized *mise-en-scène* which enacts many of the film's implications. Shakespeare's romantic comedy/drama of racial-religious conflict is readable in terms of New Zealand's more hidden racial conflicts, particularly when it is remembered that the Māori prophets' indigenizings of nineteenth-century Christianity were oriented more towards Old than New Testament, conflating Māori under the new settler state and the 'Hurai' (Jews) in bondage to Pharoah.[61] Inasmuch as the cast is wholly Māori, there is no question of Māori–Pākehā divisions being literally acted out like the source's Christian–Jewish ones. Meanings here proceed implicitly, as where Hairoka/Shylock and Anatonio/Antonio meet in a gallery exhibiting Selwyn Muru's paintings of the destruction of the non-violent Parihaka settlement in 1881: with only the focus on one marked with the word 'Holocaust' uncharacteristically overt. Elsewhere, Hairoka (Waihoroi Shortland) mixes positive and negative connotations; the English and Scottish Lords mocked by Pohia/Portia (Ngārimu Daniels) and Neriha/Nerissa (Veeshayne Armstrong) are actually seen in the film, making subtle reference to the colonial heritage. The trial scene inflects the original's repeated emphasis on the 'bond' (pukapuka), suggesting, as the Māori actors explore the document's possible readings, the interrogation of another disputed agreement, the Treaty of Waitangi. If the darkest implications of clashing races are suggested by the excessive 'Holocaust' reference, the *mise-en-scène* balances them with Belmont's dreamlike Aotearoan kingdom's combination of cultivated Māori visual aesthetics with European refinements. Here crossover fairies observing the Prince of Morocco's progress recall both those in *A Midsummer Night's Dream* and the patupaiarehe (white-skinned fairyfolk); Pohia's residence, with its largely European exterior, reveals graceful interiors decorated with wooden Māori statues, weaving and designs, wood-carved windows and bone-carved artefacts, indigenous pottery, flax baskets and a European harp; costumes echoing nineteenth-century European modes (as against Venice's Elizabethan styles) are crossed with Māori garments and pendants, in one case Pohia wearing a stylized catwalk version of a Māori cloak; the vocal music is a mixture of Māori and European styles; and even the journey Anatonio (Scott Morrison) and Patanio (Te Rangihau Gilbert) take towards Venice moves through New Zealand river vistas in a ship more nineteenth century than sixteenth. The static four-and-a-half-minute shot of the carved doors ending the film forces attention on carving that may be either Venetian or Māori or both: curvilinear designs that echo the koru motif, the whole double-door design equally suggesting a close-up of a tattooed Māori face.

Māori difference? Māori aesthetics?

The idea that Māori film utilizes formal modes different from mainstream New Zealand film-making is hardly sustainable, confusing as it does content and even in certain cases some discernably different production and distribution elements, with aesthetic systems. In *Nights in the Garden of Spain*,[62] Witi Ihimaera's novel's film-lecturer hero asserts the difference of indigenous Māori film. However, the moment is anything but transparent, with the narrator himself as well as a sceptical student doubting his definition of the difference between Mita's *Mauri* and Murphy's *Utu*. Actually, he argues nothing more radical than Mita 'attempts' to create a Māori perspective, and that 'what distinguishes her film making are the nuances, the small illuminations which makes *Mauri* a truly indigenous film'. This is more modest than critical claims that *Mauri*'s Māori formal elements were misunderstood. But elements like flashbacks and narrative double time, are hardly distinctive Māori practice, and, anyway, are missing from *Ngati*, *Once Were Warriors* and *The Māori Merchant of Venice*. *Mauri*'s oddest element, the community's acceptance of the false Rewi, is more the product of an obscuring ellipsis caused by the late cutting of explanatory material than of any unfamiliar formal motion.[63] Clearly none of these films employs formal devices like those Agathe Thornton cites as structuring traditional Māori verbal arts – for example, repetition, symmetrical pairings, doublets and appositional expansions, transmuted into film form[64] – and S.M. Mead's and Joan Metge's explanations of traditional Māori concepts of time throw little light on *Mauri*'s or the other films' temporal structures.[65] Probably we are on stronger ground in seeing a tendency (shared by *Ngati*, *Mauri* and *Te Rua*) to assert the community as protagonist, though again this is hardly unknown in mainstream cinema. This, it must be stressed, is not to say that these films have no Māori specificity. That clearly exists in the narrative material, the values propounded, in cultural attitudes such as Barclay details with reference to moments in both *Ngati* and *Te Rua* in his book *Our Own Image*, in aspects of *mise-en-scène*, in uses of Māori music, in many indigenous cultural elements that intermix with basically mainstream New Zealand cinema styles, but not in a distinguishably separate aesthetic. Also, the diverseness of even the few Māori features made so far suggests that a single template is misguided, the essentialisms often risked by both Mita and Barclay as critics in their definitions of what is and is not Māori being notably different; and it would be hard to imagine, within the governing conventions of mainstream to art-house cinema, styles more different than Tamahori's in *Once Were Warriors* and Selwyn's in *The Māori Merchant of Venice*.

Coda: five films at the millennium, 2000–2004

Rain, Christine Jeffs, 2000; *Snakeskin*, Gillian Ashurst, 2000; *Christmas*, Gregory King, 2000; *Shifter*, Colin Dodson, 2000; *In My Father's Den*, Brad McGann, 2004

This brief survey of five films from the beginning of New Zealand feature production's second century avoids futuristic speculation, though certain tendencies appear so engrained that any future is likely to retain strong links with the past, even amidst the changes of digital film-making and increased transnational production. Of the films here, *Christmas* and *Shifter* constitute swervings from the mainstream enabled by new technologies, while *Rain* and *In My Father's Den* exhibit creative inflections of traditional styles and thematics by mainstream directors. *Snakeskin*'s post-modern pastiche foregrounds what is also present in the others: the local cinema's intricate relationship to cinematic movements in the wider world.

Rain (Christine Jeffs, 2000)

Kirsty Gunn's fragile novella *Rain* (1994), the events of its family melodrama glimpsed through the deliquescent light on water atmospheres of a New Zealand beach setting permeating the adolescent girl narrator's recounting of the summer holiday that ended in her little brother's death and the breakdown of her parents' marriage, ultimately derives from one of New Zealand literature's founding works, Katherine Mansfield's revolutionary micro-novella *At The Bay* (1922).

Using Gunn's novella as its base, Jeff's version rivals Mansfield's in a different semiotic mode, combining delicate, synaesthesic impressionism with vividly realized versions of the characters only fragmentarily glimpsable in Gunn's fiction: the dissatisfied, moodily yearning mother, Kate (Sarah Peirse); the melancholy father (Alistair Browning), unable to prevent her turning away; the handsome interloper Cady (Marton Csokas), accelerating the marriage's dissolution; Janey, the teenage daughter (Alicia Fulford Wyzbicki), warily watching her parents' widening incompatibility as she comes to terms with her growing sexuality; and her little brother, Jim (Aaron Murphy), whose drowning is the film's catastrophe. The art-cinema-derived delayed exposition and double-time interweavings of McGann's *In My Father's Den* (below) are easier to register in their complexity than *Rain*'s seemingly artless micro-structures, with only the occasional highly artificial monochrome shots suggesting art-film discourse. The film's most obvious achievement is, in the wake of *My Lady of the Cave* and *The End of the Golden Weather*, to capture a reality available to every New Zealand film-maker but never so realized, the febrile physical atmospheres of the New Zealand beach holiday, prismatically reflecting the turbulent emotions of the film's characters.

Three instances of *Rain*'s pictorial subtlety are, first, the physical resemblance between Ed and Cady, conveyed by an eye alert to analogy – the husband/father a heavier, wearier version of Cady, creating extra adulterous pathos (inasmuch as Kate's desire, so great that, once, after physical contact with Cady, she vomits), is less for an image replacing than repairing the husband's; second, the way in which sensations of touch (as delicate as the hole in Ada's stocking celebrated in writing about *The Piano*) underlie the visual images of Janey's fingering pine needles, then the hair of Cady's chest; third, the metamorphosis of the novella's 'Jim Little' from 'tanned dark from the sun, tumbled like a stone smoothness' to the film's boy's startling, almost surreal, whiteness, which, amidst his sunburned family, carries a weight of metaphor for innocence and vulnerability.

The narrative, framed by Janey's voiceover, stays centrally with that very typical character in New Zealand fiction and cinema, the vulnerable child here (as in *In My Father's Den*) a girl on the brink of womanhood. Janey's relationship with her mother is central, complicating her response to her own sexuality, and leading her to throw herself at Cady, with whom her mother is obsessed, in what is simultaneously an attempt to appropriate him in order to prevent the marriage's break-up, a desire to assume the mother's achieved sexuality rather than her own confused borderings on it (she wears one of her mother's dresses, altered to fit her, when she visits Cady), and her desire to defeat the mother in a sexual contest and prove herself the female sexual centre of the family.

During the family's visit to Cady's boat a miniscule incident takes place. Janey, in the sea, by the boat's stern, watched by her father and little brother, is joined by her mother, still holding her drink (an issue between daughter and mother, with Janey criticizing her drinking to her face) as she treads water near her daughter. Carefully placed on the flat sea surface in front of her, the glass begins to sink, the mother's flurried grasp at it causing her to swallow seawater, while when Janey dives to retrieve it, the kick propelling her downwards accidentally causes the mother further minor distress, prompting Cady, in Ed's momentary absence, to dive in to look after her. When Jane surfaces with the glass, holding it up in triumph, she finds Cady attending to her mother. The moment suggests an anti-version of *Whale Rider*, with here the whisky-sour glass the equivalent of the whale's tooth Paikea dives for, a talisman both of desirable adulthood and its poisons. If *Whale Rider* represents the mythmaking face of the New Zealand cinema moving into the new century, *Rain*, with its heroine's final stress on 'endurance' (with its similarities to Celia's parable of disillusion and adaptation in *In My Father's Den*), represents its more realistic, sombre face.

In My Father's Den (Brad McGann, 2004)

Like *Rain*, *In My Father's Den* is based on a novel, here by Maurice Gee, one of the country's best-known contemporary writers. The two films offer very different perspectives on screen adaptation, with *Rain* a case of less common derivation from a short story with few translatable concrete actions, thus demanding large-scale invention in the film text, while *In My Father's Den* faced the more usual problems of reduction from, filmically speaking, an excess of incident. McGann's reworking of Gee's novel (1972) opens up the most fundamental question of adaptation facing the ambitious film-maker: how to avoid secondarization by a well-known source. Whether we see the dream McGann claimed gave him his opening as actual or invented, either way it asserts filmic rather than literary origins, with the prologuing voice of Celia (Emily Barclay) immediately marking difference in the words (the film-maker's not the novelist's) beginning her short story about the townspeople experiencing the absence created when the tide goes out and never returns. The film, like its source, is most obviously structured around the mystery of Celia's disappearance and death, though moved from the novel's beginning to later in the film, so that the detective investigation is only dominant from halfway, its governing hermeneutic replaced early on by art-film-derived ambiguities of exposition, with the present-time action of Paul (Matthew McFadyen) returning after seventeen years in Europe to small-town Central Otago for his father's funeral constantly interrupted by childhood memories not wholly comprehensible till near the film's end.

No longer the novel's schoolteacher, the film's Paul is a war-zone photographer/journalist, almost the paradigm career of contemporary edginess in its combination of exposure to and passive transcription of violence. His detachedness – read until late in the film as the product of that career, rather than the career as product of the trauma involving his father – is supplemented by contemporary extremities of hard-drug-taking, and the scene where, picked up by a woman, their sexual encounter ends by her complying with his desire for erotic asphyxia almost to the point of no return.

Gee's novel's preoccupations with puritanical religion and its influences are historically central to New Zealand fiction,[66] thematics taking on literally murderous form in the protagonist's brother, Andrew, and his religion-driven killing of Celia, but such elements are lessened considerably in the reworking, with, presumably, the rationale that they have less immediate resonance in contemporary New Zealand. In the novel the mother is associated with extreme religious puritanism, the father with free-thinking detachment, and though the latter is complicatedly treated as also resulting in problems for the son there is no doubt that puritan religious mania is the primary destructive force. In the film, however, in line with the thematic of puritanism having become less central in the thirty years between novel and film, the revelations of the ending are upturned in three ways: first, Celia's death is an accident, resulting from a fall caused by Andrew's wife (Miranda Otto) angrily pushing her in the mistaken belief that she is having an affair with her husband; second, Andrew (Colin Moye) takes the blame and goes to prison, an act which may have some justice about it because it is his inability to communicate that lies at the root of the misunderstanding; and, third, the enigma of the past is revealed as the father's, not the mother's, crime – his liberal reaction to finding his son and girlfriend making love –'Long as you're cautious ... I'll be on my way', the deceptive prelude to his seduction of Jackie and paternity of Celia.

In its complexly manipulated double-time narrative, *In My Father's Den* compares with Ward's *The Navigator*, though its play on familiar territories, family melodrama's buried secrets, the near-banal revelation of the bad father, small-town restlessness and the call of the larger world, the plot of the cosmopolitan expatriate returning to his origins, and the ambiguous relationship between the older man and adolescent girl places its art-film fragmentations in more easily approachable contexts than Ward's, allowing it a large-scale local success at the box office as well as earning it critical esteem.

At the same time it might seem disappointing that so much formal virtuosity should deliver up a solution to the mysteries of the mother's suicide, Celia's parentage and Paul's emotional frigidity as simple as the sexually voracious father, seducer of his son's girlfriend. In fact the bad father is doubled, as if for emphasis, in Jackie's unpleasant younger lover, Jeff, with his improper interest in Celia. McGann on the DVD release explains his reworking of the solution to Celia's death as a conscious reaction away from the detective story's pinning of the crime on a single character, preferring an ending in which accident prevails. This is odd in that the film actually seems to reach back, like some 1980s films, to the irresistibly blameable figure of the bad father. However, it may be that, while doing this, the narrative nevertheless in part resists some of its imposed post-patriarchal simplicities, since the father is also connected with various objects and statements that place him in an at least partially positive light – the globe, the gift to his son of the atlas, later handed on by Paul to Celia, which connect with the son's movement into the outer world (making him, whatever his crime, a vital part of the film's always present thematics of staying, going and returning, so important still in the New Zealand experience), the picture of 'Hope', his recitation of Baxter's 'High Country Weather' while he traces the boy's fingers over the map, and his advice to the boy about not being afraid of opportunity – while further dialogue set in the past between Jackie and Paul suggests that Paul's detachment, seen as a problem by other characters, the narrative and finally by Paul himself, precedes the traumatic incident which causes him to leave home.

Snakeskin (Gillian Ashurst, 2000)

The wittily ingenious opening – the antithesis of the flat afflicted monologues beginning both *Rain* and *In My Father's Den* – created by car headlights picking out of the darkness road signs inscribed with the credits, suggests the playful, allusive nature of the film, which begins its narrative with Melanie Lynskey (Pauline in *Heavenly Creatures*), as Alice, announcing her thralldom to American popular culture ('My first role model was Princess Leia, my second and third was Thelma and Louise'). This casting intertextually recalls the Borovnian and 'Fourth World' fantasies with which she and Kate

Winslet as Juliet transformed mundane early 1950s Christchurch. 'It seemed to me like the safest fucking place in the world, and I hated it' is Alice's verdict even fifty years on. Here Lynskey, now a mildly glamorous minor Hollywood starlet, retains linking elements of glum provincial resentment as she dresses to meet her more mildly fantasizing law-student friend, Johnny (Dean O'Gorman), attempting to transcend his kiwi-quotidian real name of Craig, for a ritual spin in his renovated red 1975 Chrysler Valiant along a local imagined Route 66. The credit sequence's illuminated signs (their curving bends ahead arrows foreshadowing the rattlesnake tattoo on Seth's arm which springs to alarming life later on) immediately announce the film's self-consciousness, by invoking, along with ironic allusions to New Zealand as the literally serpentless Eden, the American road movie so influential on New Zealand contemporary film-making. The title *Snakeskin*, as Philip Matthews reminds us, is itself an allusion to the snakeskin jacket that Sailor (Nicolas Cage) wears in David Lynch's *Wild at Heart* (1990)[67] with its various allusions to *The Wizard of Oz*, though Alice here suggests Lewis Carroll rather than Frank Baum as the genius of its road trip. This trip through the looking glass, entering a weird parallel New Zealand, also calls up the criminal couples of Hollywood films, especially Bonny and Clyde, and Mickey and Mallory in *Natural Born Killers*, the latter pair unmistakeable alluded to when Alice and Seth in grainy CCTV images rob a shop at gunpoint, shooting up the counter girl.

Picking up the literalization of Alice's dreams of violent freedom – Seth (Boyd Kestner), a snakeskin-booted and -jacketed hitchhiking piece of modern mythology,, who appears with oneiric inevitability to answer Alice's prayers – the pair's, now trio's, road trip begins, with Johnny/Craig finding himself marginalized by Alice's quickly demonstrated erotic preference for Seth. As the meta-narrative unfolds, Alice and Johnny enter a dream trajectory turning to nightmare with their drug-supplying, gun-toting pick-up, a nightmare climaxing in the locus of everyday bloodletting, the abattoir. As they drive through the sparsely populated South Island from day to deep night, the comic and minatory continually coalesce. Sheepskin-coated drinkers at a country-town bar metamorphose momentarily into sheep; another bar hosts a hallucinogenic 'mushroom ball'; a field of sunflowers perform the Nancy Sinatra number 'Sugartown' before withering to a desiccated wasteland when Alice blasts one of them in target practice; the rattlesnake on Seth's arm leaps to alarming life.

Seth's past criminal and erotic activities dictate that the trip becomes a chase, as he is pursued by three white New Zealand youths who have, in a search for meaning equivalent to Alice's and Johnny's, abysmally translated themselves into the violence and racism of English proletarian skinheads, led by the raging Speed (Oliver Driver). Also pursuing Seth is Tama (Gordon Hatfield) an aggressive (and minor-league drug-criminal) Māori, who in an encounter again both comic and minatory has objected to the plastic tiki in Johnny's car, hanging beside miniatures of Elvis and Marilyn, explained to him by Alice as 'the patron saints of America guarding us on our journey', generating his ominous reply 'Well, they may look after you in the big city, girl, but you're on my land now'. Speed (Oliver Driver) is out to kill Seth, for reasons obscure till their homosexual liaison is revealed. (Seth is evidently the exteriorization of Speed's repressed desires too ('He said I was the best fuck he'd ever had ... he just didn't know he'd like it so much'). Tama pursues him with dual motivations: Seth's obscure involvement in his brother's road death years before, and his cheating on a drug deal involving Tama's friend Nelson (Taika Cohen) and his girlfriend Daisy (Jody Rimmer), whose version of a travelling ice-cream van sells drugs rather than confectionaries, replacing the label 'Mr Whippy' with 'Mr Trippy'.

Snakeskin is more than a New Zealand accented pastiche of Lynch's *Wild at Heart*; it imagines an intensely local world into a jocosely sinister inflection, an act of reimagining not copying: Mr Trippy's girl selling drugs to a tourist about to bungee jump; an old recording of a venerable local pop song 'When My Wahine Does The Poi' playing in a cafe; Tama trying to convey a dying message to Nelson, also a Māori, who, however, cannot understand him because he speaks in Māori; and the major parties in the road chase forming a trio antically embodying the mixture of primary influences contesting mainstream New Zealand culture: the American, the British and the Māori (as stated more soberly in Horrocks's survey of the contemporary scene in his 'New Zealand Cinema: Cultures, Policies, Films').[68]

In *Snakeskin*'s abattoir climax, as Alice shoots Seth, he spectrally dematerializes. Then, in the dawn, having kissed the dead Johnny, she sends him and the car to a blazing funeral. Walking along the road, wearing the snakeskin jacket, she hitches a ride from the Japanese tourist who has made various narrative appearances, now in possession of a yellow mini like the one in *Goodbye Pork Pie*, to see which has apparently been his reason for visiting New Zealand. Alice's voiceover speaks of a 'strange wisdom' she has gained, as a result of which 'I could see deep into the soul of any stranger and I could become anything they wanted'. The statement is opaque, but reveals itself to a little meditation, as the closure of the film's framing allegory. A chastened Alice, if not leaving behind, at least relativizes her dreams of becoming something else – particularly American – and realizes that, in the post-modern world where identities are unceasingly interchanged, she (or New Zealand itself, as much as any postmodern anywhere) may be the object as well as the dreamer of fantasies, as witness the Japanese tourist's fascination with *Goodbye Pork Pie*.

Christmas (Gregory King, 2000)

On one its websites the New Zealand Film Archive's collection of 'Christmas Home Movies' is advertised as 'celebrat[ing] the New Zealand family Christmas: on holiday with the children at the beach, the bach, the motor camp or at home over the long summer months'.[69] Such nostalgia informs with varying degrees of irony *The End of the Golden Weather*, *Rain* and one of *Channelling Baby*'s more optimistic moments, where Bunnie and Geoff's decision to marry takes place on a beach, aurally counterpointed by the cricket commentaries which with other summer-sports broadcasts are a familiar radio accompaniment of the holiday period. Their equivalent, emanating from the sitting-room television just outside the cinema audience's view, is heard at the beginning of *Christmas*, a film playing against familiar images of pleasure, relaxation and family unity, in the suburban gathering of its dysfunctional underclass family, seemingly too exhausted to venture more than spasmodically outdoors, in a narrative largely acted out in kitchen, bedrooms, TV living room, and the much sought after lavatory, as distinct from the beach world of *The End of the Golden Weather* and *Rain*.

On the DVD release, the director aligns himself with European cinema's 'rigorous intelligence and examination' behind films which are 'not merely the products of entertainment', hoping that his own film's shocking, scatological aspects are not gratuitous 'but hooked into a larger picture', which he can push the audience into 'completing'. This suggests that *Christmas*'s blackly comic and scatological incidents at least implicitly relate to a larger social picture, not underlined overtly by any character's critical awareness, but, ironically, by the counterpoint of other background broadcasts: not so much the obvious ironies of the Queen's Message's homily to the family in good and bad times, as the radio's economic reports with their share prices and portfolios (markers of the newer privatized New Zealand, increasingly divided into haves and have nots). These ironize the lives of the Māori–Pākehā family at the film's centre, crossing the racial divide, with the whole family (Māori father, Pākehā mother, and four children so different-looking that they might be unrelated) united by their low socio-economic status, a reminder of how marginal a place critique of socio-economic inequalities has ever had in the New Zealand cinema. Indeed, outside of Hayward's *On The Friendly Road* (1936) and Gaylene Preston's *Ruby and Rata* and *Bread and Roses*, one can only think of Robert Steele's short film *Indictment!* (1950), which powerfully exposed aged homelessness in Auckland's meaner streets. In *Christmas*, the market report over the final credits segues into a discussion about a charity Town Hall Christmas meal 'to make sure a thousand people don't have a terrible Christmas', emphasizing the necessity for charity in a society used to thinking itself without such needs.

The film's narrative enacts no sustained plot over its five-day time span, only the naturalistic if seldom low-keyed interaction of the family group, with Keri (David Hornblow), the oldest son, returning after an unexplained absence of years to join his non-communicating parents (Tony Waerea and Darien Takle), his troubled siblings – Richard (Czahn Armstrong), gay, masturbating over a male pin-up and on drugs; the semi-catatonic Donna (Kate Sullivan), and the older, spectacularly foul-mouthed Megan (Helen Pearse Otene) with her unappealing partner Brett (Matthew Sutherland) – and Megan's children. Amidst the rowdy bonhomie, flare-ups and occasional violence, almost all the characters are caught in moments of trancelike solitude where their lack of emotional, as well as obvious monetary, sustenance is imaged. By the end of the film the youngest son is lying dead, of an overdose, and Donna has had a miscarriage. Keri, the most sensitized, in one scene just looks at his mother asleep in the parents' bedroom, in another reaches out to touch the face of his sleeping father (who only seems aroused from torpor by his ownership of a new car), as if in both cases trying to express a difficult love, or in the case of the father, the wish for love. In the crowded house, the lavatory, often in high angle views, functions as a place – apart from its obvious purposes, including Donna's morning-sickness vomiting and Keri's discovery of anal bleeding – for escape, solitary grief, or, in the end, death. With Keri discovering blood from his anus on the lavatory paper, in another scene rushing into the shrubbery to defecate, and in another bending over to thrust a suppository up himself, a motif of bodily waste is foregrounded, repeated in the gobs of blood on the shower floor when Donna miscarries, readable metaphorically in relation to the social text.

The film's quick shooting schedule, along with King's preference for inference over statement and for ambiguous foreground rather than carefully constructed background, leaves the text full of unexplained elements. Where has Keri been all the years? Prison? How ill is he?

Why has the father returned? Is the source of Megan's epically foul-mouthed aggression her fear that Brett will leave her? These may all be instances of King's determination that the audience should complete the picture, but many audiences may find such withholdings alienating in a negative sense. *Christmas* is in many respects roughly made, and less rigorous than the models King refers to, but it has major virtues, especially given New Zealand cinema's all but complete eschewing of social critique and the underclass, kept at arm's length by still-surviving egalitarian myths.

Shifter (Colin Hodson, 2000)

Shifter is one of several films – along with *Uncomfortable/ Comfortable* (Campbell Walker, 1998), *OFF* (Colin Hodson, 2002), *Why Can't I Stop This Uncontrollable Dancing?* (Campbell Walker, 2003) – from the Gordon Productions Collective, a group of Wellington film-makers (primarily the director/actors Colin Hodson and Campbell Walker), whose films differentiate themselves from the commercial mainstream: first, by emphasizing unhierarchical group activity – in *Shifter* the screenplay credit reads: 'text: cast and crew'; and, second, by their utilization of cheap digital technology to enable improvisatory features on miniscule budgets, like the NZ$110 shooting costs (!) and NZ$2,500 postproduction claimed for *Shifter*. This frugality creates the possibility, that as Lawrence McDonald optimistically put it, 'it could well be that we have reached the point where Alexandre Astruc's dream of Le Caméra Stylo, is beginning finally to become something of a local reality'.[70] Of necessity this involves practices antithetical to mainstream production's: non-professional actors, borrowed rather than hired equipment, shooting over days rather than weeks, doing without lighting, and an acceptance of the 'aleatory' (indeed, a willingness to alter plot and characters in line with the logistical hazards of non-professional production). The director, Colin Hodson, emphasizing 'chance' in the film's Press and Publicity release (23 July 2000), noted that its ending, in which Shifter fails to find his old girlfriend, was conditioned by the actress playing her being unavailable the day it was shot. These are, largely, production conditions similar to those under which Peter Jackson made over several years his first feature *Bad Taste*. However, there such constraints were undesired, and, far from providing a philosophical basis for future film-making, were abandoned as soon as there was finance to make films differently, whereas the conditions in which *Shifter* was made were embraced as a 'guerilla' attack on normal film production and funding practices (Press and Publicity release, 23 July 2003).

'Guerilla' cinema suggests political dimensions, but, beyond the politics of cinema, the Gordon productions feel entirely apolitical, a microcosmic world of shared short-stay flats, whose almost albinoid twenty-something inhabitants hardly interact with the urban macrocosm. In *OFF* this microcosm abuts on the criminal underworld of hard-drug usage, but morality is hardly invoked, though Bill Gosden remarks on the film's divulging of 'the self-centredness of the users'.[71] However, one might feel that drug usage – with its passivity, its rhythms of quiescence, only broken by the need of a fix, the rituals of which parallel the coffee-drinking, record-playing and desultory conversations of the other films – is only a hyperbole of their rather aimless, patiently scrutinized, retracted life rhythms. Hodson names John Cassavetes as a primary influence: 'I was trying to get at a similar rawness to what he does'.[72] The comparison holds in a shared rejection of mainstream smoothness, but otherwise suggests more differences than similarities. Cassavetes' films are centred on the traumas of middle-aged protagonists facing failure, decline and death (*Husbands* is paradigmatic, with its three middle-aged men on an intoxicated razzle after a friend's funeral), cornered by life but still full of desperate energy, reflected in the forcefulness of the shooting style. Anything like the moments in *Husbands* where the men, after comparing their youthful sporting hopes, reenact them on the basketball court, is unthinkable in the passive flat-bound world of the Aro Valley.

It would be a mistake, though, to flatten all the Gordon films into an undifferentiated pattern: *Uncomfortable/Comfortable* is a witty minimalist anti-romantic comedy of cohabitation; *Why Can't I Stop This Uncontrollable Dancing?* is the most virtuosic of these minimalist films, most of it extended, patient 'real-time' takes, as long as ten minutes, of Leah (Nia Robyn), listening repeatedly to recorded phone messages from her drunken, aggressive ex-boyfriend. *OFF* differs from the others in its quick subjective flashbacks and 'telegraphic narrative techniques the other films eschewed'.[73] *Shifter*'s specificity is built around 'The Shifter' (as he calls himself) moving through a 'molecular structure of small scale incident', a 'loose set of 13 episodes'[74] – drifting from flat to flat; ambivalent social interactions; multiple frustrations, such as losing a job opportunity through confused telephone numbers, failing to get sex with different girls, victimized by what may be an erotic practical joke set up to mock his libido – where, typically, it is difficult to separate external reality and the protagonist's projections. The incidents' deliberate unfinishednesses are recorded with a vocabulary of imperfect handheld camera, long takes, deliberately imprecise reframings, slight variations of focus, lightly disturbing jump cuts, and occasional shots without apparent narrative rationale. The director's description invokes 'unlocatable anxiety', 'paranoia' and 'dread', though this understates the way pervasive quotidian comedy (his bad dream is about a rabbit; a girl he has designs on lectures him self-absorbedly about her erotic preference for women over men) modifies such implications. 'As he tries to focus his dread (and thus contain it in one place), Shifter finds himself on an endless loop because each situation he attributes to his paranoia does not satisfactorily explain his anxiety.'[75] The film's post-credits testament 'Shifter was entirely filmed in an urban environment, somewhere', at first sight paradoxical since the film's locality is so specifically Wellington, is taken up by the Vancouver International Film Festival 2000 statement, saying that the film shows 'the alienated cinema of the Pacific rim stretches as far south as New Zealand' (video release cover), in other words a local inflection of a widespread genre of international non-commercial cinema. Undoubtedly important – along with Rachel Douglas's *Blessed*, Alexander Greenhough's *I Think I'm Going* and Florian Habicht's very different *Woodenhead* – in initiating and exemplifying alternative feature film making possibilities – both organizational and stylistic – outside the mainstream, the group and its individual members' progress will be fascinating to gauge, as will that of other related film-makers. Will there be further refinement of the minimalist, micro-realist base (such as in the *Dogme* movement)? Or will less-effective repetition result, dictated by the films' necessarily limited milieu? Will interesting divagations develop, like the anti-realist sky-travelling woman who links the characters connected with the brothel in Rachel Douglas' *Blessed*? Or will difference be threatened by larger budgets and the temptations of incorporation into the mainstream with the better-known of the film-makers?

Notes

1 Kai Jensen, *Whole Men: The Masculine Tradition in New Zealand Literature*, Auckland University Press, Auckland, 1996, especially 78–9, 103–4.
2 Jane Kelsey, *The New Zealand Experiment: A World Model for Structural Adjustment?*, Auckland University Press, Auckland, and Bridget Williams Books, 1995, 85.
3 *Ibid.*, especially 9, 10, 87, 118, 127, 348, 350, 352.
4 Roger Horrocks, 'New Zealand Cinema: Cultures, Policies, Films', 136.
5 *Ibid.*, 137.
6 David Grant, *Bulls, Bears and Elephants: A History of the New Zealand Stock Exchange*, Victoria University Press, Wellington, 1997, 312.

7 Belich, *Paradise Reforged*, 228.
8 King, *The Penguin History of New Zealand*, 369.
9 Thanks to Ivan Mladec, New Zealand Film Commission, for these figures.
10 *Channelling Baby* press kit, NZFA.
11 *ON FILM*, March 2004, 9.
12 *National Business Review*, 15 March 1996, 13.
13 Richard deCordova, *Picture Personalities: The Emergence of the Star System in America*, University of Illinois Press, Chicago and Urbana, 1990.
14 *Weekend Herald*, 16–17 November 2002; *Sunday Star Times*, H23/4, 20 April 2003, 23–4; 'Philip Matthews Talks to Danielle Cormack [Film star]', *NZ Listener*, 15 January 2000, 8–9.
15 'Bianca Zander Talks to Karl Urban [serious ac-taw]', *NZ Listener*, 24 February 2001, 10–11, 'The Price of Fame', *Herald*, section D, 15–16 July 2000.
16 Karen Holden, 'Demi God turns Human', *Sunday Star Times*, F1, 31 October 1999; *NZ Listener*, 20 November 1999, 12; Diane Wichtel, 'The Credible Hulk', *NZ Listener*, 8 September 2000.
17 Bruce Babington, 'Bugger Me Days or Carry Me Back: Time, Place and Genre in the Films of John Reid', in Ian Conrich and Stuart Murray, eds, *New Zealand Film Makers*, Wayne State University Press, Detroit, 2007.
18 Quoted by John Downie, *The Navigator: A Mediaeval Odyssey*, Flicks Books, Trowbridge, 2000, 2.
19 'A Dialogue with Discrepancy: Vincent Ward Discusses *The Navigator*', *Illusions* 10, 1989, 11.
20 *Grace*, October/November 1988.
21 Ann Hardy, 'Word Wars in Suburbia: A Reconsideration of Ruby and Rata', *Illusions* 20, 1992, 3–9.
22 Ann Hardy, 'Send a Gorilla: Out of Control', *Illusions* 10, 1989, 6.
23 Pattrick Smellie, 'Pool – a Metaphor for Life', *Stickmen* Publicity Report, *Stickmen* material, NZFA.
24 Philip Matthews, 'Table Manners', *NZ Listener*, 20 January 2001, 54.
25 For a documentary on dairying's importance to New Zealand, see the NZ Government Publicity Office's poetically titled *The Milky Way: Dairying in New Zealand* (1927).
26 Arthur Schopenhauer, 'Supplement to Book Four', *The World as Will and Idea*, Everyman/J.M. Dent, 1995, 263–6.
27 Michael Walker, 'Melodrama and the American Cinema', *Movie* 29/30, 16–17.
28 Roger Horrocks, 'Alternatives: Experimental Film Making in New Zealand', in Bieringa and Dennis, 57–87.
29 Steve Neale, *Genre and Hollywood*, Routledge, London, 2000, 196, summarizing numerous sources.
30 Thomas Elsaesser, 'Tales of Sound and Fury', reprinted in Christine Gledhill, ed., *Home Is Where The Heart Is: Studies in Melodrama and The Woman's Film*, BFI, London, 1987, especially 48–52.
31 Bruce Babington, 'Anchor Me in the Middle of Your Deep Blue Sea: Gayle

Preston, Perfect Strangers and Ambivalent Romance', *Illusions* 36, 12–15.
32 Richard Dyer 'Entertainment and Utopia', *Movie* 24, 1977, 2–13.
33 Peter Wells, the director of *Desperate Remedies*, has a screenwriting credit.
34 Barbara Cairns and Helen Martin, *Shadows On The Wall: A Study of Seven New Zealand Feature Films*, Longman Paul, Auckland, 1994, 306.
35 Peter Wells, 'Glamour on the Slopes or: The Films We Wanted to Live', in Bierienga and Dennis, 174.
36 *Ibid.*, 176.
37 Peter Wells, *Frock Attacks! Wig Wars!* Working Papers No. 1, Centre for Film, Television and Media Studies, Auckland University, 1977.
38 Noted too by Jocelyn Robson and Beverley Zalcock, *Girls' Own Stories: Australian and New Zealand Women's Films*, Scarlet Press, London, 1997, 28–9.
39 *City Voice*, 25 November 1999.
40 Owen Hughes, the producer, quoted in the booklet *Memory and Desire*, La Semaine de la Critique, Cannes Film Festival, 1998, *Memory and Desire* material, NZFA.
41 Peter Wells, 'Of Memory and Desire', *Dangerous Desires*, Minerva, London, 1995. On the incident, see *Woman's Day*, 2 November 1988, 31.
42 Jane Sayles, 'The Gendered Sublime in *Memory and Desire*', *Illusions* 28, 1999, 2–9.
43 S. Freud, 'Mourning and Melancholia', *The Standard Edition of the Complete Psychological Works of Sigmund Freud*, vol. XIV, The Hogarth Press, London, 1957, 243–58.
44 *NZ Herald*, 27 September 1960.
45 Also Babington, *Illusions* 36, 12–15.
46 These and other terms structure the later 'Aotearoa' section of *Naming The Other*.
47 850,000 theatrical viewers, box office of NZ$6.4 million, Australian takings of A$8million, and US of $21million: Shelton, 176.
48 Sarah Stuart, 'Riding to a Wave of Triumph', *Sunday Star Times*, 9 September 2002.
49 Witi Ihimaera, *The Whale Rider*, Harcourt, New York, 1987.
50 Barry Barclay, 'Among Landscapes', in Bieringa and Dennis, 123.
51 Martin and Edwards, 128.
52 Merata Mita, 'The Soul and the Image', in Bieringa and Dennis, 49.
53 Barry Barclay, 'Celebrating Fourth Cinema', *Illusions* 35, 2003, 7–11.
54 Apirana Taylor, 'Chugda Popoy Ugh Cha Cha', *One Hundred Leaves of Love*, Penguin (NZ), Auckland, 1986.
55 Barry Barclay, *Our Own Image*, Longman Paul, Auckland, 1990, especially 48–73 and 74ff.
56 The film played in New Zealand for more than a year with audiences of over a million: Shelton, 142.
57 Alan Duff, *Once Were Warriors*, Vintage, London, 1995, 191.
58 Apirana Taylor, 'Alan Duff the Writer and His Film', *Te Maori News*, 24

February 1994.
59 'The Woman Behind The Warriors', *Evening Post*, 14 May 1994.
60 See Geoff Mayer, 'Going Home: Once Were Warriors', *Metro Magazine* 100, 3–6; Nicholas Reid, 'Once were Warriors', *North and South*, June 1994, 128; and Brian McDonnell, 'Once were Warriors: Confrontational Novel Becomes Blockbuster Film', *Metro Magazine* 101, 7–9.
61 Judith Binney, 'Ancestral Voices: Maori Prophet Leaders', Keith Sinclair, ed., *The Oxford Illustrated History of New Zealand*, Oxford University Press, Auckland, 1990.
62 Witi Ihimaera, *Nights in the Gardens of Spain*, Secker and Warburg New Zealand, Auckland, 1995, 184–5.
63 *Mauri*'s Presentation Booklet, *Mauri* material, NZFA.
64 Agathe Thornton, *Maori Oral Literature As Seen By a Classicist*, Huia Publishers, Wellington, 1990.
65 S.M. Mead, 'Ka Tupu te Toi Whakairo Aotearoa: Becoming Maori Art', in *Te Maori: Maori Art from New Zealand Collections*, Heinemann (New Zealand) in association with The American Federation of Arts, Auckland, 1984, 64; Joan Metge, *The Maoris of New Zealand*, Routledge and Kegan Paul, London, rev.ed., 1976, 68–70.
66 Patrick Evans notes the prevalence in New Zealand fiction of 'parents who are puritans, and children who are alienated': 'The Provincial Dilemma: After The God Boy', *Landfall* 17, 1976, 34.
67 Philip Matthews, 'Route 666', *NZ Listener*, 3 November 2001, 52.
68 Horrocks, 'New Zealand Cinema: Cultures, Policies, Films', 132.
69 'Christmas Home Movies', http://filmarchive.org.nz/search/catplus/cat-plus-xmas.php (accessed 20 April 2007).
70 Lawrence McDonald, 'One from Cult Classic pictures, another from Gordon Productions: *Shifter* and *The Shirt*', *Illusions* 31, 2000, 24.
71 Note for New Zealand International Film Festival, 2002.
72 *City Voice*, 20 July 2000.
73 Note for New Zealand International Film Festival, 2002.
74 McDonald, *Illusions* 31, 26
75 *Shifter*, Press and Publicity, 23 July 2003, NZFA.

7

Wandering stars: New Zealand cinema on the world screen – Vincent Ward, Peter Jackson, Jane Campion

> Pine for the needles brown and warm,
> think of your nameless native hills,
> The seagulls landward blown by storm,
> the rabbit that the black dog kills.
> (A.R.D. Fairburn 'To An Expatriate')
>
> don't anchor here in the desert –
> the fishing isn't so good:
> take a ticket for Megalopolis,
> don't stay in this neighbourhood!
> (A.R.D. Fairburn, 'I'm Older than You, Please Listen')

Delaying consideration of the three best known New Zealand film-makers of all until this book's coda is a decision made for two main reasons. The usual approaches to New Zealand film history have been criticized as 'linear exercises ... working their way quickly down a list until the magical year of 1977 when their paragraphs start to get longer'.[1] A parallel pitfall is an account of the contemporary period wholly dominated by a few figures and texts, such as *Vigil*, *The Navigator*, *An Angel at My Table*, *The Piano*, *Heavenly Creatures* and the *Lord of the Rings* trilogy. This book has been organized to avoid rendering the many strands of the New Zealand feature film largely invisible, either by skimping its pre-1977 life, or over-prioritizing the three directors who, for many overseas, embody the New Zealand cinema. Something to be remembered in balancing this strategy's losses (readings of the films listed above) against its gains is that the volume of analysis devoted to them probably already exceeds that on all other local films and film-makers combined, making detailed textual discussion of them here less pressing than with others. This last part views the three together within the context of New Zealand film-making, and the ever present thematic of expatriatism, rather than viewing New Zealand film-making as an adjunct to them, important and definitive though they are.

In fact none of them relates simply to the category 'New Zealand cinema'. Only Jackson is actually resident in New Zealand and making all his films there, while Campion left in her early twenties for Australia, where she made her earliest films and first two features. Her New Zealand works, *An Angel at My Table* (1990) and *The Piano* (1993), are a brief interlude between long periods of production outside New Zealand, by a film-maker now self-defined as Australian. Ward – after his short films, *A State of Siege* (1978) and *In Spring One Plants Alone* (1982) and the two features *Vigil* (1984) and *The Navigator (1987)* – left New Zealand for the larger budgets of *Map of the Human Heart* (1993) and *What Dreams May Come* (1998), though he has recently returned to make *River Queen* (2006). All three raise complicated questions about national cinema, since they all have to be in some respects perceived in transnational terms, with Ward's *Map of the Human Heart* an extreme of internationally diffuse co-production financed from the UK, France, Australia and Canada. To paraphrase Dana Polan on Campion: her film *Holy Smoke* (1999) displays alongside its main Australian setting 'post-national' tendencies, exhibiting 'a vulnerable geography of fleeting connection' as it moves between national boundaries (Australia, India, the US)[2] – true earlier of *The Portrait of a Lady*'s (1996) characters' movements between England, Italy and the US, rooted in an earlier era's internationality, further inflected by its Australian star and prologue, the movement (though not Campion's trajectory which at that point intersects with Hollywood) only halting for the moment in the New York of *In The Cut* (2003). Ward's first post-New-Zealand film (though *The Navigator* survived on Australian finance), *Map of The Human Heart* (1998), is dominated by Arvik's journeyings from the Arctic to Montreal to London to saturation-bombed Dresden back to final displacement in the Arctic, a pattern symptomatic of the others, for example *The Navigator*'s fantastic journey between medieval Cumbria and 1980s Auckland, and Chris's progress through metaphysical geographies, the heavens and hells of *What Dreams May Come*. Ward's own peripatetic career has the film-maker, like Campion, mirroring his narratives' transshiftings. Notably, Ward's biographical 'legend' has *The Navigator*'s conception occurring as the New Zealander abroad, trapped trying to cross a German *autobahn* on foot, makes the comparison with what a medieval visitor might feel.[3] The situation's symbolics resonate, invoking displacement, wandering, and the geographical and temporal meeting of old and new worlds, all anchored in something as mundane and simultaneously extraordinary as the New Zealander's ritual OE (overseas experience) and an implicit New Zealand naïveté and experimentalism.

Ward's and Campion's literal expatriatism replays a constant thematic of New Zealandness, not just the need to experience the larger centres, and places of Pākehā origin, but, in a small, often parochial country, the pull on, sometimes the necessity for, the talented to seek larger environments. The two New Zealand artists most celebrated in the twentieth-century international canon, Katherine Mansfield and Len Lye, were both expatriates. Ward's reflections on his film beginnings suggest difficulties including but exceeding the economic. 'It's very hard to do it financially. So if you want to make a film that's scaled larger than a very small intimate drama, it becomes very difficult and you're totally at the mercy of the fluctuating New Zealand market-place. You can find yourself out of work for years', he begins, adding that 'if you make more than two or three films you're in danger of getting both knocked and institutionalized, and you're at risk of not growing ... There are many people who make one or two films in New Zealand, and that's it. Very few can stay and make more than two'.[4] Had the various expatriate New Zealand film-makers (including directors Andrew Adamson and Martin Campbell, who moved away before significant involvement in the home film scene) stayed in the home industry, with its disregarded underside of experienced film-makers shelved after a few films, there is no guarantee that they might not have ended as neglected as some talented domestic practitioners. Equally, New Zealand's expanding reputation for digital expertise looks at present more likely to benefit off-shore film-makers than smaller budgeted locals.

Jackson, who has stayed and made ten films (nine features, four of them on an enormous scale) over some nineteen years, is the overwhelming exception to both amputated home careers and literal expatriatism, achieved in his later phase through what might be described as a paradoxical mixture of local rootedness and internal emigration, in some ways paralleling that of the local popular writers who have been staple contributors to the Anglo-American popular fiction described by James Belich as 'pan-British', magnified by the 'globalisation of American culture'. To compare Jackson with Edith Lyttleton or Ngaio Marsh might appear odd, but Belich does so provokingly,[5] albeit that Jackson's conquest of his greater global market is on an unprecedented scale. His work since *Heavenly Creatures*, his last feature with New Zealand content, now exists, with its enormous American financing, in an economic dimension far removed from other New Zealand film-making, and at a seemingly growing distance from any localness of content, somewhat ironized by the adoption of the *Lord of the Rings* trilogy as a national patriotic-touristic landscape project. While Ward and Campion belong to new art-house cinema (with the possibility of 'cross-over' as with *The Piano*'s popular success), Jackson now reaches past post-family audience sectorings to the hugest mass appeal, with his films the centre of associated sub-industries of director's cut and special effects revelations DVDs, 'making-of' television and book spin-offs, and electronic games based on *The Lord of the Rings* and *King Kong*. These last obviously signal differences from Ward and Campion – it is difficult to imagine electronic games based on *The Navigator* (taking the part of Griffin, escape the Queenfish and find the Cathedral?) or *An Angel At My Table* (get Janet to 'Mirror City' avoiding ECT and a lobotomy?). Yet the differences are not always absolute, as *What Dreams May Come*'s Oscar for best visual effects and nomination for best art direction show. It should also be remembered that both Ward and Campion operate in the part-commodified world of international art-house cinema, utilizing budgets and stars demanding substantial returns, if from smaller audiences, and pressuring the adoption (which may not be alien to either, since neither is a theoretical or systematic artist) of the mainstream-moderated pleasures of that mode of cinema – for an epitome of which compare Ward's more radical early work *The Navigator* with the later *What Dreams May Come*, or Campion's *Sweetie* with the generically underwritten *In The Cut*.

Vincent Ward

A State of Siege, 1978; *In Spring One Plants Alone*, 1982; *Vigil*, 1984; *The Navigator*, 1987; *Map of the Human Heart*, 1993; *What Dreams May Come*, 1998; *River Queen*, 2006

In his book *Edge of the Earth* (a title conjoining metaphysical motifs with New Zealand's geography and Michael Powell's film *The Edge of the World*, 1938, set on another outpost, the Shetland island of Hirta), Ward presents a heightened 'legend' of origins. His narrative of his parents' intersecting lines of fateful journeyings (Ireland to New Zealand, Germany to the Middle East, and the world war that effected their meeting), enabling the artist's birth, enacts a compelling version of Manhire's poet's New Zealand of 'diversities, disjunctions, juxtapositions and incongruities'.[6] Mythically bare, the narrative then fixes on the compelling image of the solitary child reading *Ivanhoe* amidst the bloodiness and harshness of sheep farming, a paradigm of the intersection of disparate worlds so often staged in his films. Just as that account is shaped by the film *Vigil* which arose from it, even a recent website description of Ward filming the *River Queen*'s last shots cannot resist placing him back within his own films, 'himself, alone, mid winter, freezing, and waist-deep in the middle of the River Thames. He was so intent on his work he didn't notice the rising tide and his possessions from the bank behind him being swept away downstream', reportage obviously shaped by Griffin's trance that begins *The Navigator*.[7] The report contracts a fascinating melange of intersections: the New Zealander in London; the entranced director recalling the visionary Griffin, but while practising an intensely technological art; the River Thames as the Whanganui River, with the conflation of the two significant in a new film bringing together Ward's deep sympathy with Māori (at the centre of *In Spring One Plants Alone*) with his insistence on the complexity of the Pākehā English/Celtic/European heritage, sometimes slighted in newer concerns with the country's Pacificness.[8]

The most quoted intersection of places and epochs in his films is Ward's explanation of the colours of *The Navigator*'s Auckland nighttime sequences in terms of Chartres cathedral's stained glass and the Duc De Berri's *Très riches heures*.[9] But such intersections are not unidirectional. Ward's films' solitary characters in their hyperbolically hostile environments (think of the grandfather's opening words in *Vigil* about the South Pole getting closer and the often-noted medieval-like winter clothing worn by *Vigil's* characters), besieged by metaphysical thematics and by constant journeying between geographical and temporal worlds, can be viewed as grounded in geographic and psychic New Zealand realities, not least in local visual and verbal versions of the sublime (the painters van der Velden and McCahon, and the poets Brasch, Baxter and Curnow). *Vigil's* wind-battered Uruti Valley and *The Navigator*'s frozen Lake Harris, with their elemental harshness, seem analogues of the primal situations in which religions were born, making Ward's art that rarest of things (paralleled only by McCahon's painting and Baxter's poetry) in New Zealand's dominantly secular culture, an art that constantly invokes religious questions even if offering no affirmations – as in Toss's theological discussion with Ethan about whether God cares ('do the hills care? Does the sky care?'), which ends with the pair chucking their bowls of beans at God, ('beans in yer face!', 'beans up yer bum!').

Alongside his statement of the difficulties of New Zealand filmmaking, Ward also stated his past's inescapability. 'It is the country and the family and the people I come from that give my stories their shape. And that I cannot escape'.[10] Such links, if tenuous in *What Dreams May Come*, are traceable in *Map of the Human Heart*'s saga of Arvik, the mixed-race Inuit 'Holy Boy', which even though it lacks literal New Zealand connections is shadowed throughout by local elements (beyond the childhood, isolation and journeying motifs common in New Zealand art) paralleling Inuit and Māori – greeting through touching noses, facial tattoos, Arvik's tuberculosis (the Māori disease of the past), fighting for Britain in the war like many Māori, and where Arvik, having received an American-football-like pass, running with the ball, looks more like a rugby player. Arvik's fate is to live in two worlds, belonging wholly to neither, suggesting the Māori but also the Pākehā New Zealander, positioned between new and old worlds, present and past, the parallelisms augmented by the presence of the white New Zealander 'Farm Boy' in Arvik's RAF squadron.

In 1980, Ward visited the Museum of Modern Art in New York to view silent films, a visit which confirmed his student instinct for visual narrative. 'Often minimal means create great results and lack of sound can create a film with a concentration and focus that is greater than anything that has all the luxuries of Dolby'.[11] Proto-artist figures abound in his films, but the clearest allegorization of cinema is when Ethan in *Vigil* blacks out the windows and, like a projectionist, manipulates light onto bottles and glasses, producing a play of shifting blues and purples which he explains to the entranced Toss as 'magic'. This enactment of 'minimal means' for 'great results' suggests a tension in the artist attempting both to resist and cultivate a highly commodified medium. As his films have become more expensive, does the ethic of poor means and film-making as a kind of purgatorial journey of hardship, both implicit guarantors of their ultimate non-commodification, get left behind? Had *Alien III* been made with Ward's quixotic wooden Hieronymus-Bosch-like planet, monks and medieval incarnations of the alien, might it not have been more expensive than the *Alien III* made after he left? In the light of these questions, *River Queen*'s saga of production problems (replaying, it might seem, Méliès' struggles of 1912) involving the director's temporary removal from the project, may, whatever its effects on the film, have its own subterranean meanings. Perhaps all one can say to resolve the paradox is that Ward's much anecdotalized obsessional perfectionism over casting and sites, and even his later special effects, expensive though they are, relate more to the mysteries of Ethan's light show – and even at least tangentially to the theory of 'transcendental style' applied by Paul Schrader to such more stylistically severe artists as Ozu, Dreyer and Bresson[12], even though connection to that definition may be strained to breaking point by *What Dreams May Come*'s lushness, than to the hyper-materiality of most Hollywood spectacles.

Peter Jackson

Bad Taste, 1987; *Meet The Feebles*, 1989; *Braindead*, 1992; *Heavenly Creatures*, 1994; *Forgotten Silver* (with Costa Botes), 1995; *The Frighteners*, 1996; *The Lord of the Rings: The Fellowship of the Ring*, 2001; *The Two Towers*, 2002; *The Return of the King*, 2003; *King Kong*, 2005

Like Ward's, Jackson's biographical 'legend' presents a gifted, obsessive child – replacing *Ivanhoe* with *The Seventh Voyage of Sinbad* and the original *King Kong*, Sir Walter Scott with Ray Harryhausen and Willis O'Brien – in which the precocious eight-year-old, armed with his 8mm movie camera, replicates the special effects of the films that first moved him.[13] Jackson's 'mocumentary' *Forgotten Silver* (1995), made with Costa Botes, purports to rediscover a great pioneer filmmaker, Colin McKenzie, who in the 1920s out Hollywooded Hollywood in unlikely New Zealand. Its play on antipodean DIY mythologies not only refracts early local film-makers' generally more technological than aesthetic interests, with Colin making the world's first sound feature with so little attention to communication that he neglects to realize that his Chinese-speaking actors will not be understood, but is also a ludic self-projection in which Colin's graduation from inventor to artist parallels Jackson's own. *Forgotten Silver* was made between *Heavenly Creatures* (1994) – his last New Zealand feature in terms of content (Figure 20) – and *The Frighteners* (1996), the

20. Pauline (Melanie Lynskey, left) and Juliet (Kate Winslet) recreate for the 1990s, 1950s *folie à deux* and suburban matricide in Jackson's masterpiece *Heavenly Creatures* (1996).

later career's harbinger, transforming Wellington and Lyttelton into 'Fairwater', USA. Though the spoof burlesques Hayward's 'community comedies', Colin's masterwork *Salome* calls up not Hayward but Hollywood through early epic DeMille, even down to the supposed West Coast bush discovery of the film's monumental set, paralleling the discovery of the Egyptian city set of *The Ten Commandments* (1923), buried in the Californian Guadalupe Dunes. Without suggesting prophetic foresight, one can hardly fail to note the fulfilment of the scenario in the touristic traffic that now inspects the sites of *The Lord of the Rings*.

Jackson's extraordinary achievement in turning a minor province of the Hollywood empire into its temporary second centre is not only unprecedented but unlikely to be rivalled. To say this is to stress that his present position depends on numerous interwoven conditions into which he has perfectly fitted – Hollywood's contemporary post-studio dependence on the one-off blockbuster; Jackson's not just high competence in, but consuming desire to work with, the digitally enhanced, model-dominated, blue- and green-screen apparatus of a certain kind of film-making, which can make actual location irrelevant; entrepreneurial and aesthetic capacities combined to a rare degree; and his team's ability to add many extra notches to the offshore desirability of New Zealand as a film-making site through the ultra-competitive Weta digital studios.

All this has brought to fruition the childhood obsession with metamorphic effects, a continued foundational presence from the visceral prosthetics of the early horror comedies *Bad Taste* and *Braindead*, to *Meet The Feebles*' gross interstitial puppets, to the Fourth and Borovnian worlds in *Heavenly Creatures*, up to the digitalized Altdorferian battle vistas of *The Lord of the Rings* and the replication of 1930s New York in *King Kong*, and, apparently, the invention to come of Heaven in *Lovely Bones*, now in preproduction, a project bringing Jackson and the Ward of *What Dreams May Come* into proximity. While there are aspects of Jackson's art reminiscent of a child with a huge toy box performing conjuring tricks, only the most puritanical theories of filmic realism neglect the originary place of Georges Méliès' technological conjurings alongside the Lumières' actuality shooting as one of the twin determinants of all later mainstream cinema, or underestimate the primary place of wonder in audience reactions. The question 'how?' is built as an almost inevitable response into Jackson's aesthetics (how is that image possible? How can Gollum with no profilmic reality in the ordinary sense assume greater screen reality than the actors around him?), enabling a sub-industry of revelations of technological illusionism. While an art based solely on 'how' is likely to be limited, to disregard the 'how' component is to oversimplify spectatorial response to technical inventiveness in every art form. Another precondition of Jackson's success has been his profound ingestion of Hollywood tradition on a scale that makes, say, Donaldson's and Murphy's look time-bound and limited. This can be seen both in *King Kong*'s virtuosic pastiche of 1930s modes, and in *Heavenly Creature*'s daring, equally virtuosic resurrection of the bricolistic energies of the 1940s–1950s musical in sequences like the ecstatically cut and choreographed 'Donkey Serenade', built around recordings by Mario Lanza (whose Hollywood career ended, like the MGM musical's prime, before Jackson was born). Equally, if one formal strategy, in its embodying the dynamics of popular film and cinematic rather than literary storytelling, is associated with Hollywood above all others, it is cross-cutting between different dynamically intersecting narrative events and spaces (alternate syntagma). There have been few instances which combine the locomotive and conceptual intersections which found their first apotheoses in *Birth of a Nation* and *Intolerance* respectively as brilliantly as the opening and close of *Heavenly Creatures* which intercut, first, the girls running from the scene of the mother's murder, and then the murder itself with the monochrome mind-screen sequences of the girls rushing towards first their seeming salvation, then separation. At the same time, Jackson's great skills are not wholly kinetic and visual, but narrative and structural (even, in combination with his screenwriters, verbal), offering, as one of the chief critics of the sometimes low standards of New Zealand screenwriting, lessons more directly imitable than most of those implicit in his work.

The question of how to look at Jackson's later films (as distinct from registering the entrepreneurial phenomenon) has been important to New Zealand critics, often preoccupied with questions of self-definition. Curiously, because of its pivotal chronological position, and literal Americanization of New Zealand sites, it has been Jackson's most inferior film *The Frighteners* (as much a compendium of his banalities as *Heavenly Creatures* is of his abilities) on which most critical energy has been expended, reading its few tiny markers of New Zealand origins (paralleled in *King Kong* by the interior of Auckland Civic Theatre where Kong is displayed and a crate labelled 'Sumatran Rat Monkey', alluding to *Braindead*) and small parts for a few New Zealand actors as constituting a 'palimpsestic' (double) as distinct from 'mimetic' (that is, wholly Americanized) text. The problem here is that these markers, so minute that most escape even clued-up New

Zealand observers, are invisible to other viewers, so that rather than staging decipherable resistance to the dominant they are more like private jokes, making it difficult to take the weight of theory erected on a flimsy text seriously.[14] Nevertheless, the discussion raises the question whether Jackson is to be viewed post *Frighteners* as wholly reproducing/being reproduced by Hollywood or in more complex terms? As regards the latter, for instance, it is arguable that only a director positioned outside of Hollywood (wholly inside and yet significantly outside) – and more precisely with intimate cultural relation to the very English elements of Tolkien, necessitating the presence of many British actors and atmospheres: 'Better Briton' as well as 'Better Angeleno' – could have made *The Lord of the Rings* so successfully.

While it is arguable that Jackson's unprecedented entrepreneurial achievement outweighs his aesthetic ones (other New Zealanders have made major films, even, thinking of *Heavenly Creatures*, masterpieces, but none has ever approached his present commercial power), two things should be remembered. The first is that it is still early enough for developments as surprising as those of his earlier career, though (in many New Zealand eyes) the most desired – a return to 'New Zealand' subjects like the ANZACs Gallipoli film speculated recently on internet sites, a supposed favourite project shelved since 1988 when, it is claimed, postponed because of the success of *Saving Private Ryan*[15] – may become increasingly difficult because of the huge market pressures surrounding him (the attractions of unmetamorphosed New Zealand settings and characters for art-house audiences not being replicated in the largest market), unless one envisions a future regime of alternation between mass international audience projects and less certainly profitable New Zealand films financed by the former. The second is that the last few years' aggrandizements have momentarily obscured many of the earlier films' significances by seeing them primarily as means to the ends of *The Lord of the Rings* and *King Kong* – the comic 'bad taste' films achieving international recognition through the splatter horror/cult film route, and *Heavenly Creatures* gaining more prestigious international audiences through the art-house circuit – as launch pads, rather than as the remarkable works that they are in themselves, epitomes in their different ways of the possibilities of New Zealand cinema successfully finding significant overseas audiences without diminishing local interests.

Jane Campion

Peel, 1982; *Passionless Moments*, 1983; *A Girl's Own Story*, 1984; *After Hours*, 1984; *Two Friends*, 1986; *Sweetie*, 1989; *An Angel at My Table*, 1990; *The Piano*, 1992; *The Portrait of a Lady*, 1996; *Holy Smoke*, 1999; *In The Cut*, 2003

If Ward is the icon of an almost archaic solitary vision emerging from New Zealand backwaters gravitating to a highly commodified art form, and Jackson the (willingly) cinematically colonized become recolonizer to such a degree as to be for the moment synonymous with Hollywood, Campion represents – far more than Lina Wertmuller, Chantal Ackerman, Gillian Armstrong, Sally Potter, Agnes Varda or others – the popular international triumph of the female art-house director. Her emergence retrospectively possesses cultural and temporal logics, influenced by, and in turn influencing, her twin environments, New Zealand and Australia, with their similar strong late 1970s–early 1980s feminist activity[16] and film industries rapidly opening up to female directors (less through institutional means in New Zealand than in Australia with its Women's Film Fund and AFC Women's Programme, but in pragmatic terms as, if not more, successfully).

All of Campion's features and her short *A Girl's Own Story* (1986) centre around female protagonists, embodiments – in the cadences of one of her films' sources, James' *The Portrait of a Lady* – of 'the conception of a certain young woman affronting her destiny'.[17] It is axiomatic that while Campion's films profoundly engage feminist interest through female protagonists, female desire and the female gaze, in ways that simultaneously conform to and subvert mainstream cinema's structures,[18] they also resist programmatic feminism (like Robin Wood's rather obtuse unhappiness with Campion's not making the 'lesbian' Henrietta more prominent in *The Portrait*)[19] through their heroines' overriding desire for heterosexual love. This desire is often as dangerous as dominating, reaching its apogee in the intersecting love and serial murderer plots in *In The Cut* (2003): the suspicion held by Franny (Meg Ryan) that her policeman-lover may be the killer; her step-sister Pauline's romantic degradation and murder; the red phallic lighthouse – definitely not Virginia Woolf's – at which the murderer nearly kills Franny; and her fantasy of the skating father's blades 'disarticulating' the mother's limbs (a variant of Stewart chopping off Ada's finger and the Bluebeard shadow play in *The Piano*). Whether the danger of the 'disarticulating' male is literal or a metaphor for the perils represented by the patriarchal other in sexual relations, the male's dangerousness is complemented by the unruly female psyche, which as often as not, outside *The Piano*'s optimistic solutions, exerts its freedoms self-destructively, a potentiality insinuated in the seemingly wholly blissful contemporary Australian prologue to *The Portrait* in the narcissism of the girls' reduction of the other to mirrors reflecting ideal selves. The 1980s–1990s influences of 'second-wave' feminism were particularly dramatic in New Zealand, where, as Siegfried diagnosed back in 1899 (contemplating the colony's early achievement of women's suffrage), the impact of determined interest groups on a small society could be formidable.[20] But, as stressed in chapter 6, the cinematic effects – headed by Campion – were, though very real, unpredictable and often at odds with the theorizing which encouraged them. Campion's quixotic post-film novelization of *The Piano* is most interesting in its seemingly determined obstruction of the sexual-political appropriation of the films' ambiguities characteristic of much analytical work on the film.[21]

When she returned to her original environment, Campion's first New Zealand film, *An Angel at My Table*, was well received. However, *The Piano*'s reception, though mostly as rapturous as elsewhere, had difficult aspects created by the writer-director's unguardedly old-fashioned use of Māori as background figures (in spite of the presence of distinguished Māori advisors, whose role and opinions have never been really clarified) at a time when questions of representation were domestically contentious.[22] There was further controversy over the influence of Jane Mander's novel *The Story of a New Zealand River* on the film, even accusations of plagiarism, when in fact the interconnections are interesting, but oblique. Under the weight of controversy, Campion may have felt that making New Zealand films was too burdensome, with the worries, in returning to a country where she had not resided for a long time, of misjudging contexts, and of facing the complicated responses greeting the returning successful expatriate; though, significantly, her Australian career had already been consolidated with *Sweetie* (1989), and she returned with an Australian screenwriter (Laura Jones for *Angel*) and producer (Jan Chapman for *The Piano*). Whatever the interaction of causes, Campion's own future trajectory was significantly opposite to the one in *An Angel at My Table*, where the novelist returns to her homeland from abroad to practise her art.

The earlier work (a three-part television film, later released as a feature) was adapted from the novelist Janet Frame's autobiography of a traumatic early life, marked by long-term incarceration in mental hospitals, up to her first literary successes. The only one of her films constructed round a literal artist figure, *Angel* is untypical Campion in another way – Janet's lack of beauty; her morbid shyness; her characteristic position throughout the film looking enviously in at worlds barred to her, at the physically beautiful, socially confident and outwardly more poetic (she would have no place among the girls in *Portrait of a Lady*'s prologue) – contrast extremely not only with Campion's later heroines, but also with the heroine of *Angel*'s Australian cinema equivalent, Sybylla (Judy Davis) in *My Brilliant Career* (Gillian Armstrong, 1979), who chooses art over a highly desirable romantic marriage but, charismatically beautiful as she is, actually has both choices. By contrast, Janet's destiny is to discover painfully her métier's dependence on abandoning her hopeless desires for social and sexual acceptance for the solitary art world of 'Mirror City'. Profoundly different from the charismatic sexual heroines of Campion's later works, she is also, as a reclusive solitary artist, profoundly distanced from Campion's own collaborative art, almost a frenzy of social relations on set (reproducing the theatrical family environment that she came from) on the evidence of the documentary *Portrait: Jane Campion and The Portrait of a Lady*, attached to the film on DVD. *Angel* is thus a meditation on an imagined, or hidden, more constricted self, which we might feel the temptation to allegorize as Campion's (as distinct from Ward's or Jackson's) New Zealand, beguiling enough to draw the director back for a while early in her career, but not to hold her. One of Campion's most overt inventions in *Angel* is the linking music and singing of Burns' 'Duncan Gray ', with the words, 'You may go to France for me, / Ha ha the wooing o'it' placed as epigraph to part 3. Sung (in a memory sequence) by the four sisters lying in the sun on a cliff top looking out to sea, the courtship ironies of the song are largely jettisoned, with the words 'You may go to France for me' again emphasized, suggesting Janet's overseas journeyings as done on behalf of her unfulfilled dead sisters. One of the film's most quietly ecstatic moments, Campion's addition is simultaneously a quintessentially New Zealand image of at-homeness, but also, in its looking out ambivalently towards ocean distances, of a yearning for elsewhere.

This closing paragraph has, with pleasing synchronicity, been written on the day (24 January 2006) of *River Queen*'s New Zealand premiere, with Ward – doing what Campion seems unlikely to do again, returning temporarily to the New Zealand cinema – echoing Hayward's words of more than 65 years before, quoted at the beginning of chapter 3, by saying that 'New Zealand has many hidden stories –"beneath every roadside alongside every river" – that rival anything created in Hollywood'. This statement was made, however, in the context of often hostile reviews, a reminder of the more than economic difficulties local film-makers may face. Campion's more definitive expatriatism is, like Ward's more wavering exile and Jackson's resistance to departure – characteristic both of New Zealand's cinematic and larger histories, a contemporary post-colonial manifestation of that significant colonial 'cultural overproduction' of talent in many fields defined by Belich in *Reforging Paradise*:[23] hardly to be agonized over, but accepted as one of several routes followed by those struggling with the problems of working in a small, precarious cinema.

Notes

1 Lawrence McDonald, review of *Naming the Other*, *Illusions* 25, 1996, 53.
2 Dana Polan, *Jane Campion*, BFI, London, 155.
3 Vincent Ward with Alison Carter, Geoff Chapple and Louis Nowra, *Edge of the Earth: Stories and Images from the Antipodes*, Heinemann Reed, Auckland, 1990, 83–4.
4 Vincent Ward, 'Perimeter, an Interview', Dennis and Bieringa, 90.
5 Belich, *Reforging Paradise*, 338–41.
6 Bill Manhire, quoted in Nick Perry, 'Antipodean Camp', *Hyperreality and Global Culture*, Routledge, London, 1988, 14.
7 www.talkfilm.co.uk/articles/268 (accessed 3 January 2006).
8 For example, 'A Dialogue with Discrepancy: Vincent Ward Discusses *The Navigator*', *Illusions* 10, 1989, 13.
9 Ward, *ibid.*, 10.
10 Ward, *Edge of the Earth*, 76.
11 Ward, 'Perimeter, an Interview', 90.
12 Paul Schrader, *Transcendental Style in Film: Ozu, Bresson, Dreyer*, Da Capo Press, New York, 1972.
13 See Ian Pryor, *Peter Jackson: From Prince of Splatter to Lord of the Rings*, Random House New Zealand, Auckland, 2003.
14 Especially Rebecca Robinson, 'Authenticity, Mimicry, Industry: *The Frighteners* as Cultural Palimpsest', *Illusions* 28, 1999, 2–9.
15 Ian Prior, 340, also 337 and 338 on the *Bad Taste 2* and *Jean Batten* ideas.
16 An early instance of the intersection of feminism with film is found in Susan Davis, Alison Maclean and Helen Todd, 'She Through He: Images of Women in New Zealand Feature Films', *Alternative Cinema* 11.4, 1983–84, 5–7.
17 Henry James, 'Preface', *The Portrait of a Lady*, The World's Classics, Oxford University Press, 1960 [1881], xx.
18 Stella Bruzzi,'Tempestuous Petticoats: Costume and Desire in *The Piano*', *Screen* 36.3, 1995, 257–66.
19 Robin Wood, *The Wings of the Dove*, BFI, London, 1999, 11.
20 Siegfried, 280–3.
21 Jane Campion and Kate Pullinger, *The Piano: A Novel*, Bloomsbury, London, 1994.

22 For example, Leonie Pihama, 'Are Films Dangerous? A Maori Woman's Perspective on *The Piano*', reprinted in *Jane Campion's The Piano*, ed. H. Margolis, Cambridge University Press, Cambridge, 2000.
23 Belich *Reforging Paradise*, 326–43.

Filmography of fiction feature films

(New Zealand unless otherwise stated. The overseas films listed are by New Zealand film-makers, or important in the argument of the text. The list also contains a number of early New Zealand 'proto-features' of historical significance.)

Absent Without Leave, John Laing, 1993.
The Adventures of Algy (Aust.), Beaumont Smith, 1925.
Alex (NZ/Aust.), Megan Simpson, 1992.
Alien III (US), David Fincher, 1992.
Along Came a Spider (US), Lee Tamahori, 2001.
Among the Cinders (NZ/Ger.), Rolf Haedrich, 1984.
Anagram, Gerben Cath, 1991.
An Angel at My Table, Jane Campion, 1990.
Angel Mine, David Blyth, 1978.
Arriving Tuesday, Richard Riddiford, 1986.
L'avventura (It.), Michelangelo Antonioni, 1961.
Bad Blood (NZ/UK), Mike Newell, 1981.
Bad Taste, Peter Jackson, 1986.
The Battle of Treasure Island, Gavin Scott, 2005.
Battletruck, Harley Kokliss, 1982.
The Betrayer (Aust.), Beaumont Smith, 1921 (lost).
Beyond Reasonable Doubt, John Laing, 1980.
Birth of a Nation (US), D.W. Griffith, 1915.
Blessed, Rachel Douglas, 2002.
Blind Side (US), Geoff Murphy, 1993.
The Bloke from Freeman's Bay, Rudall Hayward, 1921 (lost).
Bonjour Timothy, Wayne Tourell, (NZ /Can.), 1995.
The Bounty (US), Roger Donaldson, 1984.
Braindead, Peter Jackson, 1992.
Bread and Roses, Gaylene Preston, 1993.
Bridge to Nowhere, Ian Mune, 1986.

Broken Barrier, Roger Mirams and John O'Shea, 1952.
Broken English, Gregor Nicholas, 1996.
The Bush Cinderella, Rudall Hayward, 1927.
Came a Hot Friday, Ian Mune, 1984.
Carbine's Heritage, Edwin Coubray, 1927 (lost).
Carry Me Back, John Reid, 1982.
Cave In, Rex Piano, 2003.
Channelling Baby, Christine Parker, 1999.
Chicken (NZ/Ger.), Grant LaHood, 1996.
Chill Factor (US/NZ), David L. Stanton, 1988.
Christmas, Gregory King, 2003.
Chunuk Bair, Dale Bradley, 1991.
The Climb (NZ/France), Bob Swaim, 1997.
Cocktail (US), Roger Donaldson, 1988.
Constance, Bruce Morrison, 1984.
Cops and Robbers (NZ/Aust.), Murray Reece, 1994.
Crooked Earth, Sam Pillsbury, 2001.
Crush, Alison MacLean, 1992.
Cupid's Prey, Dale Bradley, 2003.
Dangerous Orphans, John Laing, 1987.
A Daughter of Christchurch, Rudall Hayward, 1928.
A Daughter of Dunedin, Rudall Hayward, 1928.
Dead Kids (NZ/Aust.), Michael Laughlin, 1983.
Death Warmed Up, David Blyth, 1984.
Desperate Remedies, Stewart Main and Peter Wells, 1993.
The Devil's Pit, a.k.a. *Taranga*, a.k.a. *Under the Southern Cross* (US), Lew Collins, 1928–1929.
Die Another Day (UK/US), Lee Tamahori, 2002.
Don't Let It Get You, John O'Shea, 1964.
Down On The Farm, Stewart Pitt, 1935 (out-takes only).
The End of the Golden Weather, Ian Mune, 1991.
Exposure (NZ/US/Ger.), David Blyth, 2000.
The Fellowship of the Ring (NZ/US), Peter Jackson, 2001.
Fifty Ways of Saying Fabulous, Stewart Main, 2005.
Flight of the Albatross (NZ /Ger.), Werner Meyer, 1996.
Flying Fox in a Freedom Tree, Martyn Sanderson, 1990.
Footrot Flats: The Dog's ~~Tail~~ Tale, Murray Ball, 1986.
The Footstep Man, Leon Narbey, 1992.
For Good, Stuart McKenzie, 2003.
Fracture, Larry Parr, 2004.
Freejack (US), Geoff Murphy, 1992.
The Frighteners (US/NZ), Peter Jackson, 1996.

The Getaway (US) Roger Donaldson, 1994.
A Girl of the Bush (Aust.), Franklyn Barrett, 1921.
Goodbye Pork Pie, Geoff Murphy, 1980
The Grasscutter (NZ/UK), Ian Mune, 1988.
Green Dolphin Street (US), Victor Saville, 1947.
Gupta Versus Gordon, Jitendra Pal, 2003.
Hamilton Talks, Rudall Hayward, 1934.
Heart of the Stag, Michael Firth, 1984.
Heaven, Scott Reynolds, 1999.
Heavenly Creatures (NZ/UK/Ger.), Peter Jackson, 1994.
Hei Tiki: A Saga of the Maoris (US), Alexander Markey, 1935.
Her Majesty (US), Mark J. Gordon, 2005.
Hinemoa, George Tarr, 1914 (lost).
Hinemoa (US), Gaston Méliès, 1913 (lost).
Holy Smoke (US/Aust.), Jane Campion, 1999.
Hopeless, Phil Hickey, 2000.
Hot Target, a.k.a. *Restless*, Denis Lewiston, 1985.
How Chief Te Ponga Won His Bride (US), Gaston Méliès, 1913 (lost).
I Think I'm Going, Alexander Greenhough, 2003.
Illustrious Energy, Leon Narbey, 1988.
In My Father's Den (NZ/UK), Brad McGann, 2004.
In The Cut (US), Jane Campion, 2003.
Iris, Tony Isaac, 1984.
The Irrefutable Truth About Demons, Glenn Standring, 2000.
Jack Be Nimble, Garth Maxwell, 1993.
Jack Brown Genius, Tony Hiles, 1994.
Jesus' Son (US), Alison MacLean, 1999.
Jubilee, Michael Hurst, 2000.
Kid's World, Dale Bradley, 2001.
King Kong (NZ/US), Peter Jackson, 2005.
Kingpin, Mike Walker, 1985.
Kiwi Safari, a.k.a. *Lost Valley* (NZ/US), Dale Bradley, 1997.
Kombi Nation, Grant LaHood, 2003.
Kung Fu Vampire Killers, Phil Davison, 2002.
Landfall, Paul Maunder, 1977.
The Last Tattoo, John Reid, 1995.
The Leading Edge, Michael Firth, 1987.
Leave All Fair, John Reid, 1985.
The Lie of the Land, Grahame J. McLean, 1987.
Loaded (NZ/UK), Anna Campion, 1995.
The Locals, Greg Page, 2003.
The Lost Tribe, John Laing, 1985.

Loved By a Maori Chieftess (US), Gaston Méliès, 1913 (lost).
The Lunatics' Ball, Michael Thorp, 1999.
Magik and Rose, Vanessa Alexander, 1999.
A Maori Maid's Love (Aust.), Raymond Longford, 1916 (lost).
The Maori Merchant of Venice (Te Tangata Whai Rawa O Weniti), Don C. Selwyn, 2001.
Map of the Human Heart (Aust./UK/Can./Fr.), Vincent Ward, 1993.
Mark II, John Anderson, 1986.
Mauri, Merata Mita, 1988.
Meet the Feebles, Peter Jackson, 1990.
Memory and Desire, Nicky Caro, 1997.
Mesmerized (UK/NZ), Michael Laughlin, 1984.
Middle Age Spread, John Reid, 1979.
The Monster of Treasure Island, Michael Hurst, 2005.
The Mystery of Treasure Island, Michael Hurst, 2005.
Mr Wrong, Gaylene Preston, 1985.
Mulholland Falls (US), Lee Tamahori, 1996.
The Mutiny of the Bounty (Aust.), Raymond Longford, 1916 (lost).
My Lady of the Cave, Rudall Hayward, 1922.
The Navigator, Vincent Ward, 1987.
Nemesis Game (NZ/UK/Can.), Jesse Warn, 2005.
Never Say Die, Geoff Murphy, 1988.
Next of Kin (Aust./NZ), Tony Williams, 1982.
Ngati, Barry Barclay, 1987.
No One Can Hear You, John Laing, 2001.
No Way Out (US) Roger Donaldson, 1987.
OFF, Colin Hodson, 2002.
Old Scores (NZ/Wales), Alan Clayton, 1991.
Once Were Warriors, Lee Tamahori, 1994.
On Our Selection (Aust.), Raymond Longford, 1920.
On The Friendly Road, Rudall Hayward, 1936.
Orphans and Angels, Harold Brodie, 2003.
Other Halves, John Laing, 1984.
Pallet on the Floor, Lynton Butler, 1986.
Perfect Strangers, Gaylene Preston, 2004.
Phar Lap's Son?, Dr A.L. Lewis, 1936 (lost).
The Piano, Jane Campion (NZ/France/Aust.), 1992.
Pictures, Michael Black, 1981.
The Portrait of a Lady (UK/US), Jane Campion, 1996.
The Price of Milk, Harry Sinclair, 2000.
Prisoners, Peter Werner, 1982 (unreleased).
Queen City Rocker, Bruce Morrison, 1986.

The Quiet Earth, Geoff Murphy, 1985.
Race for the Yankee Zephyr (NZ/Aust.), David Hemmings, 1981.
Rain, Christine Jeffs, 2001.
Rangi's Catch (UK), Michael Forlong, 1973.
Restless, a.k.a. *Hot Target*, Denis Lewiston, 1985.
The Return of the King (NZ/US), Peter Jackson, 2003.
The Returning, John Day, 1991.
Rewi's Last Stand, Rudall Hayward, 1925 (fragments extant).
Rewi's Last Stand, a.k.a. *The Last Stand*, Rudall Hayward, 1940.
The Romance of Hine-moa (UK), Gustav Pauli 1925/27 (first reel extant).
The Romance of Sleepy Hollow, Henry J. Makepeace, 1923 (lost).
Ruby and Rata, Gaylene Preston, 1990.
Runaway, John O'Shea, 1964.
Savage Honeymoon (NZ/UK), Mark Beesley, 1999.
Savage Islands, a.k.a. *Nate and Hayes* (NZ/US), Ferdinand Fairfax, 1983.
Saving Grace, Costa Botes, 1987.
The Scarecrow, Sam Pillsbury, 1982.
Scarfies (NZ/UK), Robert Sarkies, 1999.
Second Time Lucky (Aust./NZ), Michael Anderson, 1984.
Secrets (NZ/Aust.), Michael Pattinson, 1993.
The Seekers (UK), Ken Annakin, 1954.
Send a Gorilla, Melanie Read, 1988.
The Sentimental Bloke (Aust.), Raymond Longford, 1919.
Shaker Run (NZ/US), Bruce Morrison, 1985.
Shifter, Colin Hodson, 2000.
The Shirt, John Laing, 2000.
Should I Be Good?, Grahame J. McLean, 1985.
The Silent One, Yvonne MacKay, 1984.
Skin Deep, Geoff Steven, 1978.
Smash Palace, Roger Donaldson, 1981.
Snakeskin (NZ/UK), Gillian Ashhurst, 2001.
A Soldier's Tale, Larry Parr, 1988.
Solo, Tony Williams, 1977.
Sons for the Return Home, Paul Maunder, 1979.
Spinster, a.k.a. *Two Loves* (US), Charles Walters, 1961.
Spooked, Geoff Murphy, 2004.
Squeeze, Richard Turner, 1980.
Starlight Hotel, Sam Pillsbury, 1987.
Stickmen (NZ/UK), Hamish Rothwell, 2003.
Strata, Geoff Steven, 1983.

Sweetie (Aust.), Jane Campion, 1989.
Sylvia, Michael Firth, 1985.
Sylvia, Christine Jeffs (UK), 2003.
Tabu (US), F.W. Murnau and Robert Flaherty, 1931.
A Takapuna Scandal, Rudall Hayward, 1928.
The Te Kooti Trail, Rudall Hayward, 1927.
Terror Peak (NZ/US), Dale Bradley, 2003.
Te Rua (NZ/Ger.), Barry Barclay, 1991.
The Test (Aust.), Rawdon Blandford, 1916 (lost).
Test Pictures: Eleven Vignettes From a Relationship, Geoff Steven, 1975.
Thirteen Days (US), Roger Donaldson, 2001.
This is Not a Love Story, Keith Hill, 2003.
To Love a Maori, Rudall Hayward, 1972.
Tongan Ninja, Jason Stutter, 2002.
Topless Women Talk About Their Lives, Harry Sinclair, 1997.
Toy Love, Harry Sinclair, 2003.
Trespasses, Peter Sharp, 1984.
Trial Run, Melanie Reid, 1984.
The Two Towers (NZ/US), Peter Jackson, 2002.
The Ugly, Scott Reynolds, 1997.
Uncomfortable, Comfortable, Campbell Walker, 1999.
Under the Southern Cross (UK), Gustav Pauli, 1927.
Until They Sail (US), Robert Wise, 1957.
User Friendly, Gregor Nicholas, 1990.
Utu, Geoff Murphy, 1983.
Venus of the South Seas (US), James R. Sullivan, 1924.
Via Satellite, Anthony McCarten, 1988.
Vigil, Vincent Ward, 1984.
The Vector File (NZ/Ger.), Eliot Christopher, 2002.
The Wagon And The Star, J.J.W. Pollard, 1936 (one reel surviving).
The Waiting Place, Cristobal Araus Lobos, 2001.
Whale Rider (NZ/Ger.), Niki Caro, 2003.
What Dreams May Come (US), Vincent Ward, 1998.
When Love Comes, Garth Maxwell, 1998.
When Strangers Appear, a.k.a. *Shearer's Breakfast* (NZ/Aust./US), Scott Reynolds, 2001.
White Sands (US), Roger Donaldson, 1992.
The Whole of the Moon (NZ/Can.), Ian Mune, 1996.
Why Can't I Stop This Uncontrollable Dancing?, Campbell Walker, 2003.
Wild Blue, Dale G. Bradley, 2000.

Wild Horses, Derek Morton, 1984.
Wild Man, Geoff Murphy, 1977.
A Woman of Good Character, a.k.a. *It's Lizzie to Those Close*, David Blyth, 1983.
Woodenhead, Florian Habicht, 2003.
Worzel Gummidge Down Under, James Hill, 1986.
Young Guns II (US), Geoff Murphy, 1990.
Zilch!, Richard Riddiford, 1989

Select bibliography

(For reasons of space this is very selective indeed, a basic guide for beginners, rather than a comprehensive account. Many items omitted here, especially film periodical articles, are referred to in footnotes to the text.)

Barclay, Barry, *Our Own Image*, Longman Paul, Auckland, 1990.
Baxter, James K., *Collected Poems*, ed. J.E. Weir, Oxford University Press in association with Price Milburn, Wellington, New York, 1979.
Belich, James, *Making Peoples*, Allen Lane/The Penguin Press, Harmondsworth, 1996.
Belich, James, *Paradise Reforged*, Allen Lane/The Penguin Press, Harmondsworth, 2001.
Binney, Judith, *Redemption Songs: A Life of Te Kooti Arikirangi Te Turuki*, Auckland University Press with Bridget Williams Books, Auckland, 1995.
Blythe, Martin, *Naming the Other: Images of the Maori in New Zealand Film and Television*, The Scarecrow Press, Metuchen, NJ, 1994.
Cairns, Barbara and Martin, Helen, *Shadows on the Wall: A Study of Seven New Zealand Feature Films*, Longman Paul, Auckland, 1994.
Cowan, James, *The Adventures of Kimble Bent: A Story of Wild Life in the New Zealand Bush*, Whitcombe and Tombs Ltd, London, Wellington, etc., 1911. (Reprint published by Capper Press, Christchurch, 1975.)
Cowan, James, *The New Zealand Wars: A History of the Maori Campaign and the Pioneering Period*, 2 vols, P.O. Hasselberg, Govt Printers, Wellington, 1983 [1922, 1923].
Curnow, Allen, *The Penguin Book of New Zealand Verse*, Penguin Books, Harmondsworth, 1960.
Curnow, Allen, *Selected Poems 1940–1989*, Penguin Books, Harmondsworth, 1990.

Dennis, Jonathan, ed., *The Tin Shed: The Origins of the National Film Unit*, The New Zealand Film Archive, Wellington, 1981.

Dennis, Jonathan, ed., *Aotearoa and the Sentimental Strine: Making Films in Australia and New Zealand in the Silent Period*, Moa Books, Wellington, 1993.

Dennis, Jonathan, and Bieringa, Jan, eds, *Film in Aotearoa New Zealand*, Victoria University Press, Wellington, revised edition, 1996 [1992].

Dennis, Jonathan, and Toffetti, Sergio, *Te Ao Marama: Il mondo della luce: Cinema della Nuova Zelanda*, Nuove Muse, Torino, 1989.

Department of Internal Affairs, *The Dictionary of New Zealand Biography*, 3 vols, Department of Internal Affairs, Wellington, 1990.

Devanny, Jean, *The Butcher Shop*, Auckland University Press, Auckland, 1981 [1926].

Duff, Alan, *Once Were Warriors*, Vintage, Random House, London, 1995.

Duff, Alan, *What Becomes of the Broken- Hearted?*, Vintage, Random House, Australia, 1996.

Edwards, Sam, and Martin, Helen, *New Zealand Film 1912-1996*, Oxford University Press (NZ), Auckland, 1997.

Fairburn, A.R.D., *Selected Poems*, ed. Mac Jackson, Victoria University Press, Wellington, 1995.

Frame Janet, *An Angel at My Table: An Autobiography: Volume Two*, Hutchinson Group (NZ) Ltd, Auckland, 1984.

Frame, Janet, *The Envoy From Mirror City: An Autobiography: Volume Three*, Century Hutchinson New Zealand Limited, Auckland, 1986.

Frame, Janet, *To The Is-land: An Autobiography: Volume One*, Women's Press Limited, London, 1993, in association with Hutchinson Group (NZ) Limited.

Gerstner, David, and Greenlees, Sarah, 'Cinema by Fits and Starts: New Zealand Film Practices in the Twentieth Century', *CineAction* 51 (February 2000), 37–47.

Glover, Denis, *Enter Without Knocking*, Pegasus Press, Christchurch, 1971.

Horrocks, Roger, 'Directed by Tony Williams', *Islands* 22, 6.4, 1977, 458–72.

Horrocks, Roger, 'Surviving in Films: The Career of a New Zealand Film-Maker', *Islands* 20, 6.2, 1977, 136–60.

Horrocks, Roger, 'New Zealand Cinema: Cultures, Policies, Films', in Verhoeven, Deb, ed., *Twin Peeks: Australian and New Zealand*

Feature Films, Damned Publishing, Melbourne, 1999, 129–37.

Hyde, Robin, *The Godwits Fly*, Auckland University Press, Auckland, 1994 [1938].

Ihimaera, Witi, *The Whale Rider*, Harcourt, Orlando, FL, 1987.

King, Michael, *The Penguin History of New Zealand*, Penguin Books (NZ), Auckland, 2003.

McDonald, Lawrence, 'A Book Review of *Film in Aotearoa New Zealand* that Ended up as an Essay on Film in Aotearoa New Zealand', *Illusions* 21/22, 1993, 59–60.

Mander, Jane, *The Story of a New Zealand River*, Vintage, Random House New Zealand, 1999 [1920].

Maning, Frederick Edward, *Old New Zealand*, Whitcombe and Tombs Ltd, Christchurch, Auckland, Wellington, Dunedin, 1930 [1863].

Mansfield, Katherine, *Katherine Mansfield: Undiscovered Country, The New Zealand Stories*, ed. Ian A. Gordon, Longman, London, 1974.

Mason, Bruce, *The End of the Golden Weather*, Price Milburn, Wellington, 1962.

Metge, Joan, *The Maoris of New Zealand*, Routledge and Kegan Paul, London, rev. ed., 1976.

Mirams, Gordon, *Speaking Candidly: Films and People in New Zealand*, Paul's Book Arcade, Hamilton, 1945.

Morrieson, Ronald Hugh, *The Scarecrow*, Penguin Books (NZ), Auckland, 1971.

Morrieson, Ronald Hugh, *Came a Hot Friday*, Penguin Books, Auckland, 1981.

Morrissey, Michael, ed., *The Flamingo Book of New Zealand Short Stories*, rev. ed., HarperCollins New Zealand, Auckland, 2004.

Mulgan, John, *Man Alone*, Paul's Book Arcade, Hamilton, 1960 [1939].

Oliver, W.H., and Williams, B.R., *The Oxford History of New Zealand*, Clarendon and Oxford University Press, London, 1981.

Orsman, Harry, ed., *Dictionary of New Zealand English*, Oxford University Press, Oxford, 1998.

O'Shea, John, *Don't Let It Get You: Memories – Documents*, Victoria University Press, Wellington, 1999.

Perry, Nick, 'Antipodean Camp', *Hyperreality and Global Culture*, Routledge, London, 1988.

Perry, Nick, *The Dominion of Signs: Television, Advertising and Other New Zealand Fictions*, Auckland University Press, Auckland, 1994.

Price, Simon, *New Zealand's First Talkies: Early Film-Making in Otago and Southland 1896–1939*, Otago Heritage Books, Dunedin North, 1996.

Reid, Nicholas, *A Decade of New Zealand Film: 'Sleeping Dogs' to 'Came a Hot Friday'*, John McIndoe, Dunedin, 1986.

Sargeson, Frank, *Collected Stories: 1935–1963*, Blackwood and Janet Paul, Auckland, 1964.

Sheppard, Deborah, *Reframing: A History of New Zealand Film Women*, HarperCollins Publishers New Zealand, Auckland, 2000.

Siegfried, André, *Democracy in New Zealand*, trans. E.V. Burns, G. Bell & Sons Ltd, London, 1914.

Sinclair, Keith, *A History of New Zealand*, Penguin, Harmondsworth, 1959.

Sinclair, Keith, *A Destiny Apart: New Zealand's Search for National Identity*, Unwin Paperbacks in association with Port Nicholson Press, Wellington, 1986.

Sinclair, Keith, ed., *The Illustrated History of New Zealand*, Oxford University Press, Auckland, 1990.

Smith, Philippa Mein, *A Concise History of New Zealand*, Cambridge University Press, Cambridge, 2005.

Sowry, Clive, *Film Making in New Zealand: A Brief Historical Survey*, New Zealand Film Archive, Wellington, 1984.

Sturm, Terry, ed., *The Oxford History of New Zealand Literature in English*, Oxford University Press, Auckland, 1991.

Vaggioli, Dom Felice, *History of New Zealand and its Inhabitants*, trans. John Crockett, University of Otago Press, Dunedin, 2000 [1896].

Index

Note: page numbers in *italics* refer to illustrations

action-adventure/action-thriller 122, 189
actors and stars 9, 116–18, 187–9
  'demi-stars' and 'demi-star' discourses 188–9
  factors inhibiting stardom 188
  iconic character actors 116–17
Adventures of Algy, The (dir. Beaumont Smith) 41, 42–5, 46, 52, 58, 66, 166
Adventures of Kimble Bent, The book (author, Cowan) 56–7, 159
Adventures in Maoriland: Alexander Markey and the Making of Hei Tiki (dir. Steven) 39–41
Alexander, Vanessa 12–14, 196
Angel Mine (dir. Blyth) 114–15, 121, 211
Angel at My Table, An (dir. Campion) 9, 115, 190, 193, 260, 268, 269
'Antipodean Camp' 15, 21–2
Antonioni, Michelangelo (*L'avventura*) 97–8
Arriving Tuesday (dir. Riddiford) 201–2, 206, 224–5
art or experimental film 129–30, 194–6, 220, 243, 246, 251–3
art-house cinema 1, 9, 10, 13, 260, 262, 266, 267
Austen, Dale 3, 6, 60, *61*, 117
Australian connections 3–4, 6, 16, 18, 21–2, 23–4, 41–4, 63, 116, 166, 267–9
auteurism 18–19, 22–3, 175, 257–70 *passim*

Bad Blood (dir. Newell) 119, 134, 153, 166–8, 190
Bad Taste (dir. Jackson) 191, 251, 263, 264
Barclay, Barry 87–8, 90, 187, 230–6 *passim*, 242
Barry, Tony 133, *135*, 142, 210
Baxter, James K. 24, 86, 170, 225, 246, 261
Bayler, Terence 89, 91
beach as filmic site 58–9, 72, 120, 196, 204–5, 243–4, 249
Belich, James 57, 67, 94–5, 270
Best, Elsdon 37, 38
biculturalism 80, 85, 87–8, 111, 155, 157, 158, 198–9, 224–6
biopics 113–14, 122, 190
Braindead (dir. Jackson) 191, 263, 264, 265
Brasch, Charles 102, 261
Broken Barrier (dir. O'Shea) 50, 82, 85, 88–96, *89*, 98, *99*, 104, 105, 106, 110, 111, 120, 132

Broken English (dir. Nicholas) 82, 182, 183–4, 208, 224, 225
budgets 11–14, 114–15, 129, 185, 259, 260, 262
Bush Cinderella, The (dir. Hayward) 5, 45, 46, 55, 58, 60–3, *61*, 66, 117, 190

Came a Hot Friday, book (author, Morrieson) 15
Came a Hot Friday, film (dir. Mune) 15, 114, 115, 124, 125, 127–8, 135, 224, 225
Campion, Jane 18, 23, 179, 186, 194, 257–60, 267–70
Caro, Niki 14, 23, 179, 182, 186, 194, 220–2, 227–9, 230
Carry Me Back (dir. Reid) 24, 124, 125, 126, 134, 135, 182, 197
CGI and special effects cinema 10, 259, 260, 264–5
Channelling Baby (dir. Parker) 186, 190, 208, 209, 219–20, 214, 215, 249
child- and adolescent-centred films 192–4
children's films 194
Christmas (dir. King) 242, 249–51
cinemagoing statistics 1
Cinema of Unease (dir. Neill and Rymer) 19–20, 167
variants of 20–1
comedy 123–9, 196–208
'community comedies' 44, 63–6
'old' comedy 196–9
romantic/sex comedy 190, 201–8
social comedy 197–9, 200–1
Constance (dir. Morrison) 121, 170–2
co-production, foreign funding 7, 11, 185, 242

Cormack, Danielle 188, 204–5, 206, 208, 219
Coubray, Edwin 30, 39, 50–1
Cowan, James 24, 33, 56–7, 73 156, 159, 160
'crew culture' 63, 123–9 *passim*, 135–6, 196, 198
crime films 122, 191
Crooked Earth (dir. Pillsbury) 224, 225, 226–7
Crump, Barry 85, 96, 103, 132, 134
Crush (dir. Maclean) 171, 190, 193, 208, 209, 214, 217–19
Curnow, Allen 2, 127, 133, 261
Curtis, Cliff 188, 198, 216, 217, 225

definitions of New Zealand films 17–19
Desperate Remedies (dir. Wells and Main) 180–1, 208, 209, 212, 214, 215–7
Devanny, Jean 24, 157, 180
Devil's Pit, The (dir. Collins) 36–9 *passim*
directors 115–16, 186–7
documentary traditions 2–3, 6, 30–1, 46–7, 85–7, 91, 95
Donaldson, Roger 9, 18, 19, 23, 124, 137–41, 265
Don't Let it Get You (dir. O'Shea) 85, 87, 94, 103–10, *106*, 111, 132, 190
Duff, Alan 24, 237–40 *passim*

early attempts to create industry 4–6
early exhibition 29–30
early local film-makers 28–9, 30
early 'scenics' and 'actualities' 28–9

early sound features 50–2, 79–81
End of the Golden Weather, The (dir. Mune) 115, 193, 243, 249
European art cinema 2, 96–8, 115, 121, 131, 249–51
expatriatism 8–9, 115, 116, 186, 257–70 *passim*

Fairburn, A.R.D. 225, 257
farming/the farm, 30, 43, 45–6, 51–2, 60–1, 95, 126, 206–7, 210–11, 231
feminism/feminist criticism 157, 170–1, 172–5, 180, 226, 228, 267–8
'feminization' of New Zealand film 101, 113–14, 168–9, 172–5, 186, 238–9
film festivals and prizes 2, 115, 185–6
Footstep Man, The (dir. Narbey) 13–14, 120, 179, 208, 209, 213–15
Forgotten Silver (dir. Jackson and Botes) 64, 263–4
Frame, Janet 118, 268, 269
freezing works 65, 128–9, 136, 207, 232–3, 247–8
Frighteners, The (dir. Jackson) 187, 191, 263, 265

genre 22–3, 121–3, 189–91
  generic hybrids 22
'geomentalities' and 'psychogeographies' 118–21
Girl's Own Story, A (dir. Campion) 267
'glocalism' 16, 188, *221*, 228, 235
Glover, Denis 198, 207
Gollum 19, 264
Goodbye Pork Pie (dir. Murphy) 50, 132, 134, *135*, 136, 138, 141–7, 161, 249
Gordon Productions 251–3
Graham, Stan 134, 166–8
Grey, Sir George 47–9
Grierson, John 2, 69, 94
Griffith, D.W. 62–3, 68, 73, 265

Habicht, Florian 104, 195–6
Hayward, Ramai Te Miha 56, 75, 76, 79, 103, 132
Hayward, Rudall 3, 4, 5, 6, 11, 23, 30–1, 35, 41, 55–84, *56*, 88–9, 103–4, 155, 157, 159–60
Heart of the Stag (dir. Firth) 169–70
Heavenly Creatures (dir. Jackson) 9, 190, 208, 209, 210, 246, 257, 259, *263*, 265
Hei Tiki (dir. Markey) 36, 37, 38, 39–41, 47
Hinemoa (dir. Méliès) 31, 33, 35, 47, 49, 50
Hinemoa (dir. Tarr) 4, 5, 41, 46–50, *48*
Hollywood influences 2, 3, 6, 13, 136, 142, 171, 246–9, 265
'home', 'homies' and early Anglo-New Zealand themes 6, 44, 45–6, 52, 62, 71–2
home viewing revolution 186–7
Horomona, Māta 34–6
horror films 122, 191–2
  international niche horror market 10, 191
How Chief Te Ponga Won His Bride (dir. Méliès) 31, 33, 34–5
Hunn Report 24, 90–1, 93–4

Illustrious Energy (dir. Narbey) 182–3

In the Cut (dir. Campion) 258, 260, 267
In My Father's Den (dir. McGann) 20, 108, 119, 185, 210, 214, 242, 243, 244–6
integrationism 74–5, 76–9 *passim*, 74–5, 77, 79, 81–2, 90–1, 88–96, 103–10 *passim*, 111, 154, 224
international interest in New Zealand cinema 115, 154, 186, 187
Irrefutable Truth About Demons, The (dir. Standring) 191–2

Jack Be Nimble (dir. Maxwell) 193, 208, 209, 210–11, 212
Jackson, Peter 8, 9, 11, 23, 251, 257–60, 263–6, 270
James, Billy T. 110, 196, 199
James, Vera 117
Jeffs, Christine, 23, 194, 242
Johnson, Kelly 133, *135*, 142, 168
Jones, Lloyd v, 24–5
Jubilee (dir. Hurst) 196, 198–9
Julian, Rupert 117

Kā, Wi Kuki 116, 231, 232–3
King, Gregory 242, 249–51
King, Michael 24, 92, 95
King Kong (dir. Jackson) 260, 263, 264, 265
'Kiwi Gothic' 15, 128–9
Knight, Stanley 76, 132

land, expropriation of Māori 68, 95, 180, 208, 226–7, 242
landscape in New Zealand film 32, 36–7, 118–21
Last Tattoo, The (dir. Reid) 86, 120, 190–1
Lawrence, Bruno 9, 133, 144, 147–54 *passim*, *149*, 160–6 *passim*, *163*, 169–70, 189
'left-hand-drive' films 187, 189–90
Lord of the Rings, The (dir. Jackson) 8, 19, 37, 118, 137, 187, 259, 260, 264
Loved by a Maori Chieftess (dir. Méliès) 31, 33–4, 35
low budget film-making 11–14, 49, 55, 64, 68, 92, 96, 108, 114–15, 194–6
low cost digitals 11, 184–5, 251–3
low pay in industry 8, 12–14
Lynskey, Melanie 246, 247, *263*

McCahon, Colin 110, 214, 261
McGann, Brad 242, 244–6
Maclean, Alison 186, 194, 209–10, 217–19
Magik and Rose (dir. Alexander) 12–14, 196, 202
Mair, Gilbert 67, 69, 74–5, 76–7, 155, 156, 157, 158, 159
male melodrama 148–54
Man Alone book (author, Mulgan) 133–4
'Man Alone' myth 98, 100, 138, 140, 161, 163, 164
Mander, Jane v, 24, 118, 268
Manhire, Bill 22, 260
Maning, F.E. (Old New Zealand) 57, 103
Mansfield, Katherine 130, 242–3, 259
Māori film aesthetics 241–2
Māori-made films 20–1, 230–42
Maoriland romances 22, 36, 37–41
modern inflection of 225–6
Maori Merchant of Venice, The (dir. Selwyn) 240–1, 242
Maori Television 226, 230, 235

Map of the Human Heart (dir. Ward) 258, 260, 261–2
Markey, Alexander 36, 37, 38, 39–41, 47, 119
masculinity/masculinism 65–6, 101, 113, 123–4, 133–6, 137–54 *passim*, 169–70, 203–4
Mason, R.A.K 81, 168
mateship 94, 105, 135, 138, 140, 168
Mauri (dir. Mita) 11, 20, 119, 193, 230–4, *232*, 241
Maxwell, Garth 23, 104, 186, 210–13
Méliès, Gaston 4, 19, 31–7, 47, 49, 50, 262
melodrama/psychodrama 57–63, 122, 195, 208–24
Memory and Desire (dir. Caro) 182, 190, 208, 210, 220–2, *221*, 230
Middle Age Spread (dir. Reid) 124, 125
Mirams, Gordon v, 1–3, 52
Mirams, Roger 85, 86
Mita, Merata 20–1, 187, 207, 230–4 *passim*, 241, 242
Morrieson, Ronald Hugh 15, 88, 124, 127, 128–9
Morrison, Bruce 116, 170–1
Morrison, Howard 24, 94, 103–11 *passim*
Morrison, Temuera 225, 226, 237–9, *238*
Mr Wrong (dir. Preston) 113, 172, 174–5, 179, 222
Mulgan, John 118, 133–4
multicultural films 182–4
Mune, Ian 15, 115, 138, 187, 189, 193
Murphy, Geoff 9, 18, 19, 23, *135*, 141–7, 154–60, *156*, 160–6, *163*, 231, 241, 265
musicals 103–10, 190, 212–13, 265
My Lady of the Cave (dir. Hayward) 41, 47, 55, 57–60, 62, 63, 64, 182, 190, 243
mythologies of New Zealand film 14–15

Narbey, Leon 13–14, 182, 187, 213–15
national cinema 15–17, 23–4, 257–8
National Film Unit 2, 85, 87, 91
Navigator, The (dir. Ward) 18, 162, 194, 195, 245–6, 258, 260, 261
Neill, Sam 9, 116, 117–18, 133, 138, 222, 223, 228
'New Right' influenced films 180–2, 199–201
New Zealand Film Commission 6–7, 17–18, 137
New Zealand Wars films 55, 67–9, 123, 190, 224–5
Ngārimu, Kay 89, 91
Ngata, Sir Āpirana 73, 95
Ngati (dir. Barclay) 87, 120, 192, 194, 230–4, 241, 242
niche marketing 10, 13, 201

'off shore' film-making 10–11, 31–46, 114, 185, 229–30, 265–6
Old Scores (dir. Clayton) 166, 196, 197–8
Once Were Warriors (dir. Tamahori) 10, 50, 121, 227, 237–40, *238*, 242
On the Friendly Road (dir. Hayward) 55, 79–81, 250

O'Shea, John 4, 23, 85–111, 86
Owen, Rena 120, 188, 212–13, 225, 237–9, 238

Pacific Films 85, 86–7, 168
Pākehā self-definition through Māori 44–5, 74, 78, 225
Pallet on the Floor (dir. Butler) 128–9, 196, 224
Pauli, Gustav 36, 37, 38, 45–6, 66
Perfect Strangers (dir. Preston) 104, 190, 208, 210, 214, 222–4
Perry, Joseph 28
Piano, The (dir. Campion) 18, 59, 227, 243, 258, 260, 267, 268
Pilcher, Leo 76, 132
Pillsbury, Sam 88, 226
pioneer period films 41–2, 68–79, 123, 154–60, 215–17, 224–5
Portrait of a Lady, The (dir. Campion) 258, 269
post-modernism, post-modern pastiche 242, 246–9
Preston, Gaylene 14, 104, 113, 115, 121, 160, 181, 186, 187, 190, 199–201, 217, 222–24
Price of Milk, The (dir. Sinclair) 46, 183, 202, 204–8, *207*
producers 116, 187
production statistics 7–8, 184–5

Quiet Earth, The (dir. Murphy) 135, 136, *163*, 160–6, 224, 225

Rain (dir. Jeffs) 242–4, 246, 249
Read, Melanie 115, 202–3
Reid, J.C. 2–3, 123–4
Reid, John 24, 114, 115–16, 126, 190–91

Return of the King, The (dir. Jackson) 263
Rewi's Last Stand
    (dir. Hayward, 1925) 5, 55, 67, 75, 155, 156
    (dir. Hayward, 1940) 3, 55, 57, 67, 69, 75–9, 103, 155–6
Riddiford, Richard 121, 186, 196, 202, 224
River Queen (Ward) 9, 11, 185, 258, 260, 262, 264
road movies 23, 103, 120, 148, 168, 247
romance/woman's film 60, 170–2, 217–24
Romance of Hine-moa, The (dir. Pauli) 36, 37, 38, 40
Rotorua as film site 11, 28, 33, 36–7, 47, 94, 104, 106, 108, 119
Ruby and Rata (dir. Preston) 181, 199–201, 224, 225, 250
Runaway (dir. O'Shea) 85, 96–103, 104, 110, 132, 134

Samoan-oriented films 87, 122, 182
Sargeson, Frank 124, 132, 183
Scarecrow, The, book (author, Morrieson) 88
Scarecrow, The, film (dir. Pillsbury) 15, 88
Scrimgeour, Rev. Colin 79–81
selling of New Zealand films 115, 185–6
Selwyn, Don 127, 141, 240–1, 242
Send a Gorilla (dir. Read) 181, 202–3
settler romances 41–6
Shifter (dir. Hodson) 195, 242, 251–3
Siegfried, André (*Democracy in*

New Zealand) 24, 36, 51, 268
Sinclair, Harry 23, 187, 204–8
Sinclair, Keith 24, 57
Sleeping Dogs (dir. Donaldson) 6, 15, 118, 132, 134, 136, 137–41, 153, 160
smallness of industry and related problems 8–14, 259
Smash Palace (dir. Donaldson) 9, 19, 21, 114, 115, 119, 134, 135, 140, 144, 147–54, *149*
Smith, Beaumont 41, 55, 117
Smith, Kevin 188–9, 199, 216, 217, 219
Snakeskin (dir. Ashurst) 20, 171, 185, 246–9
social problem or social revelation films 79–83, 88–96, 122
Solo (dir. Williams) 7, 168–69
sport in New Zealand films 6, 24, 93, 103, 147, 166, 189, 190, 193, 197–8, 199, 203–4, 249, 262
Steven, Geoff 6, 39, 41, 113, 124, 125–6, 129–30, 131, 168
Stickmen (dir. Rothwell) 24, 121, 181, 185, 196, 203–4
Stuart, Bathie 42–5 *passim*, 117
suburbs, suburbanization 120–1

Tabu (dir. Murnau and Flaherty) 35–7
Tamahori, Lee 121, 186, 237–40 *passim*, 242
Tangata Whenua (TV) 87, 90
Tarr, George 5, 41, 46–50
Tawhai-Rogers, Hera *48*, 49–50
tax break period 7, 17, 114
tax incentives, levies 8
teenpics 189, 191, 194
Te Kanawa, Kiri 96, 98–9, 104, *105*, 106, 110

Te Kooti 67–72 *passim*, 155
Te Kooti Trail, The (dir. Hayward) 46, 52, 55, 67–74, *68, 69, 70*, 75, 79, 155, 158
Te Reo (Māori language) 74, 77, 95, 109, 156, 180, 240–1, 248
Te Rua (dir. Barclay) 87, 88, 120, 199, 234–6, 241, 242
Test Pictures (dir. Steven) 129–30
theories and generative critical metaphors 20–2
To Love a Maori (dir. Hayward) 55, 81–3, 224
Topless Women Talk about their Lives (dir. Sinclair) 196, 204–5, 208
tourism and film 6, 17, 19, 29, 94, 259, 264
Toy Love (dir. Sinclair) 204, 205–6
Trial Run (dir. Read) 172–5
'two-culture' films 224–30
Two Towers, The (dir. Jackson) 119, 261

Under the Southern Cross (dir. Pauli) 45–6, 52, 66
Urban, Karl 9, 188
Utu (dir. Murphy) 115, 118, 119, 134, 136, 154–60, *156*, 224, 225, 241

Vigil (dir. Ward) 114, 115, 119, 130, *131*, 157, 158, 260, 261, 262

Waitangi Tribunal, Treaty of Waitangi 31, 31, 154–5, 207, 229
Wallace, Anzac 160, 231, 232
Warbrick, Patiti 38, *70*, 71
Ward, Vincent 9, 18, 114, 116,

130, 193, 194, 257–60, 269–70
war films 189, 190–1
Wells, Peter 23, 186, 221–2
West, Hazel 59
Weta digital workshop 264
whakapapas (genealogies) 106, 184, 197
Whale Rider (dir. Caro) 10, 185, 186, 194, 224, 226, 227–9, 230, 238, 244
Whale Rider, The book (author, Ihimaera) 14, 36, 228–9
What Dreams May Come (dir. Ward) 258, 260, 261, 262, 264
When Love Comes (dir. Maxwell) 104, 120, 190, 208, 212–13
Whitehouse, A.H. 28
Wilder, George 24–5, 126
Williams, Tony 6, 86, 87, 99, 104, 105, 114, 168–9
Woodenhead (dir. Habicht) 104, 195–6, 253

Xena: Warrior Princess 185

Zilch! (dir. Riddiford) 121, 181–2, 189, 196, 199

EU authorised representative for GPSR:
Easy Access System Europe, Mustamäe tee 50,
10621 Tallinn, Estonia
gpsr.requests@easproject.com

www.ingramcontent.com/pod-product-compliance
Lightning Source LLC
Chambersburg PA
CBHW070937230426
43666CB00011B/2473